ENVIRONMENTAL LAW FOR TRANSITIONS TO SUSTAINABILITY

European Environmental Law Forum Series, Volume 7

ENVIRONMENTAL LAW FOR TRANSITIONS TO SUSTAINABILITY

Edited by
Marlon Boeve
Sanne Akerboom
Chris Backes
Marleen van Rijswick

INTERSENTIA
Cambridge – Antwerp – Chicago

Intersentia Ltd
8 Wellington Mews
Wellington Street | Cambridge
CB1 1HW | United Kingdom
Tel: +44 1223 736 170
Email: mail@intersentia.co.uk
www.intersentia.com | www.intersentia.co.uk

Distribution for the UK and
Rest of the World (incl. Eastern Europe)
NBN International
1 Deltic Avenue, Rooksley
Milton Keynes MK13 8LD
United Kingdom
Tel: +44 1752 202 301 | Fax: +44 1752 202 331
Email: orders@nbninternational.com

Distribution for Europe
Lefebvre Sarrut Belgium NV
Hoogstraat 139/6
1000 Brussels
Belgium
Tel: +32 (0)800 39 067
Email: mail@intersentia.be

Distribution for the USA and Canada
Independent Publishers Group
Order Department
814 North Franklin Street
Chicago, IL 60610
USA
Tel: +1 800 888 4741 (toll free) | Fax: +1 312 337 5985
Email: orders@ipgbook.com

Environmental Law for Transitions to Sustainability

Image on cover: Wang An Qi / Shutterstock

ISBN 978-1-78068-929-6
D/2021/7849/35
NUR 823

British Library Cataloguing in Publication Data. A catalogue record for this book is available from the British Library.

CONTENTS

LIST OF AUTHORS

Sanne Akerboom
Assistant Professor of Law and Politics of the Energy Transition, Copernicus Institute of Sustainable Development (Faculty of Geosciences), Utrecht University, the Netherlands

Chris Backes
Professor of Environmental and Planning Law, Utrecht Centre for Water, Oceans and Sustainability Law, Utrecht University, the Netherlands

Mariusz Baran
Associate Professor at the Chair of Environmental Law Faculty of Law and Administration, Jagiellonian University Krakow, Poland

Marlon Boeve
Assistant Professor of Environmental and Planning Law, Utrecht Centre for Water, Oceans and Sustainability Law, Utrecht University, the Netherlands

L.S. (Lolke) Braaksma
Doctoral Candidate within the Research Programmes Law on Energy and Sustainability and Public Trust and Public Law, University of Groningen, the Netherlands

Robert Esser
Chair for German, European and International Criminal Law, Criminal Procedure Law and Economic Criminal Law, University of Passau, Germany; Research Center Human Rights in Criminal Proceedings (HRCP)

Isna Fatimah
Researcher, Indonesian Center for Environmental Law, Indonesia

Matteo Fermeglia
Assistant Professor of International and European Environmental Law, Hasselt University, Belgium

Valerie Fogleman
Professor of Law, Cardiff University School of Law and Politics, Wales, United Kingdom; Consultant, Stevens & Bolton LLP, England, United Kingdom

Sofia Fotopoulou
Doctoral Candidate, National and Kapodistrian University of Athens, Greece

Stefano Giacomelli
Scientific Collaborator, Faculty of Communication, Culture and Society, USI Università della Svizzera italiana, Lugano, Switzerland

Michael Gibbert
Full Professor, Faculty of Communication, Culture and Society, USI Università della Svizzera italiana, Lugano, Switzerland

Carola Glinski
Associate Professor, Centre for Private Governance (CEPRI), University of Copenhagen, Denmark

Shin-ya Hieda
Curator, Toyohashi Museum of Natural History, Japan

Theodoros G. Iliopoulos
Doctoral Candidate in Energy and Environmental Law, Hasselt University, Belgium

Georgios Kalogerakis
Doctoral Candidate, National and Kapodistrian University of Athens, Greece

Kenji Kamigawara
Professor, Graduate School of Environmental Science, University of Shiga Prefecture, Japan

Naomi Luhde-Thompson
Doctoral Candidate, Birmingham University, United Kingdom

Mathias N. Müller
Doctoral Candidate, Maastricht University, Netherlands

Beltrán Puentes Cociña
Doctoral Candidate, University of Santiago de Compostela, Spain

Trevor Renals
Senior Technical Adviser, Environment Agency, United Kingdom

Alistair Rieu-Clarke
Professor, Northumbria University, Newcastle

Marleen van Rijswick
Professor of European and Dutch Water Law and Director, Utrecht Centre for Water, Oceans and Sustainability Law, Utrecht University, the Netherlands

Martyna Robakowska
Doctoral Candidate, Adam Mickiewicz University, Poznań, Poland; Associate in the Environmental Law Practice of Wardyński & Partners

Hendrik Schoukens
Postdoctoral Researcher, Department of European, Public and International Law, Ghent University, Belgium

Alexander Solntsev
Associate Professor and Deputy Head of the Department of International Law, People's Friendship University of Russia (RUDN), Moscow, Russia

Anna Vanhellemont
Doctoral Candidate in Environmental Law, Hasselt University, Belgium

INTRODUCTION

Marlon Boeve, Sanne Akerboom, Chris Backes
and Marleen van Rijswick

1. ENVIRONMENTAL LAW FOR TRANSITIONS TO SUSTAINABILITY

In 2019 the European Environment Agency concluded that the European Union faces major environmental challenges if it is to achieve its self-imposed sustainability goals with its overall 2050 aim of 'living well, within the limits of our planet.'[1] These challenges are not about single issues such as reducing air pollution or better nature protection. Rather, Europe's persistent environmental challenges are systemic, in the sense that they are tied in complex ways to prevailing economic, technological and social systems. These interlinkages often make it hard to effectuate rapid reductions in environmental pressures and to get societal support for the required measures.

Over the last few decades, environmental law has significantly contributed to limiting pollution and decoupling economic growth from negative environmental effects. However, for advanced economies in Europe and elsewhere, reconciling high levels of human development (living well) with environmental sustainability (living within environmental limits) is expected to require a five-fold or even ten-fold improvement in environmental performance. Moreover, in some areas, like biodiversity loss, we have already gone beyond the capacity of our world.[2] The current challenges require considering out-of-the-box solutions, integrated and inclusive approaches by both public and private actors and cross-border sets of instruments. Therefore, the EU (and the international community) must find new ways to achieve

---

1 European Environment Agency, The European Environment – State and Outlook 2020. Knowledge for transition to a sustainable Europe, Luxembourg 2019, p. 9.

2 The International Resource Panel: 'Global Resources Outlook 2019: Natural Resources for the Future We Want', https://www.resourcepanel.org/reports/global-resources-outlook; Global Footprint Network, 'National Footprint and Biocapacity Accounts', https://www.footprintnetwork.org; European Commission, 'The Green Deal', 11 December 2019, COM(2019), 640 final, p. 1; J. Randers, J. Rockström, P.-E. Stoknes, U. Goluke, D. Collste, S. Cornell and J. Donges, 'Achieving the 17 Sustainable Development Goals within 9 planetary boundaries' (2019) 2 *Global Sustainability* E24, doi:10.1017/sus.2019.22.

fundamental transitions to sustainability in core systems, entailing 'profound changes in dominant institutions, practices, technologies, policies, lifestyles and thinking'.[3]

In order to promote the legal discussion about ways to achieve fundamental transitions to sustainability, Utrecht University hosted the Seventh European Environmental Law Forum (EELF) Conference from 28 to 30 August 2019. The central question of the conference was what support law can offer to facilitate or even accelerate these transformation processes and how it can provide guidance on the different pathways to sustainability. Which kind of law do we need to encourage innovations for more sustainable solutions? How can innovation be ensured, without endangering public health and safety and environmental quality?

During the conference, contributors focused on this central question, as well as more specific questions in the areas of: transition from a linear to circular economy; transition to a low-carbon economy in order to comply with the Paris Agreement; transition to halt biodiversity loss; and transition to a holistic management of water resources to achieve water security in urban, rural and coastal areas.

This book offers a selection of contributions presented at the 2019 EELF conference at Utrecht University. All contributions were subject to a peer review process.[4] In the first part of the book, contributions deal with the central theme and explore fundamental concepts, for instance the concept of sustainability in environmental law (Vanhellemont). In the following three parts contributions focus on: (Part II) tools for compliance with the Paris Agreement; (Part III) tools for halting the loss of biodiversity; and (Part IV) tools for achieving water security.

2. PART I: TOOLS IN GENERAL

For a long time, the first and foremost aim of environmental law has been to reduce pollution caused by human activities, especially emissions into air and water and other forms of pollution. This seems to be insufficient to achieve a sustainable economy as the over-exploitation of the ecosystem and climate change is not prevented by emission control. Systemic changes in our way of producing, consuming and living are required, including a transition from a

---

3 European Environment Agency, 'The European Environment – State and Outlook 2020. Knowledge for transition to a sustainable Europe', Luxembourg 2019, p. 24.

4 The summaries of the chapters are based on their introductions.

linear economy to a circular economy where all steps of the product life cycle need to be addressed. Law should encourage disruptive or breakthrough innovations for more sustainable technologies and processes. What kind of law will best serve this aim? Does existing law discourage sustainable innovations and solutions? Vanhellemont (Chapter 1) discusses several achievements and challenges concerning the implementation of the concept of sustainability in environmental law. Although the principle of sustainability was introduced in European Union Law over 20 years ago, it has not yet been fully implemented in environmental legislation. This can hamper a truly sustainable policy and further options to implement the concept of sustainability in EU environmental law are explored, including a clarification of the term 'sustainability', operationalising Article 11 TFEU which lays down the principle of integration and sustainable development, introducing a general duty of care and prioritising the environmental Sustainable Development Goals.

After this discussion on the implementation of the general concept of sustainability in EU law, Chapters 2, 3 and 4 focus on more specific legal frameworks and concepts and on the question of whether they support the transition process to sustainability.

Braaksma, in Chapter 2, analyses a relatively new policy instrument used by Member States of the European Union to achieve environmental objectives: the programmatic approach. He argues that this approach, as a concept, is supportive to implementing sustainability theories such as the ecosystem approach and adaptive management. The chapter explores the legal implications and challenges of the programmatic approach when used to support the transition to sustainability. Braaksma concludes that these challenges mainly revolve around reconciling a holistic and adaptive approach with key legal values, such as legal certainty.

Puentes Cocina's contribution (Chapter 3) discusses whether a paradigm shift is necessary to foster transition processes and whether such a paradigm shift can already be observed in recent amendments of EU environmental law. He focuses his analysis on the example of the transition to a circular economy. The EU waste package of 2018 was the first legislative endorsement of the circular economy political strategy launched by the European Commission. Puentes Cocina analyses whether the package implies a paradigm shift or only strengthens the old waste law. He concludes that the circular economy has not brought a new paradigm in waste law. The EU will have to move into less explored territories to achieve innovative legal reforms, like the broader concept of 'the circular economy of products.'

In Chapter 4, Glinski focuses on the contribution of private governance systems to a more effective environmental protection. The chapter critically analyses the capacity of the European Union sustainability certification of biofuels and the 'Forest Stewardship Council' to ensure sustainable production patterns and a sustainable transnational production chain. Glinski concludes that shortcomings and challenges of private environmental governance can only partly be remedied through amendments to private systems and an 'ideal' public and private framework. They cannot replace but only complement public law resource management and ecosystem protection.

In Chapter 5, Luhde-Thompson takes a more socio-legal approach, looking at the role of 'facts' in environmental decision-making. The chapter identifies the gaps and weaknesses in relation to the information upon which environmental decision-making relies. To that end Luhde-Thompson takes the decision-making on shale gas exploration and extraction in the UK as an example. Her conclusion is that there is a need for a reframing of the informational base of environmental decision-making, demanding a larger role for the use of independent and objective evidence.

3. PART II: TOOLS FOR COMPLIANCE WITH THE PARIS AGREEMENT

Legal approaches to enforcing reduction of greenhouse gas emissions are diverse. Market-based instruments like emission trading schemes compete with taxing or more traditional command and control approaches. What can we learn from the successes or failures of these instruments in the last decades? Which legal instruments do in fact foster innovative technologies to decarbonise?

A broad perspective is taken in the contribution of Solntsev (Chapter 6). Climate change is integrated into many international documents. The year 2015 was indicative in this regard: the binding Paris Agreement was adopted, along with two soft law strategic documents (SDGs and the Sendai Framework). These documents require periodic reporting by states. Solntsev states that there is an increasing tendency for various state bodies to prepare reports on various international acts that provide incomplete or contradictory information, hindering proper assessment of the actual situation of the combat against climate change. As an example, Solntsev examines the interconnection of the three aforementioned international documents that are aimed at increasing the cooperation of states when combatting climate change. The chapter analyses what this interconnection looks like (with a special focus on disaster risk reduction), what problems are visible when analysing the reports and what can be done to increase efficiency.

Muller reflects in Chapter 7 on the EU Emission Trading System, launched in 2005 as one of the key instruments of the EU's efforts to reduce greenhouse gas emissions. So far, the literature has mostly focused on weaknesses in the system, suggesting improvements. Muller takes an original approach and examines whether we are actually in a position to reflect on the EU ETS compliance cycle at all. The chapter explores to what extent the right to access environmental information can be used to reflect on the successes and failures of the EU ETS compliance cycle.

More recently, the new Renewable Energy Directive 2018/2001 (RED II) came into force. This directive establishes a common framework for the promotion of energy from renewable sources. In Chapter 8, Iliopoulos discusses to what extent the provisions identify the main actors that will spearhead the EU low-carbon energy transition. A distinction is made between bigger actors, like big companies and investment funds, and small actors, like households and operators of small-scale installations. The chapter argues that the transition to a sustainable future needs instruments suitable for both categories. Iliopoulos concludes that the EU legal framework allows Member States to determine who will be the front runners of their national efforts. Differences between national legal orders are expected to reveal best practices and have a 'learning-by-doing' effect.

In Chapter 9, Fermeglia looks at a more economic instrument: the Energy Return On Energy Investment (EROI) metric. This instrument provides a numerical quantification of the net-energy benefits associated with the exploitation of an energy source. Although EROI calculation methods have been developed and refined over time, EROI's policy implications as a tool to shape the EU's energy and climate policies remain largely unexplored. The chapter explores the legal consequences of embedding EROI as part of the conceptual toolbox in two relevant EU environmental and climate policies: financing of low-carbon innovation through the EU ETS, and spatial planning under the SEA and EIA Directives.

In Chapter 10, Isna moves to the issue of who will or should be the drivers of innovative sustainable solutions: national governments, local communities or perhaps private actors? Indonesia has pledged an ambitious goal for climate change mitigation by restoring agriculture, forestry and land-use sectors that have been transformed into concession areas to their original carbon dioxide absorbing state. The question is: who should be responsible for restoring these areas? The chapter explores the possibility of using legal constructions to attribute the 'responsibility-to-restore' to private entities.

4. PART III: TOOLS FOR HALTING THE LOSS OF BIODIVERSITY

Worldwide, biodiversity is declining rapidly. In the EU, most of the protected species and also most of the protected habitat-types are in an unfavourable conservation status. The policy aim of the EU to stop biodiversity loss by 2020 is not within reach. Has law failed? Does EU law address the main drivers of biodiversity loss, and does it do so effectively? Or would fundamentally different legal regimes be needed to stop biodiversity loss and to work towards an effective protection of nature as the basis for our future living?

In Chapter 11, Schoukens focuses on a novel movement built on the premise that nature is to be regarded as a 'rights holder'. This 'right of nature movement' which is taking root in several countries, entails a more eco-centric and holistic worldview, challenging human exceptionalism. The chapter aims to critically engage with this idea of granting legal rights to nature, exploring not only its potential for ensuring better protection of biodiversity in the EU, but also its inherent limitations.

Fogleman offers in Chapter 12 a comparative analysis of the selection of endangered species to be protected by nature conservation legislation and the establishment of areas of natural habitat to protect them in the US and the EU. The chapter compares the different approaches in the Endangered Species Act (ESA) in the United States and the Birds Directive and Habitat Directive in the European Union, as well as their implementation. The analysis shows that the ESA's approach has not proven to be resilient. Looking at the future, the Birds Directive and Habitats Directive seem effective, the revisions to the regulations under the ESA, however, risk reducing its effectiveness.

As part of this theme three contributions have been included dealing with issues regarding national law, which, in our opinion, provide relevant learnings also at European or international level.

In Chapter 13, Esser approaches the issue of biodiversity loss from another domain of law: he examines in what way criminal law could deliver a successful contribution to the transition processes needed for sustainable future development. The chapter first analyses a traditional national (in this case German) criminal law approach and then focuses on European criminal law as a possible tool for stopping biodiversity loss.

Giacomelli and Gibbert (Chapter 14) focus on a specific issue regarding the overabundance of ungulates, particularly wild boars. In Italy, these ungulates not only cause substantial damage to biodiversity, they also put the distribution of legislative power between the Central State and the Regions to a test. The authors discuss a recent case of the Italian Constitutional Court on this matter. This, relatively simple decision constitutes a case study with wider ramifications for other countries where wildlife is publicly owned.

Kamigawara, Hieda and Renals provide, in Chapter 15, an insight into the way England manages invasive alien plants. Invasive alien species (IAS) are a major cause of biodiversity loss, and many countries have introduced legislation to manage IAS, such as the prohibition on selling and on releasing certain species into the wild. In addition, England has developed the concept of 'landowner responsibility'. The chapter discusses the development of this concept and concludes that it is an important element of the scheme for collaboration among stakeholders in managing IAS in England, and can contribute to strengthening collaborative management in other countries.

5. PART IV: TOOLS FOR ACHIEVING WATER SECURITY

This theme is dedicated to the transitions to a sustainable management of water resources. It encompasses four contributions which highlight this topic from different perspectives and levels.

In Chapter 16, Rieu-Clarke discusses the significant innovation offered by the new reporting mechanism under the UNECE Water Convention. This mechanism allows countries sharing transboundary waters to collectively monitor the implementation of transboundary water-sharing commitments in a systematic and transparent manner. The chapter shows that while certain aspects of the mechanism might be improved, it is likely to offer an important means by which parties to the Water Convention can measure progress towards sustainable development within the transboundary water context for many years to come.

Two chapters within this theme focus on EU law.

In Chapter 17, Baran discusses the legal problems concerning the concept of 'water damage' as defined in the Environmental Liability Directive (2004/35). The chapter seeks an answer to the question whether the definition of 'water damage' is an effective tool to remedy water damage. The chapter analyses the relevant provisions of Directive 2000/60 and the previous case law of the EU Court of Justice interpreting these provisions. This allows an evaluation of the EU legislator's cohesive approach in the scope of defining 'environmental damage' (as regards water damage) in Article 2(5) of the Environmental Liability Directive with reference to the Water Framework Directive.

In Chapter 18, Kalogerakis and Fotopoulou address the question whether the current EU legal framework is sufficient for the protection of the marine environment. The main piece of EU legislation for the conservation of (marine) biodiversity is still the Habitats Directive. The chapter examines whether a higher – or at least equal – level of marine environmental protection can be achieved through other EU legislative acts mainly oriented toward sustainable management of marine resources. The authors conclude that the legal deficiencies of the Habitats Directive cannot be covered with the implementation of other EU Law aiming mainly at the transition to sustainability and that there is a need for a new legal framework.

Finally, in Chapter 19, Robakowska gives a national, Polish, perspective on the topic. The main aim of the new Polish Water Law Act (2018) was to ensure the full implementation of the Water Framework Directive. One of the most controversial of introduced changes concerned the system of incurring fees for water services. Under the new laws, these fees fall generally into two components – the variable one, dependant on the actual scope of provided water services, and the fixed one calculated solely on the basis of individual water permit wording. However, this approach does not encourage businesses to apply more sustainable business operation models, and raises considerable doubts as to the conformity of Polish water-pricing policy with the Water Framework Directive.

The overview of the different chapters shows a broad and fragmented picture of possible pathways to sustainability and the role that law can play in this transition. It is clear that law, until now, has only played a limited role and should be further developed and improved to better align with the more general aim to move towards a sustainable society. This entails both improvement of the legal instruments and better coordination or alignment of responsibilities. It also requires more multi- or interdisciplinary or even transdisciplinary cooperation, aiming at achieving the goal of a sustainable society. It is clear that the challenges are complex and need expertise from different disciplines and actors as well as governance levels. We wish you a pleasant read and we hope this book serves its purpose as an inspiration for further discussion on the role of law as a tool for supporting the transition to a sustainable future. We look forward to meeting you at one of the next EELF conferences.

PART I

TOOLS IN GENERAL

TOWARDS MORE SUSTAINABLE EU ENVIRONMENTAL LAW

Anna Vanhellemont

1. INTRODUCTION

Environmental law is characterised by its very broad subject and objective, requiring an overarching, global and long-term approach. The concept of sustainability fits in very well with this approach, as it is the basis for attaining the protection of ecological integrity, while both considering the capacity of the ecosystems (their natural assets and biological diversity) and acknowledging that humans are part of these ecosystems (considering present and future generations).[1] A sustainability approach creates a bridge between the individual entitlement of humans to the environment and their responsibility for the commons. Sustainability is based on three pillars that should be balanced: people, planet and profit (i.e. social, environmental and economic concerns).

Although the principle of sustainability was introduced into European Union (EU) law over 20 years ago, it has not yet been fully implemented in environmental legislation. Fundamental issues in the approach to environmental law, both in recent times and during the first stages of development of environmental legislation, still hamper an actually sustainable policy. Overall, there seems to be an imbalance between the three sustainability pillars. This includes issues of compartmentalisation, fragmentation and an overall anthropocentric view on the environment. The concept of environmental reductionism also arises in this discussion, or as Klaus Bosselmann puts it 'a number of *trees* have been saved, but the *forest* is disappearing'.[2]

The main research question in this contribution is: Which options exist to fully implement the concept of sustainability in EU environmental law? This question falls within the general theme of the conference book, as it concerns the role that environmental law can play in the fundamental transition to a

1 J.H. Jans and H.H.B. Vedder, *European Environmental Law*, 4th ed., Europa Law Publishing, Groningen 2012, p. 8.

2 K. Bosselmann, 'Losing the Forest in the Trees: Environmental Reductionism in the Law' (2010) 2 *Sustainability* 2424, 2424.

sustainable future. First, the introduction of the concept of sustainability in EU environmental legislation is discussed, including the past and planned steps towards the implementation of this principle to attain a more sustainable EU environmental policy. The chapter will assess several specific examples of what has already been achieved and question whether these initiatives have indeed led to more sustainability. This includes discussing the theory and intentions behind these initiatives, but also looking into their value in practice. For example: do they actually lead to more integration and a balance between the three sustainability pillars? Second, the issues and challenges that remain for a sustainable approach to EU environmental law are investigated. Third, the chapter will examine opportunities to further implement the principle of sustainability in EU environmental law. This will not entail a specific or detailed discussion of different pieces of EU environmental legislation, but focuses on a fundamental discussion of EU environmental law, considering more radical and substantive changes.

2. SUSTAINABILITY IN EU ENVIRONMENTAL LAW

2.1. GENERAL CONSIDERATIONS ON SUSTAINABLE DEVELOPMENT

Already at the 1992 Rio Earth Summit, sustainable development was made the centrepiece of international and domestic environmental policy.[3] Subsequently, the objective of sustainable development was first introduced into the Treaties of the EU in 1999, in the Preamble to the Treaty on the European Union (TEU), Article 3 TEU and Article 11 of the Treaty on the Functioning of the European Union (TFEU).

A clear definition of the concept in the EU was never provided. However, the European Council did mention seven priority areas of sustainable development, including specific measures to address them: climate change and clean technologies, sustainable transport, sustainable consumption and production, conservation and management of natural resources, public health, social inclusion, demography and migration, and global poverty and the challenges of sustainable development.[4] Sustainable development can be considered to be 'the improvement to the standard of living and welfare of the relevant populations within the limits of the capacity of the ecosystems, by maintaining natural assets and their biological diversity for the benefit of

3 B.J. Richardson and S. Wood, 'Environmental Law for Sustainability' in B.J. Richardson and S. Wood (eds.), *Environmental Law for Sustainability*, Hart Publishing, Oxford 2006, p. 1.

4 L. Krämer, *EU Environmental Law*, 8th ed., Sweet & Maxwell, London 2016, p. 10.

present and future generations'.[5] It is mainly based on the principle of intergenerational equity, which requires that the next generation receives a stock of assets at least equivalent to our own, also taking into account the growing population.[6] In short, it can be defined as meeting the needs of the current generation without compromising those of future generations,[7] an idea that can also be found in the title of the seventh Environment Action Programme (EAP): 'Living well, within the limits of our planet'.[8] Sustainable development also takes centre stage in the Europe 2020 Strategy for smart, sustainable and inclusive growth[9] and was the subject of the previous EU Sustainable Development Strategy which was first launched in 2001.[10]

These definitions show that the concept of sustainable development is quite vague and broad. Its vagueness has been criticised, as it can be considered a way of downplaying the concept and importance of sustainability. The aforementioned definitions are believed to illustrate the weak version of sustainability, viewing ecological sustainability separately from economic and social sustainability.[11] Strong sustainability, on the other hand, entails that the preservation of the Earth's ecosystems should be considered the core principle of sustainable development, imposing necessary limits on both economic and social development.[12]

Closely linked with the principle of sustainable development is the concept of integrated decision-making,[13] both concerning environmental issues themselves and the incorporation of environmental, social and economic considerations and goals into all decisions.[14] Integration can be considered an important first

---

5 J.H. Jans and H.H.B. Vedder, *European Environmental Law*, 4th ed., Europa Law Publishing, Groningen 2012, p. 8.

6 M.S. Peters and M. Komar, 'Achieving Sustainability through Effective Mechanisms of Environmental Impact Assessment and Strategic Environmental Assessment' (2013) *EEELR (European Energy and Environmental Law Review)*, 79, 79–83.

7 This definition is also provided by the 1987 Brundtland Report, released by the World Commission on Environment and Development, titled 'Our Common Future'.

8 European Parliament and Council, Decision No 1386/2013/EU on a General Union Environment Action Programme to 2020 'Living well, within the limits of our planet', [2013] OJ L 354, 171–200.

9 Commission, 'A strategy for smart, sustainable and inclusive growth' (Communication), COM(2010) 2020 final.

10 This strategy was revised in 2006 and reviewed in 2009: see COM/2001/0264 final, COM(2009) 400 final and COM(2010) 2020 final.

11 K. Bosselmann, *The Principle of Sustainability: Transforming law and governance*, 2nd ed., Routledge, Abingdon 2016, p. 2.

12 K. Bosselmann, 'Losing the Forest in the Trees: Environmental Reductionism in the Law' (2010) 2 *Sustainability* 2424, 2437.

13 On the topic of integration, see: N. Dhondt, *Integration of Environmental Protection into Other EC Policies: Legal Theory and Practice*, Europa Law Publishing, Groningen 2003.

14 J.C. Dernbach and J.A. Mintz, 'Environmental Laws and Sustainability: An Introduction', (2011) 3 *Sustainability* 532, 531–540.

step towards sustainable development.[15] Furthermore, when considering the aforementioned strong version of sustainability, sustainability of ecological systems should be considered the bottom line in this integrated approach. Merely considering the ecological, economic and social dimensions simultaneously would not be sufficient to attain actually sustainable development.[16]

2.2. ACHIEVEMENTS OF SUSTAINABILITY IN EU ENVIRONMENTAL LEGISLATION

This section will look into several concrete examples of sustainability in EU environmental law, ranging from the broader development of legislation to very specific concepts that embrace sustainable development. This is in no way a limitative list and solely serves an illustrative purpose. Throughout, any critical questions or comments that arise are noted, and will be discussed further in the chapter.

2.2.1. Article 11 TFEU

The most obvious way in which sustainability is inscribed in EU environmental law is Article 11 TFEU. This article lays down the duty to integrate environmental protection requirements into other EU policies and activities, particularly with a view to promoting sustainable development. In theory, the codification of the principle of sustainable development in the TFEU could have significant implications for both the EU institutions and the Member States.[17] However, the question arises whether in practice Article 11 TFEU is actually operationalised and if it can be used as a tool to ensure more sustainable EU law and policy. Specifically, what does this obligation to integrate environmental considerations entail? Earlier research by Dhondt on (former) Article 6 EC concluded that the provision not only contains an active responsibility for the EU institutions, but also lays down a passive obligation for Member States not to adopt policies that would hinder the achievement and observance of environmental objectives and principles.[18] Dhondt also stresses that the integration principle entails that environmental protection

---

15 K. Bosselmann, *The Principle of Sustainability: Transforming law and governance*, 2nd ed., Routledge, Abingdon 2016, p. 2.

16 K. Bosselmann, 'Losing the Forest in the Trees: Environmental Reductionism in the Law' (2010) 2 *Sustainability* 2424, 2437–2438.

17 On this topic, see: B. Sjåfjell, 'The Legal Significance of Article 11 TFEU for EU Institutions and Member States' in B. Sjåfjell and A. Wiesbrock (eds.), *The Greening of European Business under EU Law: Taking Article 11 TFEU Seriously*, Routledge, Abingdon 2015, pp. 51–72.

18 N. Dhondt, *Integration of Environmental Protection into Other EC Policies: Legal Theory and Practice*, Europa Law Publishing, Groningen 2003, p. 108.

as an EU objective is placed on the same level as economic concerns.[19] Furthermore, she proposes the use of a 'strong interpretation' of the principle. This means that the institutions must pursue environmental objectives both when taking environmental action (based on powers to develop and implement an environmental policy) and any other policy action (based on other powers, for example in the field of agriculture, energy and transport). Such action should also be based on the environmental principles and take into account the environmental criteria.[20]

2.2.2. *'No Net Loss' and 'Ecological Impact Neutrality' Approach*

Two concrete concepts fit in naturally with the idea of sustainability: the 'no net loss' principle and the 'ecological impact neutrality' approach. The principle of no net loss cannot be found in EU environmental legislation,[21] but was officially introduced into EU environmental policy with the Biodiversity Strategy.[22] Action 7 under Target 2 lays down the objective of no net loss of biodiversity and ecosystem services.[23] The no net loss principle entails that biodiversity losses in one area are balanced by a gain elsewhere, provided that this does not lead to impairment of existing biodiversity as protected by EU nature legislation.[24] The term 'ecological impact neutrality approach' is also not used as such in EU environmental legislation. McGillivray describes the ecological impact neutrality approach as 'an ethos under which natural resources may only be interfered with if functional equivalents are provided'.[25]

A very clear example where these concepts are reflected in EU environmental legislation is the compensation mechanism in Article 6(4) of the Habitats Directive,[26] which states:

> If, in spite of a negative assessment of the implications for the site and in the absence of alternative solutions, a plan or project must nevertheless be carried out for imperative

19 Ibid. at p. 109.

20 Ibid. at pp. 109–110.

21 Literature on the no net loss principle: H. Schoukens and A. Cliquet, 'Biodiversity offsetting and restoration under the European Union Habitats Directive: balancing between no net loss and deathbed conservation' (2016) 21(4) *Ecology and Society* 10; M. Maron et al., 'The many meanings of no net loss in environmental policy' (2018) 1 *Nature Sustainability* 19.

22 On the topic of introducing an EU no net loss initiative: IEEP, 'Policy Options for an EU No Net Loss Initiative' (Final Report), ENV.B2/SER/2012/0028.

23 Commission, 'Our life insurance, our capital: an EU biodiversity strategy to 2020' (Communication), COM(2011) 244 final, p. 12.

24 IEEP, 'Policy Options for an EU No Net Loss Initiative' (Final Report), ENV.B2/SER/2012/0028, Executive Summary, p. 11.

25 D. McGillivray, 'Compensating Biodiversity Loss: The EU Commission's Approach to Compensation under Article 6 of the Habitats Directive' (2012) 24(3) *Journal of Environmental Law* 417, 417–418.

26 Council Directive 92/43/EEC of 21 May 1992 on the conservation of natural habitats and of wild fauna and flora.

> reasons of overriding public interest, including those of a social or economic nature, the Member State shall take *all compensatory measures necessary to ensure that the overall coherence of Natura 2000 is protected*. It shall inform the Commission of the compensatory measures adopted.
>
> Where the site concerned hosts a priority natural habitat type and/or a priority species, the only considerations which may be raised are those relating to human health or public safety, to beneficial consequences of primary importance for the environment or, further to an opinion from the Commission, to other imperative reasons of overriding public interest (emphasis added).

The aim of the compensatory measures under the Habitats Directive is to maintain the overall coherence of Natura 2000, including measures that ensure on-site and in-kind compensation. Furthermore, the link should be made with the global coherence of Natura 2000 and the coherence between the affected site and the created or restored compensatory habitat.[27] Framed by the ecological impact neutrality approach, the system of compensation under the Habitats Directive seems to be ecologically driven and is thus based on the strong notion of the concept of sustainability.[28] When a plan or project has an adverse ecological impact that cannot be avoided, reduced or mitigated, it can only be carried through when steps are taken to ensure no net loss of nature conservation interests.[29] However, even though the provision is based on 'strong sustainability' as defined by Bosselmann, the system still provides for social or economic public interests to override ecological interests in the first subparagraph. Only in relation to priority habitat types or species is the option to deviate from the primary principle of nature conservation limited to more imperative reasons of public interest, such as human health or public safety.

The question arises whether the no net loss principle is or should be limited to the EU's biodiversity policy. Could a similar, generally applicable principle ensure a more sustainable approach to environmental mitigation? Moreover, could such a principle serve as the first step towards a general duty of care for the environment or even a basic prohibition on causing harm to the environment?

2.2.3. Environmental Assessments

Two other important instruments to promote sustainability are the Environmental Impact Assessment Directive[30] and the Strategic Environmental

---

[27] G. Van Hoorick, 'Compensatory Measures in European Nature Conservation Law' (2014) 10(2) *Utrecht Law Review* 161, 164.

[28] D. McGillivray, 'Compensating Biodiversity Loss: The EU Commission's Approach to Compensation under Article 6 of the Habitats Directive' (2012) 24(3) *Journal of Environmental Law* 417, 421.

[29] https://ec.europa.eu/environment/nature/biodiversity/nnl/index_en.htm.

Assessment Directive.[31] These are both proactive tools (unlike retrospective tools, such as ecological footprint analysis and sustainability audits), which are considered effective mitigation mechanisms.[32] One of the main objectives of strategic environmental assessments is the integration of environmental considerations into the preparation and adoption of plans and programmes in order to promote sustainable development.[33] References to sustainability in EU policy are also made for environmental impact assessments.[34] The value of environmental impact assessments in the achievement of sustainable development has been the subject of research for many years.[35] Although the usefulness of this tool for the promotion of sustainable development is clear, is found that sometimes in practice it does not fully attain this goal yet.[36]

2.2.4. Developments in Certain Policies

Overall, a more integrated approach has been taken recently in EU environmental law, partly overcoming the fragmented sectoral approach. Examples include the seventh EAP, the Water Framework Directive (WFD) and the Industrial Emissions Directive (IED).

As mentioned above, the seventh EAP already reflects the idea of sustainability in its title. Furthermore, it not only contains goals towards 2020, but also looks further and lays down where the EU should be in 2050. Sustainable development is central to this long-term vision.[37] The development

---

30 Directive 2011/92 of the European Parliament and of the Council of 13 December 2011 on the assessment of the effects of certain public and private projects on the environment, [2011] OJ L26, pp. 1–21 (EIAD).

31 Directive 2001/42/EC of the European Parliament and of the Council of 27 June 2001 on the assessment of the effects of certain plans and programmes on the environment, [2001] OJ L197, pp. 30–37 (SEAD).

32 M.S. Peters and M. Komar, 'Achieving Sustainability through Effective Mechanisms of Environmental Impact Assessment and Strategic Environmental Assessment' (2013) *EEELR* 79, 79–80.

33 Article 1 SEAD.

34 Recitals (8), (9) and (17) EIAD.

35 See for example: K. Joseph et al., 'Environmental Impact Assessment as a Tool for Sustainable Development' in W.L. Filho (ed.), *Encyclopedia of Sustainability in Higher Education*, Springer, New York 2018; T. Mingjing et al., 'Strategic Environmental Assessment and Sustainable Development', *IOP Conference Series Earth and Environmental Science* (2018) 133; B. Soni et al., 'Environmental Impact Assessment: Tool for Sustainable Development' (2010) 16(2) *Ecology, Environment and Conservation Paper* 249–253.

36 For example, at national level in the case of Sweden: S. Bruhn-Tysk and M. Eklund, 'Environmental impact assessment – a tool for sustainable development? A case study of biofuelled energy plants in Sweden' (2002) 22(2) *Environmental Impact Assessment Review* 129–144.

37 European Parliament and Council, Decision No. 1386/2013/EU on a General Union Environment Action Programme to 2020 'Living well, within the limits of our planet', [2013] OJ L354, pp. 171–200, 176.

of EU legislation concerning water also shows positive steps towards more sustainability. The current WFD is said to lay the foundation for a modern, holistic and ambitious EU water policy.[38] It entails an innovative and far-seeing integrative dimension and aims to protect EU waters in a sustainable way.[39] The ambition of the WFD was to replace the fragmented system of water-related directives with one integrated water management system.[40] However, there are still several separate environmental directives on water in force.[41] Similarly, the 2010 Industrial Emissions Directive is based on an integrated approach, meaning that permits should take into account the entire environmental performance of an industrial plant. It recasts seven former directives, creating an integrated system of pollution control.

Overall, the current system of EU environmental law is still rather fragmented and incoherent. Will this integrative evolution stay limited to certain acts and policies, or should a complete overhaul of the current framework of EU environmental law follow?[42] Could further internal harmonisation of EU environmental legislation lead to more sustainability?

2.3. FUTURE STEPS TOWARDS MORE SUSTAINABILITY

The United Nations 2030 Agenda for Sustainable Development includes 17 Sustainable Development Goals (SDGs) and 169 targets. It is clearly based on the weak version of sustainability, urging integration in a balanced manner of the three dimensions of sustainable development (i.e. economic, social and environmental),[43] without clear prioritisation. Several SDGs have a stronger focus on the environmental aspect of sustainability. For example, SDG 6 focuses on sustainable management of water, SDG 14 concerns the 'sustainable

---

38 H. Josefsson and L. Baaner, 'The Water Framework Directive – A Directive for the Twenty-First Century?' (2011) 23(3) *Journal of Environmental Law* 464, 463–486.

39 D. Grimeaud, 'The EC Water Framework Directive – An Instrument for Integrating Water Policy' (2004) 13 *RECIEL (Review of European Comparative and International Environmental Law)* 27, 28.

40 For a complete initial discussion of the sustainability aspects of the 2001 Water Framework Directive, see: D. Grimeaud, 'Reforming EU Water Law: Towards Sustainability?' (2001) 10 Issue 2 *EEELR* (41–51), Issue 3 (88–97), Issue 4 (125–134).

41 For an overview see Figure 4.2 in H.F.M.W. Van Rijswick and A.M. Keessen, 'The EU approach for Integrated Water Resource Management: Transposing the EU Water Framework Directive within a national context – key insights from experience' in A. Rieu-Clarke, A. Allan and S. Hendry (eds.), *Routledge Handbook of Water Law and Policy*, Routledge, London 2017, p. 56.

42 For example: a framework act on biodiversity and/or ecosystems could overcome fragmentation in this field and also fill in certain gaps in legislation.

43 Preamble, United Nations, 'Transforming Our World: the 2030 Agenda for Sustainable Development', A/RES/70/1.

use' of the oceans, seas and marine resources, and SDG 15 covers 'terrestrial ecosystems', specifically mentioning forests, desertification, land degradation and biodiversity loss. This again shows the problematic fragmentary view on the environment and evokes the question of what importance will be given to these separate goals. Which SDGs will be prioritised in this integration model where all goals are essentially linked?

The EU Commission has communicated its strategy for implementing the SDGs in 2016, aiming to fully integrate the goals into the European policy framework and current Commission priorities.[44] The Commission expressly states that 'protecting the environment is key for the quality of life of current and future generations'.[45] However, throughout this document, the environment is solely mentioned in relation to economic gains. For example: 'maintenance and improvement of our natural resource base is also essential for our economic sectors to deliver their services'.[46] Furthermore, none of the Commission's 2014–2019 priorities reflected the need for a stronger environmental policy *per se*, except for a mention of its circular economy strategy[47] and plastics strategy,[48] always linked with potential economic growth.[49] The priority mostly linked with the environmental SDGs is 'jobs, growth and investment; a stronger global actor'.[50] On a positive note, the Commission's new priorities for 2019–2024 seem to focus more on the environment as such. The so-called 'European Green Deal' is the first priority. It intends to 'make Europe climate-neutral and protect our natural habitat', including actions in biodiversity policy and eliminating pollution.[51] This seems to be a positive development, as it can be considered strange (at best) that there previously was no focus on protection of the environment as such.

Overall, the contents of the SDGs are admirable. However, it remains to be seen how they will be implemented and what the effects in practice will be. The question of prioritisation of environmental SDGs can be asked on both levels. How will the EU decide what importance (or more practically speaking: what funding) will be allocated to the environmental goals while implementing

44 Commission, 'Next steps for a sustainable European future. European action for sustainability' (Communication), COM(2016) 739 final.

45 COM(2016) 739 final, p. 5.

46 COM(2016) 739 final, p. 9.

47 For the most recent version of this strategy, see: Commission, 'A new Circular Economy Action Plan. For a cleaner and more competitive Europe' (Communication), COM(2020) 98 final.

48 Commission, 'A European Strategy for Plastics in a Circular Economy' (Communication), COM(2018) 28 final.

49 European Parliament, 'The Juncker Commission's ten priorities. An end-of-term assessment' (In-Depth Analysis), PE 637.943 – May 2019, pp. 4–5.

50 Commission, 'Key European action supporting the 2030 Agenda and the Sustainable Development Goals' (Staff Working Document), SWD(2016) 390 final, pp. 21, 50, 53.

51 https://ec.europa.eu/info/strategy/priorities-2019-2024/european-green-deal_en.

the SDGs in its policies? Which SDGs deserve the main focus and how is this reflected in current practices?,[52][53] Also, due to the non-binding nature of the SDGS, what happens if the EU just does not comply?

3. REMAINING ISSUES AND CHALLENGES FOR A SUSTAINABLE APPROACH

As illustrated above, many positive strides have been taken and EU environmental legislation has helped majorly in limiting pollution and assessing environmental issues. However, we are consistently not meeting several environmental targets (e.g. concerning biodiversity)[54] and (global) environmental disasters keep occurring. Instead of looking at specific issues in EU environmental legislation, this section will now briefly discuss several more systemic problems as well as some comments related to the approach to environmental law.

3.1. LACK OF CLARITY

Overall, vagueness surrounds the concept and policy on sustainable development. Leading back to the development of the EU Treaties' amendments, there has been a lack of clarity on what sustainability actually entails. Besides uncertainty concerning the contents of Article 11 TFEU, its legal value and effects are also unclear. Since 'integrated' is not defined in the article, or elsewhere in the Treaty, what does it entail?[55] Which specific obligations can be deduced

---

52 Research on prioritisation of SDGs in a private or corporate environment has already been done, see for example: I. Masayoshi et al., 'The process of selecting and prioritising corporate sustainability issues: Insights for achieving the Sustainable Development Goals' (2019) 236 *Journal of Cleaner Production* 117661. Also, research on ways how to set policy priorities has occurred, see for example: M.H. El-Maghrabi et al., 'Sustainable Development Goal Diagnostics. An Application of Network Theory and Complexity Measures to Set Country Priorities' (World Bank, June 2018) *Policy Research Working Paper 8481*, https://openknowledge.worldbank.org/handle/10986/29934.

53 This question was raised by Robin Kundis Craig in her keynote speech titled 'How Do We Think About Transitioning to Sustainability in the Middle of a Transformation? Implications for Environmental and Natural Resources Law in the Anthropocene' at the 7th EELF Conference in 2019.

54 See for example: European Environment Agency, 'Environmental indicator report 2018. In support to the monitoring of the Seventh Environment Action Programme' (Report), No. 19/2018.

55 L. Krämer, 'Giving a voice to the environment by challenging the practice of integrating environmental requirements into other EU policies' in S. Kingston (ed.), *European Perspectives on Environmental Law and Governance*, Routledge, London 2013, p. 84.

from this provision? How should policy-makers comply with the environmental considerations of the concept of sustainability? The aforementioned research by Dhondt already provides some answers concerning the integration principle. However, although this research dates from 2003, no policy action has been taken in this regard. The same can be said for the implementation of the SDGs. It seems that a lot of discretion is left to policy-makers, and there are no guidelines or evidence on whether and how to prioritise one goal above another. Furthermore, as the SDGs are not legally binding and cannot be enforced as such, the question arises what their actual implications will be.[56]

3.2. COMPARTMENTALISATION

There is a clear issue of compartmentalisation, which means that there is a separation between environmental, social and economic policies.[57] Article 11 TFEU, which codifies the integration principle and also puts forth sustainable development, is in place to try and merge these fields. As mentioned above, the precise legal status of this article and its legal implications for decision-makers are not clear. The current conventional view is that Article 11 TFEU does not constitute a general principle and should be considered a purely programmatic provision.[58] However, limiting the value of Article 11 TFEU to a merely programmatic provision is too restrictive. The case law of the European Court of Justice seems to give more practical effect to the integration principle, and it has even obtained constitutional status in several Member States.[59] Nevertheless, the question remains what the practical implications are for the adoption of new legislation or other activities. Even though sustainable development is mentioned throughout EU policy documents, it is rarely used as a *legal standard* in EU secondary legislation. The practical effect of Article 11 TFEU has even been called underwhelming[60] and described by Krämer as 'a historic monument in the Treaty, which everybody looks at, nods at, and then goes away and forgets'.[61]

---

56 This was stated in the keynote speech of Robin Kundis at the EELF Conference (see n. 53 above).

57 These issues are also discussed in: N. Dhondt, *Integration of Environmental Protection into Other EC Policies: Legal Theory and Practice*, Europa Law Publishing, Groningen 2003 and S.R.W Van Hees, *Innovative Ocean Renewable Energy & EU Law*, Utrecht University 2018.

58 S. Kingston, *Greening EU competition law and policy*, Cambridge University Press, Cambridge 2012, p. 107.

59 Ibid. at pp. 108–109.

60 Ibid. at p. 112.

61 L. Krämer, 'Sustainable Development in EC Law' in H. Bugge and C. Voigt (eds.), *Sustainable Development in International and National Law*, Europa Law Publishing, Groningen 2008, p. 394.

3.3. FRAGMENTATION

EU environmental law itself also faces structural issues, which can be brought back to fragmentation in the approach and in legislation concerning the environment. These structural issues lead to other problems, which must be confronted in order to move towards more sustainable law.

On the one hand, there is the sectoral approach that has been used since the conception of EU environmental law, developing legislation *ad hoc* to react to certain events or to counter issues. On the other hand, there is a clear fixation on specific aspects of the environment, which leads to separation and prioritisation of certain environmental topics instead of considering the environment as a whole.[62] Overall, a case-by-case approach can be seen in dealing with environmental problems. This leads to what has been called the splintered fallacy, namely 'the tendency to splinter each problem into discrete pieces to be dealt with one at a time'.[63] Fragmentation also leads to inconsistencies and incoherence between different pieces of environmental legislation and can thus hamper the realisation of an integrated or ecosystem approach.[64]

Furthermore, this fragmented approach can be noticed in the way in which the concept of sustainable development is being implemented in existing EU (environmental) law. There has been no comprehensive overhaul of the current framework in the interest of sustainability. This may be referred to as the marginal fallacy, namely 'the belief that we can achieve sustainability by tinkering at the margins of the existing social, economic and legal systems'.[65]

3.4. ANTHROPOCENTRIC AND UTILITARIAN VIEW

Furthermore, there currently is an anthropocentric and utilitarian view on the environment. This can both be seen in the use of the term 'natural resources', which has a clear economic connotation, and the fact that there seems to be a right to use and alter the environment.[66] This utilitarian view can even be

---

62 Consequently, this can lead to a system where environmental pollution is pushed towards other 'sectors' of the environment, because there is no transsectoral approach to environmental protection.

63 R.M. Bratspies, 'Sustainability: Can Law Meet the Challenge' (2011) 34 *Suffolk Transnational Law Review* 283, 304.

64 See on this topic: F.M. Platjouw, *Environmental Law & The Ecosystem Approach. The Need for Consistency and Coherence in Environmental Law for the Maintenance of Ecosystem Integrity*, Thesis, University of Oslo, 2015, https://www.jus.uio.no/english/research/areas/natural-resources/projects/consistency/froukje/.

65 R.M. Bratspies, 'Sustainability: Can Law Meet the Challenge' (2011) 34 *Suffolk Transnational Law Review* 283, 304.

66 K. Bosselmann, 'Losing the Forest in the Trees: Environmental Reductionism in the Law' (2010) 2 *Sustainability* 2424, 2432.

seen in the SDGs: for example the 'sustainable use of marine resources'. As mentioned above, environmental law seems to be based on the assumption that there is a fundamental right to use and alter the environment. However, there is currently no duty in return (e.g. a general duty of care or a duty to focus on sustainable use).[67]

4. FULLY EMBRACING THE CONCEPT OF SUSTAINABILITY

Even though the achievements of EU environmental legislation should not be overlooked, these successes are mostly outdone by failures in the system as a whole. It is high time to adopt a broader view, instead of trying to mitigate environmental issues on a case-by-case basis. This section will look into several options to create this shift towards more sustainable EU environmental legislation, focusing primarily on fundamental changes in the law and its approach to the environment.

Before going into these suggestions, the primary question is whether there is a need to adopt *new* legislation or other instruments to attain this goal, or whether *existing* legislation can be reviewed or applied in accordance with the principle of sustainability. It seems that the improvement and adaptation of existing legislation could suffice, provided that it is done in accordance with a strong vision of sustainability and integration. The necessary basic tools for sustainability in EU environmental law are available (e.g. Article 11 TFEU), but they have to be put to work. The purely formal use of terms such as 'sustainable development' and 'integration' does not suffice. Central should be a shift in approach and a different view on the environment altogether. This entails changing our perspective on environmental law from anthropocentric to ecocentric, meaning that the environment, including humans, and ecological integrity take centre stage. Overall, further (internal) harmonisation of the existing body of EU environmental law would also help in overcoming issues of fragmentation.

4.1. CLARIFY 'SUSTAINABILITY'[68]

There is no legal definition of sustainable development in the system of EU law. Overall, the commonly agreed definition from the Brundtland Report is

---

67 K. Bosselmann, 'A vulnerable environment: contextualising law with sustainability' (2011) 2(1) *Journal of Human Rights and the Environment* 45, 50.

68 On the topic of providing a clear and workable definition of sustainability, see: S.R.W. Van Hees, 'Sustainable Development in the EU: Redefining and Operationalizing the Concept' (2014) 10(2) *Utrecht Law Review* 60–76.

followed, as mentioned above in section 2.1.[69] The implications of the principle for EU policy are unclear: how should policy-makers or decision-takers apply the idea of sustainability or sustainable development?

The option exists to introduce a more specific definition of sustainability or sustainable development into EU environmental legislation. This would surely reflect its importance and confirm that it is not just a vague concept. Van Hees has provided such a workable and clear definition, which clarifies what is required from policy-makers in light of sustainable development.[70] However, defining the concept in EU law is not necessary *per se* and may not lead to improvements in practice. Providing a specific legal definition would prove a difficult task and might lead to even more discussion on what the principle really entails. Merely formulating clear guidelines and sharing best practices or experiences in applying the principle could in itself lead to greater clarity and better implementation altogether. A step in this direction was also made by Van Hees, who drafted a framework for the application of his proposed definition. This includes a method for decision-makers to implement sustainable development in their work.[71]

4.2. OPERATIONALISE ARTICLE 11 TFEU[72]

Based on the considerations in the previous sections, a stronger interpretation of Article 11 TFEU could lead to actually operationalising the article and giving more weight to sustainable development and environmental considerations throughout EU policy. This could overcome the aforementioned issues of compartmentalisation and fragmentation, as it would lead to actual integration.

The obligations enshrined in Article 11 TFEU should be clarified, both in terms of law-making and enforcing legislation. The importance of this article in reaching actual sustainable development cannot be overlooked, and its practical implications should be brought up to par with its textual contents and underlying aims. Regarding the enforceability of Article 11 TFEU, it may also be time for a stricter approach. It seems that currently the article may only be used as a standard for reviewing EU legislation when ecological interests have

---

69 See n. 7 above.

70 S.R.W. Van Hees, 'Sustainable Development in the EU: Redefining and Operationalizing the Concept' (2014) 10(2) *Utrecht Law Review* 60, 75.

71 Ibid. at 72–73.

72 On this topic: L. Krämer, 'Giving a voice to the environment by challenging the practice of integrating environmental requirements into other EU policies' in S. Kingston (ed.), *European Perspectives on Environmental Law and Governance*, Routledge, London 2013, pp. 87–98.

manifestly *not* been taken into account or when they have been completely disregarded. A lot of discretion is left to the EU institutions in this regard.[73] Currently, not a single measure has been annulled based on an infringement of Article 11 TFEU.[74]

If sustainability and our environment are to be taken seriously, the value of Article 11 TFEU has to be acknowledged in practice. Merely considering environmental factors in decision-making and not actually acting upon these environmental and sustainability considerations is not sufficient to meet the integration requirements.

4.3. GENERAL DUTY OF CARE

To mitigate the current utilitarian approach to the environment, the introduction of a right to use the environment in a sustainable manner can be put forth. Instead of relying on existing views of how the environment fits in with economic and social needs, this idea of 'sustainable use' should be clearly defined.[75] If not, the current unsustainable state will stagnate and there will be no progress in protecting the environment.

Going even further, the option to introduce a general duty of care for the environment in EU law can be put forth. This would entail a more proactive and preventative approach, by causing a shift from what should *not* be done (e.g. cause environmental harm, pollute ...) to what *should* be done (i.e. refrain from interventions that may alter or harm the environment). Any interventions found necessary should then be compensated for accordingly. Based on the sustainability principle, such compensations should be based on a goal of no net loss and taking into account an ecosystem approach.

Of course, serious questions arise on how such a duty should be phrased, and to which standard of care or 'sustainable use' everyone should be held. Defining and inscribing this principle in EU environmental law should be done rigorously, keeping in mind the potential legal effects and considering whether enforcing it would in fact be possible. At least, such a provision could fill in the gaps in current environmental protection in the law. In this way, it would serve as an additional contribution to, and guarantee of the implementation of the

---

73 J. Nowag, 'Article 11 TFEU and Environmental Rights' in S. Bogojevic and R. Rayfuse (eds.), *Environmental Rights in Europe and Beyond*, Hart Publishing, 2018, pp. 170–171.

74 J. Nowag, 'Article 11 TFEU and Environmental Rights' in S. Bogojevic and R. Rayfuse (eds.), *Environmental Rights in Europe and Beyond*, Hart Publishing, 2018, p. 163.

75 K. Bosselmann, 'Losing the Forest in the Trees: Environmental Reductionism in the Law' (2010) 2 *Sustainability* 2424, 2432.

principle of sustainability,[76] overcoming the current fragmented approach and ensuring a more integrated view of environmental mitigation.

4.4. PRIORITISE ENVIRONMENTAL SDGs

The contents and implications of the SDGs are inevitably linked. Progress in one SDG could have a significant positive impact and greatly improve progress in achieving another SDG. It has been shown that the main focus and attention should be on the broader societal and environmental objectives (i.e. goals 4–16), as achieving these goals could directly lead to progress in the first three goals.[77] This leads to the question which SDGs should be prioritised in EU policy. If we base ourselves on the concentric circle (or three-nested-dependencies) model of the three pillars of sustainability (i.e. three concentric circles, economy being at the centre, then society and finally – encompassing the other two – environment), the environment requires the main focus. This does not entail that the other goals are not important or that they should not be implemented; on the contrary, progress in purely environmental SDGs will also positively affect other goals. At the international level, Bosselmann and Kim also argue that ecological integrity should be the priority goal and that other interests (e.g. socio-economic development) are subordinate. They define this main goal as 'safeguarding the integrity of Earth's life-support systems' and even go so far as to propose that it should be legally binding.[78]

5. CONCLUSION

Although sustainable development seems to take centre stage in global and EU policy, it cannot be said it has been fully implemented in the body EU environmental law. Examples exist where sustainability shines through, with the most evident example being Article 11 TFEU and several environmental policy documents. Without a doubt, there is clear value in past and current legislative action. However, several issues still stand in the way of an actually sustainable approach to the environment and environmental legislation. The lack of clarity surrounding the concept of sustainable development in EU law makes it difficult

---

76 N. Gunningnam, 'Should a general "duty of care" for the environment become a centrepiece of a "next generation" environment protection statute?' (2017) 34 *EPLJ (Environmental and Planning Law Journal)* 198, 202.

77 https://www.bath.ac.uk/announcements/focusing-on-key-sustainable-development-goals-would-boost-progress-across-all-analysis-finds/.

78 R.E. Kim and K. Bosselmann, 'Operationalizing Sustainable Development: Ecological Integrity as a Grundnorm of International Law' (2015) 24 *RECIEL* 194, 207.

to implement the principle and to know its legal value. Furthermore, the approach to environmental law is still mostly compartmentalised, fragmented and anthropocentric. The environment is not always considered in its entirety or for its inherent values. The focus so far on environmental resources, which inevitably has led to prioritising other (mainly economic) interests, is detrimental.

It is clear that the main problem is the current attitude towards the environment. Tinkering with the current body of EU environmental law through specific legislative changes is not an adequate solution for our sustainability problem. This contribution has argued that there is a need for a comprehensive overhaul and a change of perspective. Naturally, such a shift cannot be accomplished overnight. Therefore, several options were presented that support more sustainable EU environmental law. Overall, there is a need to clarify both the concept and the place of sustainable development in EU environmental law. What legal value and effects does this principle warrant? Operationalising Article 11 TFEU which lays down the principle of integration and sustainable development could itself offer a solution. Besides this, the question arises whether the idea of 'sustainable use' or a general duty of care for the environment should be inscribed in EU law. The advantage of such an obligation would be the shift towards a more proactive and preventative way of dealing with environmental harm. A more policy-oriented option is the prioritisation of environmental SDGs, as this would also serve in attaining other non-environmental goals. Nevertheless, the question of enforceability arises in all cases, ranging from the non-binding nature of the SDGs to the restricted legislative review available concerning Article 11 TFEU.

Evidently, these changes and a complete overhaul of EU environmental law with regards to sustainability will not all prove feasible or realistic in the short term. However, more immediate changes can be made in the approach and view of the environment, e.g. in current legislative action, implementation or application of EU environmental legislation. This would include adopting an integrated view and prioritising the environmental SDGs, all the while confirming the primordial significance of our environment.

THE PROGRAMMATIC APPROACH TO ACHIEVING SUSTAINABILITY IN ENVIRONMENTAL LAW

Is it Possible?

L.S. (Lolke) Braaksma

1. INTRODUCTION

Ecosystems are subjected to growing pressures.[1] As humankind's capacity to manipulate and alter ecosystems increases, more and more ecosystem goods and services are secured for socio-economic development.[2] Within scientific communities, a consensus has emerged that global environmental conditions are worsening, with humankind's over-exploitation as the main driver.[3]

Climate change and biodiversity loss are considered to be the two major environmental challenges of our era.[4] A study published in 2016 showed that the adverse impacts of this over-exploitation have already caused biodiversity to fall to unsustainable levels across more than half of the world's landmass.[5]

---

1 See e.g. S.L. Maxwell et al., 'Biodiversity: The ravages of guns, nets and bulldozers' (2016) 536 *Nature* 143–145; H.F.M.W. van Rijswick, 'The Road to Sustainability: How Environmental Law Can Deal with Complexity and Flexibility', editorial in (2012) 8(3) *Utrecht law Review* 1.

2 Daily describes ecosystem services as 'the conditions and processes through which natural ecosystems, and the species that make them up, sustain and fulfil human life', in G. Daily (ed.), *Nature's services: Societal Dependence on Natural Ecosystems*, 4th ed., Island Press, Washington D.C. 1997, idem. 3; See: Millennium Ecosystem Assessment, *Ecosystems and Human Well-Being: Synthesis*, Island Press, Washington D.C. 2005.

3 R.E. Kim, K. Bosselmann and V. Mauerhofer, *Planetary Boundaries in Post-2015 Sustainable Development Goals: Safeguarding Ecological Integrity as a Priority Goal and a Grundnorm of International Law*, Planetary Boundaries Initiative, WWF-UK 2013, 24/25.

4 K. Skogen, H. Helland and B. Kaltenborn, 'Concern about climate change, biodiversity loss, habitat degradation and landscape change: Embedded in different packages of environmental concern?' (2018) 44 *Journal for Nature Conservation* 12–20.

5 T. Newbold et al., 'Has land use pushed terrestrial biodiversity beyond the planetary boundary? A global assessment' (2016) 353 *Science* 288–291. Other environmental concerns – interconnected with these two concerns – are interference with the nitrogen and phosphorus cycles, stratospheric ozone depletion, ocean acidification, global freshwater use, changes in land use, chemical pollution, and atmospheric aerosol loading, see: R.E. Kim,

The gravity of these environmental concerns led scientists to assume that a new interval of geologic time period had begun after the 'Holocene', since humans have altered Earth's functioning so immensely. This time period is called the 'Anthropocene'.[6] While the precise consequences of this shift are uncertain, they are very likely to be catastrophic to human societies. International consensus has been reached to act fast and drastically on the myriad of environmental concerns at hand.[7]

It has been argued that current legal frameworks are inadequate to achieve sustainability.[8] Examples include provisions over-valuing political and economic objectives at the expense of environmental objectives, as well as the fragmented structure of legal frameworks, which is too centralised and places too much emphasis on uniform models and rational, linear, legal-centralist processes that assume certainty.[9] Fundamental changes are necessary to the main approaches governing social-economic systems that pursue sustainability.[10]

In the search for more sustainable management practices, numerous heterogeneous approaches are being developed and researched. The programmatic approach could be a frontrunner in this regard.[11] Examples of this approach can be found in the European Union (EU) and its Member States to achieve sectoral environmental objectives regarding, for instance, water quality, air quality and the conservation of Natura 2000 sites.[12] In the Netherlands, the most notable examples of the programmatic approach are the National Air Quality Cooperation Programme (NAQCP) and the (former) Programmatic Approach to Nitrogen (PAN).[13] These integrated approaches have the two-fold

K. Bosselmann and V. Mauerhofer, *Planetary Boundaries in Post-2015 Sustainable Development Goals: Safeguarding Ecological Integrity as a Priority Goal and a Grundnorm of International Law*, Planetary Boundaries Initiative, WWF-UK 2013, idem. 5.

6 See e.g. E.C. Ellis, *Anthropocene: A Very Short Introduction*, Oxford University Press, Oxford 2018.

7 See e.g. the United Nations Framework Convention on Climate Change (UNFCCC), COP 21, the Paris Agreement.

8 See e.g. K.N. Lee, 'Deliberately Seeking Sustainability in the Columbia River Basin' in L.H. Gunderson, C.S. Holling and S.S. Light (eds.), *Barriers and Bridges to Renewal of Regional Ecosystems*, Columbia University Press, New York 1995.

9 See e.g. F.M. Platjouw, *Environmental Law and the Ecosystem Approach: Maintaining Ecological Integrity Through Consistency in Law*, Routledge: Earthscan, London 2016.

10 See e.g. K.N. Lee, 'Deliberately Seeking Sustainability in the Columbia River Basin' in L.H. Gunderson, C.S. Holling and S.S. Light (eds.), *Barriers and Bridges to Renewal of Regional Ecosystems*, Columbia University Press, New York 1995.

11 See e.g. R.H.W. Frins and L.J.M. Timmermans, 'De bestuursrechtelijke toekomst programmatisch aangepakt' in R.J.N. Schlössels, B.A. Beijen, A.M.M.M. Bots and J.A.F. Peters (eds.), *In het nu ... wat worden zal: Over toekomstig bestuursrecht*, Kluwer, Deventer 2018, idem. 135–158.

12 See e.g. A.A. Freriks and H.F.M.W. van Rijswick, 'Programmatische aanpak stikstof en programmatische aanpak water: van tweeën een?' (2015) 9 *Tijdschrift voor Agrarisch Recht* 399.

13 *Dutch Government Gazette* 2015, 16320; *Dutch Government Gazette* 2009, 11559.

objective of achieving environmental objectives whilst allowing new economic development to take place.[14] The future Dutch Environment and Planning Act, which is anticipated to come into force in 2022, introduces a generic version of the programmatic approach, allowing this approach to be used for practically every component of the physical environment.[15]

This chapter aims to explore the legal implications and challenges of the programmatic approach when used to support the transition to sustainability. It begins by setting out the pathways to manage the environment sustainably and continues by providing an overview of what is required as a basis for environmental law to enable the transition towards this ideal. This points towards the application of the programmatic approach with a set of prerequisites (section 2). After that, EU and Dutch legal frameworks are discussed and analysed in light of this normative framework. The result will be an overview of the main legal implications and challenges when using the programmatic approach to strive for sustainability (section 3).[16] Finally, general conclusions are drawn (section 4).

2. THE PROGRAMMATIC APPROACH: A PROMISING APPROACH TO PURSUE SUSTAINABILITY

2.1. SETTING THE STAGE: SUSTAINABILITY AND SUSTAINABLE DEVELOPMENT

The dedication to move towards sustainability – the goal of a human-ecosystem equilibrium – can be observed in all sectors of society nowadays. Sustainable development – the holistic approach and temporal processes that lead us to sustainability – is regarded, in turn, as the main paradigm to act upon environmental concerns.[17] The concept of sustainable development gained worldwide attention with the publication of the Brundtland report, where it is defined as '[d]evelopment that meets the needs of the present without

---

14 A reduction of administrative costs is also mentioned as an objective of the programmatic approach, see e.g. *Dutch Government Gazette* 2015, 16320, idem. 31.

15 *Governmental Gazette* 2016, 156; *Parliamentary Papers II* 2020/21, 33118, no. 160. The physical environment is defined in article 1.2 of this Act and includes nature, water, infrastructure, housing, parking, recreation and mobility.

16 This part is delineated by only taking examples from regulations to achieve objectives regarding air quality, water quality and Natura 2000 sites.

17 See e.g. K. Bosselmann, *The Principle of Sustainability*, Routledge: Taylor & Francis, London 2016; M. Leach, I. Scoones and A. Stirling, *Dynamic sustainabilities: technology, environment, social justice*, Earthscan, London 2010. Some argue that the paradigm of sustainability should be replaced by resilience, see e.g. R.K. Craig and M.H. Benson, 'Replacing Sustainability' (2013) 46(4) *Akron Law Review* 841.

compromising the ability of future generations to meet their own needs.'[18] It is generally understood that sustainable development requires a balancing act between environmental, social and economic dimensions to attain a harmonious co-existence between them. The exact meaning of sustainable development is, however, contested and uncertain.[19] There is, for example, discussion on how different interests should be valued and weighed, both on an abstract level as well as in concrete cases.[20]

This chapter does not try to settle the debate on the precise implications of sustainable development. Instead, this concept is operationalised by discussing the conditions necessary to pursue sustainability. To this end, the concept of environmental utilisation space (EUS) is used, which illustrates that there are limits to the pressures that ecosystems can endure (section 2.2). Subsequently, the ecosystem approach and adaptive management are discussed, offering pathways to manage ecosystems sustainably (section 2.3). The section ends by providing the elements needed in light of these theories, resulting in a normative framework of the programmatic approach (section 2.4).

2.2. THE CONCEPT OF ENVIRONMENTAL UTILISATION SPACE

The concept of environmental utilisation space (EUS) represents the idea that exploitation ceilings can be formulated for the sustainable use of (non-)renewable environmental goods and of the natural environment as a sink for emissions.[21] Opschoor defines EUS as 'the locus of all feasible combinations of environmental services that represent steady states in terms of levels of relevant environmental quality and stocks of renewable sources.'[22] In other words: the EUS concept reflects the limits of the services provided by ecosystems and the capacity to absorb waste and pollution and regenerate.[23]

---

18 Report of the World Commission on Environment and Development, *Our Common Future*, United Nations General Assembly, Annex to document A/42/427, 1987, idem. 37.

19 J.M. Mog, 'Managing Development Programs for Sustainability: Integrating Development and Research Through Adaptive Management' (2006) 19(6) *Society and Natural Resources* 531.

20 There is, for example, discussion on placing an equal value on environmental, social and economic interests ('weak' sustainable development), instead of acknowledging that humans are dependent on nature, that humans are a part of nature and that ecosystems and elements of them have a value in themselves, which results in prioritising environmental interests above environmental and social interests ('strong' sustainable development).

21 V. Beekman, 'Environmental Utilization Space Between Science and Politics' (2004) 17(3) *Journal of Agricultural and Environmental Ethics* 293, 294.

22 J.B. Opschoor and R. Weterings, 'Environmental utilisation space: An introduction' (1994) 9(5) *Tijdschrift voor Milieukunde* 198, 199.

23 See also: L.S. Braaksma and K.J. de Graaf, 'Managing Environmental Utilisation Space in the Dutch Environment and Planning Act' in H. Tegner Anker and B.E. Olsen (eds.), *Sustainable*

The innovative part of the EUS concept is that it became clearer that there are, at all times, limits to the amount of environmental pressure that the ecosystems can take without damaging these systems or the life support processes that they enable.[24] De Bruyn gives the following example: one should not harvest more from the stock than the stock grows each year, or the next year will return a lower available stock for providing environmental services.[25] Beekman notes that the EUS concept embraces two striking features, namely intergenerational egalitarianism in the distribution of environmental goods *and* an egalitarian distribution of environmental utilisation space among the members of the current generation.[26]

From the above it becomes clear that there are boundaries to the environmental pressures ecosystems can take, and that, therefore, polluting rights are scarce. Now, the question rises as to how ecosystems should be managed to pursue sustainability and what that implies for the legal framework.

2.3. THE ECOSYSTEM APPROACH AND ADAPTIVE MANAGEMENT

The ecosystem approach has been described as a strategy for the integrated management of land, water and living resources that promotes conservation and sustainable use in an equitable way.[27] Trouwborst argues that, throughout the variety of definitions for an ecosystem approach, three core elements are substantially agreed upon. These elements are: (1) a holistic management of human activities (2) which is based on the best available knowledge on the components, structure and dynamics of ecosystems (3) and is aimed at satisfying human needs in a way that does not compromise the integrity or health of ecosystems.[28] Platjouw adheres to these elements and elaborates on the holistic

---

Management of Natural Resources: Legal Instruments and Approaches, Intersentia, Vol 5 European Environmental Law Forum Series, Cambridge 2018, idem. 142.

24 J.B. Opschoor and R. Weterings, 'Environmental utilisation space: An introduction' (1994) 9(5) *Tijdschrift voor Milieukunde* 198.

25 S.M. de Bruyn, *Economic Growth and the Environment: An Empirical Analysis*, Springer, Dordrecht 2000, idem. 29.

26 V. Beekman, 'Environmental Utilization Space Between Science and Politics' (2004) 17(3) *Journal of Agricultural and Environmental Ethics* 293, 294–295.

27 See the Convention on Biological Diversity, www.cbd.com; D.E.J. Currie, *Ecosystem-Based Management in Multilateral Environmental Agreement: Progress towards Adopting the Ecosystem Approach in the International Management of Living Marine Resources*, World Wildlife Fund 2007, idem. 1–2.

28 A. Trouwborst, 'The Precautionary Principle and the Ecosystem Approach in International Law: Differences, Similarities and Linkages' (2009) 18(1) *Review of European Community & International Environmental Law* 26.

element and integrative element.[29] The holistic element in environmental law refers to the idea that ecosystems should be seen and protected as a whole, whereas the integrative element aims to couple the sustainable use of ecosystem goods while maintaining the integrity of those ecosystems.[30]

The ecosystem approach requires adaptive management to deal with the complex and dynamic nature of ecosystems and the absence of complete knowledge or understanding of their functioning. One of the key objectives of the ecosystem approach is the maintenance of ecosystem integrity.[31] The ecosystem approach does not preclude other management and conservation approaches, such as single-species conservation programmes, but aims to integrate all these approaches and other methodologies to deal with complex situations. A comprehensive set of (various) measures have to be put in place on national, regional, local, and other scales to be effective.[32] Slocombe argues that adaptive management allows for the flexibility and inclusiveness to deal with constant environmental, societal and political change, which is necessary to adopt an ecosystem approach.[33]

The concept of resilience is – together with experimental science, systems theory and industrial ecology – considered the origin of adaptive management.[34] The idea of adaptive management was proposed by Holling in 1978, and has been developed further ever since.[35] Allen and Garmestani describe adaptive management theory as

> the process of defining and bounding the management problem, identifying and representing what we know through models of dynamics that identify assumptions and predictions so experience can further learning, identifying possible sources of uncertainty and alternate hypotheses and designing policies to allow continued resource management while enhancing learning.[36]

Essentially, this type of management translates essential ecological understanding based on extended studies of complex ecological systems into localised

---

29 F.M. Platjouw, *Environmental Law and the Ecosystem Approach: Maintaining Ecological Integrity Through Consistency in Law*, Routledge: Earthscan, London 2016, chapter 2.1.

30 H.D. Tolsma, *Integrated Environmental Permitting. Towards a Coherent System of Environmental Law in the Netherlands*, Europa Law Publishing, Zutphen 2019, idem. 10.

31 F.M. Platjouw, *Environmental Law and the Ecosystem Approach: Maintaining Ecological Integrity Through Consistency in Law*, Routledge: Earthscan, London 2016, idem. 71.

32 See e.g. annex 7 of the International Technical Workshop, *Biological Management of Soil Ecosystems for Sustainable Agriculture*, found on: www.fao.org.

33 D.S. Slocombe, 'FORUM: Defining Goals and Criteria for Ecosystem-Based Management' (1998) 22(4) *Environmental Management* 483–493.

34 C.R. Allen et al., 'Adaptive Management of Rangeland Systems' in D. Briske (ed.), *Rangeland Systems*, Springer Series on Environmental Management 2017, idem. 376.

35 C.S. Holling, *Adaptive Environmental Assessment and Management*, Wiley, Chichester 1978.

36 C.R. Allen and A.S. Garmestani, 'Adaptive management' in C.R. Allen and A.S. Garmestani (eds.), *Adaptive Management of Social-Ecological Systems*, Springer, Dordrecht 2015, idem. 4.

implications for human society. This is particularly the case for human learning and institutional change in a certain area.[37] The essence of adaptive management theory is an iterative, incremental, decision-making process built around a continuous flow of monitoring the effects of decisions and adjusting decisions accordingly.[38] This allows for a better response to the ecological uncertainty regarding ecosystems. Roughly three types of uncertainty can be identified, namely: imperfect knowledge, when knowledge on how ecosystems work is inadequate or inexact; incomplete knowledge, where multiple perspectives are needed to construct a full system understanding; and unpredictability, which results from the inherent variability and constant co-evolution of complex systems.[39]

A foundational premise of adaptive management is that knowledge of ecological systems is often incomplete and that, therefore, human interactions with the system should be experimental. Two frameworks to describe the processes that guide the implementation of adaptive management in resource systems can be distinguished: passive and active adaptive management.[40] Passive adaptive management can be described as the '*traditional prescription*'-type of management in which the best possible predictive model is designed. This model should be acted upon until evidence shows that the model is outdated.[41] This style unintentionally leads to additional knowledge about resource management, but it does not pursue such learning. Active adaptive management, in contrast, takes a more experimental route by pursuing management interventions which lead to learning. The key difference between these two frameworks ultimately comes down to the way uncertainty is recognised and treated.[42]

The literature seems to be rather clear on the general steps to be taken for passive- and active adaptive management.[43] The first step is to define goals and objectives; the second step is to formulate a plan and policies to reach these goals and objectives; the third step is to implement them; the fourth step is to evaluate, and lastly; the fifth step is to see what lessons can be learned

37 J. Jiggins and N. Röling, 'Adaptive Management: Potential and Limitations for Ecological Governance of Forests in a Context Normative Pluriformity' in J.A.E. Oglethorpe (ed.), *Adaptive Management: From Theory to Practice*, IUCN, Gland/Cambridge 2002, idem. 94.

38 J.B. Ruhl, 'Panarchy and the Law' (2012) 17(3) *Ecology and Society* 31.

39 L. Hasselman, 'Adaptive management; adaptive co-management; adaptive governance: what's the difference?' (2017) 24(1) *Australasian Journal of Environmental Management* 31.

40 See e.g. B. Williams, 'Passive and active adaptive management: Approaches and an example' (2011) 92(5) *Journal of Environmental Management* 1371.

41 C.J. Walters, *Adaptive Management of Renewable Resources*, Macmillan Publishers, Basingstoke 1986, idem. vii.

42 B. Williams, 'Passive and active adaptive management: Approaches and an example' (2011) 92(5) *Journal of Environmental Management* 1371.

43 See e.g. D.D. Murphy and P. Weiland, 'Science and structured decision-making: Fulfilling the promise of adaptive management for imperiled species' (2014) 4(3) *Journal of Environmental Studies and Sciences* 200.

(which can lead to a feedback loop to step two) to define a new or changed plan and policies.

In short, the ecosystem approach and adaptive management requires (1) environmental quality objectives, set on the basis of available knowledge on the components, structure and dynamics of ecosystems, which aim to satisfy human needs in a way that does not compromise the integrity or health of ecosystems, together with (2) a coordinated and integrated approach of land-use management and (3) the constant generation and incorporation of new sustainability knowledge and, finally, (4) adaptation of land-use decisions to best available knowledge.[44]

2.4. A NORMATIVE FRAMEWORK FOR THE PROGRAMMATIC APPROACH

The programmatic approach as a policy instrument can be supportive to pursue sustainability. This chapter defines this approach as 'an integrated, cyclic decision-making process – following a structured, multistep protocol – which contains the use of plans and programmes to achieve environmental objectives within a certain time frame.' Some readers will recognise similarities between this definition and definitions of adaptive management. This is no surprise, as the idea of the programmatic approach can be regarded as a novel adaptive management strategy.[45]

Similar steps can be identified when using the programmatic approach compared to adaptive management. The first is to identify the environmental objectives for the compartments of the environment that have to be achieved within a set time frame. The second step is to design a coherent and consistent plan and/or programme, which includes selecting the measures to improve the quality of the environment as well as a framework to influence the permissibility of new socio-economic developments. The third is to conduct interim monitoring, and evaluate whether the plan and/or programme concerned is on track to achieve the environmental objectives. The fourth step is to adapt the plan and/or programme: this means it is modified when interim monitoring results or new scientific knowledge indicates that the environmental objectives are not achievable within the set time frame.

---

44 See also: H.F.M.W. van Rijswick et al., *Rechtsvergleichende Studie zu Instrumenten eines nachhaltigen Landmanagements Comparative Law Analysis on Instruments for Sustainable Land Management (CLAIM)*, Leibniz-Zentrum für Agrarlandschaftsforschung (ZALF) e.V. 2015.

45 See also: H. Schoukens, 'The quest for the Holy Grail and the Dutch Integrated Approach to Nitrogen: how to align adaptive management strategies with the EU Nature Directives?' (2018) 15(2) *Journal for European Environmental & Planning Law* 171.

In addition, as a prerequisite, the accompanying legal frameworks should support the programmatic approach. These frameworks should therefore include a coherent and consistent set of provisions to, *inter alia*, (re)distribute environmental utilisation space, to revoke permits, and to monitor, evaluate and adapt the plan or programme. Next to that, the legal frameworks should also include other elements necessary in a constitutional democracy: *inter alia*, norms regarding transparency, participation, legal protection, streamlined decision-making processes and providing compensatory measures when permits which allow detrimental activities are revoked.[46]

3. THE PROGRAMMATIC APPROACH IN EU AND DUTCH ENVIRONMENTAL LAW: LEGAL IMPLICATIONS AND CHALLENGES

3.1. INTRODUCTION

From the above, the requirements the programmatic approach should adhere to from theory, have become relatively clear. Now it is time to analyse the legal implications and challenges which emerge when this normative-laden approach is implemented within EU and Dutch legal frameworks.[47] This analysis will be done on a conceptual level and in line with the four stages of the programmatic approach as identified in section 2.4 above. At the end of each stage, examples of legal implications and challenges that arise from current legal frameworks will be provided. Monitoring and evaluating are discussed together with the adaptive element, as this element on its own is less interesting from a legal point of view. The analysis is, therefore, undertaken for environmental objectives (section 3.2), plans and programmes, (section 3.3) and monitoring, evaluation and adaptation (section 3.4).

3.2. SETTING ENVIRONMENTAL OBJECTIVES

3.2.1. The Regime for Formulating Objectives

Article 192 Treaty on the Functioning of the European Union (TFEU) stipulates that EU environmental policy and law aims to preserve, protect and improve

[46] See e.g. R. Bellamy, 'Constitutional Democracy' in M.T. Gibbons (ed.), *The Encyclopedia of Political Thought*, Wiley-Blackwell, Hooken NJ/Oxford 2014; These legal frameworks should be based on environmental principles, see e.g. G.A. Biezeveld, *Onze ecologische voetafdruk. Hoe het milieurecht kan helpen die te verkleinen*, Europa Law Publishing, Groningen 2009.

[47] See also: F.A.G. Groothuijse and R. Uylenburg, 'Everything according to plan? Achieving environmental quality standards by a programmatic approach' in M. Peeters and R. Uylenburg, *EU Environmental Legislation. Legal Perspectives on Regulatory Strategies*, Edward Elgar, Cheltenham 2014.

the quality of the environment. Often, policies based on this provision require a certain quality of some aspect of the environment that must be achieved within a time frame, the so-called environmental quality standard (EQS). Although EU environmental law does not provide for a uniform definition of EQSs, such a standard can generally be defined as a value or quality that specifies the status of a specific component of the ecosystem, such as air, soil or water, which has to be achieved by Member States.[48] An example of an EQS can be found in Article 2(35) of the Water Framework Directive where it is defined as 'the concentration of a particular pollutant or group of pollutants in water, sediment or biota which should not be exceeded in order to protect human health and the environment.'[49]

Member States often enjoy a considerable amount of discretion to choose how they want to achieve EQSs.[50] A Member State can, for example, decide to halt issuing permits for new activities that are detrimental to the environment. It may also decide to reduce the emissions of current detrimental activities by (partly) revoking the permit necessary to conduct the activity, thereby reducing the detrimental effects of that activity. This strategy can also be used sometimes to offset (or to compensate for) the detrimental effects of a new project. Another route is to prescribe improvement measures when permitting a new project (mitigation), such as filters to reduce emissions into the air. Other measures are to (let third parties) carry out measures that improve the quality of the environment.

This type of thinking in environmental law is typically referred to as the goal-based approach: goals are specified in EU and/or national law, and it is more or less left to the public authorities of the Member States to decide how to achieve them. Goal-based approaches

> consist of norms, which operate at different levels: the goals setting the high-level objectives; the functional requirements including the criteria to be met to fulfill the goals; and the regulations that set out the detailed requirements for meeting the functional requirements and the goals.[51]

---

48 See for another definition: F.A.G. Groothuijse and R. Uylenburg, 'Everything according to plan? Achieving environmental quality standards by a programmatic approach' in M. Peeters and R. Uylenburg, *EU Environmental Legislation. Legal Perspectives on Regulatory Strategies*, Edward Elgar, Cheltenham 2014, idem. 117–118.

49 Directive 2000/60/EC of the European Parliament and of the Council of 23 October establishing a framework for Community action in the field of water policy.

50 M.N. Boeve and G.M. van den Broek, 'The Programmatic Approach; a Flexible and Complex Tool to Achieve Environmental Quality Standards' (2012) 8(3) *Utrecht Law Review* 74; Article 288 TFEU.

51 T. Henriksen, 'Protecting Polar Environments: Coherency in Regulating Arctic Shipping' in R. Rayfuse (ed.), *Research Handbook on International Marine Environmental Law*, Edward Elgar, Cheltenham 2015, idem. 370.

In this context, the distinction between emission limit values (ELVs) and EQSs is crucial. ELVs are not aimed at achieving a certain quality of a component of the ecosystem within a certain time frame, but rather at limiting the emissions of polluting substances in the environment at the source to a certain level. Just like EQSs, ELVs are not uniformly defined in EU law. ELVs are defined in the IE Directive as 'the mass, expressed in terms of certain specific parameters, concentration and/or level of an emission, which may not be exceeded during one or more periods of time.'[52]

It is not necessarily the case that achieving the ELVs will result in achieving a certain EQS. Groothuijse and Uylenburg point out the possibility that all individual point sources comply with an applicable ELV set for a certain substance, but that the EQS for the same substance is nevertheless exceeded because of other diffuse pollution sources that are not directly linked to a specific point source.[53] An ELV, therefore, does not determine the maximum concentration of emissions of a certain substance in component of the environment. There is, of course, a substantial link between controlling ELVs and the EQSs, as it will be easier to achieve EQSs when the emissions of point sources are limited. Legal frameworks can provide a link between the ELVs and EQSs in the assessment criteria for a permit for a specific detrimental activity.[54]

The EUS concept is also relevant in this regard. The EQSs are supposed to set concrete requirements on what a good state of water quality entails. This means that a ceiling must be created, which, together with knowing (or using models to estimate) the current state of the quality of the environment and how it is influenced by prescribing ELVs and other factors, means that – at least in theory – the EUS can be determined for a component of the environment.

3.2.2. *Examples of Legal Implications and Challenges*

Several examples of legal implications and challenges can be identified when setting environmental objectives with a programmatic approach to pursue sustainability. One lies in taking into account all components of the ecosystem.[55] EQSs are not always based on the pressures that the environment can take, as the maximum environmental pressure is expressed in legally binding norms which are often – if not always – influenced by socio-economic interests.

---

52 Article 3 under 5 of the IE Directive.

53 F.A.G. Groothuijse and R. Uylenburg, 'Everything according to plan? Achieving environmental quality standards by a programmatic approach' in M. Peeters and R. Uylenburg, *EU Environmental Legislation. Legal Perspectives on Regulatory Strategies*, Edward Elgar, Cheltenham 2014, §1.

54 Ibid.

55 R.T. Lackey, 'Seven pillars of ecosystem management' (1998) 40(1–3) *Landscape and Urban Planning* 21–30.

This means that the legal leeway does not necessarily correspond with the capacity of ecosystems and, consequently, that the ecological EUS is at odds with the legal EUS.[56] Examples of this include the fact that EQSs can be different throughout the territories of the Member States and are often regulated in a fragmented manner without being coordinated well with each other. Current EQSs, therefore, often do not take into account the environment as a whole.[57]

A second example concerns to what extent derogating from these objectives should be made possible. Current legal frameworks often include a certain room for derogation.[58] This could allow for a No Net Loss (NNL) approach or a per balance system,[59] and can allow Member States to avoid an economic lockdown when there is no EUS left.[60] In theory, these possibilities to derogate could be used in accordance with active adaptive management; that is, to experiment and to learn. But to what extent do current legal frameworks allow for such flexibility, and to what extent should additional legal guarantees be implemented to reduce the risk of not achieving environmental objectives within the time frame?[61]

The last example addressed here is what happens when a programmatic approach fails. This question is particularly relevant in the Netherlands at the moment, as the Administrative Jurisdiction Division of the Council of State concluded that the PAN was unlawful in light of Article 6 of the Habitat Directive.[62] The decision illustrates how EU legal frameworks can provide for more legal guarantees to achieve environmental objectives than some Member

56 K.J. de Graaf, F.M. Platjouw and H.D. Tolsma, 'The future Dutch Environment and Planning Act in light of the ecosystem approach' (2018) 29(Part B) *Ecosystem Services* 306–314.

57 See in this regard also: F.M. Platjouw, 'Environmental Law and the Ecosystem Approach: Maintaining Ecological Integrity Through Consistency in Law', Routledge: Earthscan, London 2016; R. Giljam, *Towards Ecological Governance in EU Energy Law. With a Focus on Biomass Regulation and the Use of 'Best Available Techniques'*, PhD University of Groningen 2019.

58 See on this e.g. M.M. Bogaart, *Flexible directives: towards a better environment? An analysis of the balance between flexibility for Member States and harmonisation regarding the effective protection of European Union's waters and air*, PhD University of Amsterdam 2017.

59 M.N. Boeve and G.M. van den Broek, 'The Programmatic Approach; a Flexible and Complex Tool to Achieve Environmental Quality Standards' (2012) 8(3) *Utrecht Law Review* 78; L. Squintani and H.F.M.W. van Rijswick, 'Improving Legal Certainty and Adaptability in the Programmatic Approach' (2016) 28 *Journal of Environmental Law* 443, 445.

60 See e.g. E.T. Schutte-Postma, 'Luchtkwaliteit en EU; Europese achtergronden van het Besluit luchtkwaliteit' in S.T. Ramnewash-Oemrawsigh (ed.), *Regeling inzake luchtkwaliteit; Nederland op slot?*, Vereniging voor Milieurecht, BJu 2006/1.

61 Significant efforts have already been made to analyse these aspects in EU environmental Directives, see e.g. S. van Holten and H.F.M.W. van Rijswick, 'The consequences of a governance approach in European Environmental directives for flexibility, effectiveness and legitimacy' in M. Peeters and R. Uylenburg, *EU Environmental Legislation. Legal Perspectives on Regulatory Strategies*, Edward Elgar, Cheltenham 2014.

62 Administrative Jurisdiction Division of the Council of State (Afdeling bestuursrechtspraak van de Raad van State (ABRvS)) 29 May 2019, ECLI:NL:RVS:2019:1603 and ECLI:NL:RVS:2019:1604.

States are willing to require. The aftermath of this decision is still ongoing. Questions include to what extent permits that have been granted under this programmatic approach should be revoked in order to still achieve the environmental objectives, and under what circumstances new permits could be granted.[63]

3.3. DESIGNING PLANS AND PROGRAMMES

3.3.1. *Typology of Plans and Programmes*

Plans and programmes have been used for decades, both as a requirement under EU directives as well as by the Member States themselves to achieve environmental objectives.[64] They can be defined as 'a package of policy intentions and measures that serve to achieve and retain environmental values and goals in the physical environment.'[65] They are prepared for agriculture, forestry, fisheries, energy, industry, transport, waste management, water management, telecommunications, tourism, town and country planning or land-use planning.[66]

Squintani and Van Rijswick distinguish three types of plans and programmes required under EU environmental legislation.[67] The first type includes plans and programmes that are required to obtain information about Member States' compliance with EU environmental goals. In the second place, there are plans and programmes used as a tool to achieve EU environmental goals by inducing Member States to set up the groundwork for environmental policy. For the third type, plans and programmes are the only instruments required to achieve these goals. These authors only regard the latter two types as plans or programmes with a programmatic approach. The reason for this seems to be that these plans and programmes directly influence the available EUS in a particular component of the environment.

---

63 See e.g. R. Kegge and A. Drahmann, 'The Programmatic Approach: Finding the Right Balance between the Precautionary Principle and the Right to Conduct a Business', (2020) 17(1) *Journal for European Environmental & Planning Law* 76–98.

64 See e.g. A.A. Freriks and H.F.M.W. van Rijswick, 'Programmatische aanpak stikstof en programmatische aanpak water: van tweeën een?' (2015) 9 *Tijdschrift voor Agrarisch Recht* 399.

65 This definition is used by the Dutch legislator in the future Environment and Planning Act. For an EU definition see article 2 of Directive 2001/42/EC of the European Parliament and of the Council of 27 June 2001 on the assessment of the effects of certain plans and programmes on the environment (SEA Directive).

66 See article 3 of the SEA Directive.

67 L. Squintani and H.F.M.W. van Rijswick, 'Improving Legal Certainty and Adaptability in the Programmatic Approach' (2016) 28 *Journal of Environmental Law* 443, 444.

The difference between the two latter types of programmatic approaches is whether or not they have a delinking effect. A delinking effect in this regard means that the connection between the EQS and the authorisation of a specific project affecting this standard is missing, and that the plan or programme is used by the public authority as the sole reference when assessing whether a request for a permit is eligible to be granted. When plans and programmes are just one of the instruments to achieve EU environmental goals, they have a linkage and therefore have no delinking effect; whereas if the plan or programme is the *only* instrument to achieve these goals, such a linkage between the EQSs and allowing new activities to take place is missing, thus having a delinking effect.[68]

The distinction can be regarded as a sliding scale, as it depends on the specific legal regime to what extent public authorities have to take into account the trade-offs and other considerations made in the plan and programmes when granting or rejecting permits.

3.3.2. *Examples of Legal Implications and Challenges*

Designing the legal frameworks to allow for plans and programmes that support the transition to sustainability is not an easy task. It includes coming up with fair and just mechanisms to (re-)distribute environmental utilisation space, building in legal guarantees which ensure that measures being put into the plan or programme are being realised, and revoking permits for detrimental activities when necessary, with or without compensation.[69]

Another point of interest is how norms regarding transparency, participation and legal protection should be used in the programmatic approach. In fact, multiple analyses have been conducted to align the programmatic approach with the norms from the Aarhus Convention and the EU legal framework on, for instance, the principle of effective legal protection.[70] Although effective participation of the public and stakeholders is needed for the programmatic approach to function properly, the question remains what these formal elements should entail to be effective, as it will probably be less effective when long procedures impair the functioning of the plans and programmes. Decision-making procedures should be streamlined to allow the plan and/or programme to function properly, but should also allow the public and

68 Ibid. idem. 445.

69 See e.g. R. Kegge and A. Drahmann, 'The Programmatic Approach: Finding the Right Balance between the Precautionary Principle and the Right to Conduct a Business' (2020) 17(1) *Journal for European Environmental & Planning Law* 76–98.

70 See e.g. L. Squintani and E.J.H. Plambeck, 'Judicial Protection against Plans and Programmes Affecting the Environment: A Backdoor Solution to Get an Answer from Luxembourg' (2016) 13(3/4) *Journal for European Environmental Law & Planning Law* 294–324.

stakeholders to stand up for their rights and influence the contents of a plan or programme.[71]

3.4. MONITORING, EVALUATING AND ADAPTIVE CAPACITY

3.4.1. *Monitoring for Effectiveness*

Obligations to monitor, evaluate and, when necessary to adapt plans and programmes can be found throughout EU environmental directives.[72] For example, both the Dutch PAN and NAQPC provide for annual monitoring obligations with possibilities to add extra measures or limit the available EUS when interim results show that the environmental objectives are not reached within the set time frame.[73] It can even be required to revoke given authorisations when the evaluation concludes that environmental objectives will not be achieved with the added measures or when the environmental utilisation space is diminished.[74]

3.4.2. *Examples of Legal Implications and Challenges*

Just like in the United States, where adaptive management approaches have been used for decades, attempts to integrate adaptive management strategies are often attempts to fit adaptive management within existing legal mandates and protocols.[75] Benson and Schultz state in this regard that 'adaptive management is being thrown like a blanket on top of existing authorizations and requirements, with little attention to how practitioners balance this new mandate in relation to other legal and institutional requirements.'[76]

---

71 See for suggestions to reconcile these elements: L. Squintani and H.F.M.W. van Rijswick, 'Improving Legal Certainty and Adaptability in the Programmatic Approach' (2016) 28 *Journal of Environmental Law* 443, §4.

72 See on this e.g. B.A. Beijen, H.F.M.W. van Rijswick and H.T. Anker, 'The Importance of Monitoring for the Effectiveness of Environmental Directives, A Comparison of Monitoring Obligations in European Environmental Directives' (2014) 10(2) *Utrecht Law Review* 126–135.

73 Administrative Jurisdiction Division of the Council of State (Afdeling bestuursrechtspraak van de Raad van State (ABRvS)) 17 May 2017, ECLI:NL:RVS:2017:1259, §§6.6 and 6.11.

74 See also: R. Kegge and A. Drahmann, 'The Programmatic Approach: Finding the Right Balance between the Precautionary Principle and the Right to Conduct a Business' (2020) 17(1) *Journal for European Environmental & Planning Law* 76–98, §3.

75 M.H. Benson and C. Schultz, 'Adaptive Management and Law' in C.R. Allen and A.S. Garmestani (eds.), *Adaptive Management of Social-Ecological Systems*, Springer, Dordrecht 2015, idem. 41.

76 Ibid.

Nevertheless, implementing an adaptive approach in a legal system based on legal values such as legal certainty, finality and stationarity is challenging.[77] Adapting means moving away from front-ended decision-making procedures and embracing the dynamics of ecosystems, but is simultaneously at odds with the need for finality and legal certainty of stakeholders.[78] Also on this point, further research is required in order to strike an appropriate balance between the opposed interests.[79]

4. CONCLUSION AND DISCUSSION

This chapter explored some of the main legal implications and challenges on a conceptual level that arise when pursuing sustainability with the programmatic approach. In this regard, the words of Advocate General Kokott in her conclusion on the Dutch Programmatic Approach on Nitrogen say it all: '(...) whilst a programmatic integrated planning approach is to be welcomed, there is still room for improvement in its practical implementation.'[80]

Current programmatic approaches do not necessarily meet the criteria that are needed to be ecologically sound. However, in light of the above, when sustainable environmental objectives are pursued, the programmatic approach could be deemed a valuable policy instrument. The legal implications and challenges indicated in this chapter mainly revolve around reconciling a holistic and adaptive approach with key legal values, such as legal certainty and finality.[81]

A considerable amount of research has already been conducted on the question concerning to what extent current EU and Dutch legal frameworks allow for a programmatic approach. Provided that this approach can support sustainability theories, perhaps an additional question that should be asked is how current legal frameworks should be designed to sufficiently implement these theories with the programmatic approach.

---

77 M.F. Frohlich, C. Jacobson, P. Fidelman and T.F. Smith, 'The relationship between adaptive management of social-ecological systems and law: a systematic review' (2018) 23(2) *Ecology and Society* 23.

78 See also: L. Squintani and H.F.M.W. van Rijswick, 'Improving Legal Certainty and Adaptability in the Programmatic Approach' (2016) 28 *Journal of Environmental Law* 443–470.

79 Lessons may be learnt from experiences from the United States in this regard, see e.g. C.R. Allen and A.S. Garmestani (eds.), *Adaptive Management of Social-Ecological Systems* Springer, Dordrecht 2015.

80 Conclusion A-G J. Kokott, 25 July 2018 in Joined Cases C-293/17 and C-294/17, ECLI:EU:C:2018:622.

81 M.F. Frohlich et al., 'The relationship between adaptive management of social-ecological systems and law: a systematic review' (2018) 23(2) *Ecology and Society* 23, under 'Legal barriers to adaptive management'.

AN ANALYSIS OF THE CIRCULAR ECONOMY LEGISLATIVE PACKAGE

A New Paradigm vs The Old Waste Law

Beltrán PUENTES COCIÑA

1. INTRODUCTION

Adopted by the European Parliament and the Council on 30 May 2018, the waste package was the first legislative endorsement of the circular economy political strategy launched by the European Commission in 2015.[1] Indeed, this is the first time that the principle of circular economy has been written into an EU legal binding instrument. Its adoption allowed the Juncker Commission to see the first legislative acts of its major environmental project published before the end of the mandate.

The circular economy legislative package consists of four directives[2] that reform the European regulatory framework for the waste sector. Here, we will focus on the modifications that Directive (EU) 2018/851 made to

1 As part of its Circular Economy Action Plan [Communication from the Commission to the European Parliament, the Council, the European Economic and Social Committee and the Committee of the Regions. *Closing the loop. An EU action plan for the Circular Economy*, COM(2015) 614 final], the Commission adopted on 2 December 2015 a package of legislative proposals on waste.

2 These are the four directives adopted:

- Directive (EU) 2018/851 of the European Parliament and of the Council of 30 May 2018 amending Directive 2008/98/EC on waste [OJ L150, 14.6.2018, pp. 109–140].
- Directive (EU) 2018/850 of the European Parliament and of the Council of 30 May 2018 amending Directive 1999/31/EC on the landfill of waste [OJ L150, 14.6.2018, pp. 100–108].
- Directive (EU) 2018/852 of the European Parliament and of the Council of 30 May 2018 amending Directive 94/62/EC on packaging and packaging waste [OJ L150, 14.6.2018, pp. 141–154].
- Directive (EU) 2018/849 of the European Parliament and of the Council of 30 May 2018 amending Directives 2000/53/EC on end-of-life vehicles, 2006/66/EC on batteries and accumulators and waste batteries and accumulators, and 2012/19/EU on waste electrical and electronic equipment [OJ L150, 14.6.2018, pp. 93–99].

Directive 2008/98/EC on waste, known as the Waste Framework Directive (WFD).[3] It should be noted that about three-quarters of the WFD has been modified (31 of the 47 articles have been replaced or added in, along with two new annexes). In this sense, the reform raises, first, a question regarding legislative technique. Such a thorough revision of the regulatory framework on waste could have been done through a new framework directive that more ambitiously and thoroughly examined its relationship with other regulatory sectors (product legislation, eco-design, materials or chemical substances).

Nonetheless, the present work raises a more specific question concerning the extent to which the approval of the legislative package has contributed to the introduction of a new sustainability paradigm[4] by incorporating the new principle of the circular economy into European waste law. It should be recalled that the circular economy strategy sought to bring about 'systemic change', as stated in the Action Plan for the circular economy that was presented in 2015, along with the legislative reform proposals.

In other words: has the new regulatory framework introduced substantial changes to the legal regime of waste which, in their development by national or regional competent authorities, will lead to significant change in existing waste management and prevention policies? Or to the contrary, does the reform merely aim at providing new or updated monitoring mechanisms to improve effectiveness and compliance with regard to waste law, rather than introducing any substantially new measures?

2. MAIN REFORMS

I will now point out the key elements of the WFD reform, introduced by Directive (EU) 2018/851, sticking to the most relevant aspects for answering the questions raised and determining to what extent they correspond to the Commission proposals.[5]

2.1. ALIGNMENT OF DEFINITIONS

The first aspect to be highlighted is the effort at regulatory simplification and alignment of definitions, as reflected in Directive (EU) 2018/851. The glossary in Article 3 WFD was expanded to hold new definitions and concepts, outline

---

3 Directive 2008/98/EC of the European Parliament and of the Council of 19 November 2008 on waste and repealing certain Directives [OJ L312, 22.11.2008, pp. 3–30].

4 M. Geissdoerfer, P. Savaget, N.M.P. Bocken and E.J. Hultink, 'The Circular Economy – A New Sustainability Paradigm?' (2017) 143 *Journal of Cleaner Production* 757–768.

5 Proposal for a Directive of the European Parliament and of the Council amending Directive 2008/98/EC on waste [Brussels, 2.12.2015. COM(2015) 595 final].

some existing definitions and compile some that were scattered among other directives in the sector.

Definitions of material concepts ('non-hazardous waste', 'municipal waste', 'construction and demolition waste', 'food waste') were introduced, while others ('bio-waste') were updated. These terms classify waste by its origin (municipal, construction and demolition, food) or composition (hazardous, non-hazardous, biodegradable). The concepts are used to specify the scope of the regulatory measures,[6] to facilitate and harmonise the adoption of policies and measures for different waste streams by the competent governments.

Some new functional concepts relating to waste operations were also included, albeit modified from the Commission's proposals. The definitions of 'material recovery' (as preferred over energy recovery) and 'backfilling' (as a specific form of recycling) were introduced. The concept of 'waste management' was also modulated, with explicit reference to 'sorting' as part of the recovery process. However, the Commission's proposal to revise the definition of 'preparing for re-use' was left out.

Finally, the concept of 'extended producer responsibility scheme' was introduced. The definition mentions the obligation of Member States to ensure that producers take responsibility for waste management. The terminology rather imprecisely states that this consists of 'a set of measures taken by Member States to ensure that producers of products bear financial responsibility or financial and organisational responsibility for the management of the waste stage of a product's life cycle'. In simpler terms, this refers to the costs of waste management.

2.2. MEASURES TO PROMOTE THE WASTE HIERARCHY

The new Article 4(3) WFD requires Member States to promote the application of the old principle of the waste hierarchy: 'Member States shall make use of economic instruments and other measures to provide incentives for the application of the waste hierarchy, such as those indicated in Annex IVa or other appropriate instruments and measures'. Economic incentives are key instruments to promote circular economy. They play a crucial role by embedding resource efficiency in the decision-making of economic actors.[7]

Accordingly, Annex IVa contains an extensive list of examples of economic instruments and other measures Member States can apply to complement the

6 N. de Sadeleer, *Droit des déchets de l'UE. De l'élimination à l'économie circulaire*, Bruylant, Brussels 2016, p. 245.

7 T. Domenech and B. Bahn-Walkowiak, 'Transition Towards a Resource Efficient Circular Economy in Europe: Policy Lessons from the EU and the Member States' (2019) 155 *Ecological Economics* 7, 14.

waste prevention measures mentioned in WFD Annex IV. Some of the most relevant are:

- charges and restrictions for the landfilling and incineration of waste;
- 'pay-as-you-throw' schemes that charge waste producers on the basis of the waste generated;
- fiscal incentives for donation of products; deposit-refund schemes; and
- fiscal measures to promote the uptake of products and materials that are prepared for re-use or recycled.

As with the preventive measures compiled in Annex IV, those contained in the new Annex IVa to promote the waste hierarchy constitute little more than suggestions for national or regional governments to incorporate into the drafting of their waste prevention programmes or waste management plans. The discretionary nature of their adoption, the extensive list of examples, the variety of instruments and the inclusion of voluntary instruments (e.g. the 'continued promotion of dialogue and co-operation between all stakeholders in waste management, the promotion of voluntary agreements and waste reporting by business') make this list a loose or non-binding standard for the governments responsible for implementing waste policies.

In this author's opinion, this list of recommendations is in practice intended to guide the action of governments and administrations with the greatest deficiencies in the implementation of waste legislation and policies. It could even be considered a sort of soft law embedded in a legislative act (strictly speaking, the text of a directive would be hard law). Indeed, these lists of examples can be considered to perform the functions of soft law technique, acting as guidelines for the implementation or development of waste policies.[8]

2.3. MINIMUM MEASURES IN THE FIELD OF PREVENTION

Reducing the waste generated at source and the hazardous content of that waste is regarded as the highest priority according to the waste hierarchy established in Article 4 WFD. However, it is widely acknowledged that waste policies have been so far focused on recycling.[9] The directive hardly included any specific

[8] For a more extensive study on the functions of soft law, see C. van Dam, 'EU Administrative Soft Law and the Separation of Powers' in H.-M. ten Napel and W. Voermans, *The Powers That Be. Rethinking the Separation of Powers. A Leiden Response to Möllers*, Leiden University Press, Leiden 2016, pp. 191–213.

[9] European Environmental Bureau (EEB), *A circular economy within ecological limits: Why we need to set targets to reduce EU resource consumption and waste generation in the new Circular Economy Action Plan*, 14 February 2020, p. 8.

rules and obligations to prevent the generation of waste – beyond obliging Member States to draw up prevention programmes, whose implementation has been unequal and inconsistent. This lack of concreteness is common in relation to the environmental principle of prevention. Although it is seen a cornerstone of environmental law and an omnipresent principle, it often remains elusive and difficult to pinpoint.[10]

Until the reform, Article 9 WFD simply entrusted the Commission with various tasks: to prepare a report on waste generation and to adopt an action plan to change consumption patterns, both by 2011, and to set prevention targets for 2020. The targets were abandoned and development of these tasks by the Commission has been ineffective and without impact.

To replace this deficient preventive model, the new Article 9(1) WFD now establishes a series of minimum measures to be taken by Member States to avoid waste generation. However, as with the two annexes mentioned previously, the measures seem to be too generic, not allowing for the attribution of responsibility in the event of non-compliance by the Member States. Some of them are declarations of will or overall goals, rather than specific measures.

Significantly, no quantitative prevention targets have been set (i.e. waste generation targets). The European Environmental Bureau (EEB)[11] has recently argued for setting targets on waste generation in the new Circular Economy Action Plan (the European Green Deal[12] of the Von der Leyen Commission has announced the forthcoming publication of a new CEAP). They could be based on those already existing in some European countries and regions (e.g. France, Italy and Flanders). Their setting could help to control the rates of waste generation, which exceed their historical maximum every year,[13] since 'targets play a crucial role for the emergence and diffusion of innovations'.[14]

However, the positive aspect is that these measures of Article 9(1) are established as the minimum content of waste prevention programmes (see section 2.8 below) and many refer to production and design phases or the activities of product reuse and repair. For instance: (a) promote and support sustainable production and consumption models; (b) encourage the design,

---

10 L.-A. Duvic-Paoli, 'Principle of prevention' in L. Krämer and E. Orlando (eds.), *Principles of Environmental Law*, Elgar Encyclopedia of Environmental Law Series, Vol. 6, Edward Elgar, Cheltenham/Northampton MA 2018, pp. 161–173 at 162.

11 See n. 9 above, p. 8.

12 Communication from the Commission to the European Parliament, the European Council, the Council, the European Economic and Social Committee and the Committee of the Regions. *The European Green Deal*. [Brussels, 11.12.2019, COM(2019) 640 final].

13 Approximately 2.6 billion tonnes of waste were generated in the EU-28 in 2014 [Eurostat, waste statistics, 2014]. This is the highest amount of waste ever recorded [European Parliament, *Towards a circular economy – waste management in the EU*, September 2017, p. 31].

14 H. Wilts, N. Von Gries and B. Bahn-Walkowiak, 'From Waste Management to Resource Efficiency – The Need for Policy Mixes' (2016) 8(7) *Sustainability* 622, p. 8.

manufacturing and use of products that are resource-efficient, durable (including in terms of life span and absence of planned obsolescence), reparable, re-usable and upgradable; (c) target products containing critical raw materials to prevent that those materials become waste; (d) encourage the re-use of products and the setting up of systems promoting repair and re-use activities; (e) encourage the availability of spare parts, instruction manuals, technical information, or other instruments, equipment or software enabling the repair and re-use of products.

Most of the other measures relate directly to the reduction of waste generated, although some propose interesting solutions to tackle waste production, such as market restrictions. In this respect, Member States are encouraged to identify products that are the main sources of littering, notably in natural and marine environments, and take appropriate measures to prevent and reduce litter from such products. If market restrictions are chosen, it is noted that they should be proportionate and non-discriminatory.

This is a similar approach to the one adopted in the recent single-use plastics directive.[15] Although it is not the only measure it contains, the directive is known by this name because it prohibits the placing on the market of certain plastic products that are among the items that most frequently contaminate European beaches and for which good, plastic-free alternatives exist (plastic cutlery, plastics plates, plastic straws, food containers made of expanded polystyrene, beverage containers and cups for beverages made of expanded polystyrene, products made from oxo-degradable plastic, and cotton bud sticks made of plastic). In addition, Member States must take the necessary measures to achieve a quantitative reduction in the consumption of other products (food containers made of plastic and plastic cups for beverages).

2.4. UPDATING TARGETS FOR PREPARING FOR RE-USE AND RECYCLING

The targets for preparing for re-use and recycling, which had to be renewed by 2020, have been updated. According to Article 11(2) WFD, preparation for re-use and recycling of municipal waste shall be increased to a minimum of 55 per cent by weight by 2025, 60 per cent by 2030 and 65 per cent by 2035.

A problem for the use of such quantitative targets is the huge variations between Member States in waste management rates. For instance, the rate of municipal waste recycled or composted varies from 66 per cent in Germany

[15] Directive (EU) 2019/904 of the European Parliament and of the Council of 5 June 2019 on the reduction of the impact of certain plastic products on the environment [OJ L155, 12.6.2019, pp. 1–19].

to 15 per cent in Romania.[16] It seems that waste management is only weakly influenced by the European common regulatory framework.[17] Considering the difficulties of achieving the new ambitious targets, certain underperforming Member States will be allowed to extend the target deadlines by a maximum of five years, provided that certain requirements set out in Article 11 WFD, paragraphs 3, 4 and 5 are met.

A more ambitious reform could have included specific targets for preparation for re-use of certain types of waste. An example of these can be found in the Spanish Waste Electrical Electronic Equipment (WEEE) legislation. Spain became the first European country to set targets for preparation for re-use with the approval of Royal Decree 110/2015 of 20 February on WEEE. The targets, more than their ambition, are remarkable for their symbolic value: 3 per cent or 4 per cent of the collected equipment, depending on the category, has to be prepared for reuse.

2.5. PROMOTING USE OF SECONDARY RAW MATERIALS AND BY-PRODUCTS

Directive (EU) 2018/851 also amended Article 6 WFD, which governs the regime for declaring the end-of-waste status. Until the reform, the article only regulated the abandonment of the waste status, allowing it under certain conditions. With the new wording, Member States must not only allow it but take appropriate measures to ensure that recovered materials cease to be waste, provided that certain requirements are met. Thus, the new wording seeks to promote the abandonment of waste status for substances (a) that are to be used for specific purposes, (b) for which there is a market or demand, (c) that meet the technical requirements for the specific purposes and comply with current legislation and products standards, and (d) that will not result in adverse environmental or health impacts if used.

Furthermore, Article 6(2) WFD strengthens the Commission's powers to adopt implementing acts that establish detailed criteria for applying the end-of-waste status to certain waste streams. In this sense, specific criteria should at least be developed for aggregates, paper, tyres and textiles. However, the powers granted to the Commission have been reduced with respect to its aspirations. The executive arm of the EU, in its 2015 proposal for legislative reform, proposed granting itself powers to adopt not implementing but delegated acts.

Similarly, the amendment to Article 5 WFD aims to promote the use of by-products: substances or objects resulting from production processes not primarily intended to produce them, but which can be used for another purpose.

---

16 Eurostat. Municipal waste by waste operations. Data of 2014.

17 H. Wilts, N. Von Gries and B. Bahn-Walkowiak, n. 14 above, p. 6.

The new wording of the provision requires Member States to take appropriate measures to ensure the recognition of by-products when certain conditions are met: (a) the further use of the substance or object is certain, (b) the substance or object can be used directly without further processing, beyond normal industrial practice, (c) the substance or object is produced as an integral part of a production process, and (d) its further use is lawful, in accordance with specific legislation on products and environmental and health protection.

The Commission's powers in this area were also strengthened (Article 5, paragraph 2 WFD) but its proposal to do so through delegated acts was abandoned. In the final wording, the Commission is given the faculty to adopt implementing acts that lay down detailed criteria regarding the uniform application of by-product conditions. To this end, the European executive body should take as a starting point the most stringent and environmentally protective criteria among those adopted by the Member States, giving priority to the usual practices of industrial symbiosis in developing the detailed criteria.

2.6. REINFORCEMENT OF EXTENDED PRODUCER RESPONSIBILITY

The new Article 8a WFD introduces minimum operational requirements that Member States must meet if they choose to establish an extended producer responsibility (EPR) scheme. Most importantly, it requires Member States to ensure that, in the case of collective fulfilment of EPR obligations, producers are given incentives to design their products in such a way that they incorporate increased options for recycling, re-use and repair.

Until the reform, the link between producer responsibility and product design was treated superficially and was left to the will of Member States. The previous wording of Article 8(2) WFD stated that 'Member States may take appropriate measures to encourage the design of products in order to reduce their environmental impacts and the generation of waste in the course of the production and subsequent use of products'. Now, new Article 8a WFD, paragraph 4(b), establishes that the financial contributions must be 'modulated, where possible, for individual products or groups of similar products, notably by taking into account their durability, reparability, re-usability and recyclability and the presence of hazardous substances, thereby taking a life-cycle approach'. The modulation of contributions to EPR systems can be a decisive step towards more durable, reusable and repairable products. This could overcome Wilts et al.'s criticism of collective schemes:

> Such an approach helps to reduce costs but it lowers the ambition for the individual companies to develop more circular products: The company would have to bear the

costs for design and production changes, while the benefits of the reduced end-of-life costs would be shared with all other companies in the market.[18]

While strengthening the role of EPR systems, this measure connects with the essential idea of the EPR principle: creating green design incentives for manufacturers by establishing a link between product design and management costs.[19] The development of the EPR concept may be viewed in the context of a general shift in environmental law and policy-making 'from command and control towards instruments such as economic and informational tools, which leave more flexibility in how the set policy objectives are to be achieved'.[20]

The Commission is also given power to adopt harmonised criteria for the uniform application of Article 8a. These would modulate the producer contributions for each product, or group of products in case of collective compliance with EPR obligations, so as to avoid distortions in the functioning of the internal market. These implementation acts would be adopted in accordance with the examination procedure referred to in Article 39(2) WFD.

2.7. AMENDED SYSTEM FOR CALCULATING ACHIEVEMENT OF TARGETS

For proper assessment, objective calculation rules were introduced. They establish detailed criteria by which the various Member States will quantify their outcomes in a homogeneous manner (Article 11a WFD). These rules must also be expanded by the Commission through implementing acts that establish a common methodology for calculating the weight of recycled metals. Similarly, a delegated act must establish a system for calculating, verifying and reporting the weight of materials or substances that are disposed of after a sorting operation and not subsequently recycled.

Adoption of Directive (EU) 2018/851 also implies incorporating homogeneous calculation rules into the WFD, to measure achievement of the targets for preparing for re-use and recycling of municipal waste by 2025, 2030 and 2035. For uniform application of these criteria, new powers are also given to the Commission, which will have to issue rules for calculating the weight of recycled metals and bio-waste separated at source, in accordance with

18 H. Wilts, N. Von Gries and B. Bahn-Walkowiak, n. 14 above, p. 12.

19 C. Dalhammar, 'Extended Producer Responsibility' in L. Krämer and E. Orlando (eds.), *Principles of Environmental Law*, Elgar Encyclopedia of Environmental Law Series, Vol. 6, Edward Elgar, Cheltenham/Northampton MA 2018, pp. 208–218.

20 H. Kalimo, R. Lifset, C. Van Rossem, L. Van Wassenhove, A. Atasu and K. Mayers, 'Greening the Economy through Design Incentives: Allocating Extend Producer Responsibility' (2012) 21(6) *European Energy and Environmental Law Review* 274–305.

Article 11a, paragraphs 6 and 9. Powers are also delegated to the Commission to complete the rules for calculating, verifying and reporting the weight of materials or substances that are disposed of after a sorting operation and not recycled afterwards (paragraph 10).

2.8. STRENGTHENING OF MANAGEMENT PLANS AND PREVENTION PROGRAMMES

With the transposition of Directive (EU) 2018/851, the content of the instruments that Member States are required to draw up for waste management planning and waste prevention will be harmonised and extended. The current wide variations between Member States' documents may be the reason for setting these new minimum contents. For instance, the prevention programmes show considerable differences in detail, coverage, objectives, time horizons and extent (from the 4–6 pages of the Finnish and Norwegian programmes to the 200 pages of the detailed Bulgarian programme).[21]

The content of the waste prevention programmes will be expanded (Article 29 WFD). From the entry into force of the national rule that transposes the Directive, the programmes must include at least all the preventive measures provided for in Article 9(1) WFD (see section 2.3 above). They will also contain information about how the instruments and measures included in Annexes IV and IVa contribute to waste prevention. Additionally, specific national programmes to prevent food waste must be adopted.

Concerning management plans, new wording of Article 28 WFD emphasises identification of the main disposal and recovery facilities, attention to waste streams containing significant amounts of key raw materials, and how to assess the need to close existing facilities. The plans should also incorporate ways of ensuring that no waste suitable for recovery is accepted in landfills. This involves assessing existing collection systems, verifying total land and material coverage, and including measures to improve their operation, combat and prevent all forms of waste disposal and clean up dispersed waste. There must also be qualitative or quantitative indicators and targets.

Once again, executive powers are assigned to the Commission to establish the format for communicating data on the adoption and revision of management plans and prevention programmes. The role of the European Environment Agency as the assessing body for plans and programmes is also strengthened through the task of publishing a bi-annual progress report.

---

[21] European Environment Agency (EEA), *Waste Prevention in Europe – the status in 2014*, Copenhagen 2015.

2.9. INCREASED REPORTING AND CONTROL OBLIGATIONS

Article 37 WFD has been completely amended to introduce a new data reporting system, which supersedes the excessively bureaucratic and inefficient system that required reports from Member States every three years. The new wording establishes that Member States shall report to the Commission on the achievement of the targets for preparing for re-use and recycling, providing data for each calendar year. The data shall be communicated electronically within 18 months of the end of each year, in a format determined by the Commission through implementing acts, accompanied by a quality control report and a report on measures taken.

Subsequently, the Commission shall publish a report containing a review of the reported data and an assessment of the data with regard to collection, organisation, sources, methodology, thoroughness, reliability, timeliness and consistency. Obligations to evaluate and monitor the achievement of the objectives are also reinforced with the introduction of early warning reports (Article 11b). These are studies that the Commission will carry out three years prior to the expiration deadlines established in Article 11.

3. CONCLUSIONS

The circular economy legislative package aims to introduce the new circular economy paradigm into the old waste law. To this end, the toolbox of WFD has been reviewed and expanded.

The greatest novelties lie in the introduction of some relatively new instruments. One highlight is the introduction of a list of economic instruments that Member States can adopt to implement the waste hierarchy, as well as a list of minimum measures on prevention. Both catalogues have been criticised for their lack of concreteness and non-binding nature. Other instruments that have been introduced are the early warning reports – to be drawn up by the Commission in the event of the prospect of non-compliance by a Member State with the quantitative targets – and the modification of data calculation and reporting systems.

Some existing instruments have also been updated. In this regard, the minimum content of both prevention programmes and waste management plans has been expanded, the quantitative targets for preparing for re-use and recycling have been updated and the collective EPR schemes have been strengthened and harmonised. Another key aspect is the strengthening of the Commission powers to issue delegated or implementing acts in relevant matters (end-of-waste status, by-products or EPR systems). In addition, the alignment and simplification of concepts and definitions also contributes to a more effective implementation of waste law.

An analysis of this toolbox shows that all these elements aim to improve implementation of waste policies. The new or updated instruments address better compliance with traditional principles that have been in force in waste legislation for decades – waste hierarchy, prevention, the polluter-pays. Aiming for a greater effectiveness of waste hierarchy, they seek to prioritise waste prevention and to improve waste management in the EU.[22]

However, we must also point out that some elements of the package refer to a more in-depth review of waste law, linking it to other sectors such as product design and reuse or repair activities. This could mean a broader and more useful view of the concept of the circular economy. As Backes noted, 'even more important than the discussion on waste law may be the questions related to product design and to the use of products'.[23]

This is the case with new Article 8a WFD, which seeks to link producer responsibility to product design by modulating producers' contributions to EPR collective schemes according to the product's characteristics. Similarly, Article 9 WFD calls on Member States to adopt preventive measures, by promoting the design of products that are durable, material efficient, repairable, reusable and upgradable, along with other measures that affect production and use of products. These elements call for a broader concept of the circular economy, which must involve not only change in waste management but also in production and consumption patterns. The recent directive on single-use plastics[24] and the directive on contracts for the sale of goods[25] are two examples of how the concept could be evolved.

However, these innovative elements are only a small part of the WFD reform and run contrary to abandoning the idea of setting prevention and preparation for re-use quantitative targets or lowering the Commission's aspirations to take more ambitious measures through delegated acts. An analysis of the *entire* package shows a not so ambitious view of the circular economy, which should be more than a demanding update of waste legislation garnished with specific measures in other sectors.[26]

---

22 According to Santamaría Arinas, it was symptomatic that the VII Programme implied that the problem of the waste regulatory sector lies in its effective application rather than in the need for its reform [R.J. Santamaría Arinas, 'Aproximación jurídica a las medidas de la Unión Europea para la economía circular' (2016) 117 *Revista Ambienta* 36, p. 45].

23 Ch.W. Backes, *Law for a Circular Economy*, Eleven International Publishing, The Hague 2017, p. 15, available at: www.uu.nl/sites/default/files/rgl-ucowsl-backes-law_for_a_circular_economy.pdf.

24 Directive (EU) 2019/904 of the European Parliament and of the Council of 5 June 2019 on the reduction of the impact of certain plastic products on the environment [OJ L155, 12.6.2019, pp. 1–19].

25 Directive (EU) 2019/771 of the European Parliament and of the Council of 20 May 2019 on certain aspects concerning contracts for the sale of goods, amending Regulation (EU) 2017/2394 and Directive 2009/22/EC, and repealing Directive 1999/44/EC.

26 A. Nogueira López, 'Cuadrar el círculo' in (2019) 3 *InDret – Revista para el análisis del Derecho* 23.

Recalling the thesis put forth in the introduction of this chapter, it can be concluded that the package seeks mainly to promote a higher degree of effectiveness of waste law, through updated instruments and new tools for monitoring waste policies. Although some elements seem to have an impact on production and design policies, the truth is that no new principles or substantive relevant rules have been added.[27] We can conclude that the introduction of the principle of circular economy in the waste sector has only served, roughly speaking, to strengthen the old waste law.

A similarly critical view is shared by Domenech and Bahn-Walkowiak:

> While the roadmap is a comprehensive visioning exercise that tackles all key areas, the circular economy package is limited in its scope and weak in terms of instrumentation (no hard-binding objectives apart from those on waste; measures very much rely on adaptation of existing instruments, e.g. eco design, rather than other economic instruments).

They also consider that

> progress in recycling and reuse of materials are certainly in the right direction to increase the circularity of the system and work towards closing the loops of production and consumption processes by providing alternative sources of resources to maintain the actual physical stock of societies, but these measures are clearly insufficient if they just supplement rather than substitute primary material consumption.[28]

The circular economy has not brought a new paradigm in waste law. To achieve innovative legal reforms, the EU will have to move into less explored territories. From the old waste law to a broader concept: the circular economy of products.[29] We will have to rely on further reforms concerning eco-design and use of products, to see if this new environmental paradigm can bring about the desired systemic change.

This chapter shows how the role of law is crucial in the adoption of innovative sustainability strategies. In this regard, it has shown how recent changes in

---

[27] According to J.F. Alenza, the circular economy does not represent an indispensable value as a legal principle, especially when compared to classical legal principles and values [J.F. Alenza García, 'La economía circular en el Derecho ambiental' (2019) 35 *Revista Electrónica De Derecho Ambiental*].

[28] T. Domenech and B. Bahn-Walkowiak, n. 7 above, pp. 17–18.

[29] This is the path mapped out in a recent report of the European Economic and Social Committee (EESC), which notes that the circular economy has already moved beyond recycling and waste management into a new and more critical stage under the business sector initiative. The EESC encouraged the incoming Commission to ensure that this broadening of the concept is reflected in any circular economy package. [Opinion of the European Economic and Social Committee on 'Developing synergies across different circular economy roadmaps' (own-initiative opinion), EESC 2019/02078, OJ C14, 15.1.2020, pp. 29–33].

the waste legal regime seek to promote a greater degree of effectiveness in the implementation of waste policies, through new or renewed instruments. In addition, it concludes that disruptive decisions need to be made in the field of the circular economy as long as the old waste law is not sufficient to promote a paradigm shift. Furthermore, the greatest possibilities for innovation seem to lie in areas that are not covered by waste law, such as product design or consumption. Therefore, a correct interaction between the different legal areas is also necessary in order to draw up cohesive, breakthrough and powerful strategies.

PRECONDITIONS AND CONSTRAINTS OF EFFECTIVE PRIVATE ENVIRONMENTAL GOVERNANCE

Carola GLINSKI

1. INTRODUCTION

Environmental law, in particular the traditional administrative law approach, often suffers from an effectiveness and enforcement problem. Therefore, and accompanying a general (neo-)liberal turn in law, environmental law has in the last few decades increasingly embraced private environmental governance instruments such as business self-regulation, private standards or sustainability certification based on information and market mechanisms.

The expectation was that rules and standards set up by practice itself and/or with the inclusion of various stakeholders and driven by market forces would provide for more effective, prompter, more flexible, more problem-adequate and better accepted answers to environmental problems and would face fewer enforcement problems than the classical environmental law regulatory approach. This applies in particular to the protection of ecosystems and the environment at global level where effective public international law agreements are difficult to agree upon and where private governance provides for a means to bridge national jurisdictional borders and to achieve sustainable transnational production chains.

This chapter critically analyses the capacity of private standardisation and certification systems to ensure sustainable production patterns and a sustainable (transnational) production chain, using as examples the European sustainability certification of bio-fuels and the 'Forest Stewardship Council'. Both are elaborate transnational (public-)private governance systems aiming at the protection of ecosystems. At the same time, both systems face enormous challenges with regard to their effectiveness and reliability, and thereby provide exemplary insights. Thereby, the role of law, and legal challenges and constraints are explored, in particular in the relevant (public or private) framework systems as a (potential) safeguard for adequate substantive as well as procedural standards.

The chapter briefly describes the two systems with their main substantial and procedural requirements, before it evaluates their functioning in practice as well as their structural problems concerning implementation, compliance control and enforcement (Sections 2., 3. and 4.). It then elaborates the legal challenges arising from that, for the environmental governance systems themselves as well as for the legal systems in which they are embedded. Three types of challenges are addressed: challenges with regard to an adequate and effective framework (Section 5.1.), those relating to the general legal and factual empowerment of stakeholders (Section 5.2.) as well as the need for a progressive interpretation in particular of tort law, which should 'take private governance seriously' (Section 5.3).

2. CERTIFICATION OF BIO-FUELS

2.1. THE SYSTEM

Within the European strategy to combat climate change, the Renewable Energies Directive promotes the use of bio-fuels, bio-liquids and biomass. Article 3(4) of Directive 2009/28/EC ('RED I')[1] requires Member States to ensure a share of at least 10 per cent of energy from renewable sources in their final energy consumption in the transport sector in 2020.[2]

The European certification system is meant to guarantee the sustainability of the promoted bio-fuels, in particular their positive greenhouse gas balance, namely that the reduction in GHGs emissions realised by the use of bio-fuels rather than fossil fuels is not invalidated by negative impacts on greenhouse gas stocks, on environmental protection and biodiversity through (direct or indirect) land use changes. One focus lies on the global South where bio-liquids such as palm- and soy oil can be produced cheaper and more efficiently.[3]

---

1 For the sake of illustration, this chapter uses the experience with the old promotion system of the first Renewable Energy Directive 2009/28/EC (RED I) on the promotion of the use of energy from renewable sources, [2009] OJ L140/16. Meanwhile, based upon these experiences, the system has been amended twice, by Directive (EU) 2015/1513, [2015] OJ L239/1, and by the new Directive (EU) 2018/2001 on the promotion of the use of energy from renewable sources (recast), [2018] OJ L328/82 (RED II), which has to be implemented by 30 June 2021.

2 Art. 25(1) Directive 2018/2001 has amended this target to at least a 14% share by 2030, which, however, also includes renewable liquids and gaseous transport fuels of non-biological origin and recycled carbon fuels.

3 The EU would not even be able to produce the necessary amount of biomass on its own territory, See S. Ponte and C. Daugbjerg, 'Biofuel Sustainability and the Formation of Transnational Hybrid Governance' (2015) 24 *Environmental Policy* 96 ff. The main exporters were Argentina, Indonesia, the United States and Brazil; see European Commission, *Technical assessment of the EU biofuels sustainability and feasibility of 10% renewable energy in transport*, SWD(2015) 117 final, 3.

To this end, Article 17 RED I codified sustainability criteria, namely greenhouse gas emission-saving requirements as well as the prohibition on taking bio-fuels into account which have been obtained from land with high biodiversity value in 2008 or from land with a high carbon stock such as primary forests, highly bio-diverse grasslands, wetlands or peatlands. In addition to that, agricultural raw materials cultivated in the EU have to be produced in accordance with the requirements and standards for good environmental and agricultural practice, Article 17(6).

Adherence to these criteria within the transnational supply chain for bio-fuels must be ensured by way of a multi-level compliance system in accordance with Article 18 RED I. This compliance system can either be based on a national standardisation scheme or on a private 'voluntary' standardisation scheme recognised by the European Commission. These schemes must concretise and implement the sustainability requirements. The standardisation schemes, for their part, have to provide for independent auditing and certification by a private certification body.

In order to be recognised by the European Commission,[4] private voluntary schemes have to apply the substantive requirements correctly, provide for accurate data, comply with the methodological requirements concerning measurement, and provide for adequate standards of reliability and transparency such as an internal documentation management. Moreover, they must ensure independent auditing of economic operators (by a certification body) before they can participate in the scheme, as well as at least annual audits, Article 18(4) RED I.[5]

Certification bodies and auditors must possess sufficient capabilities and expertise to ensure sustainability. They comply with these requirements when they follow the ISO 19011 standard on quality and/or environmental management auditing. The main requirements are that audits must be planned, conducted and reported properly, and that risk assessments and verification measures are carried out.[6]

That system, however, proved not to be sufficiently reliable, and it contributed to significant land-use changes, in particular in the global South, where former tropical rain forest was (directly or indirectly) turned into palm oil plantations.[7]

---

4 The recognition of voluntary schemes is an implementing act by the Commission in terms of Art. 291 TFEU, following the advisory procedure of Art. 4 of Regulation (EU) No. 182/2011 laying down the rules and general principles concerning the Commission's exercise of implementing powers, [2011] OJ L 55/13. See also Art. 13(1)(a) of Reg (EU) No. 182/2011. Thereunder, the Commission has to take into consideration the opinion of the Committee on the Sustainability of Biofuels and Bioliquids, see Arts. 18(6) and 25(3) Renewable Energy Directive.

5 See also European Commission, Communication on voluntary Schemes and default values in the EU biofuels and bioliquids sustainability schemes, [2010] OJ C 160/1.

6 ibid, section 2.2.2.

7 See e.g. European Council of Auditors, *The EU system for the certification of sustainable biofuels, Special Report 18/2016* (Luxembourg, 2016).

2.2. STRUCTURAL PROBLEMS

With regard to substantive requirements, the original RED I sustainability criteria have been criticised for being too broad. References to 'highly biodiverse grasslands' or 'high ecological value' have led to quite different interpretations by the various schemes or resulted in complete ignorance of the criteria. Also, the lack of a definition of 'waste' led to the declaration of virgin oil as waste oil.[8]

Further, the criteria neither required any standards for good environmental or agricultural practice outside the EU, nor an environmental impact assessment. The sustainability criteria covered neither environmental problems in relation to transportation and the further processing of the fuel nor additional socio-economic considerations such as labour conditions, land rights, other community rights, or food security.

Most importantly, RED I did not address the issue of indirect land-use changes. Indirect land-use changes occur when energy crops do not directly replace land of high ecological value but replace food crops, which then, in turn, are grown on land of formerly high ecological value, leading to deforestation and to the destruction of natural lands and biodiversity. The use of palm oil in particular has been heavily criticised from the beginning by NGOs, academics and not least the European Parliament.[9] Consequently, the audit team of the European Court of Auditors

> found that the assessments carried out by the Commission as a basis for the recognition of voluntary schemes did not adequately cover some important aspects necessary to ensure the sustainability of biofuels. In particular, the Commission did not require voluntary schemes to verify that the biofuel production they certify does not cause significant risks of negative socio-economic effects, such as land tenure conflicts, forced/child labour, poor working conditions for farmers and dangers to

---

8 For a critique, see the European Council of Auditors (above n. 7), pp. 25 f.; see also S. Romppanen, 'The EU's Biofuels: Certified as Sustainable?' (2012) 3(3) *Renewable Energy Law and Policy Review* 173 at 177; A. Schmeichel, *Towards Sustainability of Biomass Importation – An Assessment of the EU Renewable Energy Directive*, Europa Law Publishing, Groningen 2014, pp. 167 ff. Concretising acts by the Commission – such as the Communication on voluntary schemes and default values in the EU biofuels and bioliquids sustainability schemes, [2010] OJ C 160/1, the Communication on the practical implementation of the EU biofuels and bioliquids sustainability scheme and on counting rules for biofuels, [2010] OJ C 160/8, and the Commission note on 'Verification of the chain of custody of biofuels made from waste and processing residues' (10 October 2014); available at: https://ec.europa.eu/energy/sites/ener/files/documents/2014_letter_wastes_residues.pdf, – came relatively late, and they still left a lot of room for interpretation.

9 See, for example, C. Bowyer, *Anticipated Indirect Land Use Change Associated with Expanded Use of Biofuels and Bioliquids in the EU – An Analysis of the National Renewable Energy Action Plans* (Institute of European Environmental Policy, November 2010); see also recital (74) RED I.

> health and safety. Similarly, the impact of indirect land-use changes (ILUC) on the sustainability of biofuels is not covered by this assessment. Although we acknowledge the technical difficulties in assessing the impact of ILUC, the relevance of the EU sustainability certification system is undermined without this information.[10]

This ambiguity of the standards and their loopholes are also reflected in the implementation by the various private schemes, which not only differ in their definitions of excluded areas of high ecological value but also have taken considerably differing approaches to additional social requirements. Only a number of multi-stakeholder roundtable schemes set up at least some requirements in these respects, whereas industry-driven schemes neglected them.[11]

The enforcement system has triggered serious criticism as well. NGOs have criticised the procedure for the recognition of voluntary schemes for its lack of transparency and public participation.[12] The European Court of Auditors found that voluntary schemes were recognised despite the fact that they applied inappropriate verification procedures that did not ensure compliance of economic operators with the substantive requirements.[13] It further complained that the RED I did not require the European Commission to exercise supervision over voluntary schemes once they are recognised; with the consequence that no monitoring was undertaken even where it would have been easy to do so with a simple review of the schemes' websites. Moreover, no complaints system was in place that could have alerted the Commission.[14]

Two critical points have been highlighted with regard to certification bodies. Firstly, the European Commission's recognition does not extend to certification bodies; nor are they subject to any Commission assessment.[15] Moreover, the RED I did not establish particular requirements concerning the institutional set-up of certifiers or the independence and transparency of the audits, for example by way of inclusion of stakeholders.[16]

---

10 See European Court of Auditors (above n. 7), p. 35.

11 For details, see Schmeichel (above n. 8), pp. 167 ff.

12 Several NGOs tried to get access to documents relating to the recognition of voluntary schemes and, failing to obtain them, claimed an infringement of their right of access to environmental information. The General Court, however, dismissed the claim for procedural reasons; see Case T-278/11 *Client Earth et al. v. Commission*, ECLI:EU:T:2012:593; see also Schmeichel (above n. 8), p. 134.

13 European Court of Auditors (above n. 7), p. 25.

14 European Court of Auditors (above n. 7), pp. 29 f.

15 For critique, see Schmeichel (above n. 8), pp. 136 f. In this regard, the Commission seems to be more concerned with avoiding 'excessive administrative burden' than with strict control of the activities of economic operators, see the Staff Working Document accompanying the Renewable Energy Progress Report of 27/3/2013, SWD(2013) 102 final, p. 17.

16 For critique, see S. Romppanen, *New governance in context: Evaluating the EU biofuels regime*, Dissertation, University of Eastern Finland, 2015, p. 49.

Procedural shortcomings concerning the recognition and supervision of voluntary schemes and certification bodies of course have an impact on the proper implementation of the substantive sustainability requirements by the voluntary schemes. Without supervision of the voluntary schemes following their recognition, there is no guarantee that they will really provide 'accurate data'.[17] Indeed, the special report of the European Court of Auditors concluded that, 'because of weaknesses in the Commission's recognition procedure and subsequent supervision of voluntary schemes, the EU certification system for the sustainability of biofuels is not fully reliable.'[18]

In fact, voluntary schemes significantly differ not only in their substantive standards but also in their transparency, public participation, inclusion of stakeholders, fees, resources and expertise, and required verification procedures.[19] The intensity of control that individual certification bodies have exercised in practice is unclear, because the European Commission has not controlled their activities. One may suspect that they also differ in relation to fees and to the intensity of control exercised, as the audit team of the European Court of Auditors suggested.[20]

Economic operators that have a choice between private schemes with differing protection requirements and enforcement standards will often opt for the private system and/or certification body that delivers the desired result at the lowest costs. Or, in case of rejection, the operator may simply switch scheme.[21] As a consequence, a race to the bottom between private systems has been observed, to the disadvantage of schemes with comprehensive standards and intense control. This can be illustrated by the German national scheme, which was the first to be set up under the RED I and which exercised tight control over voluntary schemes and certification bodies. Whereas in 2011, it also had a 33 per cent share of participants from other EU Member States and 11 per cent from third countries, the number of participants decreased continuously whereas participation in the Commission's newly recognised private voluntary schemes increased.[22]

---

17 See Schmeichel (above n. 8), p. 135.

18 European Court of Auditors (above n. 7), p. 8.

19 See e.g. the overview of voluntary schemes at: https://ec.europa.eu/energy/sites/ener/files/documents/voluntary_schemes_overview_dec17.pdf; see also J. Hamelmann, *Certification of biofuels within the Directive 2009/28/EC: A comparative analysis of certification schemes*, Bachelor's Thesis University of Twente, 2016, pp. 30 ff.; for critique, see European Court of Auditors (above n. 7), p. 25.

20 European Court of Auditors (above n. 7), p. 32.

21 On 'scheme shopping', see European Court of Auditors (above n. 7), p. 32, see also Hamelmann (above n. 19), p. 45.

22 See C. Glinski, 'Certification of the Sustainability of Biofuels in Global Supply Chains' in P. Rott (ed.), *Certification – Trust, Accountability, Liability*, Springer, Cham 2019, pp. 163, 178 ff., with further references.

3. FOREST STEWARDSHIP COUNCIL (FSC)

3.1. THE SYSTEM

The Forest Stewardship Council (FSC) is a private standardisation scheme for sustainable forestry based on membership. It sets standards for 'environmentally appropriate, socially beneficial and economically viable management of the world's forests'.[23] It has a three-chamber membership structure, with economic, social and environmental representatives respectively, which is further divided into Northern and Southern sub-chambers with equal voting power.[24] The substantive provisions consist of 10 very general requirements for economic operators relating to applicable laws; social and economic well-being of workers and local communities; indigenous peoples' rights; and forest management with a long-term economic, environmental and social perspective; maintaining, conserving and/or restoring ecosystem services and environmental values; and applying a management system based upon an impact assessment, monitoring and the precautionary approach. These principles are further concretised by criteria and implementing documents.[25] The concretisation of these principles is decentralised at the national or regional level.[26]

The development of standards follows the FSC's tripartite structure and must be carried out in a transparent, independent and participatory manner based on public notice and comment procedures. The ISEAL Code of Good Practice for Setting Social and Environmental Standards[27] and the ISO definition for consensus[28] must be applied.[29]

---

23 See the mission statement at: https://www.fsc.org/en/about-us.

24 See https://fsc.org/en/governance-strategy.

25 See Forest Stewardship Council, *FSC International Standards, FSC Principles and Criteria for Forest Stewardship*, FSC-STD-01-001 V5-2 EN, 2015, available at: https://fsc.org/en/document-centre/documents/resource/392 with further references.

26 See Forest Stewardship Council, *Structure and Content of National Forest Stewardship Standards*, FSC-STD-60-002 (V1-0) EN, 2009, available at: https://fsc.org/en/document-centre/documents/resource/261.

27 ISEAL Code of Good Practice for Setting Social and Environmental Standards, January 2004, s. 5.

28 ISO (ISO/IEC Guide 2:1996): 3.1 'Consensus: General agreement, characterized by the absence of sustained opposition to substantial issues by any important part of the concerned interests and by a process seeking to take into account the views of interested parties, particularly those directly affected, and to reconcile any conflicting arguments. Note – Consensus need not imply unanimity.'

29 For further details, see E. Meidinger, 'The Administrative Law of Global Private-Public Regulation: the Case of Forestry' (2006) 17 *European Journal of International Law* 47, 61 ff.; E. Meidinger, 'Multi-Interest Self-Governance through Global Product Certification Programmes' in O. Dilling, M. Herberg and G. Winter (eds.), *Responsible Business, Self-Governance and the Law in Transnational Economic Transactions*, Hart Publishing, Oxford 2008, pp. 259, 265 ff.

The FSC applies its own process for the accreditation of certification bodies (with the possibility of suspending accreditation[30]) and regulates the certification procedure in detail. This applies to forest certification as well as supply chain certification. Notable safeguards against fraud or at least a biased approach are included: the assessment of economic actors must be based upon a review by an interdisciplinary team including forestry, biology and social science experts and upon consultation with stakeholders, and the assessment report must be peer reviewed by two or three independent specialists.[31]

The FSC's compliance system is based on the incentive of being entitled to use the certificate, the FSC logo, for the marketing of timber products. In case of non-adherence to the standards, the certificate and/or the membership can be revoked. The FSC also provides for a complaints procedure, which is, however, only open to members.[32]

Thus, the FSC has established an impressive and elaborate governance structure, which is dedicated to procedural justice with participatory and inclusive structures in place, and it has therefore been reviewed quite positively by legal scholars.[33]

3.2. PROBLEMS IN PRACTICE

Nevertheless, in practice, numerous cases of unsustainable certification have been revealed that undermine the reliability of the certificate as such. Identified shortcomings relate to the reliability of the (concretised) standards as well as to the monitoring of compliance and to enforcement.[34]

---

30 See Forest Stewardship Council, *General requirements for FSC accredited certification bodies*, FSC-STD-20-001 V4-0 EN, available at: https://fsc.org/en/document-centre/documents/resource/280, paras. 5.4.4. f.; see also Meidinger, 'Multi-Interest Self-Governance' (above n. 29), pp. 267 f.

31 See Forest Stewardship Council, *Forest management evaluations*, FSC-STD-20-007 (V3-0) EN, 2009, available at: https://fsc.org/en/document-centre/documents/resource/279.

32 For an overview of the governance structure of the FSC, see e.g. Meidinger, 'Multi-Interest Self-Governance' (above n. 29); K. Nowrot, 'Forest Stewardship Council' in C. Tietje and A. Brouder (eds.), *Handbook of Transnational Economic Governance Regimes*, Martinus Nijhoff Publishers, Leiden 2009, pp. 865 ff.

33 See only Meidinger, 'Multi-Interest Self-Governance' (above n. 29) and Nowrot (above n. 32).

34 The analysis of the aforementioned problems is based on the Deutsche Welle documentary 'Die Ausbeutung der Urwälder', 2019, available at: https://www.dw.com/de/die-ausbeutung-der-urw%C3%A4lder/av-49725929; in English 'Stripping the Jungle', available at: https://www.youtube.com/watch?v=GMp0IFAV41Q, as well as an answering statement by the FSC which does not neglect the described problems but criticises the one-sidedness of the documentary which also refers to problems which lie outside of the FCS's competence and which does not describe the positive impacts of the scheme. The multiplicity of problems and shortcomings has even led to the foundation of a group named 'FSC Watch', see https://fsc-watch.com/about.

Examples of ecologically inadequate forestry standards have been identified with regard to Nordic forests as well as to tropical rainforests, as the following examples will illustrate. In Nordic forests, five per cent of the trees must be preserved in order to provide habitats for species until the forests have recovered. This has been criticised by ecologists as insufficient and unrealistic as forest recovery processes take up to 100 years.[35] The standards for sustainable harvesting in tropical rainforests allow for single trees to be harvested, which also leads to unsustainable consequences: the rainforest is cut into pieces by roads for transportation and invaded by noise which affects species and ecosystems severely. Moreover, this practice leads harvesters to focus on valuable species of trees, the number of which is at risk of being reduced below crucial amounts for mutual fertilisation.[36] Certificates have been granted for eucalyptus plantations with an enormous and unsustainable need for water and nutrition, damaging water balance and surrounding ecosystems.

Although the FSC is based upon an equal tripartite structure between social, economic and environmental interests, ecologically inadequate standards can be explained by the structural disadvantage of environmental interests. Practice has shown that in concrete standards-setting at decentralised level, due to its economic power, the interests of the timber business regularly prevail.[37] In various regions of the world, social and environmental representatives were even bribed, threatened or killed.

Similar observations have been made on certification. Although the FSC framework provides detailed requirements for certification bodies to be accredited and laudable procedural safeguards for reliable certification, detrimental forestry practices – e.g. those which did not comply with indigenous peoples' rights and which applied low labour standards – became certified in different parts of the world. Other problems relate to illegal cutting, smuggling and mixing of timber, (unidentified) false declaration of the origin of timber, and as a result its false FSC certification. Local certifiers – in particular those working in circumstances with weak public governance structures – have been bribed,

---

35 On the insufficiency of the 5% rule, see M. Elbakidze, P. Angelstam, K. Andersson, M. Nordberg and Y. Pautov, 'How does forest certification contribute to boreal biodiversity conservation? Standards and outcomes in Sweden and NW Russia' (2011) 262 *Forest Ecology & Management* 1983.

36 On the impact of selective harvesting in Indonesia see A. Insya, H.H. de Iongh, W. Kustiawan and G.R. de Snoo, 'Structure, composition and diversity of plant communities in FSC-certified, selectively logged forests of different ages compared to primary forest' (2014) 23 *Biodiversity Conservation* 2445.

37 On the difficulty of applying an ecologic perspective at the concretising level and on other difficulties with fair and equal representation of the various stakeholders, see also H. Garrelts and M. Flitner, 'Governance Issues in the Ecosystem Approach: what lessons from the Forest Stewardship Council?' (2011) 130 *European Journal of Forest Research* 395, 396 ff., 400 ff.; on the prevailing economic rationale of forestry companies, see also J. Johansson, 'Towards democratic and effective forest governance? The discursive legitimation of forest certification in northern Sweden' (2014) 19 *Local Environment* 803, 812 ff.

threatened or even killed, or they lack the means to identify smuggled and mixed timber. Another reason could be that the FSC does not sufficiently monitor the activities of acknowledged certification bodies. Also, NGOs complained that companies choose their own certifiers, that audits are non-transparent and that NGOs do not have access to the auditing procedure.[38]

Although the FSC provides for sanctions and a complaints procedure, a number of serious infringements of FSC requirements have not led to the withdrawal of the certificate or the termination of the membership of the perpetrators.

Voluntariness and competition among different private framework systems: here, FSC international with other forestry certification programmes, does not work in favour of high standards, reliable control and effective enforcement either.[39] The FSC's reluctance to impose sanctions on non-complying economic actors has been justified with the argument that the FSC does not want to lose members and that low standards and low adherence are better for the environment than no standards in the event of economic operators leaving the system.[40]

At the same time, an increased demand for tropical timber due to its perceived sustainability has been observed in Western societies.[41]

4. INTERIM CONCLUSION

The foregoing has shown that transnational private environmental governance systems face serious shortcomings and challenges at both the substantive and the procedural levels. These include low and imprecise standards that are ill-equipped to address the complexity of sustainability or ecological problems at stake, dysfunctional procedural structures and weak enforcement mechanisms. This is further reinforced by asymmetric incentives towards economic efficiency in a competitive environment and the structural weakness of representatives of environmental interests.

5. LEGAL CHALLENGES

Following from that, the legal challenges to the promotion of effective private environmental governance are threefold. Firstly, an adequate and effective

---

38 For Sweden, see e.g. also Johansson (above n. 37), 816.

39 See Meidinger, 'The Administrative Law of Global Private-Public Regulation' (above n. 29), 53 ff.

40 K. Carstensen, the Director General of FSC International, in the Deutsche Welle documentary 'Die Ausbeutung der Urwälder' (above n. 34).

41 ibid.

framework with clear and encompassing sustainability standards must be in place, which pre-structures and controls the private governance systems. Secondly, in order to ensure the proper (i.e. impartial, independent and balanced) functioning of the private systems themselves, environmental stakeholders must be empowered, *de jure* and *de facto*. Therefore, thirdly, the law, in particular private law, should take private environmental governance seriously and provide for adequate (external) legal remedies for non-compliance.

5.1. AN ADEQUATE AND EFFECTIVE GOVERNANCE FRAMEWORK

The regulatory frameworks – be it a public law framework such as the EU framework for the promotion of renewable energies, or be it a privately organised private law framework such as that of the FSC International[42] – face the challenge to provide for sufficiently precise and adequate requirements in substantive as well as in procedural regard. Further, they should have in place an effective administrative control mechanism throughout the whole 'compliance chain', including the standardisation and certification schemes.

Where (transnational) framework systems leave leeway for implementation, their ambiguity and loopholes are often reflected in significantly differing (transnational or national) private standardisation and certification systems. In case of competition between private governance systems, these differences could result in a race to the bottom, to the disadvantage of schemes with comprehensive standards and intense control, as shown above.

5.1.1. Substantive Standards

Based upon this insight, the new RED II has amended substantial and procedural requirements for bio-fuels certification. The substantive criteria for sustainable production of biomass, now Article 29(2)-(9) RED II, have not been concretised in the relevant respects and still remain vague. However, they take a more comprehensive approach insofar as they not only include bio-fuels and bio-liquids but also other biomass used for energy production – Article 7(1) subparagraph 4, Article 29. This, however, comes at the ecological price of the inclusion of wood ('forest biomass') into the promotion system. Consequently, requirements for sustainable forestry and land-use change criteria have been included in Article 29(6) and (7).

---

42 In fact, the FSC framework has often been compared to a public administrative law framework, see only Meidinger, 'The Administrative Law of Global Private-Public Regulation' (above n. 29).

Most importantly, in order to address the issue of indirect land-use changes, Article 26 RED II introduces a ceiling for conventional bio-fuels, and Article 25(1) subparagraph 4 a minimum share of advanced bio-fuels. Under Article 26(1), bio-fuels, bio-liquids and biomass fuels produced from food and feed crops may only contribute to a maximum of 7 per cent (or a maximum of a 1 per cent increase as compared to 2020 if lower than 7 per cent) to the 14 per cent renewable energy goal in the transport sector by 2030 set out in Article 25(1). By virtue of these amendments, the share of 'high indirect land-use change-risk' bio-fuels, bio-liquids or biomass fuels (such as those from palm oil) may not exceed the level of consumption in 2019 and from 2023 until 2030 at the latest gradually decrease to 0 per cent – Article 26(2).[43] Furthermore, greenhouse gas-saving requirements have been increased – Article 29(10).[44] In contrast, suggestions of the European Parliament to phase out bio-fuels and bio-liquids produced from palm oil completely in 2021[45] have not made it into the final RED II.

5.1.2. Compliance Procedure

Article 30 RED II has also amended the verification of compliance procedures applying to voluntary private systems, auditing and certification bodies and economic operators themselves. Article 30(4), (7) and (8) require the recognised voluntary schemes to implement adequate standards of reliability, transparency, independent auditing and assurances of the reliability of the materials as concretised by the Commission. Where a Member State raises concerns that a private voluntary scheme is not operating properly, the Commission shall investigate the matter and take appropriate steps, Article 30(8) subparagraph 2.[46] Article 30(5) subparagraph 2 has introduced detailed reporting requirements for recognised voluntary schemes, and the reports must be made public.[47]

---

43 See also Commission Delegated Regulation (EU) 2019/807 as regards the determination of high indirect land-use change-risk feedstock for which a significant expansion of the production area into land with high carbon stock is observed and the certification of low indirect land-use change-risk biofuels, bioliquids and biomass fuels, [2019] OJ L 133/1.

44 Due to their political urgency, these aspects had already been addressed by Directive (EU) 2015/1513 See also the impact assessment by the Commission, SWD(2012) 343 final; recital (5) of Directive (EU) 2015/1513; Glinski (above n. 22), pp. 180 f.

45 European Parliament doc. A8-0066/2017; European Parliament doc. P8_TA-PROV(2018)0009 of 17/1/2018, Amendment 307 on Art. 7(1) subpara. 4 of the Commission proposal.

46 This seems to be another consequence of the findings of the audit team of the European Court of Auditors, demonstrating that trust in the European Commission's engagement to investigate the effectiveness of voluntary schemes is limited.

47 These reporting requirements had already been introduced by Directive (EU) 2015/1513 into Article 18(5) subpara. 2 and (6) subpara. 2 RED I (as amended). The requirement in Article 18(6) subpara. 3(a) to (k) RED I (as amended) that these reports should provide the basis of a detailed analysis by the Commission concerning the functioning of these schemes, has not been taken over.

Certification bodies, for their part, must be supervised by the competent authorities of the Member States; a system that exists in Germany.[48] They must submit, upon request, all relevant data; and the voluntary schemes shall be informed of any non-conformity without delay, Article 30(9) subparagraph 2. Article 30(3) requires Member States to ensure that economic operators submit reliable information concerning greenhouse gas savings and that they arrange for adequate standards of auditing.

In addition, RED II has strengthened national schemes. Article 30(6) requires the Commission to prioritise national schemes and provides for their mutual recognition amongst Member States.

These amendments are important steps in the right direction. However, in particular, criticism relating to the absence of (public) participation and the inclusion of stakeholders has not been accommodated, either through the approval of voluntary schemes or in their supervision. Also, no mandatory inclusion of stakeholders in the certification procedure, namely in the auditing of economic operators, has been introduced. Another option would have been to entitle persons having sufficient interest in environmental decision-making (namely environmental organisations) to request the European Commission to take action in case of the breach or the imminent threat of a breach of certification requirements.[49]

5.2. THE FUNCTIONING OF PRIVATE SYSTEMS: EMPOWERMENT OF STAKEHOLDERS

In order to ensure the functioning of the private systems themselves, environmental stakeholders must be empowered.

As the European bio-fuels system has shown, pluralistic multi-stakeholder approaches often apply more ambitious standards and more reliable procedures. This multi-stakeholder approach is also reflected in the tripartite structure of the FSC.

These two examples reflect a general observation with regard to the standardisation of environmental (and also health and safety) issues: Standardisation is always a balancing act between (optimal) environmental protection and business interests and affordability. The relevant body may lean more towards less restrictive requirements, in particular when it is dominated

48 See § 55 *Verordnung über Anforderungen an eine nachhaltige Herstellung von Biokraftstoffen* of 30 September 2009.

49 A comparable provision has, for example, been introduced in Art. 25 of Regulation (EU) No 1257/2013 on ship recycling in order to ensure the reliability of the certification of ship recycling facilities.

by industry representatives.[50] This applies even more when standardisation schemes compete with each other.

Comparable considerations apply to certification: Although based on the idea of private expertise, professional integrity, independence and impartiality, the structure of private certification of transnational supply chains is often dysfunctional. The practice that the economic operator chooses the certification body, that certification is based upon a contractual relationship between the certifier and the economic operator and that it is the economic operator who pays for the certification, provides for an asymmetric incentive to please the economic operator, which poses a serious threat to impartiality.[51] Again, this is reinforced by the competition among certification bodies.[52]

Consequently, numerous standardising bodies as well as referring to legal frameworks have set up elaborate requirements for expertise and procedural justice relating to transparency, openness, plurality, public comment procedures and consensus, among them the FSC itself.

With regard to certification, typical safeguards are independence (from the manufacturer), professional integrity, financial independence, impartiality, expertise and sufficient resources, which are also in principle reflected in both systems. Noteworthy in this regard is that the requirement to include (environmental) stakeholders in the certification process is part of the FSC requirements but not of the EU bio-fuels compliance system.

At the same time – due to the structural disadvantage of environmental versus economic interests, for example, in relation to financial and personal resources and access to information, which is particularly salient in transnational structures[53] – pluralistic structures and procedures do not necessarily provide safeguards for high standards and reliable enforcement,[54] as the example of the

---

50 See also G. Lübbe-Wolff, 'Verfassungsrechtliche Fragen der Normsetzung und der Normkonkretisierung im Umweltrecht' (1991) 6 *Zeitschrift für Gesetzgebung* 235; P. Verbruggen, 'Tort Liability for Standards Development in the United States and European Union' (2018) *Tilburg Private Law Working Paper* 12/2018, p. 3.

51 See, for example, G. Wagner, 'Marktaufsichtshaftung produktsicherheitsrechtlicher Zertifizierungsstellen' (2018) *Juristenzeitung* 130, 135 f.; C. Glinski and P. Rott, 'Regulating Certification Bodies in the Field of Medical Devices: The PIP Breast Implants Litigation and beyond' (2019) 27(2) *European Review of Private Law* 403, 423 ff.; both in relation to medical devices.

52 On competition between certification bodies, see also G. von Wangenheim, 'Certification as Solution to the Asymmetric Information Problem?' in Rott (ed.), *Certification* (above n. 22), pp. 11, 19.

53 On the International Standardisation Organization (ISO), see, for example, J. Clapp, 'The Privatization of Global Environmental Governance: ISO 14000 and the Developing World' (1998) 4 *Global Governance* 302. See also H. Schepel, *The Constitution of Private Governance*, Hart Publishing, Oxford 2005, pp. 185 ff. On the FSC, see Garrelts and Flitner (above n. 37), 396 ff.

54 See also Lübbe-Wolff (above n. 50), 248; B. van Leeuwen, *European Standardisation of Services and its Impact on Private Law*, Hart Publishing, Oxford 2017, pp. 62 f.

FSC has shown. Codifying participatory rights for environmental stakeholders is a necessary but not a sufficient precondition for effective private environmental governance. Therefore, legal orders which rely (to a certain extent) on private environmental governance, at the same time have to strengthen environmental stakeholders *de facto*, in particular financially.

As we have seen in the case of the FSC, private governance systems often mirror the national or local public governance deficiencies or power imbalances that they mean to bridge. The less standing and the less legal protection environmental interests enjoy in the national or local system, the more important it is for the transnational system to compensate for these shortcomings. This not only entails detailed requirements but also an effective complaints procedure which is accessible for all interested parties (including environmental or development organisations in the North)[55] and which provides for effective remedies.

5.3. TAKING PRIVATE GOVERNANCE SERIOUSLY

Finally, the law, and in particular private law, should take private governance seriously, in order to accommodate the public interest role of standardisation and certification, to compensate for the structural imbalance inherent in these systems and to provide for adequate remedies. This applies in particular to the question of (tort) liability of standardisation and certification bodies, but also to the use of unfair commercial practices law as a remedy for 'green-washing.'

5.3.1. Liability

In the past, a number of scandals relating to the certification of highly unsafe products or production conditions have brought the issue of liability of certification bodies onto the table.[56] Although, for a long time, liability towards

---

55 Thus going beyond the complaints procedure of the FSC.

56 See the recent liability actions of victims against TÜV Süd for having certified a highly instable dam of a goldmine in Brazil, the collapse of which caused hundreds of deaths and enormous environmental destruction, see N.N., 'Opfer der Schlammlawine verklagen TÜV Süd', *ZEIT* of 25/10/2019, available at: https://www.zeit.de/gesellschaft/zeitgeschehen/2019-10/brasilien-schlammlawine-klage-tuev-sued-opfer. Other cases relate to the certification of unsafe vessels by classification societies, on which see V. Ulfbeck and A. Møllmann, 'Public Function Liability of Classification Societies' in P. Rott (ed.), *Certification* (above n. 22), pp. 213 ff.; J. de Bruyne, 'Liability of Classification Societies: Cases, Challenges and Future Perspectives' (2014) 45 *Journal of Maritime Law & Commerce* 181 ff. See also the case of *RINA*, on which see CJEU, Judgment of 7 May 2020, Case C-641/18 *LG v. Rina SpA, Ente Registro Italiano Navale*, ECLI:EU:C:2020:349; or the fire safety certification at Ali Enterprises, a textile producer for the Western market, in Pakistan by RINA; on which see C. Glinski and P. Rott, 'The role and liability of certification organisations in transnational value chains' (2018) 23 *Deakin Law Review* 83; T. van Ho and C. Terwindt, 'Assessing the Duty of Care for Social Auditors' (2019) 27 *European Review of Private Law* 379 ff.

third parties had not even been discussed, litigation against TÜV Rheinland in the PIP breast implants scandal appears to have been a game changer.[57] Meanwhile, a number of tort lawyers argue in favour of tort liability of certification bodies. The public interests at stake induce the need for liability,[58] as the classical approach towards the mutual interplay and compensation between public and private law[59] requires complementarity between public law prevention and private (tort) law compensation.[60] At the same time, tort liability has a preventive effect in increasing the diligence of potential tortfeasors. Without the threat of liability, the asymmetric incentive and threat to impartiality prevails, due to the contractual relationship with the economic operator that asks for certification.[61]

These arguments also apply to health and safety as well as sustainability certification in transnational supply chains. While the European bio-fuels certification scheme already provides for a public law framework, the reliability of which is at stake, certain private (public interest) standardisation schemes such as the FSC have assumed a comparable public role.[62]

Doctrinally, liability can be achieved with a progressive interpretation of tort law requirements such as the 'duty of care' or the 'breach of a statutory duty' that are meant to protect the victim or the environment.[63] Another possibility would be to interpret the certification contract as a 'contract with protective effect on third parties'.[64]

The legal challenge arising from private international law – according to which regularly the tort law of the country applies where the damage has occurred,[65] thus the foreign legal order – can be answered with so-called

---

57 See Case C-219/15 *Elisabeth Schmitt v. TÜV Rheinland LGA Products GmbH*, ECLI:EU:C:2017:128. Cases in Germany and France are still pending; for details, see Glinski and Rott (above n. 51), with further references. On the PIP breast implants scandal, see also P. Rott, 'Certification of Medical Devices – Lessons from the PIP Scandal' in Rott (ed.), *Certification* (above n. 22) pp. 189 ff.

58 See S. Unger, 'Herstellerbegleitung oder Marktüberwachung? Zur Haftung "benannter Stellen" im Medizinproduktrecht' (2017) *Europäische Zeitschrift für Wirtschaftsrecht* 299, 300 ff.

59 See only W. Hoffmann-Riem, 'Öffentliches Recht und Privatrecht als wechselseitige Auffangordnungen – Systematisierung und Entwicklungsperspektiven' in W. Hoffmann-Riem and E. Schmidt-Aßmann (eds.), *Öffentliches Recht und Privatrecht als wechselseitige Auffangordnungen*, Nomos, Baden-Baden 1996, pp. 261 ff.

60 G. Brüggemeier, 'Luxemburg locuta, causa finita? – Eine Nachbetrachtung der juristischen Behandlung der sogenannten PIP-Affäre in Deutschland' (2018) *Juristenzeitung* 191, 194 f.

61 Wagner (above n. 51), 135 f.

62 For details, see Glinski and Rott (above n. 56), 107 ff.

63 See Brüggemeier (above n. 60), 195.

64 For details relating to the German and English legal system, see Glinski and Rott (above n. 56) with further references. The German Federal Supreme Courts recently rejected this for the certification of medical devices, see BGH, 27 February 2020, VII ZR151/18 (2020) *Neue Juristische Wochenschrift* 1514.

65 For the EU, see Art. 4(1) of Regulation (EC) 864/2007 on the law applicable to non-contractual obligations (Rome II), [2007] OJ L199/40.

'overriding mandatory provisions', which make the provisions of the standards framework (including a liability provision) applicable irrespective of the otherwise applicable tort law.[66]

In the same way, the liability of standardisation organisations towards victims of products or production methods which cause harm because the standards are defective is being discussed;[67] and again, the idea is that third-party liability should have a preventive effect and provide a safeguard against adverse incentives stemming, for example, from competition for members or users. Liability of standardisation organisations is, however, more difficult to establish than liability of certification organisations. Counter-arguments relate to the voluntariness of the use of private standards, which leave the responsibility for damaging practices either with the public body providing the relevant legal framework or with the economic operator causing the damage. Moreover, liability risks can have a chilling effect against private (public interest) standardisation.[68]

Remedies in the case of bio-fuels and sustainable forestry could relate to damages for the destruction or deprivation of land that forms the basis of the livelihood of local people. Often, health issues caused by environmental degradation are at stake as well.[69] Finally, one could think of broader damage claims relating to (pure) ecological damage;[70] which would yet have to be introduced in many legal systems.

5.3.2. 'Green-Washing'

Another risk to the effectiveness of private environmental governance systems is the so-called 'green-washing' of environmentally detrimental practices with the perceived reliability of sustainability certificates. For example, the perceived reliability of the FSC label has led to increased demand for (certified) tropical timber in industrialised countries.

---

66 This legislative technique has been used in the French Code de Commerce, which in Art. L 225-102-4, -5 has introduced binding Corporate Social Responsibility requirements for (bigger) companies accompanied by liability for non-adherence. See also the Swiss *Konzernverantwortungsinitiative* (Corporate Responsibility Initiative), which is still pending; R. Klinger, M. Krajewski, D. Krebs and C. Hartmann, *Verankerung menschenrechtlicher Sorgfaltspflichten von Unternehmen im deutschen Recht*, 2016, available at: https://germanwatch.org/de/11970.

67 See P. Verbruggen, 'Good Governance of Private Standardization and the Role of Tort Law' (2019) *European Review of Private Law* 325; C. Glinski and P. Rott, 'Liability for Deficient Product Safety Standards' in C. Cauffmann and M. Eliantonio (eds.), *Standardisation as regulatory technique in the process of European integration: voluntary, inclusive and legitimate?*, Edward Elgar, Cheltenham 2020, pp. 131 ff.

68 See Glinski and Rott (above n. 67) with further references.

69 Although recitals (81 ff) of Directive (EU) 2018/201 only mention the climate effects of indirect land-use change.

70 See also recital (42) of Directive (EU) 2018/201, referring to environmental sustainability.

This risk of (detrimental) market effects can be addressed by unfair commercial practices law,[71] which has always been applied to misleading environmental statements or labels.[72]

In fact, the UK Advertising Standards Authority has already addressed the practice of economic operators to publish their participation in voluntary schemes under the EU bio-fuels framework. The courts have held that a reference to the participation in the 'Roundtable on Sustainable Palm Oil' was misleading if it was mentioned in conjunction with the purported sustainable production of the company.[73] The case also illustrates the importance of legal standing of environmental organisations, as the complaint to the Advertising Standards Authority had been made by the environmental organisation Friends of the Earth.

6. CONCLUSION

This chapter has shown that transnational private environmental governance systems face serious shortcomings and challenges at both the substantive and the procedural levels. Too low or imprecise substantive standards can, in principle, be addressed by the framework systems, although such a centralised approach is somewhat in tension with the aim to provide for a decentralised, bottom-up development of locally (and thus also ecologically) adequate standards that is inherent in the FSC structure. Framework systems can also, in principle, provide for precise procedural requirements for implementing bodies and improve their compliance structures and monitoring mechanisms, for example, by way of an extension to certification bodies, as the EU bio-fuels system has shown.

At the same time, there are also serious constraints on the coverage of private regulation and certification of sustainable production chains. As both the EU bio-fuel system and the FSC have shown, the certification of an individual production site, method or chain can address neither complex ecosystem protection, resource management or land planning issues nor related socio-economic effects, and can thus not replace complex political planning and the balancing of interests by the state or the international community. The problem of indirect land-use changes related to the promotion of bio-fuels provides an illustration. As it could not be addressed by the governance framework, the EU legislator finally decided to eliminate high-risk production chains from the system altogether.

---

71 Under national law implementing Directive 2005/29/EC concerning unfair business-to-consumer commercial practices in the internal market, [2005] OJ L 149/22.

72 See C. Glinski, *Die rechtliche Bedeutung der privaten Regulierung globaler Produktionsstandards*, Nomos, Baden-Baden 2010, pp. 196 ff.

73 See the ASA Ruling in *Malaysia Palm Oil Council* of 9 September 2009, quoted by A. Beckers, *Enforcing Corporate Social Responsibility Codes*, Hart Publishing, Oxford 2015, p. 199.

Moreover, as, in particular, the experiences with the FSC have shown, private governance systems often mirror the national or local public governance deficiencies or power imbalances that they are meant to overcome, and they perform best 'in the shadow of the law' of a functioning legal system.[74] Centralised monitoring carried out by the framework system, accompanied by effective complaints and sanctions mechanisms, can compensate to a certain extent for public governance deficiencies.

Nevertheless, the functioning of private environmental governance systems relies heavily on environmental stakeholders that traditionally suffer from structural disadvantages in relation to their financial and personal resources as well as their access to information, and therefore require support in this regard.

In order to compensate for the structural imbalance and the asymmetric incentives in favour of economic interests inherent in private systems in a competitive environment, and also to provide for adequate remedies, legal orders 'should take private governance seriously'. This applies in particular to the (progressive) interpretation of tort law with regard to the potential liability of standardisation and certification bodies. Detrimental market effects of unreliable environmental certificates can be addressed by unfair commercial practices law.

Even such 'ideal' internal and external legal conditions, however, cannot entirely rule out the market logics that impact on private environmental governance systems. Thus, they cannot replace but rather only complement comprehensive public law ecosystem protection and resource management.

[74] See also Garrelts and Flitner (above n. 37), 400.

WHY REALITY AND TRUTH MATTER IN ENVIRONMENTAL LAW

Naomi LUHDE-THOMPSON

1. INTRODUCTION

The coining of the term 'alternative facts' by the US presidential office in 2017 has attracted intense public scrutiny and criticism.[1] In thinking about environmental law, and the way 'facts' are used, a re-examination of the perspectives of both governmental and non-governmental participants in environmental decision-making highlights some gaps and weaknesses in relation to these 'facts'. Information and evidence are treated differently depending on the rules that govern development decision-making. For example, the scientific reality of what is required to secure climate mitigation in order to remain within the limits set by the Paris Agreement[2] should inform the relevant laws of decision-making. As the EU and the UK make fundamental transitions from a high carbon economy to a low or net zero carbon economy,[3] so the law needs to support this transition. If law is to do this effectively, then this involves rethinking the evidential basis of environmental decision-making. This imperative is clear given that the EU and UK may not be doing enough to achieve the Paris Agreement commitments.[4] By taking the example of decision-making on shale gas extraction in England, the contention is that the current laws of environmental decision-making

1 K. Conway, Counselor to the US President, phrase coined in an interview on 22 January 2017 with *Meet the Press*, a weekly television news programme on NBC.

2 Adoption of the Paris Agreement under the United Nations Framework Convention on Climate Change, Decision 1/CP.21, entered into force on 4 November 2016.

3 Proposal for a Regulation of the European Parliament and of the Council establishing the framework for achieving climate neutrality and amending Regulation (EU) 2018/1999 (European Climate Law) COM/2020/80 final; The Climate Change Act 2008, section 1.

4 V. Masson-Delmotte, P. Zhai, H.-O. Pörtner, D. Roberts, J. Skea, P.R. Shukla, A. Pirani, W. Moufouma-Okia, C. Péan, R. Pidcock, S. Connors, J.B.R. Matthews, Y. Chen, X. Zhou, M.I. Gomis, E. Lonnoy, T. Maycock, M. Tignor and T. Waterfield (eds.), *Global Warming of 1.5°C – An IPCC Special Report on the impacts of global warming of 1.5°C above pre-industrial levels and related global greenhouse gas emission pathways, in the context of strengthening the global response to the threat of climate change, sustainable development, and efforts to eradicate poverty*, IPCC, 2018.

may be hampering sustainable outcomes. The question posed in this chapter is to what extent effective outcomes for sustainable solutions of development decision-making may be undermined by the nature and limitations of the 'facts' upon which these decisions rely. What is the 'reality' described within the decision-making frame? What 'truths' are being denied? And why does 'reality and truth' matter in law for sustainable transitions?

2. THE IMPORTANCE OF 'FACTS' IN MAKING DECISIONS

While the establishment of 'fact' in the rules-based decision-making processes that abound in Europe has not descended into an 'alternative' universe, in highly contentious areas of decision-making such as that on shale gas, the entry of political ideology into the policy frame has caused some discomfort.[5] Shale gas is a natural gas that is found in shale formations that requires specific extraction techniques, and is different to conventional gas that is found in highly permeable reservoir rock and is therefore more easily extractable. Assessing the policy frame shows that some shale gas development rules, such as those in England on land-use planning, have been driven by political motivation and not necessarily consistently with the whole body of relevant evidence.[6] Similarly, development consent processes on extraction within the EU and UK more broadly rely upon information largely generated by the private sector[7] as the basis for making decisions that will impact upon environmental objectives, such as reducing climate changing emissions and pollution.[8] Policy frames such as that for shale gas exploration and extraction – popularly known as 'fracking – in England emphasise some evidence while ruling out other evidence pertaining to environmental impact.[9] In 2019, a moratorium was declared for the second time due to public and political pressure on shale gas extraction in England.[10] When combined with the use of evidence from the promoter of the project, the key question arises: to what extent does this constellation undermine the robustness

---

5 M. Cotton, 'Stakeholder perspectives on shale gas fracking: A Q-method study of environmental discourses' (2015) 47 *EP (Environment and Planning)* 1944–1962.

6 Department for Communities and Local Government, *Planning Practice Guidance for Onshore Oil and Gas*, DCLG, London 2013.

7 For example, in the submission of an application for consent by the private sector.

8 Mediating conflicting interests through land use planning see B. Cullingworth and V. Nadin, *Town and Country Planning in the UK*, 14th ed., Routledge, London/New York 2006, p. 4.

9 Secretary of State for Energy and Climate Change, Amber Rudd, *Shale Gas/Oil Policy Written Statement*, 16 September 2015, Hansard Col. 36WS. E. Stokes, 'Regulatory domain and regulatory dexterity: critiquing the UK governance of "fracking"' (2016) 79(6) *Modern Law Review* 961–986.

10 Secretary of State and Minister for Business, Energy, and Industrial Strategy, Andrea Leadsom, Kwasi Kwarteng, *Government ends support for fracking*, Press release, 2 November 2019.

of this and other similar development processes for the purpose of securing environmental protection outcomes? And how could this impact the role of law in transitioning towards sustainable solutions in this area?

3. 'FACTS' AND SECURING SUSTAINABLE SOLUTIONS IN DEVELOPMENT DECISION-MAKING

The environment has been impacted substantially, and at an increasingly accelerated pace since the industrial revolution. Within the EU and UK, despite policy development on environmental protection across all sectors, the issues of biodiversity loss and diffuse pollution, including from climate changing emissions, remain as persistent and severe challenges.[11] The European Environment Agency (EEA) has identified 'serious gaps between the state of the environment and existing EU near- and long-term policy targets',[12] suggesting that the existing and proposed political system's capacity to deal with the environmental problems faced by the EU and its Member States is inadequate. In this context, it is incumbent to consider the shortcomings of the existing development decision-making system if improvements are to be made to reverse current trends with the urgency required.[13] Given the state of the environment, it is argued that environmental law needs a continuing assessment of its impact and effectiveness in securing sustainable outcomes.

An examination of the evidence on which decisions rely provides a useful entry point to test the basis of certain types of environmental decisions. Consider the energy minerals extraction decision-making process. Is it sufficient to rely upon information largely generated by the private sector in making decisions that will impact upon environmental objectives such as greenhouse gas emissions reduction? While each Member State has their own rules and regulations concerning land use, the general neo-liberal trend in land use planning decision-making in England has become less to command and control development and more to invite market input.[14] Expertise for energy

---

[11] European Environment Agency, *The European environment – state and outlook 2020*, 2019.

[12] Ibid. Foreword, p. 7.

[13] T.M. Lenton, J. Rockström, O. Gaffney, S. Rahmstorf, K. Richardson, W. Steffen and H.J. Schellnhuber, 'Climate tipping points – too risky to bet against' (2019) 575 *Nature* 7784.

[14] H. Campbell and R. Marshall, 'Moral obligations, planning, and the public interest: A commentary on current British practice' (2000) 27(2) *EP (Environment and Planning B: Planning and Design)* 297–312; A. Lord and M. Tewdwr-Jones, 'Is Planning "Under Attack"? Chronicling the Deregulation of Urban and Environmental Planning in England' (2014) 22(2) *EPS (European Planning Studies)* 345–361; P. Allmendinger and G. Haughton, 'The Evolution and Trajectories of English Spatial Governance: 'Neoliberal' Episodes in Planning' (2013) 28(1) *PPR (Planning Practice & Research)* 6–26.

infrastructure development is largely held by the private sector, and this may affect the value placed on lay input in decision-making processes.[15]

Learning and scientific understanding, broadly contemplated as a result of social process in science and technology studies,[16] are nuanced in a development decision-making process. Lay understandings of science are quite profound, and more seated in the real world, whereas scientists understand the science but not necessarily the context in which the science is then applied.[17] Taking inspiration from Jasanoff's theory of co-production, that 'scientific knowledge … both embeds and is embedded in social practices, identities, norms, conventions, discourses, instruments and institutions',[18] this chapter examines the way evidence is used in the shale gas decision-making process in England. It considers the differing perspectives of varied participants in the process on the evidence that is being utilised, and whether this evidential knowledge is 'co-produced' as Jasanoff suggests, or remains dissonant. The question is how science, in the form of evidence, is being used in a highly politicised and contested decision-making process, where environmental protection and economic growth aims collide.

Drawing upon thinking on the interaction between science and governance, the shale gas exploration and extraction decision-making process, as governed by a plethora of rules and regulations, provides the opportunity to examine the 'reasoning' that is taking place within this forum.[19] Reasoning could be described as the process of reaching conclusions using publicly shared values, whereas decision-making could be described as the conclusion based on judgement.[20] The subject of investigation is how this reasoning is faring in securing environmental protection, as the value placed upon different bodies of evidence is heavily contested. It is also to consider the extent to which middle ground and mediated solutions emerge that may not have been built on completely scientific bases.[21] Co-production allows for a lack of data, whilst describing a process where a consensus can be reached and has some form of social licence attached to the basis of decision-making.[22] The values that are placed upon private or corporate

---

15 M. Aitken, 'Wind Power Planning Controversies and the Construction of "Expert" and "Lay" Knowledges' (2009) 18(1) *Science as Culture* 47–64.

16 S. Jasanoff, 'A Field of Its Own: The Emergence of Science and Technology Studies' in R. Frodeman (ed.), *The Oxford Handbook of Interdisciplinarity*, 2nd ed., Oxford University Press, Oxford 2017.

17 A. Saltelli and M. Giampetro, 'What is wrong with evidence based policy, and how can it be improved?' (2017) 91 Futures 62–71.

18 S. Jasanoff (ed.), *States of Knowledge*, Routledge, Abingdon (Oxon) 2004, p. 3.

19 S. Jasanoff, *Science and Public Reason*, Routledge, Abingdon (Oxon) 2012, p. 5; and also J. Rawls, *A Theory of Justice*, Harvard University Press, Cambridge MA 1971 on public reason.

20 P. N. Johnson-Laird and E. Shafir, 'The interaction between reasoning and decision making: an introduction' (1993) 49 *Cognition* 1–9.

21 S. Jasanoff, *Science and Public Reason*, Routledge, Abingdon (Oxon) 2012, p. 15.

22 Y. Rydin, L. Natarajan, M. Lee and S. Lock, 'Black-boxing the Evidence: Planning Regulation and Major Renewable Energy Infrastructure Projects in England and Wales' (2018) 19(2)

'expertise' may or may not result in the co-production of knowledge, depending on whether consensus can be built.

Reaching consensus on knowledge is an important part of establishing a basis for decision-making. In shale gas cases, where the development is hotly contested,[23] the gap between 'reality' and 'truth' in the decision-making frame may hinder the co-production of knowledge. Essentially promoters and objectors may not agree on whether or not shale gas reduces emissions overall (by replacing other more polluting sources of fossil fuels)[24] or whether it is an additional source of emissions,[25] with an unknown set of risks of greater polluting emissions.[26] The same goes for water pollution impacts, with promoters and objectors failing to agree on the level of risk of groundwater pollution,[27] and on the ability of the regulatory system to deal with the waste water produced.[28] Establishing the 'facts' in this example is contested. It can also be seen that the conflict over the establishment of 'facts' derives in part from the perceived environmental outcome of the development decision-making process, and therefore undermines the achievement of objectively sustainable solutions.

4. THE ROLE OF LAW IN TRANSITIONING TOWARDS SUSTAINABLE SOLUTIONS

Law sets out the rules of the development decision-making process in this instance. In general, these laws controlling development contain aims to mitigate environmental, social and economic impacts.[29] Fisher, Scotford and Barritt, make a case for the disruptive nature of climate change as an issue where environmental 'facts' are the basis of disputes, and posit that there is therefore a need for change in legal frameworks, despite their nature being deeply imbued with principles of stability.[30] As Fisher has previously pointed out, 'scientific

Planning Theory & Practice 218–234; R.G. Boutilier, 'Frequently asked questions about the social licence to operate' (2014) 32(4) *Impact Assessment and Project Appraisal* 263–272.

23 Y. Beebeejaun, 'Questioning the local: environmental regulation, shale gas extraction, and the politics of scale' (2019) 24(8) *Local Environment* 777 789.

24 UKOOG, 'General Emissions', (http://www.ukoog.org.uk/12thpres.htm).

25 J. Broderick and K. Anderson, *Natural gas and climate change*, Report commissioned for Friends of the Earth Europe, Tyndall Centre, University of Manchester 2017.

26 R. Howarth, R. Santoro, A. Ingraffea, 'Methane and the Greenhouse-Gas Footprint of Natural Gas from Shale Formations' (2011) 106(4) *Climatic Change* 679–690.

27 BBC, 'Fracking "could put gas and chemicals" in drinking water', 19 July 2013, BBC.

28 Friends of the Earth, *Consultation response – objection to Preston New Road application*, (2015).

29 W. Upton, QC, 'What is the Purpose of Planning Policy? Reflections on the Revised National Planning Policy Framework 2018' (2019) 31 *JEL (Journal of Environmental Law)* 135–149.

30 E. Fisher, E. Scotford and E. Barritt, 'The Legally Disruptive Nature of Climate Change' (2017) 80(2) *MLR (Modern Law Review)* 173–201, at 181.

uncertainty and socio-political conflict make it difficult to develop a robust factual base for decision-making'.[31] If the basis of decision-making is weak rather than robust, then the contested nature of the development may remain, and negative environmental consequences such as those already noted with regard to climate change emissions will persist.[32] How this contributes to the failure to achieve sustainable solutions may not seem immediately obvious, but on a closer examination of the approval or refusal of shale gas exploration and exploitation in England, a clear gap can be discerned between the observed impacts on the environment, and what is and what is not taken into account in the decision-making process. Considering how law can support the transition to sustainable solutions in the fora of development decision-making more broadly could be informed by these reflections, in an attempt to secure more sustainable outcomes in similar regimes.

5. RESEARCH METHODOLOGY

The research design has its roots in critical realism,[33] and more specifically in examining the causes of outcomes. The field research was designed to elicit insights into the way information and evidence are produced and used in the decision-making process under scrutiny.[34] The use of evidence in environmental and planning law in England as the area for investigation in this chapter allows for an examination of a specific area of law in action, through taking a socio-legal approach.[35] Analysing the production and use of knowledge, described as evidence in the decision-making process for shale gas, requires an empirical approach, as it is the operation of the law in the real world that is under examination.[36] The premise is that to assess the effectiveness of laws in transitioning to sustainable solutions, it is essential to examine how existing laws that influence the achievement of sustainability are currently operating. Any flaws or gaps that were provisionally identified and are presented here aim to help inform drafting of similar future laws so that they are more effective

31 E. Fisher, 'Environmental Law as "Hot" Law' (2013) 25(3) *JEL (Journal of Environmental Law)* 347, 350–351.

32 N. Luhde-Thompson, 'Changing Decisions on Energy Generating Infrastructure: Can the European Union's New Energy Package Deliver the Radical Transformation Needed?' (2019) 3 *Oil, Gas & Energy Law*.

33 B. Danermark, M. Ekström, L. Jakobsen and J.C. Karlsson, *Explaining society: Critical realism in the social sciences*, Routledge, London/New York 2002.

34 The semi-structured interviews were collected as part of PhD field research conducted under the aegis and ethical approval of Birmingham Law School in 2019.

35 D.N. Schiff, 'Socio-Legal Theory: Social Structure and Law' (1976) 39(3) *MLR* 287–310.

36 P. Cane and H.M. Kritzer (eds.), 'Empirical Legal Research and Policy-making' in *The Oxford Handbook of Empirical Legal Research*, Oxford Handbooks Online, 2010.

and more robust at achieving sustainable outcomes. The research used shale gas extraction decisions as a case study because it is contested in terms of its environmental sustainability. Shale gas extraction in the US has proven environmental impacts,[37] but industry points to its lower climate change impact in comparison to coal.[38] Whether or not these acknowledged environmental impacts are acceptable, or can be minimised to acceptable levels, can be viewed as either an objective matter in relation to environmental limits, or a political matter in relation to commitments such as the Paris Agreement.

In the fieldwork, semi-structured interviews were conducted and recorded to collect data for this analysis. A number of individuals, drawn from industry, from the relevant regulatory bodies, and lay people who had some sort of contact with the shale gas development (this varied widely) were interviewed for their view on the information available, the sources of information, and what 'counted' or was 'of influence' in the decision-making process.[39] Interviewing them elicited perspectives on the type, value and treatment of evidence within the process. The aim of the research was to identify any gaps or weaknesses of the regulatory system and its application in practice that may have affected the evidence on which decisions were being made. Empirical documentary data consisting of the documentation produced within and for the decision-making process by Government, agencies, developers and lay people was also examined. Using this empirical documentary data and a set of associated stakeholder interviews on the shale gas decision-making process in England, it is possible to gain an insight into how evidence is perceived and utilised. The findings suggest that there may be a selective approach to the evidence which is associated with the strong political and ideological motivation behind shale gas policy, resulting in uncertain outcomes for environmental protection.

6. EXAMINING 'TRUTH' AND 'REALITY' IN DECISION-MAKING

With regard to development decision-making within the EU and UK, the matter of the scientific evidence basis for these decisions becomes very important.

---

37 United States Environmental Protection Agency, *Hydraulic Fracturing for Oil and Gas and Its Potential Impact on Drinking Water Resources in the United States*, US EPA, 2016.

38 International Energy Agency, *Golden Rules for a Golden Age of Gas: World Energy Outlook Special Report*, IEA, 2013.

39 Twenty individuals were interviewed; eight interviews were conducted in person, and the remainder by telephone. The research questions were semi-structured as a topic list. Only one area of the topic list, 'information' is the subject of the findings presented here. Each interviewee is assigned a transcript code for the purposes of referencing. The field research was conducted as part of the author's overall research PhD in 2019 under the aegis of Birmingham Law School, Birmingham, UK.

Observed scientific data collected from the environment tells us that it is changing – that there is less biodiversity, that there is pollution of environmental media: the air, land, water and sea. It is also obvious that this trend is in one direction – there is less and less biodiversity broadly speaking, and there is more pollution, even if the increase in pollution is slowing in some areas.[40] This could be characterised as a 'reality' in the empirical sense. Between this reality of environmental degradation, and that on which decisions are based, there is a gap. This gap arises because what is taken into account and what is disregarded in a decision-making process is defined by the rules. These rules may exclude information not on a scientific basis but on a policy basis, which may be politically influenced. The reality within the process is different to the external reality. And in this difference, this gap, environmental impacts could multiply. The relevant rules, conventions and biases operate as a construct that loosens the connection between observed environmental data and, for example, a development decision. What is 'truth', in the bounded space of the decision, may not be the 'whole truth' given the omission and negation of some matters by virtue of the rules governing the process. Understanding the nature, origin and limitations of the evidence, both scientific and lay – 'the truth' upon which decisions are made, as well as the artificial constructs of what is relevant or not relevant for the constructed 'reality' of a particular decision – has implications for development decision-making processes that may have to radically transform in order to secure sustainable solutions.

7. SHALE GAS DECISION-MAKING: THE CASE STUDY

In 2015, the UK Government's written ministerial statement said that '(e)xploring and developing our shale gas and oil resources could potentially bring substantial benefits and help meet our objectives for secure energy supplies, economic growth and lower carbon emissions'.[41] Planning practice guidance issued two years earlier similarly emphasised shale gas's role as a transition to lower emissions.[42] The issue of 'lower' carbon emissions is clearly a contentious one.[43] Kysar notes that evaluating policy revisits the reasons for choosing and acting in particular ways,[44] and it is important to evaluate what impact the

---

40 European Environment Agency, *The European environment – state and outlook 2020*, EEA, 2019.

41 A. Rudd, 'Shale Gas and Oil Policy Written statement', HCWS202, DECC, London 2015.

42 Department for Communities and Local Government, *Planning Practice Guidance for Onshore Oil and Gas*, DCLG, London 2013.

43 R.W. Howarth, R. Santoro and A. Ingraffea, 'Venting and leaking of methane from shale gas development: response to Cathles et al' (2012) 113 *Climatic Change* 537–549.

44 D.A. Kysar, *Regulating From Nowhere: Environmental Law and the Search for Objectivity*, Yale University Press, New Haven CT 2010, pp. 66–67.

construction of national policy in this way has on the decision-making processes that implement this policy. Both developers and planning authorities in England emphasise the 'need' for shale gas, creating a 'high bar' for environmental impacts that would have to outweigh this need.[45] Refusals of shale gas exploration consents were rare until public campaigning reached a fever pitch in Lancashire in 2015 culminating in the elected Members of the local authority Planning Committee rejecting high-profile, large-scale exploration sites, one of them against the advice of planning officers, on visual impact and transport grounds.[46] Other councils followed suit, but in the knowledge that they were likely to lose if developers appealed against these refusals, as indeed happened in relation to the Preston New Road application in Lancashire.[47] More recently, councils have attempted to defend decisions to refuse shale gas exploration on climate change grounds.[48] These planning authorities, both in terms of elected members and officers, were not necessarily assisted by the policy guidance in their decisions to refuse development. No Strategic Environmental Assessment (SEA)[49] was conducted on the policy guidance when originally formulated, as this has not usually been the case for planning policy in England,[50] although local plans do undergo SEA.[51] Arguably, without the use of this instrument to assess the policy, there may be an absence of information and public consultation, leading to a shortfall in the relevant evidence to inform the policy. Mulder points out that planning is not that scientifically certain, and there is much conflict and ambiguity involved.[52] Against that, actively promoting shale gas developments through policy, contrary to what might be scientifically certain in terms of harms, seems to go to the heart

45 Lancashire County Council, *Officer's Report Preston New Road Cuadrilla Planning Application*, Lancashire County Council, 2015 (https://www.lancashire.gov.uk).

46 Ibid, and at Lancashire County Council, Development Control Committee, *Minutes of the Meeting held on 23, 24, 25 and 29 June 2015 at 10.00 am in Council Chamber, County Hall, Preston*, (http://council.lancashire.gov.uk/documents/s67167/FinalDCminsJunewithannexs.pdf).

47 Ministry of Housing, Communities & Local Government, '*Recovered appeals: Cuadrilla Bowland Ltd and Cuadrilla Elswick Ltd* (refs: 3134386, 3130923, 3134385 and 3130924 – 6 October 2016) Decision letter and Inspector's Report on appeals relating to applications for planning permission', MHCLG, London 2016.

48 S. Mander, 'Why are Local Authorities going against UK Government on fracking?', Manchester University, 2019 (https://www.manchester.ac.uk/discover/news/why-are-local-authorities-going-against-uk-government-on-fracking).

49 Council Directive 2001/42/EC of the European Parliament and of the Council of 27 June 2001 on the assessment of the effects of certain plans and programmes on the environment [2001] OJ L197/30.

50 *Friends of the Earth Ltd v. Secretary of State for Housing, Communities and Local Government* [2019] EWHC 518 (Admin).

51 UK, The Environmental Assessment of Plans and Programmes Regulations 2004, SI 2004/1633.

52 J. De Mulder, 'The Protocol on Strategic Environmental Assessment: A Matter of Good Governance' (2011) 20(3) *Review of European Community and International Environmental Law (RECIEL)* 232.

of why environmental protection may fail to be secured through such policies and the associated processes.

8. THE NATURE OF THE EVIDENCE IN SHALE GAS DECISION-MAKING

The regulatory system for shale gas in England consists of a number of different legal requirements as follows – an exclusive licence must be granted to the operator to drill in that area,[53] then planning permission[54] and environmental permits[55] need to be obtained. The shale gas well design must be approved,[56] and be independently examined. There must be notification of the intent to drill,[57] and only when such conditions are all met will a hydraulic fracture consent be issued by the Oil and Gas Authority.[58] Planning permission is normally issued by the Minerals Planning Authority, and, if it is not a delegated decision,[59] then elected Members (councillors) on the Planning Committee will make the decision, based on the officer's report and recommendation for approval or refusal. In the case of the environmental permits, some are issued under standard rules where there is no consultation;[60] there is a three-week consultation on others, and on 'high public interest' developments there are longer consultation periods.[61] Policy guidance is issued by several UK Government departments attached to these various regulations, as well as the local Minerals Plan,[62] and guides officers and decision-makers.

In terms of public participation and the bulk of the evidence that comes into play on decisions, planning permission and environmental permits are the most important processes. The 'role of participation in the provision and interrogation

53 This is a Petroleum Exploration and Development Licence, otherwise called a PEDL and is issued by the Department for Business, Energy and Industrial Strategy.

54 By the Minerals Planning Authority, the County Council in a two-tier council area, or the Unitary Council.

55 These Environmental Permits cover waste and emissions controls, much of which are derived from European Directives and are issued by the Environment Agency in England.

56 This approval is carried out by the Health and Safety Executive in the UK.

57 This notification is sent to the British Geological Society.

58 UK's oil and gas regulator, see https://www.ogauthority.co.uk/.

59 Powers to approve land-use development can be 'delegated' to the responsible officers who are civil servants employed by the authority for certain types of development if the Council has passed an order to that effect.

60 Environment Agency, England (https://www.gov.uk/government/collections/standard-rules-environmental-permitting).

61 Environment Agency, England (https://www.gov.uk/guidance/legal-operator-and-competence-requirements-environmental-permits).

62 A legal document adopted by the Council's elected members through a specific process set out in primary and secondary legislation following an examination by an independent Government agency, The Planning Inspectorate for England and Wales.

of evidence' is recognised in good environmental governance as key to testing the information to ensure that it is robust.[63] Much has been made over the years of the evidence-based approach to land-use planning decision-making,[64] a view that has been strengthened by the role of Environmental Impact Assessment (EIA)[65] in Europe in elucidating the various environmental impacts associated with any given development. Environmental assessment in this form plays a key role in making authorities 'think'.[66,67] It has become evident that EIA has limitations,[68] not least that while these assessments contribute to a better understanding of environmental impacts, the evidence presented may also be selective,[69] and could even in some circumstances be considered biased, especially where the promoter of the project (the developer) also commissions this environmental assessment, such as in the UK.[70] The relative weight that evidence carries in a decision-making process may also be undermined by the treatment of this evidence by authorities, and by the courts.[71]

Socio-legal research into decision-making on nationally significant renewable energy infrastructure projects in England and Wales,[72] has found that Examining Authorities have 'significant freedom to shape the evidence that is provided in the examination' by requesting types of information, and a preference for 'technical forms of knowledge' with 'less-formalised knowledge' from lay and public sources not generally relied upon.[73] Freedom to shape the information brought into the process has to be set in the context that the process

---

63 L. Squintani, J. Darpö, L. Lavrysen and P. Stoll (eds.), *Managing Facts and Feelings in Environmental Governance*, Edward Elgar, Cheltenham 2019.

64 See B. Cullingworth and V. Nadin, *Town and Country Planning in the UK*, 14th ed., Routledge, London/New York 2006.

65 R.K. Morgan, 'Environmental impact assessment: the state of the art' (2012) 30(1) *Impact Assessment and Project Appraisal* 5–14.

66 J. Holder, D. Mcgillivray, 'Taking Stock' in Holder and McGillivray (eds), *Taking Stock of Environmental Assessment: Law, Policy and Practice*, Routledge, Abingdon(Oxon) 2007, 1, at 5.

67 J. De Mulder, 'The Protocol on Strategic Environmental Assessment: A Matter of Good Governance' (2011) 20(3) RECIEL 232.

68 U. Jha-Thakur and T.B. Fischer, '25 years of the UK EIA System: Strengths, weaknesses, opportunities and threats', (2016) *Environmental Impact Assessment Review*, 61, 19–26; A. Barker and C. Jones, 'A critique of the performance of EIA within the offshore oil and gas sector', (2013), *Environmental Impact Assessment Review*, 43, 31–39.

69 See for example, North Yorkshire County Council, 'Officer's report for the Planning and Regulatory Functions Committee C3/15/00971/CPO (NY/2015/0233/ENV) – Planning application to hydraulically stimulate and test the various geological formations by Third Energy' (May 2016).

70 The Town and Country Planning (Environmental Impact Assessment) Regulations 2017, SI 2017/517 (England), reg. 18(5)(a)–(b).

71 J. Litton QC, *EIA and SEA Update Presentation* (Landmark Chambers, London: 2019).

72 M. Lee, S. Lock, L. Natarajan and Y. Rydin, *Evidence, Publics and Decision-making for Major Renewable Energy Infrastructure*, UCL, London 2017.

73 M. Lee, S. Lock, L. Natarajan and Y. Rydin, 'Decision-making for Major Renewable Energy Infrastructure' (2018) 5 *Journal of Planning and Environment Law* 507.

itself is already excluding some matters, such as the question of 'need' for the development from detailed examination.[74] This change reverses the previous trend where increasing levels of scientific evidence were informing policy such as England's 2007 Planning Policy Statement 1 Supplement on Climate Change.[75]

9. PERSPECTIVES ON KNOWLEDGE IN ENVIRONMENTAL DECISION-MAKING

A number of themes emerged from the data that provide areas for reflection. The first of these is the theme of 'conflicting information' where information from lay participants, in communities affected by development, is contrary or different in some regard to that presented by the industry. The second of these themes is the matter of 'origin of information': where the information is coming from, who is presenting it, and the variation of sources. The third theme is the 'sifting of information' where some information is discarded or ruled out of the frame of reference. This can happen where either the policy rules put weight on certain issues and/or guide decision-makers away from other issues. Fourthly, there is the 'lacuna of information', where evidence is simply unavailable, either because it does not exist (where the technology is novel) or because it does not form part of the decision-making process.

10. CONFLICT IN RELATION TO THE 'FACTS'

Where the matter for decision has recognised environmental impacts, as with shale gas, conflict arises as the opposition to the development will focus on the environmental (and social and economic) impacts, and the promoters of the development (in this case Government or Industry as broad groups) focus on the economic benefits and seek to minimise the environmental impacts so that they are publicly acceptable. This conflict was characterised in the findings by politicians as a 'judgement call'[76] and by the lay people involved – many of whom cited a lack of trust in the information presented by the industry[77] – as a concern that the environmental impacts were being 'underplayed'.[78] To an extent this is axiomatic given that the promoter will have an interest in the project being approved and is likely therefore to be tempted to downplay impacts,

---

74 K. Barker, *Barker Review of Land Use Planning Final Report – Recommendations*, HM Treasury, London 2006.

75 Communities and Local Government, *Planning Policy Statement: Planning and Climate Change – Supplement to Planning Policy Statement 1*, CLG, London 2007.

76 Transcript 020.

77 Transcript 008.

78 Transcript 009.

but the decision-making process should allow for the testing of evidence.[79] This depends on the resources of the regulatory authorities being available to critically analyse, engage with, and even bring in other expert evidence to elucidate, any areas where conflict over the level of environmental impact emerges in that process. One regulator perspective was that the communities protesting against the development were not engaging in 'a very evidence-based discussion; it tends to be very assertion-based and opinion-based'.[80] While the type of knowledge held by the community is likely to be self-acquired, possibly in response to a perceived threat, rather than professionally acquired, and may not have been rigorously critiqued, it is also valid to question the industry evidence. As one of the interviewed professionals pointed out, the stereotyping of responses – 'they would say that wouldn't they?' – is used to critically dismiss community or lay responses, while the same stereotyping is not applied by regulators to similarly dismiss industry responses.[81] Conflict therefore remains in the sphere of knowledge in the shale gas decision-making process; a conflict that could translate into a greater environmental impact of the development as the technocratic approach (that favours industry) wins out over the emotional approach (that favours environmental protection).

In the 'to and fro' of evidence that occurs in the decision-making process, one lay person explained that their perception was that 'documents are produced [by developers] to discredit what I would consider valid community evidence'.[82] This may be more than a case of agreeing to disagree. The conflict may be more fundamental, in that communities are concerned about impacts on climate change,[83] wastewater,[84] and local impacts such as seismicity,[85] noise,[86] and transport,[87] while industry promoters may minimise these impacts in their evidence.[88] There may be a limited prospect of the conflict being

---

[79] see B. Cullingworth, V. Nadin, *Town and Country Planning in the UK*, 14th edn, Routledge, London/New York 2006.

[80] Transcript 004.

[81] Transcript 007.

[82] Transcript 022.

[83] R. Hayhurst, *More criticism of council advice on Preston New Road fracking plans*, Drillordrop (28 June 2015), https://drillordrop.com/2015/06/28/more-criticism-of-council-advice-on-preston-new-road-fracking-plans/.

[84] Lancashire County Council, *Annex 2: Summary of Representations to LCC/2014/0096 Preston New Road, Little Plumpton, Fylde*, LCC, 2015; M.C. O'Donnell, S.M.V. Gilfillan, K. Edlmann and C.I. Mcdermotta, 'Wastewater from hydraulic fracturing in the UK: assessing the viability and cost of management' (2018) 4 *Environment Science: Water Resource Technology* 325–335.

[85] R. Hayhurst, 'Lancashire tremors push fracking opposition to record high', *Drill or Drop* (7 November 2019), https://drillordrop.com/2019/11/07/lancashire-tremors-push-fracking-opposition-to-record-high/.

[86] Transcript 015.

[87] Lancashire County Council meeting minutes, n. 44 above.

[88] UK Onshore Oil and Gas, *Developing shale gas and maintaining the beauty of the British countryside* (2017), UKOOG.

resolved as the fundamental principle of the project is contested, even if a decision mediated through the process is arrived at. Shale gas remains a source of emissions on the face of it, and its impacts can only be minimised rather than removed entirely. Hence an impression of cognitive dissonance persists, as the internal conflict between viewpoints and evidence from sources within the process reflects the outer dissonance between a stated aim of environmental protection and a system that grants consent to developments with environmental impacts.

11. THE ORIGIN OF 'FACTS'

Where information originates from in the decision-making process shapes its content and form.[89] Across the research findings, there was consistent awareness that most of the evidence came from the developer.[90,91] In the planning process in England, this is because the evidence is submitted by the applicant for development as part of the EIA, if it applies, and if not, in the Planning Statement and any other information requested by the planning authority. For the environmental permits, these all tend to be even more technocratic, with some permits not even requiring a public consultation[92] and therefore being solely based on information from the applicant combined with the 'in-house' sources of the regulator. Given that the regulation is also informed by the industry,[93] as the best available techniques are themselves based largely on industry information,[94] this could be considered a self-reinforcing system. Community perspectives may in general view information coming from the developer with caution, considering the information as weighted towards economic benefits. The NGO perspective in this research was that regulators place more weight on economic benefits rather than environmental and social impacts,[95] emphasised by the regulators' 'economic growth duty'.[96] Regulators themselves were aware of the tilt within the system towards the developer. In the sphere of extraction health and safety, this was presented as a pragmatic approach, as it is commercial companies that explore and exploit resources of fossil fuels and consequently possess the

---

89 E.J. Rykiel et al., 'Science and Decision-making' in R. Costanza and S.E. Jorgensen (eds.), *Understanding and Solving Environmental Problems in the 21st Century: Toward a New, Integrated Hard Problem Science*, Elsevier, Amsterdam 2002, pp. 153–166.

90 Transcript 022.

91 Transcript 002.

92 Standard Rules Permit, as at n. 60 above.

93 EU Best Available Techniques reference documents (BREFs), https://www.eea.europa.eu/themes/air/links/guidance-and-tools/eu-best-available-technology-reference.

94 Transcript 003.

95 Transcript 019.

96 Deregulation Act 2015, s. 108.

information associated with those activities. A number of community and lay perspectives commented on the 'inequality of arms' whereby it was simply not possible for them to provide the same type of information as the developer due to time, resources and expertise.[97] Inevitably these different sorts of information are then treated differently within the process.

12. THE SIFTING OF FACTS

Sifting the evidence occurs both in the overall context of the decision-making process and inside it. A community perspective expressed the view that 'Government has chosen to look at one type of evidence'.[98] The failure of the UK Government to consult on its policy for shale gas extraction originally meant an opaque policy-making process, where it was unclear what evidence had been brought to bear. Many community perspectives in the research expressed concern at the equation of shale gas extraction with sustainability – sometimes relying on the evidence of polluting impacts from extensive extraction in the USA to question this equation, and broader questioning around the issue of climate change.[99] One perspective pointed out that 'the policies that control development don't reflect the evidence',[100] so what may happen is that when that evidence is then adduced as part of the later decision-making process, either the evidence is disregarded or it is deemed outside of the policy frame. An example of this is the issue of climate-changing emissions from the end use of fossil fuels, on which the most obvious candidate to exercise regulatory scrutiny at the point of extraction, the land-use planning system, may not be able in practice to properly control it.[101] As one professional pointed out, for the decision-makers, 'the extent to which they can square that circle with the scientific evidence against the policy background is a question'.[102]

13. THE DEVELOPMENT OF LACUNAE IN RELATION TO 'FACTS'

New developments and technologies inevitably bring a level of risk, given their unknown impacts. This could be styled as a knowledge lacuna.

---

97 Transcript 002.
98 Transcript 014.
99 Transcript 005.
100 Transcript 019.
101 UK Department for Communities and Local Government, *Recovered appeals: Cuadrilla Bowland Ltd and Cuadrilla Elswick Ltd (refs: 3134386, 3130923, 3134385 and 3130924 – 6 October 2016)*, (Correspondence, DCLG, London, 6 October 2016).
102 Transcript 002.

Industry perspectives on this were in favour of exploring for gas in order to acquire the necessary information.[103] Community perspectives tended to be more concerned at the experimental nature of exploration in terms of the lack of evidence or information available *before* activities commenced. Concern extended to the ability of the regulators to deal with new technologies without the information that would be available with established and well-understood activities, and the extent to which a precautionary approach is applied.[104] Regulator perspectives on this emphasised their approach as being restrictive initially so as to minimise possible impacts.[105,106]

Lacuna can emerge in these conditions because the research is not conducted on an unbiased basis (i.e. there is a commercial interest), and because the way regulation is developed is in close relationship with the regulated industry, which may mean a lack of other perspectives. The other lacuna that arose during the process was the absence of certain types of information in parts of the process – for example the lack of chemicals information in the planning process.[107] NGOs in their objections to planning applications noted the lack of EIAs in the early decisions on shale gas in England and Wales, and Broderick also commented on the gap around environmental information because of the discretionary nature of certain size developments.[108] Kotsakis notes further gaps – including in well examination, that is focused on health and safety rather than environmental impacts, and risks around the injection of fracturing fluid – considering this to point towards 'a business-friendly regulatory environment bewitched by the shale gas revolution'.[109] Chemical safety reports for those used in shale gas development may also not be fit for purpose, as they have been developed for other uses.[110]

14. CONCLUSION

From this series of snapshots, the themes that emerged from the findings were of 'conflict' between the information brought to bear, the origin of the information

---

[103] Transcript 001.

[104] J. Hawkins, 'Fracking: Minding the Gaps' (2015) 17(1) *ELR (Environmental Law Review)* 8–21.

[105] Transcript 004.

[106] Transcript 003.

[107] Transcript 019.

[108] J. Broderick et al., *Shale Gas: An Updated Assessment of Environmental and Climate Change Impacts* Tyndall Centre for Climate Change Research, Manchester, 2011, pp. 118–119.

[109] A. Kotsakis, 'The Regulation of the Technical, Environmental and Health Aspects of Current Exploratory Shale Gas Extraction in the United Kingdom: Initial Lessons for the Future of European Union Energy Policy' (2012) 21(3) *RECIEL*.

[110] See J. Broderick et al., n 108 above.

being largely from one perspective (the developer), the sifting of the evidence through ruling out or weighting certain evidence, and the lacunae where information is unavailable. These were recognised by the public and professionals, and sometimes disputed or avoided by the regulators and industry. Clearly, these themes influence the outcome of the decisions being made. In addition, these themes are the consequence of the current formulation of law and policy controlling these decisions. The 'reality' within this decision-making frame is that not all externalities were properly accounted for – such as climate changing emissions from the burning of fossil fuels at point of extraction. It is 'true' that fossil fuel extraction inevitably results in these climate-changing emissions.[111] The findings indicate that the nature and limitations of the 'facts' upon which decisions rely may in practice hamper the achievement of sustainable solutions.

Development decision-making law is an important part of societal transition to sustainability. It is within the gift of current development consent law in the broad sense to encourage certain types of development and restrict others. As the global environmental situation becomes more acute, there is more pressure to ensure that laws such as those on development decision-making mediate conflicting perspectives objectively, create a larger role for the use of independent and objective evidence, weight environmental impacts more importantly, and recognise and close politically drawn evidence gaps. The reality of the state of the environment is that policy is failing to secure the protection that is required – the example of this shale gas decision-making process shows the limitations of the real-world operation of law and policy in this area. The context of a shortening timeframe for avoiding the worst impacts of climate change, and the need to reverse environmental pollution by waste chemicals, requires a reframing of the informational base of decision-making. This is needed in order to produce a more impartially generated evidence base with a fuller and more complete account of wider contextual factors for decisions, and its materiality, by authorities and by extension, the courts. There is room for broader testing of this analysis, as the same processes apply across other land use development decision-making regimes.

[111] In the absence of commercial carbon capture and storage.

PART II

TOOLS FOR COMPLIANCE WITH THE PARIS AGREEMENT

TOWARDS A CUMULATIVE EFFECT IN COMBATING CLIMATE CHANGE WITH SPECIAL FOCUS ON DISASTER RISK REDUCTION

Paris Agreement, SDGs and the Sendai Framework

Alexander SOLNTSEV

1. INTRODUCTION

Various dimensions of the challenge of combating climate change are today reflected in many international instruments. The current level of international legal practice requires states to periodically submit reports on the fulfilment of obligations stipulated by these acts. There is a tendency for various state bodies to prepare reports on various international acts and provide incomplete or contradictory information that does not allow assessment of the real situation in the field of combating climate change and showing the interconnection of these acts. In this contribution, as a narrower example, we will examine how the problem of climate change – with special focus on disaster risk reduction – is reflected in three international documents (Sustainable Development Goals (SDGs),[1] the Paris Agreement,[2] and the Sendai Framework for Disaster Risk Reduction[3]), how states report on them (in order to highlight best practices that show the interrelation of the three documents) and what can be proposed to increase efficiency in this area of international cooperation. At the same time, the current contribution relates to the theme of the conference. Moving towards fundamental transition processes to a sustainable future requires a special

---

1 Resolution 70/1 UN General Assembly on 25 September 2015. Transforming our world: the 2030 Agenda for Sustainable Development.

2 Paris Agreement 2015, http://unfccc.int/files/essential_background/convention/application/pdf/english_paris_agreement.pdf.

3 Sendai Framework for Disaster Risk Reduction 2015–2030. https://www.undrr.org/publication/sendai-framework-disaster-risk-reduction-2015-2030. The Sendai Framework is the successor instrument to the Hyogo Framework for Action (HFA) 2005–2015: Building the Resilience of Nations and Communities to Disasters.

approach to rule-making. When discussing questions like what kind of law optimally encourages disruptive or breakthrough innovations, we should note that it is necessary to combine hard law and strategic soft law and to provide reporting mechanisms; moreover, it is important to go down to the level of the reporting criteria of states and provide a detailed manual on reporting. In this regard, we need new *international* collaborative structures that will ensure that these manuals reflect the relationship between the reports and that there are references to other international acts. At the same time, at the state level, reports are prepared by different ministries and departments, which makes it very difficult to avoid repetitions and to show consistency in solving the problem. So, we need also *national* collaborative structures. It seems that just such detailing can become a successful element on the path of the fundamental transition processes to a sustainable future.

2. CLIMATE CHANGE INTEGRATION IN THE SDGs

The internationally agreed strategic goals and objectives contained in international treaties of a *recommendatory* nature are increasingly being accepted as having significant political and instrumental value, as they are called upon to ensure a global world order together with *binding* international instruments through synergy of actions, mobilisation of all interested parties and the development of cooperation between members of the international community.

The Paris Agreement and the 2030 Agenda for Sustainable Development were adopted in 2015. The 2030 Agenda and the Paris Agreement are both universal visions and are both based on 'bottom-up' implementation, meaning that countries identify their own priorities, needs and ambitions. It should be emphasised that the legal force of these documents is different: the Paris Agreement is an international treaty with binding legal force, and the 2030 Agenda for Sustainable Development was adopted in the form of a resolution of the UN General Assembly and is therefore advisory in nature (it is worth noting that many obligations are simply collected in this document, but legally stem from other international treaties[4]). Still, the resolution emphasises: 'we reaffirm our commitment to international law and emphasize that the Agenda is to be implemented in a manner that is consistent with the rights and obligations of

---

[4] Declaration, para. 10 'The new Agenda is guided by the purposes and principles of the Charter of the United Nations, including full respect for international law. It is grounded in the Universal Declaration of Human Rights, international human rights treaties, the Millennium Declaration and the 2005 World Summit Outcome'. See: Resolution 70/1 UN General Assembly on 25 September 2015. Transforming our world: the 2030 Agenda for Sustainable Development.

States under international law'.[5] At the same time, SDGs are called nothing less than a 'Charter for people and planet in the twenty-first century' (paragraph 51 of the Declaration), which emphasises their multi-faceted and comprehensive nature. SDGs are intended as a driver for realising and mainstreaming sustainability throughout the UN system as a whole.

Climate change issues are already addressed in the Declaration preceding the SDGs, as stated in paragraph 31:

> [T]he United Nations Framework Convention on Climate Change is the primary international, intergovernmental forum for negotiating the global response to climate change. We are determined to address decisively the threat posed by climate change and environmental degradation. The global nature of climate change calls for the widest possible international cooperation aimed at accelerating the reduction of global greenhouse gas emissions and addressing adaptation to the adverse impacts of climate change.

In other words, it is emphasised that the SDGs complement the commitments of the United Nations Framework Convention on Climate Change (UNFCCC). The Paris Agreement is not mentioned because it was adopted two and a half months *after* UN General Assembly resolution 70/1.

The 2030 Agenda for Sustainable Development contains 17 goals, 169 targets and 244 indicators,[6] some of which relate to the challenge of climate change. First of all, SDG 13 tells us to 'Take urgent action to combat climate change and its impacts'.

However, all SDGs are interrelated and interdependent. It is repeatedly stated in the text of 2030 Agenda for Sustainable Development: 'They are integrated and indivisible and balance the three dimensions of sustainable development: the economic, social and environmental (Preamble, p. 1; Declaration, paragraph 5, paragraph 10, etc.); 'The interlinkages and integrated nature of the Sustainable Development Goals are of crucial importance in ensuring that the purpose of the new Agenda is realized' (Preamble, p. 2).

Many SDGs – from poverty eradication and elimination of hunger to conservation of biodiversity and protecting the oceans – will be unattainable unless the progress is made in combating climate change. Other SDGs are connected with the climate change problem: 'build the resilience of the poor and those in vulnerable situations and reduce their exposure and vulnerability to climate-related extreme events and other economic, social and environmental

---

5 Declaration, para. 18. See: Resolution 70/1 UN General Assembly on 25 September 2015. Transforming our world: the 2030 Agenda for Sustainable Development.

6 Since nine Indicators are repeated under two or three different targets, the actual total number of individual indicators in the list is 232 (see A/RES/71/313).

shocks and disasters' under SDG 1.5; 'sustainable food production systems' and 'resilient agricultural practices' under SDG 2.4; energy transitions envisaged in SDG 7 on sustainable energy for all will contribute significantly to lowering GHG emissions relative to business-as-usual pathways, thereby contributing to the objectives of the Paris Agreement; more sustainable industrialisation under SDG 9; 'substantially increase the number of cities and human settlements adopting and implementing integrated policies and plans towards inclusion, resource efficiency, mitigation and adaptation to climate change, and resilience to disasters' under SDG 11b; and changing patterns of consumption and production in line with SDG 12 can contribute towards low-emission pathways, the creation of new kinds of jobs and making long-term progress towards eradicating poverty. Thus, 7 out of 17 SDGs contain a component aimed at resolving climate issues.

We also see these interactions between different SDGs and climate change issues in the 'The Sustainable Development Goals Report 2019'. In the introduction to the annual report, the Secretary General of the United Nations, António Guterrish, explicitly states: 'Valuable opportunities exist to accelerate progress by examining interlinkages across Goals. For example, tackling climate change requires a shift to clean energy, reversing the trend in forest loss, and changing our production and consumption patterns'.[7] And further down the text we see concrete examples of 'climatization' of seven SDGs (analysis of SDG 13 is omitted in this aspect):

- As regards SDG 1, the growing impact of climate-related disasters is addressed (especially in poor countries);
- As regards SDG 2 the report addresses the need to adapt to climate change in order to increase the resilience of small food producers;
- As regards SDG 6, it is stated that water demand will increase due to climate change;
- It is noted in relation to SDG 9 that between 2010 and 2016, the carbon intensity of manufacturing industry declined at an annual rate of almost three per cent, and therefore we can talk about a general tendency to overcome the correlation between GDP growth, on the one hand, and carbon dioxide emissions, on the other hand;
- The report, in relation to SDG 11, states that cities and suburbs are the engines of economic growth: they account for about 60 per cent of global GDP, while they also account for approximately 70 per cent of global carbon emissions. It is also stated that amid a growing number of people moving to urban areas, the use of public transport helps to mitigate the effects of air pollution and climate change; and the fact is addressed that Ambient

7 The Sustainable Development Goals Report 2019. United Nations, New York 2019, p. 3. https://www.un.org/sustainabledevelopment/progress-report.

air pollution from traffic, industry, power generation, waste burning and residential fuel combustion, combined with household pollution, poses a major threat to mitigation efforts;

- In relation to SDG 14, it is noted with regret that decades of increasing carbon emissions have led to a build-up of heat in the oceans and changes in their chemical composition. The resulting adverse effects of ocean acidification, climate change (including sea-level rise), extreme weather events and coastal erosion exacerbate ongoing threats to marine and coastal resources from overfishing, pollution and habitat degradation. It is also highlighted that as the acidity of the ocean rises, its capacity to absorb CO_2 from the atmosphere decreases, hampering the ocean's role in moderating climate change.
- As regards SDG 15, it is noted that climate change is one of the main causes of decline in biodiversity loss, and that biodiversity is declining faster than at any other time in human history.

A brief analysis of the UN annual report on the implementation of the SDGs in 2019 shows that climate change issues run like a golden thread through seven of the SDGs. This report shows that the UN systematically monitors the global climate policy, which significantly complements the implementation of the UNFCCC and Paris Agreement. Moreover, the analysis above showed that the approach of the Sustainable Development Goals (2016–2030) is much better than the approach used in the Millennium Development Goals (MDGs, 2000–2015) in terms of substance. MDGs endeavour to reduce poverty and galvanise human development in developing states, while the SDGs 'aim to cover the whole sustainable development universe, which includes basically all areas of the human enterprise on Earth'.[8] While earlier all environmental issues were included in just one of the eight MDGs, and climate change was almost neglected, now within the framework of the SDGs, as has been shown above, not only are almost all 17 SDGs 'green', but eight of them also address climate issues.

3. POSSIBLE INTERACTIONS BETWEEN NDCs AND VNRs CONCERNING THE ISSUE OF CLIMATE CHANGE

One of the purpose of this contribution is to consider what issues should be raised in the preparation of NDCs (Nationally Determined Contributions) under the Paris Agreement and VNRs (voluntary national reviews) under the 2030 Agenda

[8] D. Le Blanc, 'Towards integration at last? The sustainable development goals as a network of targets', UN Department of Economic and Social Affairs 2015, p. 11.

in order to ensure policy coherence and institutional alignment, financing and other means of implementation, as well as monitoring and review of progress.

The Paris Agreement (Article 4, paragraph 2) requires each Party to prepare, communicate and maintain successive NDCs that it intends to achieve. Parties shall pursue domestic mitigation measures, with the aim of achieving the objectives of such contributions. 186 Parties have submitted their first NDCs and three Parties (Marshall Islands, Republic of Moldova, Suriname) have submitted their second nationally determined contributions to the secretariat of the UNFCCC.[9]

If we look, for example, at the NDCs of these three states, which introduced the NDC for the second time, we will see the following picture. The Republic of the Marshall Islands in their second NDC mentioned SDGs (Goals 5 and 13) to reinforce arguments regarding the relationship between gender and climate change.[10] The Republic of Suriname in their second NDC mentioned SDGs in the following context:

> Climate-resilience is key to sustainable development, and in particular to achieving the UN Sustainable Development Goals (SDGs). The mutually supporting nature of the two agendas should be clear: delivering on its NDC will help Suriname achieve the SDGs, and achieving the SDGs will facilitate Suriname's efforts to mitigate and adapt to climate change.[11]

The Government of the Republic of Moldova in their Updated Nationally Determined Contribution mentions SDGs, namely:

> The achievement of this overarching goal is dependent, to a great extent, on the measures to be implemented in key sectors of Moldova's economy that have to contribute to sectoral and overall country climate resilience and adaptation to climate change. These activities will contribute to achieving the following Sustainable Development Goals (SDG): 1.5, 9.1, 9.4, 11.2, 13.1, 13.2, 13.3, 15.2, 15.3, 15.5 and 15.9).[12]

---

9 INDCs as communicated by Parties, https://www4.unfccc.int/sites/ndcstaging/Pages/Home.aspx.

10 The Republic of the Marshall Islands. Nationally Determined Contribution (22 November 2018), para. 175, https://www4.unfccc.int/sites/ndcstaging/PublishedDocuments/Marshall%20Islands%20Second/20181122%20Marshall%20Islands%20NDC%20to%20UNFCCC%2022%20November%202018%20FINAL.pdf.

11 The Republic of Suriname. Nationally Determined Contribution 2020, p. 6 https://www4.unfccc.int/sites/ndcstaging/PublishedDocuments/Suriname%20Second/Suriname%20Second%20NDC.pdf.

12 Government of the Republic of Moldova. Updated Nationally Determined Contribution (04/03/2020), p. 38. https://www4.unfccc.int/sites/ndcstaging/PublishedDocuments/Republic%20of%20Moldova%20Second/MD_Updated_NDC_final_version_EN.pdf.

Further on, the Republic of Moldova explicitly states that:

> The National Adaptation Plan (NAP) process in the Republic of Moldova was established as a modality to assemble various adaptation efforts into coherent and sustainable national process. In its turn, the NAP was envisaged to assist the Government of Moldova to maximize synergies of existing or under development processes of NDCs, SDGs, Paris Agreement, CCAS [Climate Change Adaptation Strategy] and, to the extent possible, integrate and add value to a more sustainable and resilient development of the country.[13]

It is extremely important that the state is aware of and reports about the synergy of these processes.

It is important to reflect on the pros and cons of a closer implementation of the two international instruments. In September 2019, the Russian Federation joined the Paris Agreement and will prepare its NDC; also, Russia's first VNR is under preparation and will be presented in 2020. Thus, it is important to take into account the approach proposed in this contribution during the preparation of the Russia's reports (NDC and VNR).

4. DISASTER RISK REDUCTION AND CLIMATE CHANGE

Today, the issue of the climate change impact on the increase of disaster risk is critical. Globalisation demands that we join the dots between climate change and the rise in extreme weather events, whether it is the wildfires which threaten urban spaces in developed countries like the US and Australia, the recent flash floods and landslides which have left almost three million people in need in the Horn of Africa, the poor harvests and prolonged drought which are driving migration from countries in Central America … there are so many examples now of how the climate emergency is derailing efforts to eradicate poverty and to achieve the other SDGs.[14] As was mentioned by the Special Representative of the UN Secretary-General for Disaster Risk Reduction,

> The single most significant thing we can do to reduce disaster risk and to avoid creating future disaster risk, is to reduce greenhouse gas emissions. Limited progress

---

13 Government of the Republic of Moldova. Updated Nationally Determined Contribution (04/03/2020), p. 61. https://www4.unfccc.int/sites/ndcstaging/PublishedDocuments/Republic%20of%20Moldova%20Second/MD_Updated_NDC_final_version_EN.pdf.

14 Special Representative of the UN Secretary-General for Disaster Risk Reduction Ms. Mami Mizutori. Marrakesh Partnership. Accelerating Action to Build a Resilient 1.5° World. UNFCCC COP-25 (10 December 2019). https://www.undrr.org/news/accelerating-action-build-resilient-150-world.

> to date shows that this can be done if we scale up. If we do not act now, then we are facing a nightmare of slow but steady collapse of our natural world amidst a rise in extreme weather events which will stretch us to breaking point in terms of our ability to prepare and respond to them.[15]

The Paris Agreement addresses the issue of disaster risk reduction in Articles 7 and 8.

SDG 13 provides for a disaster risk reduction approach for three indicators (13.1.1, 13.1.2, 13.1.3).[16] We also see this problem in the 'The Sustainable Development Goals Report 2019':

> [C]limate change is already exacerbating disaster risk. From 1998 to 2017, climate-related disasters around the world accounted for 77 per cent of the nearly $3 trillion in direct economic losses from disasters. Over that period, climate-related and geophysical disasters claimed an estimated 1.3 million lives.[17]

Moreover, we see in the SDG indicators the direct link to a new strategic document that was not previously mentioned in this contribution, but was also adopted also in 2015 – the 'Sendai Framework for Disaster Risk Reduction 2015–2030'. This, on the one hand, is quite confusing, but on the other hand, we can approach this issue in a more systematic manner.

The Sendai Framework for Disaster Risk Reduction 2015–2030 was adopted at the Third UN World Conference in Sendai, Japan, on 18 March 2015. It is the outcome of stakeholder consultations initiated in March 2012 and inter-governmental negotiations from July 2014 to March 2015, supported by the United Nations Office for Disaster Risk Reduction at the request of the UN General Assembly.

With a close reading of the Sendai Framework, we see that the issue of climate change is really solidly presented in various dimensions: paragraphs 4, 6, 11, 13, 19(h), 25(b), (c), 28(b), (c), 33(a), 34(c), 42, 47(d), and 48 (c), (e).

The Preamble of the Sendai Framework states: 'Disasters, many of which are exacerbated by climate change and which are increasing in frequency and

---

15 Special Representative of the UN Secretary-General for Disaster Risk Reduction Ms. Mami Mizutori. Marrakesh Partnership. Accelerating Action to Build a Resilient 1.5° World. UNFCCC COP-25 (10 December 2019). https://www.undrr.org/news/accelerating-action-build-resilient-150-world.

16 13.1.1 'Number of deaths, missing persons and directly affected persons attributed to disasters per 100,000 population', 13.1.2 'Number of countries that adopt and implement national disaster risk reduction strategies in line with the Sendai Framework for Disaster Risk Reduction 2015–2030'; 13.1.3 'Proportion of local governments that adopt and implement local disaster risk reduction strategies in line with national disaster risk reduction strategies': see A/RES/71/313.

17 The Sustainable Development Goals Report 2019. United Nations, New York 2019, p. 48. https://www.un.org/sustainabledevelopment/progress-report/.

intensity, significantly impede progress towards sustainable development' (paragraph 4). It is explicitly emphasised in paragraph 11 that

> intergovernmental negotiations on the post 2015 development agenda, financing for development, climate change and disaster risk reduction provide the international community with a unique opportunity to enhance coherence across policies, institutions, goals, indicators and measurement systems for implementation, while respecting the respective mandates.[18]

Both the Sendai Framework and the SDG outcomes are a product of interconnected social and economic processes. As such, there is a lot of synergy between the two policy instruments. In fact, Sendai Framework monitoring is intended to complement monitoring of 11 SDG indicators in general. The part of SDG 13 that interests us is also reflected in the Sendai Framework indicators: Goal 13.1.1 – A1 and B1; Goal 13.1.2 – E1; Goal 13.1.3 – E2.

The next question that logically arises is the following: Do states mention the Sendai Framework in their NDCs under the Paris Agreement? Selective analysis of NDCs did not allow us to find any links. If we look at the second round of NDCs (Marshall Islands, Suriname and Moldova), we will see the same situation: states have repeatedly talked about disaster risk reduction and climate change,[19] but none of them mention the Sendai Framework.

A different situation arises when analysing reports on SDGs. Since the adoption of the Sendai Framework, countries have been making efforts to develop and implement national and local disaster risk reduction strategies until 2020 in accordance with its provisions. 67 of the latest reports (2017–2018) received from 70 countries describe strategies that correspond more or less to the Sendai Framework. The most difficult challenges are directing investments for disaster risk reduction to increase resilience and fostering strategic alignment of the SDGs and climate action. Many local governments have developed relevant local strategies linked to national strategies.[20]

---

18 Sendai Framework for Disaster Risk Reduction 2015–2030. https://www.undrr.org/publication/sendai-framework-disaster-risk-reduction-2015-2030.

19 The Republic of the Marshall Islands. Nationally Determined Contribution (22 November 2018) https://www4.unfccc.int/sites/ndcstaging/PublishedDocuments/Marshall%20Islands%20Second/20181122%20Marshall%20Islands%20NDC%20to%20UNFCCC%2022%20November%202018%20FINAL.pdf; The Republic of Suriname. Nationally Determined Contribution 2020, https://www4.unfccc.int/sites/ndcstaging/PublishedDocuments/Suriname%20Second/Suriname%20Second%20NDC.pdf; Government of the Republic of Moldova. Updated Nationally Determined Contribution (04/03/2020) https://www4.unfccc.int/sites/ndcstaging/PublishedDocuments/Republic%20of%20Moldova%20Second/MD_Updated_NDC_final_version_EN.pdf.

20 The Sustainable Development Goals Report 2019. United Nations, New York, 2019, p. 48. https://www.un.org/sustainabledevelopment/progress-report/.

Planning for disaster risk reduction must also include planning for climate change adaptation. All states must integrate climate change adaptation into their national disaster risk reduction strategies, and disaster risk reduction into their national adaptation plans, to ensure coherence in implementing and monitoring the Sendai Framework, the Paris Agreement and Sustainable Development Goals. Moreover, cities also should develop local disaster risk reduction and climate resilience action plans based on the Sendai Framework.

5. CONCLUSION

This contribution has provided a pragmatic approach for connecting SDG 13 to other Goals, which apply problematic approaches to climate change in an attempt to transcend the perceived policy silos within the 2030 Agenda. Moreover, a link is made between three international documents that are aimed at increasing the cooperation of states in combating climate change with a special emphasis on Disaster Risk Reduction: namely, SDGs 2015–2030, the Paris Agreement and the Sendai Framework for Disaster Risk Reduction 2015–2030.

The adoption of the 2030 Agenda and the Paris Agreement in 2015 established a strong foundation for coherent implementation of climate action and sustainable development objectives across all levels and sectors. Exploiting synergies and co-benefits and making collaborative and coordinated efforts to both achieve the SDGs and implement the Paris Agreement is critical. Taking into account decisive climate action and the SDGs together can help avoid duplication of effort and create an opportunity for more efficient budget allocation.

In general, the 2030 Agenda should serve as a regulatory framework for enhancing action towards sustainable development of the Planet. All efforts of the states should be aimed at a comprehensive interaction between the social, economic and environmental aspects of sustainability, as well as at identification of existing and potential relationships within the SDGs, and outside of them – between SDGs and other strategic documents (in this case, the Sendai Framework for Disaster Risk Reduction 2015–2030) and relevant international treaties (in this case, the 2015 Paris Agreement) in order to stimulate interaction, overcome alleged compromises and achieve a synergistic effect. This chapter attempts to contribute to the awareness of the existing links between the SDGs and other international instruments that require periodic reporting by states. The analysis of some state reports on SDGs, the Paris Agreement and the Sendai Framework, on the one hand, does not show the full picture (this chapter provides only a small sample), but, on the other hand, it shows that a number of states are aware that these documents are interrelated, and that further steps need to be taken to bring this information to all states of the world. As a result of such steps, there is a chance to count on a synergistic effect when the situation can change for the better.

DIRECTIVE 2003/4/EC AS A TOOL TO LEARN FROM THE SUCCESSES AND FAILURES OF THE EU ETS

Reflecting on the EU Emission Trading System

Mathias N. Müller

1. INTRODUCTION

The transition to a sustainable future has been on the EU's agenda for many years. One of the key challenges in this transition is to reduce greenhouse gas emissions. Since its launch in 2005, the EU Emission Trading System (EU ETS) has been one of the cornerstones of the EU's efforts to reduce greenhouse gas emissions. Now, at the end of phase 3 of the EU ETS, it is timely to ask what we can learn from its successes and failures, with a view to fine tuning and improving the system. Most literature on the EU ETS has, thus far, focused on identifying weaknesses in the system with a view to suggesting improvements. The weaknesses that have been identified by the literature are mostly structural deficits or results thereof, such as the free allocation and the large surplus of allowances and the sanctioning provisions of the EU ETS.[1] In addition, the literature has dissected the compliance cycle of the EU ETS; the set of rules that is intended to ensure that participating industries comply with their obligations.[2]

---

1 See for example C. de Perthuis and R. Trotignon, 'Allowance "surplus" and governance implications' in S.E. Weishaar (ed.), *Research Handbook on Emissions Trading*, Edward Elgar, Cheltenham 2016, pp. 161–194; J. Prentice, 'The Revision of the European Union's Emissions Trading system Ahead of the Fourth Trading Period, 2021–2030' (2018) 8 *Climate Law* 340; J. Wettestad and T. Jevnaker, *Rescuing EU Emissions Trading: the Climate Policy Flagship*, Palgrave Macmillan, London 2016; and M. Peeters and H. Chen, 'Enforcement of Emissions Trading: Sanction regimes of greenhouse gas emissions trading in the EU and China' in S.E. Weishaar (ed.), *Research Handbook on Emissions Trading*, Edward Elgar, Cheltenham 2016, pp. 111–135.

2 See for example B. Hintermann, 'Emissions trading and market manipulation' in S.E. Weishaar (ed.), *Research Handbook on Emissions Trading*, Edward Elgar, Cheltenham 2016, pp. 89–110; L.K. McAllister, 'The Enforcement Challenge of Cap-and-Trade Regulation' (2010) 40(4) *Environmental Law* 1195, p. 1199; J. van Zeben, *The Allocation of Regulatory Competence in the EU Emission Scheme*, Cambridge University Press, Cambridge 2014.

Even though these studies have contributed to a better understanding of the EU ETS and have suggested improvements, it is hardly possible to properly review, for example, the compliance cycle, since available information on the enforcement of and compliance with the EU ETS rules is mostly published in aggregated form.

However, to be able to identify aspects that need improvement, it is necessary to dig deeper. Consequently, in addition to the question of *what* we can learn from the successes and disappointments of the EU ETS, we must ask whether we are actually in a position to reflect on the EU ETS compliance cycle. The Aarhus Convention and the Access to Environmental Information (AEI) Directive set out that the public must, in principle, be given access to environmental information held by public authorities upon request.[3] Since the EU ETS ultimately aims at protecting the environment by reducing greenhouse gas emissions, requests for information related to the EU ETS generally fall under the Aarhus regime. Therefore, this contribution aims at answering the question to what extent the right to access environmental information can be used to reflect, in detail, on the successes and failures of the EU ETS compliance cycle. By answering this question, this contribution elucidates to what extent the legal right to access to environmental information can contribute to reflecting on the adequacy of existing legislation in reducing greenhouse gas emissions and the transition to a more sustainable future.

The chapter is structured as follows. First, it briefly explains the basic functioning of the EU ETS, and why it is necessary to reflect on the compliance cycle. Subsequently, it explains why the information that is publicly available is insufficient to identify elements of the compliance cycle that need improvement. Then, the main features of the right to access environmental information, as set out by the AEI Directive, are explained. Finally, using the example of information on the enforcement of and compliance with the EU ETS rules, the chapter explores to what extent the right to access to environmental information can be used to identify problems of the EU ETS that do not become apparent from the readily available information. The final section concludes and provides some reflections.

2. REFLECTIONS ON THE EU ETS

2.1. THE FUNCTIONING OF THE EU ETS

The EU ETS is a cap-and-trade system with an EU-wide cap on emissions.[4] For every tonne of CO_2 that participating installations emit, operators must

---

3 Directive 2003/4/EC of 28 January 2003 on public access to environmental information and repealing Council Directive 90/313/EEC [2003] OJ L41/26 (Directive 2003/4/EC).

4 S. Borghesi, M. Montini and A. Barreca, *The European Emission Trading System and Its Followers: Comparative Analysis and Linking Perspectives*, Springer, Heidelberg 2016, pp. 2–3;

surrender an allowance to the competent public authority.[5] Allowances are either allocated for free,[6] sold at auctions by the Member States,[7] or can be bought on the allowance market. Since operators have to pay for every tonne of CO_2 they emit, there is a clear incentive for them to reduce their emissions.[8] The tradability of allowances is what makes the system so appealing. While operators for whom it is cheaper to reduce emissions (for example by changing the mode of production) than to buy allowances will do so, operators of installations where it is more expensive to change their production in a way that emissions would be reduced will instead buy allowances.[9] Operators that have more allowances than they need to cover their emissions, can sell the excess emissions. Consequently, emissions will be reduced where it is most cost-efficient.[10] The goal of overall emission reductions is achieved by reducing the EU-wide cap every year.[11]

The compliance cycle is a set of measures that aims at ensuring the proper functioning of and compliance with the EU ETS.[12] Operators participating in the system must obtain a greenhouse gas permit from the competent

---

A.D. Ellerman, 'The EU ETS: What We Know and What We Don't Know' in M. Gronwald and B. Hintermann (eds.), *Emissions Trading as a Policy Instrument: Evaluation and Prospects*, MIT Press, Cambridge MA 2015, p. 25.

5 Directive 2003/87/EC of 13 October 2003 establishing a scheme for greenhouse gas emission allowances trading within the Union and amending Council Directive 96/61/EC [2003] OJ L275/32 (consolidated version), Article 12(3).

6 Directive 2003/87/EC of 13 October 2003 establishing a scheme for greenhouse gas emission allowances trading within the Union and amending Council Directive 96/61/EC [2003] OJ L275/32 (consolidated version), Articles 10a, 10b and 10c.

7 Directive 2003/87/EC of 13 October 2003 establishing a scheme for greenhouse gas emission allowances trading within the Union and amending Council Directive 96/61/EC [2003] OJ L275/32 (consolidated version), Article 10; auctioning is the main allocation method since 2013.

8 J. Prentice, 'The Revision of the European Union's Emissions Trading system Ahead of the Fourth Trading Period, 2021–2030' (2018) 8 *Climate Law* 340; S. Borghesi, M. Montini and A. Barreca, *The European Emission Trading System and Its Followers: Comparative Analysis and Linking Perspectives*, Springer, Heidelberg 2016, p. 3.

9 A. Lange, 'EU Emissions Trading and Regulatory Uncertainty' in M. Gronwald and B. Hintermann (eds.), *Emissions Trading as a Policy Instrument: Evaluation and Prospects*, MIT Press, Cambridge MA 2015, p. 43.

10 K. Rogge, 'Reviewing the evidence on the innovation impact of the EU Emissions Trading System' in S.E. Weishaar (ed.), *Research Handbook on Emissions Trading*, Edward Elgar, Cheltenham 2016, pp. 287–307, p. 161.

11 J. Wettestad and T. Jevnaker, *Rescuing EU Emissions Trading: the Climate Policy Flagship*, Palgrave Macmillan, London 2016, p. 3; S. Borghesi, M. Montini and A. Barreca, *The European Emission Trading System and Its Followers: Comparative Analysis and Linking Perspectives*, Springer, Heidelberg 2016, p. 6; B. Hintermann and M. Gronwald, 'The EU ETS' in M. Gronwald and B. Hintermann (eds.), *Emissions Trading as a Policy Instrument: Evaluation and Prospects*, MIT Press, Cambridge MA 2015, p. 16.

12 S. Borghesi, M. Montini and A. Barreca, *The European Emission Trading System and Its Followers: Comparative Analysis and Linking Perspectives*, Springer, Heidelberg 2016, p. 5.

national authority.[13] The greenhouse gas permit is the entry ticket to the EU ETS and ensures that the competent authority is aware of all operators that participate in the EU ETS.[14] To make sure that they surrender a sufficient number of allowances (i.e. one per tonne CO_2), operators must continuously monitor their emissions throughout the year.[15] They do so according to a monitoring plan which must be approved beforehand by the competent authority.[16] After the end of a monitoring period (one calendar year), operators must compile an emissions report in which they lay out how much CO_2 was emitted in the last year.[17] Subsequently, operators must hire a private third-party verifier to check whether the emissions report is complete and free from material misstatements.[18] The results of the verification are recorded in the verification report. If the verifier approves the emissions report, both reports are submitted to the competent public authority and the operator must, as the final step of the compliance cycle, surrender a number of allowances equal to its CO_2 emissions.[19]

2.2. REFLECTIONS ON THE COMPLIANCE CYCLE

Operators, as rational economic actors, 'base … the decision whether to comply on a comparison of the expected benefits and expected costs of noncompliance.'[20]

---

13 Directive 2003/87/EC of 13 October 2003 establishing a scheme for greenhouse gas emission allowances trading within the Union and amending Council Directive 96/61/EC [2003] OJ L275/32 (consolidated version), Article 4.

14 S. Borghesi, M. Montini and A. Barreca, *The European Emission Trading System and Its Followers: Comparative Analysis and Linking Perspectives*, Springer, Heidelberg 2016, p. 4.

15 Directive 2003/87/EC of 13 October 2003 establishing a scheme for greenhouse gas emission allowances trading within the Union and amending Council Directive 96/61/EC [2003] OJ L275/32 (consolidated version), Article 14(3).

16 Commission Implementing Regulation (EU) 2018/2066 of 19 December 2018 on the monitoring and reporting of greenhouse gas emissions pursuant to Directive 2003/87/EC of the European Parliament and of the Council and amending Commission Regulation (EU) No 601/2012 [2018] OJ L334/1, Article 11(1).

17 Commission Implementing Regulation (EU) 2018/2066 of 19 December 2018 on the monitoring and reporting of greenhouse gas emissions pursuant to Directive 2003/87/EC of the European Parliament and of the Council and amending Commission Regulation (EU) No 601/2012 [2018] OJ L334/1, Article 68(1).

18 Commission Implementing Regulation (EU) 2018/2066 of 19 December 2018 on the monitoring and reporting of greenhouse gas emissions pursuant to Directive 2003/87/EC of the European Parliament and of the Council and amending Commission Regulation (EU) No 601/2012 [2018] OJ L334/1, Article 68(1); S. Borghesi, M. Montini and A. Barreca, *The European Emission Trading System and Its Followers: Comparative Analysis and Linking Perspectives*, Springer, Heidelberg 2016, p. 5.

19 S. Borghesi, M. Montini and A. Barreca, *The European Emission Trading System and Its Followers: Comparative Analysis and Linking Perspectives*, Springer, Heidelberg 2016, p. 4.

20 J.K. Stranlund, C.A. Chavez and B.C. Field, 'Enforcing Emissions Trading programs: Theory, Practice, and Performance' (2002) 30(3) *Policy Studies Journal* 343, p. 351; L.K. McAllister, 'The Enforcement Challenge of Cap-and-Trade Regulation' (2010) 40(4) *Environmental Law* 1195, p. 1201.

Where the benefits of not complying, i.e. lower costs due to undercounting of emissions – essentially 'cheating' the system – outweigh the costs of complying, the operator will not comply.[21] Thus, the higher the price of allowances, the higher the cost of compliance and, consequently, the stronger the incentive to undercount emissions. If operators undercount their emissions, they need fewer allowances to comply. This results in a lower overall demand for allowances which leads to a lower allowance price.[22] That makes it cheaper for all operators to comply and consequently reduces the incentive to decrease emissions.[23] Moreover, where reported emissions almost reach the cap, the emissions that have actually occurred surpass the cap due to undercounting. This means that the goal of reducing overall emissions would not be achieved.[24] Thus, if only a few operators cheat, it may have serious implications for the system as a whole. The goal of the EU ETS was to reduce greenhouse gases by 21 per cent in 2020 compared to 1990 levels.[25] According to the Commission, the EU is set to surpass this target.[26] However, the Commission bases this projection on the data submitted to it by Member States. Member States in turn submit the data that they receive from operators. Thus, if operators submit false data, intentionally or not, then this could still have serious implications for the effectiveness of the EU ETS.

Therefore, it is fundamental that monitoring and reporting data is accurate and reliable.[27] The compliance cycle of the EU ETS is based on self-monitoring and reporting of emissions with subsequent verification by a private third party.[28] Verification is intended to ensure that operators correctly monitor and do not underreport their emissions.[29] The verifier plays a crucial role in the compliance cycle, since there is an incentive for underreporting, especially when allowance prices are rising, which has been the case since early 2018.[30] However, verifiers

---

21 L.K. McAllister, 'The Enforcement Challenge of Cap-and-Trade Regulation' (2010) 40(4) *Environmental Law* 1195, p. 1201.

22 L.K. McAllister, 'The Enforcement Challenge of Cap-and-Trade Regulation' (2010) 40(4) *Environmental Law* 1195, p. 1199.

23 D.M. Driesen, 'Is Emissions Trading and Economic Incentive Program: Replacing the command and Control/Economic Incentive Dichotomy' (1998) 55(2) *Washington & Lee Law Review* 289, p. 333.

24 L.K. McAllister, 'The Enforcement Challenge of Cap-and-Trade Regulation' (2010) 40(4) *Environmental Law* 1195, p. 1200.

25 https://ec.europa.eu/clima/policies/strategies/2020_en.

26 https://ec.europa.eu/clima/policies/ets_en.

27 D.M. Driesen, 'Is Emissions Trading and Economic Incentive Program: Replacing the command and Control/Economic Incentive Dichotomy' (1998) 55(2) *Washington & Lee Law Review* 289, p. 334.

28 See section 2.1.

29 Kruger and Egenhofer, 2006, p. 7; L.K. McAllister, 'The Enforcement Challenge of Cap-and-Trade Regulation' (2010) 40(4) *Environmental Law* 1195, p. 1228.

30 Between late 2011 and beginning of 2018 the price for an allowance was consistently well below 10 EUR. However, since then, the price has been increasing up to 29 EUR and has not fallen below 20 EUR since late 2018 (see https://sandbag.org.uk/carbon-price-viewer/).

are hired and paid by the operators themselves,[31] which creates a conflict of interest for verifiers. They are paid by those whom they control. In a competitive market for verification contracts, this could lead to a situation where verifiers are more lenient with operators, so that they will be contracted again in the future. This situation is the potential Achilles' heel of the EU ETS. If undercounting of emissions, intentional or not, is not discovered, the integrity of the system is compromised. Strong public enforcement possibilities could constitute a possible solution to this problem. If the public at large could access the relevant data, it would be possible to scrutinise operators and verifiers and identify potential irregularities.[32] Therefore, the next section is dedicated to identifying the information that is relevant for checking compliance.

2.3. INFORMATION READILY AVAILABLE

The key to enabling the public to identify non-compliance is the access to 'data and other information that [makes it possible] to show that a violation has occurred.'[33] Throughout the compliance cycle, a multitude of information is generated. The most relevant stages of the compliance cycle are the monitoring, reporting and verification stages. However, only information that makes it possible to link instances of non-compliance to individual installations/operators is relevant for the purpose of checking whether a particular operator has undercounted its emissions.

The information on the monitoring, reporting and verification of emissions that is publicly available is mostly of an aggregated nature. Consequently, it is not possible to check whether an individual operator has undercounted emissions. An annual report by the Commission points out general developments such as the percentage of installations using continuous emissions measurement systems, the percentage of installations that deviated from their tier and the number of countries that reported complaints about verifiers.[34] The annual report by the European Environment Agency on trends and projections in the EU ETS is equally generic, providing information on short- and long-term trends such as emissions by main activity, for the top 30 emitters and on the

31 F. Fleurke and J. Verschuuren, 'Enforcing the European Emissions Trading System within the EU Member States: A Procrustean bed?' in T. Spapens and R. White (eds.), *Environmental Crime in transnational context: Global issues in green enforcement and criminology*, Routledge Publishing, Abingdon (Oxon) 2016, p. 7.

32 L.K. McAllister, 'The Enforcement Challenge of Cap-and-Trade Regulation' (2010) 40(4) *Environmental Law* 1195, p. 1225.

33 L.K. McAllister, 'The Enforcement Challenge of Cap-and-Trade Regulation' (2010) 40(4) *Environmental Law* 1195, p. 1225.

34 European Commission, 'Report on the functioning of the European Carbon Market' COM(2018) 842 final, pp. 37–39. On the tiering system see nn. 39 and 40 below.

supply and demand of allowances.[35] The Fourth ETS Monitoring, Reporting, Accreditation & Verification (MRAV) Compliance Review goes into much more detail, scrutinising and comparing the implementation of the compliance cycle in all Member States.[36] However, it does not provide data at installation level but instead focuses on good practices, flaws, and inconsistencies across Member States. Therefore, it does not allow for checking whether an individual operator has undercounted its allowances.

Pursuant to Article 21 of the EU ETS Directive, all Member States are obliged to fill out a questionnaire on the application of the EU ETS once a year and send it to the Commission. Based on the responses, the Commission compiles a report on the application of the EU ETS Directive.[37] Unfortunately, the report aggregates the responses of the Member States, which makes it impossible to learn about individual operators. However, the responses by individual Member States are available.[38]

Two of the questions contained in the questionnaire aim at identifying certain individual installations. Therefore, they are, in principle, relevant for checking compliance by individual operators. Question 5.10 asks the Member States to list all category C[39] installations that were allowed to apply a lower tier[40] than the highest one.[41] Moreover, for each of the installations the Member State must name the affected GHG source streams, the affected monitoring parameter, the highest tier required, and the highest tier applied. This information is useful for checking whether an operator has undercounted its emissions, since applying a lower tier means that the accuracy of the monitored emissions can be lower, which in turn makes it easier to emit more than reported.[42]

---

35 European Environment Agency, 'Trends and projections in the EU ETS in 2018 – The EU Emissions Trading System in numbers', EEA Report No 14/2018, Publications Office of the European Union, Luxembourg, 2018.

36 Ecofy Germany GmbH, Fourth ETS MRAV Compliance Review – Final Report, Cologne 2015.

37 European Union, 'Application of the European Union Emission Trading System – Analysis of national responses under Article 21 of the EU ETS Directive in 2017', Publications Office of the European Union, Luxembourg 2018.

38 http://cdr.eionet.europa.eu/.

39 There are three categories of installations. Installations with average verified annual emissions of equal or less than 50,000 tonnes of $CO_{2(e)}$ fall into category A; installations with average verified annual emissions of more than 50,000 and equal to or less than 500,000 tonnes of $CO_{2(e)}$ fall into category B; and installations with average verified annual emissions of more than 500,000 tonnes of $CO_{2(e)}$ fall into category C.

40 Installations for which a calculation-based monitoring methodology is used must apply tiers. The higher the tier the higher is the required degree of certainty of monitoring methodology. Which tier needs to be applied depends on the activity that is carried out. For example, a category B installation that produces hydrogen must apply the tier for hydrogen production which allows a maximum uncertainty threshold of ±2.5%.

41 Commission Implementing Decision C(2014) 1726, Annex.

42 The more CO_2 an installation emits, the stronger the environmental effect will be, since the accuracy is based on a percentage.

Question 5.16 asks Member States to list the installations that have applied a monitoring methodology based on continuous emission measurement instead of a calculation-based monitoring methodology.[43] When trying to identify operators that potentially undercounted their emissions, knowing the monitoring methodology of a particular installation is crucial. To check whether emissions have been monitored correctly, it is necessary to know how they have been monitored. It could be that it is harder to undercount emissions if they are continuously measured instead of calculated, the reasoning being that it is harder to manipulate a measuring sensor than to tamper with numbers. However, whether this is true is uncertain.

It can be concluded that the information that is publicly available is insufficient to assess whether an operator complies with the EU ETS or whether it underreports its emissions. The reason is that the available information is mostly aggregated and, in addition, the installation-level information that is available does not allow for checking of compliance.

2.4. RELEVANT INFORMATION

To learn in detail about the failures and successes of the EU ETS compliance cycle, it is necessary for information which makes it possible to identify non-compliance and irregularities to be publicly accessible. This requires installation-level information; in other words, information that makes it possible to evaluate the compliance of *individual* installations. The EU ETS Directive contains some articles on access to information[44] that suggest that certain data related to the compliance cycle should be publicly available. The wording of Article 15a, for instance, suggests that the Member States and the Commission must publish all decisions and reports related to the quantity and allocation of allowances and to the monitoring, reporting and verification of emissions.[45] Consequently, the emissions report and verification report should be publicly available, for instance on the websites of the competent authorities. However, at least in the case of Germany and the United Kingdom, this is not

43 Commission Implementing Decision of 21 March 2014 amending Decision 2005/381/EC as regards the questionnaire for reporting on the application of Directive 2003/87/EC of the European Parliament and of the Council [2014] OJ L89/45, Annex.

44 K. MacDonald and Z. Makuch, 'Emissions trading and the Aarhus Convention: a proportionate symbiosis?' in M. Peeters and K Deketelaere (eds.), *EU Climate Change Policy: The Challenge of New Regulatory Initiatives*, Edward Elgar, Cheltenham 2006, p. 138.

45 It is unclear what exactly this article entails. See M. Peeters and M.N. Müller, 'Private Control of Public Regulation: A Smart Mix?' in J. van Erp, M. Faure, A. Nollkaemper and N. Philipsen (eds.), *Smart Mixes for Transboundary Environmental Harm*, Cambridge University Press, Cambridge 2019, for a more detailed discussion.

the case. Moreover, Article 17 sets out that 'decisions relating to the allocation of allowances … and reports of emissions required under the greenhouse gas permit and held by the competent authority' must be disclosed pursuant to the AEI Directive.[46]

The installation-level data that the Commission publishes is mostly related to annual emissions of installations. For example, the Commission publishes a compliance code list, a list of stationary installations and a verified emissions list.[47] All three of these documents provide information about individual installations which can be helpful to determine whether an operator has undercounted its emissions. The compliance code list sets out the total verified emissions per installation, total surrendered allowances and whether the number of allowances surrendered is sufficient. The list of stationary installations lists, for each installation, the name of the account holder in the Union Registry, the name and identification number of the installation, the activity carried out, the identification number of the greenhouse gas permit, the permit status[48] and the postal address of the operator/installation. The verified emissions list encompasses a lot of the information that is also contained in the list of stationary installations, but adds, regarding all installations, the number of allowances allocated free of charge, the number of allowances allocated for modernisation of electricity generation, the number of allowances allocated from the new entrants reserve, and the verified emissions.

Unfortunately, this information is not sufficient to reflect on the strengths and weaknesses of the compliance cycle of the EU ETS. It is neither possible to determine whether an operator has underreported its emissions, nor to identify the weaknesses of the compliance system that the operator in question exploited. The data necessary to perform such a test comprises the data collected throughout the monitoring process, the monitoring plan, the emissions report, the data collected throughout the verification process and the verification report. Since none of this information is publicly available, the only possibility is to request it from the body holding it.

The relevant information is partially held by the competent authority and partially by the verifier. In light of the Aarhus Convention and the AEI Directive, two essential questions arise: first, does the relevant information fall under the definition of environmental information and second, are the bodies holding the relevant information public authorities pursuant to the definition set out in the AEI Directive. It is beyond the scope of this contribution to examine

[46] Directive 2003/87/EC of 13 October 2003 establishing a scheme for greenhouse gas emission allowances trading within the Union and amending Council Directive 96/61/EC [2003] OJ L275/32 (consolidated version).

[47] Available under https://ec.europa.eu/clima/policies/ets/registry_en#tab-0-1.

[48] Active or revoked.

all the relevant forms of information individually to determine whether they fall under the definition of environmental information. Therefore, this chapter analyses whether records of site visits, as a typical example of a piece of relevant information, is environmental information. The other question is whether the bodies holding the relevant information are public authorities. With regards to the competent public authorities the answer is clearly yes. However, the case is not so clear regarding the verifier. Therefore, besides determining whether information on site visits is environmental information, the following section focuses on the question whether verifiers are 'public authorities' pursuant to the definition set out in the AEI Directive.

3. ACCESS TO THE RELEVANT INFORMATION

3.1. APPLICABILITY OF DIRECTIVE 2003/4/EC

The EU ETS Directive is based on what is now Article 192(1) TFEU.[49] Instruments based on that Article are intended to contribute to achieving the aims set out in Article 191 TFEU, which include environmental protection. Moreover, the preamble of the EU ETS Directive points out that its ultimate goal is to 'achieve a stabilisation of greenhouse gas concentrations in the atmosphere at a level which prevents dangerous anthropogenic interference with the climate system.'[50] Since the aim of the EU ETS Directive is environmental protection, requests for information related to it will generally be covered by the AEI Directive on public access to environmental information.

The AEI Directive implements the first pillar of the Aarhus Convention, giving every member of the public the right to access to environmental information that is held by a public authority. A public authority may (partially) refuse the request for information where one of the grounds of refusal applies. Consequently, three conditions must be fulfilled before the requested information must be disclosed. First, the information in question must fall within the definition of environmental information. Second, the information must be held by a public authority. Last, none of the grounds of refusal may apply. Therefore, it must be assessed whether the relevant information – in the case at hand the records of site visits – constitutes environmental information, whether the verifier falls within the definition of a public authority, and whether any of the grounds of refusal apply.

49 Formerly Article 175(1) TEC.

50 Directive 2003/87/EC of 13 October 2003 establishing a scheme for greenhouse gas emission allowances trading within the Union and amending Council Directive 96/61/EC [2003] OJ L275/32 (consolidated version), recital (3).

3.2. ENVIRONMENTAL INFORMATION

In the context of records of site visits, three sub-paragraphs of the definition of environmental information are particularly interesting. First, environmental information includes information on the state of elements of the environment such as air and atmosphere.[51] Second, information on 'factors, such as emissions, discharges and other releases … affecting or likely to affect the … environment' is environmental information.[52] Finally, information on any measure or activity that affects or is likely to affect either the elements of the environment or the environmental factors is environmental information as well.[53]

Information on greenhouse gas emissions is environmental information since those emissions affect an element of the environment – the atmosphere – by altering its composition.[54] Consequently, when assessing whether records of site visits are environmental information, the crucial question is whether site visits constitute a measure or activity that affects or is likely to affect an element of the environment or an environmental factor. The Court of Justice of the European Union (CJEU) has ruled that the definition of environmental information must be interpreted broadly.[55] Therefore, the term 'activity' should be construed widely as every human activity.[56] Consequently, site visits are an activity within the meaning of Article 2(1)(c) of the AEI Directive. The final question is whether site visits have or are likely to have an effect on the environment. In light of the CJEU's decision that the term environmental information is a broad concept, it can be argued that it is sufficient that the activity is capable of having an effect on the environment. The corresponding provision in the German national legislation has been interpreted to mean that a *potential* effect on the environment is in itself enough for an activity to be likely to affect the environment.[57] Pursuant to the broad interpretation of the concept

---

51 Directive 2003/4/EC of 28 January 2003 on public access to environmental information and repealing Council Directive 90/313/EEC [2003] OJ L41/26, Article 2(1)(a).

52 Directive 2003/4/EC of 28 January 2003 on public access to environmental information and repealing Council Directive 90/313/EEC [2003] OJ L41/26, Article 2(1)(b).

53 Directive 2003/4/EC of 28 January 2003 on public access to environmental information and repealing Council Directive 90/313/EEC [2003] OJ L41/26, Article 2(1)(c).

54 Directive 2003/4/EC of 28 January 2003 on public access to environmental information and repealing Council Directive 90/313/EEC [2003] OJ L41/26, Article 2(1)(a) and (b).

55 See for example Case C-321/96 *Mecklenburg v. Kreis Pinneberg – Der Landrat* [1998] ECR I-3824, pp. 3832–3933, para. 19; Case C-316/01 *Eva Glawischnig v Bundesminister für soziale Sicherheit und Generationen* [2003] ECR I-6009, pp. 6020–6021, para. 24.

56 The Administrative Court Düsseldorf has interpreted the German Environmental Information Act in this way (VG Düsseldorf, 15 January 2002, 3 K 5795/01, para. 17.).

57 Umweltinformationsgesetz in der Fassung der Bekanntmachung vom 27. Oktober 2014 (BGBl. I S. 1643, §2 Abs. 3 Nr. 3; R. Götze and G.-R. Engel, *Umweltinformationsgesetz*, Erich Schmidt Verlag, Berlin 2017, p. 85; O. Reid and G. Schiller 'Umweltinformationsgesetz' in M. Beckmann, W. Durner, T. Mann and M. Röckinghausen (eds) *Umweltrecht* Vol. 1, München: C.H. Beck, 2020, para. 44.

of environmental information in general, and more specifically the phrase 'likely to have an effect on the environmental factors', it can be concluded that site visits are likely to have an effect on the environmental factors, since they help to ensure that operators do not emit more than reported. Consequently, carrying out site visits can have an effect on an environmental factor, i.e. emissions. That means that records of site visits are environmental information pursuant to the definition set out in the AEI Directive.

3.3. PUBLIC AUTHORITIES

Pursuant to the AEI Directive, there are three categories of public authorities. The first category comprises classic state bodies such as governmental agencies or administrative authorities.[58] The public authorities responsible for administering the EU ETS fall under this category. The second and third categories cover private entities that qualify as 'public authority' under certain circumstances. Records of site visits are held by the verifier. Since the verifier is a formally private entity, it is necessary to establish whether the verifier constitutes a public authority pursuant to the definition set out in the AEI Directive and is consequently, in principle, obliged to disclose environmental information upon request.

3.3.1. Bodies of Public Administration

Pursuant to the second category, a private entity is considered to be a public authority if it performs 'public administrative functions under national law'.[59] The definition of the concept public administrative functions is crucial. In *Fish Legal*, the CJEU ruled that 'public administrative function' is an EU concept which must have the same meaning in all Member States.[60] It pointed out that 'only entities which, by virtue of a legal basis specifically defined in the national legislation which is applicable to them', are[61] 'vested with special powers beyond those which result from the normal rules applicable in relations between persons governed by private law'[62] constitute bodies carrying out public administrative tasks. The *Fish Legal* case concerned the question whether water companies

58 Directive 2003/4/EC of 28 January 2003 on public access to environmental information and repealing Council Directive 90/313/EEC [2003] OJ L41/26, Article 2(2)(a).

59 Directive 2003/4/EC of 28 January 2003 on public access to environmental information and repealing Council Directive 90/313/EEC [2003] OJ L41/26, Article 2(2)(b).

60 Case C-279/12 *Fish Legal and Emily Shirley v. Information Commissioner and Others* ECLI:EU:C:2013:853, para. 45.

61 Case C-279/12 *Fish Legal and Emily Shirley v. Information Commissioner and Others* ECLI:EU:C:2013:853, para. 48.

62 Case C-279/12 *Fish Legal and Emily Shirley v. Information Commissioner and Others,* ECLI:EU:C:2013:853, para. 52.

were carrying out public administrative functions. The CJEU observed that these water companies had a number of special powers under the applicable national law, such as the power of compulsory purchase, the power to make bye-laws relating to the waterway and land in their ownership, and the right to temporarily cut the public water supply.[63] It was left to the referring national court to determine whether these powers constituted 'special powers'.[64] The Upper Tribunal (Administrative Appeals Chamber) of the United Kingdom pointed out that it is not necessary that the power is unique to a particular body, sector or industry to be considered special.[65] In its assessment regarding whether the water companies' powers were special, the Upper Tribunal considered whether the powers gave each of the companies 'an ability that confers on it a practical advantage relative to the rules of private law.'[66] Moreover, it stated that a power is special where it allows the body in question to override the execution of private law powers.[67] Based on these considerations, the Upper Tribunal decided that the water companies did indeed have special powers.[68]

The question that must be answered in the context of examining whether verifiers are public authorities pursuant to Article 2(2)(b) of the AEI Directive is whether verifiers 'perform a service in the public interest and have special powers to perform this service.'[69] This question cannot be answered with certainty. On the one hand, it can be argued that verifiers, to a certain extent, have special powers, since they have wide-ranging powers such as auditing operators[70] and issuing verification reports whereby they determine whether the operator can surrender allowances and continue to participate in the EU ETS.[71] On the other hand, one can argue that a verifier only acquires its special powers *vis-à-vis* an operator once they have agreed on a verification contract. Moreover, one could invoke that verifiers do not have special powers because, even though operators must

---

63 Case C-279/12 *Fish Legal and Emily Shirley v. Information Commissioner and Others*, ECLI:EU:C:2013:853, para. 54.

64 Case C-279/12 *Fish Legal and Emily Shirley v. Information Commissioner and Others*, ECLI:EU:C:2013:853, para. 55.

65 The Upper Tribunal GIA/0979/2011 *Fish Legal v. Information Commissioner, United Utilities plc, Yorkshire Water Services Ltd and the Secretary of State for the Environment, Food and Rural Affairs* [2015] UKUT 0052 (AAC), para. 110.

66 *Fish Legal* [2015] UKUT 0052 (AAC), para. 106.

67 *Fish Legal* [2015] UKUT 0052 (AAC), para. 123.

68 *Fish Legal* [2015] UKUT 0052 (AAC), para. 130.

69 M. Peeters and M.N. Müller, 'Private Control of Public Regulation: A Smart Mix?' in J. van Erp, M. Faure, A. Nollkaemper and N. Philipsen (eds.), *Smart Mixes for Transboundary Environmental Harm*, Cambridge University Press, Cambridge 2019, p. 273.

70 Of course, verifiers do not perform a financial audit, but rather an environmental audit of the operators' emissions reports.

71 M. Peeters and M.N. Müller, 'Private Control of Public Regulation: A Smart Mix?' in J. van Erp, M. Faure, A. Nollkaemper and N. Philipsen (eds.), *Smart Mixes for Transboundary Environmental Harm*, Cambridge University Press, Cambridge 2019, pp. 273 f.

have their emissions report verified and consequently contract with a verifier, operators cannot be forced to contract with a specific verifier. In addition, even though operators and verifiers are relatively constrained by the provisions of the Monitoring and Reporting Regulation[72] and the Accreditation and Verification Regulation[73] with regards to their rights and obligations, they are nonetheless free to shape the contract between them according to their preferences within the limits of those regulations. Thus, it is at least debatable whether the verifier performs public administrative functions and is consequently a public authority pursuant to Article 2(2)(b) of the AEI Directive.

3.3.2. *Other Qualifying Bodies*

The third category of public authorities covers private entities that have 'public responsibilities or functions, or [provide] public services, relating to the environment [and are] under the control of' a body that falls within one of the first two categories of public authorities.[74] This definition contains three major elements that require further attention. First, it is necessary to determine under what conditions a responsibility, function or service (in the following subsumed under the term 'task') must be considered to be of a public nature. Second, it must be determined when a public task relates to the environment; and finally, it is essential to establish the conditions that must be fulfilled for a body to be regarded as being under the control of a public authority.

3.3.2.1. Tasks of a Public Nature

The AEI Directive does not define the term 'public' and it has not been interpreted by the CJEU. However, there have been some cases based on, and literature about, national legislation implementing the AEI Directive at the national level. They provide a good indication of the circumstances in which a task is considered to be public in nature. When assessing whether a task is of a public nature, courts examine whether the functions are typically of a governmental nature,[75]

---

72 Commission Implementing Regulation (EU) 2018/2066 of 19 December 2018 on the monitoring and reporting of greenhouse gas emissions pursuant to Directive 2003/87/EC of the European Parliament and of the Council and amending Commission Regulation (EU) No 601/2012 [2018] OJ L334/1.

73 Commission Implementing Regulation (EU) 2018/2067 of December 2018 on the verification of data and on the accreditation of verifiers pursuant to Directive 2003/87/EC of the European Parliament and of the Council [2018] OJ L334/94.

74 Directive 2003/4/EC of 28 January 2003 on public access to environmental information and repealing Council Directive 90/313/EEC [2003] OJ L41/26, Article 2(2)(c).

75 *The Port of London Authority v. Information Commissioner and Mr John Hibbert*, [2007] EA/2006/0083, para. 27; F. Elfeld, *Pflichten Privater zur Herausgabe von Umweltinformationen aus der Umsetzung der RL 2003/4/EG*, Kovač, Hamburg 2014, p. 77.

whether the functions are part of a statutory regime,[76] whether the government would be responsible for finding another body that performs the function if the body carrying them out failed to do so,[77] whether the body is licensed to carry out the task in question,[78] whether the body can freely determine the price it charges for carrying out the task,[79] whether there is a strong public interest in the performance of the task[80] and whether, under free market conditions, the task would be carried out due to its profitability.[81]

Thus, it must be determined whether the tasks of a verifier match these criteria. Evaluation of the criteria shows that some of them indicate that verification *is* a public task while others point to the opposite. The *raison d'être* of verification is to ensure that operators comply with their obligation to surrender a correct number of allowances. Ensuring compliance with legislation is typically a task carried out by the government. Moreover, verifiers must be accredited by the national accreditation body of one of the Member States. Thus, verifiers are licensed to carry out their task. There is also a strong public interest in the performance of verification, since it ensures the proper application of legislation that is intended to protect the environment, and environmental protection is in the public interest. Finally, verification is part of a statutory regime, the EU ETS compliance cycle. There would be no need for verification if the EU ETS did not exist. However, within the verification market, verifiers can freely determine the price they charge for performing the verification of emissions reports. Thus, even though created by a statutory regime, the market for verification can be considered to be a free market. Nevertheless, ensuring the correct application of legislation is ultimately the responsibility of the government. Consequently, it would be the government's

---

76 *The Port of London Authority v. Information Commissioner and Mr John Hibbert*, [2007] EA/2006/0083, para. 27; F. Elfeld, *Pflichten Privater zur Herausgabe von Umweltinformationen aus der Umsetzung der RL 2003/4/EG*, Kovač, Hamburg 2014, p. 84.

77 *The Port of London Authority v. Information Commissioner and Mr John Hibbert*, [2007] EA/2006/0083, para. 27.

78 *Smartsource v. Information Commissioner and a Group of 19 additional parties* [2011] *Journal of Planning & Environment Law (JPL)* 455, [2010] UKUT 415 (AAC), [2014] AACR 10, para. 66.

79 *Smartsource v. Information Commissioner and a Group of 19 additional parties* [2011] *JPL* 455, [2010] UKUT 415 (AAC), [2014] AACR 10, para. 66.

80 T. Schomerus and S. Clausen, 'Informationspflichten Privater nach dem neuen Umweltinformationsgesetz am Beispiel der Exportkreditversicherung' (2005) *Zeitschrift für Umweltrecht* 575, p. 578; R. Götze and G.-R. Engel, *Umweltinformationsgesetz*, Erich Schmidt Verlag, Berlin 2017, p. 85; O. Reid and G. Schiller 'Umweltinformationsgesetz' in M. Beckmann, W. Durner, T. Mann and M. Röckinghausen (eds) *Umweltrecht* Vol. 1, München: C.H. Beck, 2020, para. 21; A. Geiger, 'Das Umweltinformationsrecht der EU und seine Umsetzung in Deutschland', *Anwaltsblatt* 7/2010, 464, p. 466; and R. Götze and G.-R. Engel, *Umweltinformationsgesetz*, Erich Schmidt Verlag, Berlin 2017, pp. 63 f.

81 F. Elfeld, *Pflichten Privater zur Herausgabe von Umweltinformationen aus der Umsetzung der RL 2003/4/EG*, Kovač, Hamburg 2014, p. 85 f.

task to assign the performance of verification to another body if verifiers failed to perform verification. Thus, most of the criteria indicate that verification is a public task.

3.3.2.2. In Relation to the Environment

The second criterion is that the public task must be related to the environment. This term has not been interpreted by the CJEU, but at national level there have been some cases that dealt with this term. According to these cases, the term must be interpreted widely[82] as having a connection to the environment.[83] It is enough that the task has the potential to have an effect on the environment.[84] A relation to the environment exists if the body in question carries out public tasks that are envisaged to protect the environment.[85] Naturally, national courts do not interpret EU legislation, however, until there is a judgment of the CJEU that gives a clear EU-wide definition of this term, their interpretation of the national legislation implementing Directive 2003/4/EC provides examples of how this term can be interpreted.

The question that arises regarding the issue at hand is whether the verification of emission reports is a task that is related to the environment. Given the broad interpretation of the term 'related to the environment' set out above and the fact that the verification process is an integral part of the compliance cycle of the EU ETS, which is aimed at protecting the environment, the answer must be affirmative.

3.3.2.3. Under the Control

The third and last criterion to determine whether a private entity qualifies as a public authority set out in Article 2(2)(c) is that the private entity must be

---

82 T. Schomerus and S. Clausen, 'Informationspflichten Privater nach dem neuen Umweltinformationsgesetz am Beispiel der Exportkreditversicherung' *Zeitschrift für Umweltrecht*, 2005, p. 578; F. Elfeld, *Pflichten Privater zur Herausgabe von Umweltinformationen aus der Umsetzung der RL 2003/4/EG*, Kovač, Hamburg 2014, p. 89.

83 Decision Notice by the UK Information Commissioner, FER149772, para. 36, available at: www.ico.gov.uk.

84 BVerwG 25 March 1999, 7 C 21.98, p. 11; R. Götze and G.-R. Engel, *Umweltinformationsgesetz*, Erich Schmidt Verlag, Berlin 2017, p. 85; O. Reid and G. Schiller 'Umweltinformationsgesetz' in M. Beckmann, W. Durner, T. Mann and M. Röckinghausen (eds) *Umweltrecht* Vol. 1, München: C.H. Beck, 2020, para. 23 and A. Guckelberger, 'Geschichte des Umweltinformationsrechts und allgemeine Anspruchsvorausetzungen' (2018) 40 *Natur und Recht* 378, p. 385.

85 R. Götze and G.-R. Engel, *Umweltinformationsgesetz*, Erich Schmidt Verlag, Berlin 2017, p. 66; F. Elfeld, *Pflichten Privater zur Herausgabe von Umweltinformationen aus der Umsetzung der RL 2003/4/EG*, Kovač, Hamburg 2014, p. 92.

under the control of a body that is a public authority pursuant to Article 2(2)(a) or (b), i.e. a government body or a private body with public administrative functions. The CJEU interpreted the phrase 'under the control' in the *Fish Legal* case.[86] It concluded that an entity is under the control of a public authority where it

> does not determine in a genuinely autonomous manner the way in which it performs the functions in the environmental field which are vested in it, since a public authority ... is in a position to exert decisive influence over the entity's actions in that field.[87]

It does not matter in what way the public authority exerts the decisive influence.[88] Moreover, an entity may even be considered to be under the control of a public authority where it is a commercial company that performs a public task in relation to the environment if the performance of that task is subject to a particularly precise legal framework that lays down specific rules which the company must follow when carrying out the task.[89] For example, this could be the case where the company is supervised to ensure that it complies with the specific rules.[90]

Hence, the final question that must be answered when determining whether the verifier is a public authority pursuant to Article 2(2)(c) of the AEI Directive is whether the verifier is under the control of a body that is a public authority pursuant to Article 2(2)(a) or (b). Since the verifier is a private company that is independent from any public authority and its independence from the national accreditation body[91] is even enshrined in the Accreditation and Verification Regulation,[92] there is no public authority that 'is in a position to exert decisive influence over'[93] the verifier's activities.

However, a private party is also under the control of a public authority where the performance of its activities is subject to a particularly tight legal framework.

86 Case C-279/12 *Fish Legal and Emily Shirley v. Information Commissioner and Others*, ECLI:EU:C:2013:853, paras. 57 ff.

87 Case C-279/12 *Fish Legal and Emily Shirley v. Information Commissioner and Others*, ECLI:EU:C:2013:853, para. 68.

88 Case C-279/12 *Fish Legal and Emily Shirley v. Information Commissioner and Others*, ECLI:EU:C:2013:853, para. 69.

89 Case C-279/12 *Fish Legal and Emily Shirley v. Information Commissioner and Others*, ECLI:EU:C:2013:853, para. 71.

90 Case C-279/12 *Fish Legal and Emily Shirley v. Information Commissioner and Others*, ECLI:EU:C:2013:853, para. 71.

91 National accreditation bodies are public authorities themselves.

92 Commission Implementing Regulation (EU) 2018/2067, Article 57(1).

93 Case C-279/12 *Fish Legal and Emily Shirley v. Information Commissioner and Others*, ECLI:EU:C:2013:853, para. 68.

The verifier's obligations can be found in the Accreditation and Verification Regulation. Instead of merely providing the aim of verifying that the emissions report is free from misstatements, the regulation sets out, in detail, the different steps that the verifier has to take in the course of verifying an emissions report. The regulation stipulates that the verifier must, *inter alia*, analyse the inherent risk[94] and the control activities,[95] draw up a verification plan (the regulation also specifies what the verification plans must include),[96] verify the data in the emissions report,[97] verify whether the operator has correctly applied the monitoring methodology[98] and carry out a site visit.[99] Due to this detailed regulation of the verification process, it can well be argued that the verifier is subject to a 'particularly precise legal framework which lays down a set of rules determining the way in which [it] must perform [the verification]' when carrying out the verification of emissions reports. The result is that verifiers 'do not have genuine autonomy *vis-à-vis* the State, even if the latter is [not] in a position … to determine their day-to-day management.'[100]

That means that verifiers are under the control of a public authority pursuant to Article 2(2)(c) of the AEI Directive. Consequently, verifiers are public authorities for the sake of the AEI Directive, since they (1) carry out a public task, (2) that task relates to the environment, and (3) they are under the control of a public authority.

4. FINAL REMARKS

The aim of this contribution has been to examine to what extent the right of access to environmental information can be used to reflect, in detail,

---

94 Commission Implementing Regulation (EU) 2018/2067, Article 12; the inherent risk refers to the 'susceptibility of a parameter in the operator's … report to misstatements that could be material' (Article 3(16)).

95 Commission Implementing Regulation (EU) 2018/2067, Article 12; 'control activities' refers to 'any acts … by the operator … to mitigate inherent risks.' (Article 3(12)).

96 Commission Implementing Regulation (EU) 2018/2067 of December 2018 on the verification of data and on the accreditation of verifiers pursuant to Directive 2003/87/EC of the European Parliament and of the Council [2018] OJ L334/94, Article 13.

97 Commission Implementing Regulation (EU) 2018/2067 of December 2018 on the verification of data and on the accreditation of verifiers pursuant to Directive 2003/87/EC of the European Parliament and of the Council [2018] OJ L334/94, Article 16.

98 Commission Implementing Regulation (EU) 2018/2067 of December 2018 on the verification of data and on the accreditation of verifiers pursuant to Directive 2003/87/EC of the European Parliament and of the Council [2018] OJ L334/94, Article 17.

99 Commission Implementing Regulation (EU) 2018/2067 of December 2018 on the verification of data and on the accreditation of verifiers pursuant to Directive 2003/87/EC of the European Parliament and of the Council [2018] OJ L334/94, Article 21.

100 Case C-279/12 *Fish Legal and Emily Shirley v. Information Commissioner and Others*, ECLI:EU:C:2013:853, para. 71.

on the failures and successes of the EU ETS compliance cycle. It is a very important question, since the integrity of the EU ETS would be compromised if emissions were undercounted (section 2.2 above) and, as has been shown in section 2.3, the information that is publicly available does not suffice to adequately reflect on the successes and failures of the EU ETS, especially regarding the compliance cycle. The information that is publicly available is mostly of an aggregated nature, which makes it impossible to determine whether individual actors are complying, and consequently, it is impossible to reflect on how to improve the compliance cycle to prevent non-compliance in the future. One example of information that would be relevant for identifying individual actors that do not comply and the reasons for their non-compliance are reports of site visits that the verifier carries out in the course of the verification process.

By means of the example of reports of site visits, the third section has been dedicated to exploring to what extent environmental information can be accessed with a view to using it to identify instances of non-compliance and to reflect on the compliance cycle. It has been shown that, due to the broad definition of environmental information, it is relatively easy to argue that reports of site visits constitute environmental information pursuant to the AEI Directive.

The second central element of a request for environmental information is the question whether the body holding the information is a public authority pursuant to the definition set out in the AEI Directive. Reports of site visits are held by the verifier. Consequently, section 3.3 has analysed whether verifiers are public authorities and concluded that the verification of emissions reports is a public task since it (indirectly) protects the environment and environmental protection is in the public interest. However, according to the criteria developed by the CJEU in *Fish Legal*, verifiers do not have special powers to perform verification and consequently do not have public *administrative* functions. Nonetheless, it has been argued that verifiers' tasks are public and relate to the environment and that verifiers are under the control of a body that is a public authority pursuant to the first or second category. Therefore, it has been asserted that verifiers are public authorities pursuant to the AEI Directive.

Thus, the answer to the central question of this contribution is that the right to access environmental information can be used to reflect on the successes and failures of the EU ETS, as far as the relevant information constitutes environmental information. However, this conclusion is subject to some reservations. Besides the two elements discussed in this contribution (the definitions of 'environmental information' and 'public authority'), it is necessary to check whether one of the grounds of refusal, set out in the AEI Directive, applies. In light of that, the legislator 'should facilitate ... public disclosure [of relevant information] through appropriate statutory language, as some of [the] self-monitoring data would likely be argued to constitute confidential business information.'[101] In addition, applicants may face more practical barriers when requesting access to environmental information, such as charges levied by public authorities[102] or public authorities that simply ignore requests. Nevertheless, it is clear that the right of access to environmental is a powerful tool that may be used to check the compliance with legislation that aims at reducing the greenhouse gas emissions in the EU, which is a fundamental element of moving towards a more sustainable future.

---

101 L.K. McAllister, 'The Enforcement Challenge of Cap-and-Trade Regulation' (2010) 40(4) *Environmental Law* 1195, p. 1225.

102 Even though, public authorities are in principle allowed to levy charges, these may not be so high as to dissuade potential applicants from requesting environmental information.

FINDING THE SPEARHEAD OF THE EU LOW-CARBON ENERGY TRANSITION

Theodoros G. Iliopoulos

1. INTRODUCTION

Since the mid-2000s, and especially since the early 2010s, the terms 'low-carbon economy', 'low-carbon energy transition' and 'decarbonisation' have appeared in quite a few Commission policy documents and have encapsulated the direction of EU energy and climate change policy.[1] Most recently, the new supranational strategy that was presented in December 2019 in the Communication 'the European Green Deal' emphasised the need for a 'clean energy transition', which involves decarbonisation and an increased share of renewable energy sources, more energy efficiency and energy security, as well as the rise of a fully integrated, interconnected and digitalised European energy market.[2] In addition, given that the energy sector produces the most emissions in the European Union, with the production and use of energy accounting for more than 75 per cent of the EU's greenhouse gas emissions,[3] energy reforms are crucial in the struggle to tackle the climate change threat. Therefore, the promotion of renewable energy sources, in serving the low carbon energy transition policy objective, is a part of the overall transition to a sustainable future.

In November 2016 the EU put forward the Clean Energy Package, with the aim to bring a comprehensive update in its energy policy framework so that the low-carbon energy transition could be facilitated. The Clean Energy Package in essence constituted a set of eight legislative initiatives, which became legal

---

1 See for instance Commission, 'Accelerating Europe's transition to a low-carbon economy' (Communication) COM(2016) 500 final; Commission, 'A policy framework for climate and energy in the period from 2020 to 2030' (Communication) COM(2014) 15 final; Commission, 'A Roadmap for moving to a competitive low carbon economy in 2050' (Communication) COM(2011) 112 final.

2 Commission, 'The European Green Deal' (Communication) COM(2019) 640 final.

3 Ibid. p. 6.

acts in 2018 and 2019. One of these legal acts is the new Renewable Energy Directive 2018/2001, also known as the 'RED II', which establishes a common framework for the promotion of energy from renewable sources.[4] This chapter focuses on the RED II and especially on the rules therein relating to the support schemes for renewable energy sources ('Renewable Energy Support Schemes' (RESSs)); RESSs are defined in Article 2(5) of the RED II as instruments, schemes or mechanisms that Member States enact in order to promote the use of renewable energy sources.

Attention is called to the question to what extent the provisions on the RESS design also identify the main actors that are expected to deliver the desirable outcome, i.e. the increase in the use of renewable energy sources. The distinction made is that between bigger actors, like big companies and investment funds, and smaller actors, like households, final customers and operators of small-scale installations. The two categories of actors have different needs and possibilities, as they differ, *inter alia*, in terms of their investment capabilities and commercial profile, their degree of risk aversion, or their familiarity with the energy markets and their willingness to be actively involved in them. Accordingly, the relevant provisions of the RED II will be interpreted and the attractiveness of the RESS – as impacted in their design by EU law – to bigger and smaller actors will be assessed. The chapter argues that the transition to a sustainable future needs instruments suitable for both categories and that EU law arms Member States with the tools to provide the solutions that they deem more suitable to engage more actors in the transition process.

As for the structure of this chapter, it is divided into six sections. The first section is the introduction, where the topic is presented and the research question put forward. The second section will provide the definitions for the concepts of 'big' and 'small' players. The third section will present the supranational renewable energy law framework. The fourth section will concentrate upon the RED II rules that determine the standard design of national RESSs and will argue that they mostly deal with the engagement of bigger actors in the clean energy transition. Next, the fifth section will specifically refer to smaller actors and it will note that EU law and EU policy assign an important role to them, which is enhanced by new trends, like the rise of self-consumption and of renewable energy communities, and by RESSs that are primarily addressed to them. Last, the sixth section will conclude the chapter.

4 Article 1 of Directive (EU) 2018/2001 of the European Parliament and of the Council of 11 December 2018 on the promotion of the use of energy from renewable sources [2018] OJ L328/82 (RED II).

2. THE DISTINCTION BETWEEN BIGGER AND SMALLER ACTORS

The distinction made between big and small actors is based on the recognition that distributed generation, i.e. a decentralised and small-scale paradigm of power use and management that sites generation close to load,[5] is important to boost the deployment of renewable energy sources.[6] The potential contribution of small-scale installations to the promotion of renewable energy sources is recognised by recital 17 of the RED II, which also acknowledges that a special treatment might be necessary to ensure their participation in the energy transition. For the definition of small-scale installations, recital 17 of the RED II refers to State aid law.[7] The relevant reference in State aid law is found in the General Block Exemption Regulation 651/2014 that declares certain categories of State aid compatible with the internal market.[8] This Regulation, in Article 43, contains rules for the compatibility of 'operating aid for the promotion of energy from renewable sources in small-scale installations', from which a definition of 'small-scale installations' can be distilled. More specifically, Article 43 of the General Block Exemption Regulation applies, according to paragraph 2, to

> installations with an installed capacity of less than 500 kW for the production of energy from all renewable sources except for wind energy, for which aid shall be granted to installations with an installed capacity of less than 3 MW or with less than 3 generation units and for biofuels, for which aid shall be granted to installations with an installed capacity of less than 50 000 tonnes/year. For the purpose of calculating those maximum capacities, small scale installations with a common connection point to the electricity grid shall be considered as one installation.

Given the above, the distinction this chapter makes between bigger and smaller actors is based on the size of the renewable energy installation that they have

---

5 C. Cleveland and C. Morris, *Dictionary of Energy*, Elservier, Amsterdam 2006, p. 120.

6 Small-scale generation can rely on photovoltaic, wind, biomass or geothermal power. Commission, 'Renewable Energy: a major player in the European energy market' (Communication) COM(2012) 271 final, p. 12.

7 Recital 17 of the RED II states: 'Small-scale installations can be of great benefit to increase public acceptance and to ensure the rollout of renewable energy projects, in particular at local level. In order to ensure participation of such small-scale installations, specific conditions, including feed-in tariffs, might therefore still be necessary to ensure a positive cost-benefit ratio, in accordance with Union law relating to the electricity market. The definition of small-scale installations for the purposes of obtaining such support is important to provide legal certainty for investors. State aid rules contain definitions of small-scale installations'.

8 Commission Regulation (EU) No. 651/2014 of 17 June 2014 declaring certain categories of aid compatible with the internal market in application of Articles 107 and 108 of the Treaty [2014] OJ L187/1.

or plan to invest in. Smaller actors are those who invest in renewable energy installations with an installed capacity of less than 500 kW. Exceptionally for wind energy projects, the threshold is less than 3 MW or less than 3 generation units and, in terms of biofuels, small-scale installations are those with an installed capacity of less than 50,000 tonnes per year. In juxtaposition to smaller actors, this chapter categorises those who do not invest in small-scale installations, and those who also invest in bigger projects, in the group of bigger actors.

3. THE NEW RENEWABLE ENERGY DIRECTIVE AND THE RESSs

Promoting renewable energy sources has been acknowledged by the supranational energy and climate policy as being inextricably linked with the objectives to reduce greenhouse gas emissions and to attain the transition to a sustainable, low-carbon economy. In pursuing such objectives, the EU legislator has enacted the RED II.

The objective to promote renewable energy sources does not have a merely declaratory nature, but is expressed as a legal obligation. More specifically, Article 3(1) of the RED II states that 'Member States shall collectively ensure that the share of energy from renewable sources in the Union's gross final consumption of energy in 2030 is at least 32%'. This provision introduces an important novelty. While the former Renewable Energy Directive 2009/28/EC[9] introduced mandatory targets that were different and unique for each Member State, the RED II Union target is not converted into national targets. According to Article 3(2) of the RED II, the collective target is now binding only for the EU as a whole and Member States are bound to determine their 'national contributions' to it. Within this framework, Member States have more freedom to decide the ambition of their national energy policies, and they retain the power to decide what specific measures they will take in order to properly contribute to the attainment of the collective target.[10] Yet, according to Article 3(2) of the RED II, Member States are required to set their national contributions to the collective target and the measures that will be serving them in their integrated national energy and climate plans, widely known as NECPs. The NECPs

---

9 Directive 2009/28/EC of the European Parliament and of the Council of 23 April 2009 on the promotion of the use of energy from renewable sources and amending and subsequently repealing Directives 2001/77/EC and 2003/30/EC [2009] OJ L140/16 (RED).

10 For an analysis of the Clean Energy Package see S. Oberthür, 'Hard or Soft Governance? The EU's Climate and Energy Policy Framework for 2030' (2019) 7 *Politics Gov. (Politics and Governance)* 17; M. Ringel and M. Knodt, 'The governance of the European Energy Union: Efficiency, effectiveness and acceptance of the Winter Package 2016' (2018) 112 *Energy Policy* 209.

form part of a novel reporting and monitoring governance framework that is introduced by the new Regulation on the Governance of the Energy Union and Climate Action.[11] More specifically, the NECPs must be drafted in accordance with criteria set down by the Regulation and be submitted to the Commission. Moreover, the Regulation confers on the Commission the power to assess the level of ambition of Member States and to periodically assess the progress made towards meeting the collective target. If the targeted contributions and planned measures are estimated not to be appropriate for meeting the collective target, the Commission is empowered to issue recommendations, propose measures and exercise its powers at Union level.[12] This system is an interesting experiment, in the sense that it is hard to speculate to what extent the introduction of more stringent procedural obligations will prove sufficient to ensure that Member States' efforts will deliver the collective target. It is very much dependent on what the exact measures of the Commission will be in the event of a potential risk that the collective target is not met. The abolishment of mandatory national targets rather excludes the initiation of infringement procedures, which would have significant coercive power, but the procedural obligations give the Commission the right to intervene in national energy policies at various stages.[13] As for the EU target-setting model, it is limited to determining the target that must be reached, but it does not extend to the means that shall be used. Accordingly, Member States have been resorting to the broad category of RESSs, which have been acknowledged by the EU as pivotal for the promotion of the use of energy from renewable sources, especially for new technologies that cannot compete with energy from conventional fossil fuels yet.[14] According to EU law, a support scheme is

> any instrument, scheme or mechanism applied by a Member State, or a group of Member States, that promotes the use of energy from renewable sources by reducing the cost of that energy, increasing the price at which it can be sold, or increasing,

---

11 Regulation (EU) 2018/1999 of the European Parliament and of the Council of 11 December 2018 on the Governance of the Energy Union and Climate Action, amending Regulations (EC) No 663/2009 and (EC) No 715/2009 of the European Parliament and of the Council, Directives 94/22/EC, 98/70/EC, 2009/31/EC, 2009/73/EC, 2010/31/EU, 2012/27/EU and 2013/30/EU of the European Parliament and of the Council, Council Directives 2009/119/EC and (EU) 2015/652 and repealing Regulation (EU) No 525/2013 of the European Parliament and of the Council [2018] OJ L328/1 (Energy Governance Regulation).

12 Article 3(2) of the RED II in conjunction with Articles 3–5, 9, 29–32 and 34 of the Energy Governance Regulation.

13 A. Monti and B. Martinez Romera, 'Fifty shades of binding: Appraising the enforcement toolkit for the EU's 2030 renewable energy targets' (2020) 29(2) *RECIEL (Review of European, Comparative & International Environmental Law)* 221, at 229–231, https://onlinelibrary.wiley.com/doi/10.1111/reel.12330; S. Oberthür, 'Hard or Soft Governance? The EU's Climate and Energy Policy Framework for 2030' (2019) 7 *Politics Gov.* 17, 24.

14 See recital 16 of the RED II; recital 25 and Articles 2(k) and (l) and 3(3) of the RED.

by means of a renewable energy obligation or otherwise, the volume of such energy purchased.[15]

The definition continues with a non-exhaustive list of RESSs, which includes, but is not restricted to 'investment aid, tax exemptions or reductions, tax refunds, renewable energy obligation support schemes including those using green certificates, and direct price support schemes including feed-in tariffs and sliding or fixed premium payments'.[16] Of the various support schemes, the scientific literature has named the obligation support schemes and the direct price support schemes 'primary support schemes'.[17] This name denotes that these support schemes are the main instruments employed. Opposite to the primary support schemes are the so-called 'secondary' instruments, like subsidies, soft loans or tax exemptions, which do not constitute the main regulatory option for the promotion of renewable energy sources, but they mostly complement the primary support schemes enacted.[18]

Nevertheless, the discretion that Member States enjoy is not unlimited. First, the share of energy from renewable sources in each Member State's gross final consumption of energy shall not be lower than the 2020 national target share.[19] Thus, the 2020 national mandatory targets remain valid and they are rendered the minimum national contributions required.[20]

Last, until the RED II was enacted, support schemes' design belonged almost exclusively to the competence of Member States. There was no secondary EU law governing the support schemes and the EU could only impact on the relevant national laws by means of primary law, more specifically State aid law and the law of the free movement of goods. Yet the RED II brought

---

15 Article 2(5) of the RED II; Article 2(k) of the RED.

16 Ibid.

17 See P. Del Río and P. Mir-Artigues, 'Combinations of Support Instruments for Renewable Energy in Europe: A Review' (2014) 40 *Renew. Sust. Energ. Rev. (Renewable and Sustainable Energy Reviews)* 287; C. Huber et al., 'Economic modelling of price support mechanisms for renewable energy: Case study on Ireland' (2007) 35(2) *Energy Policy* 1172.
For another categorisation of 'support methods', see C. Battle, I.J. Pérez-Arriaga and P. Zambrano-Barragán, 'Regulatory design for RES-E support mechanisms: Learning curves, market structure, and burden-sharing' (2012) 41 *Energy Policy* 212. The authors distinguish two different types of support methods, namely indirect and direct methods. The former group is found to include implicit payments or discounts, as well as institutional support tools and positive discriminatory rules, while the latter comprises investment support and operating support mechanisms.

18 See P. Del Río and P. Mir-Artigues, 'Combinations of Support Instruments for Renewable Energy in Europe: A Review' (2014) 40 *Renew. Sust. Energ. Rev.* 287; A. Bergek, I. Mignon and G. Sundberg, 'Who invests in renewable electricity production? Empirical evidence and suggestions for further research' (2013) 56 *Energy Policy* 568.

19 See Article 3(4) and Annex I of the RED II.

20 T. Iliopoulos, 'Dilemmas on the Way to a New Renewable Energy Directive' (2018) 27 *EEELR (European Energy and Environmental Law Review)* 210.

an important novelty; it introduced secondary law provisions that relate to the design of the national support schemes. These provisions are the focus of attention for the next sections of this chapter. Accordingly, the question posed is to what extent their content also identifies the actors who will be the spearhead of the low-carbon energy transition.

4. THE SUPPORT SCHEMES' DESIGN SUITABILITY FOR BIGGER ACTORS

The RED II includes several articles that relate to RESSs. From these articles, one could highlight Article 4, which contains provisions determining the design of RESSs *stricto sensu*. Article 4 relates to the sector of electricity and adopts a rather principle-based approach; indeed, Article 4(2) of the RED II highlights the requirement that RESSs for electricity be 'market-based and market-responsive'.[21] The exact content of such indeterminate legal concepts is further elaborated in the first part of Article 4(3) of the RED II, which requires that

> '[s]upport schemes for electricity from renewable sources shall be designed so as to maximise the integration of electricity from renewable sources in the electricity market and to ensure that renewable energy producers are responding to market price signals and maximise their market revenues'.[22]

Article 4(2) and (3) entail that generators of electricity from renewable sources must not be immoderately compensated and that they must be incentivised to respond to market signals, so that their generation be integrated into the electricity market.[23] Article 4(2) and (3) of the RED II show that the lessons

---

21 Article 4(2) of the RED II reads: 'Support schemes for electricity from renewable sources shall provide incentives for the integration of electricity from renewable sources in the electricity market in a market-based and market-responsive way, while avoiding unnecessary distortions of electricity markets as well as taking into account possible system integration costs and grid stability'.

22 See also recital 16 of the RED II, which reads: 'Support schemes for electricity from renewable sources or "renewable electricity" have been demonstrated to be an effective way of fostering deployment of renewable electricity. If and when Member States decide to implement support schemes, such support should be provided in a form that is as non-distortive as possible for the functioning of electricity markets. To that end, an increasing number of Member States allocate support in a form by means of which support is granted in addition to market revenues and introduce market-based systems to determine the necessary level of support. Together with steps by which to make the market fit for increasing shares of renewable energy, such support is a key element of increasing the market integration of renewable electricity, while taking into account the different capabilities of small and large producers to respond to market signals'.

23 D. Newbery, 'Towards a green energy economy? The EU Energy Union's transition to a low-carbon zero subsidy electricity system – Lessons from the UK's Electricity Market Reform'

from the experience with the past wave of RESSs have been learned. More specifically, in the 2000s and the early 2010s most Member States had relied, in their renewable energy policies, on a certain direct price RESS, namely feed-in tariffs. Feed-in tariffs have been the most widespread RESSs, with the vast majority of Member States, but also third countries, having, at least at some point, turned to them.[24] Feed-in tariffs are long-terms contracts that oblige electricity distributors to purchase and feed into the grid the electricity generated from renewable sources at a guaranteed fixed price, which exceeds the market price.[25] Thus, feed-in tariffs reduce investment risk, as they ensure a set price will be paid to generators regardless of the market conditions. In practice, in the 2000s and early 2010s feed-in tariffs schemes mobilised more investments than planned, also in large-scale installations, which resulted in an overproduction of electricity from renewable sources in many Member States, such as Greece, Italy or Spain.[26] Nevertheless, while such an overproduction would normally lead to a decrease of the electricity price, the feed-in tariffs were not market-responsive and they kept on remunerating the generators at the fixed prices that had been agreed beforehand. Given this stable high remuneration, the generators had no incentive to react to the market signals and to reduce production, but they kept on feeding the grid with more highly priced electricity. Similarly, more investors were willing to enter and benefit from such lucrative regimes. As might be expected, such a model threatened the grid

---

(2016) 179 *Applied Energy* 1321; Commission, 'A Framework Strategy for a Resilient Energy Union with a Forward-Looking Climate Change Policy' (Communication) COM(2015) 80 final, p. 15. See also T. Iliopoulos, 'Price Support Schemes in the Service of the EU's Low-Carbon Energy Transition' in T. Zachariadis et al. (eds.), *Economic Instruments for a Low-carbon Future*, Edward Elgar, Cheltenham/Norhampton MA, 2020, pp. 2–16.

24 Bulgaria, Czechia, Hungary, Germany, Greece, Italy, Portugal, Slovakia and Spain are a few examples of Member States that have used feed-in tariffs. See P. Crossley, *Renewable Energy Law: An International Assessment*, Cambridge University Press, Cambridge 2019, pp. 176–185; S. Boemi and A. Papadopoulos, 'Times of Recession: Three Different Renewable Energy Stories from the Mediterranean Region' in E. Michalena and J. Hills (eds.), *Renewable Energy Governance*, Springer, London 2013, pp. 263–275.

25 See A. Pyrgou, A. Kylili and P. Fokaides, 'The Future of the Feed-In Tariff (FIT) Scheme in Europe: The Case of Photovoltaics' (2016) 95 *Energy Policy* 94; R. Sioshansi, 'Retail Electricity Tariff and Mechanism Design to Incentivize Distributed Renewable Generation' (2016) 95 *Energy Policy* 498; N. Atmaca and I. Lojodice, 'The Impact of Support Schemes on RES Installations and Retail Electricity Prices' (2014) 1 *RELP (Renewable Energy Law and Policy)* 67; L. Schaffer and T. Bernauer, 'Explaining Government Choices for Promoting Renewable Energy' (2014) 68 *Energy Policy* 15.

26 See for instance Νόμος [Law] 3468/2006 ΦΕΚ [OJ] 129/A'; Real Decreto [Royal Decree] 661/2007 BOE [OJ] 126, 26/05/2007. See also G. Bellantuono, 'The misguided quest for regulatory stability in the renewable energy sector' (2017) 10 *J. World Energy Law Bus. (Journal of World Energy Law and Business)* 274; P. Del Río and P. Mir-Artigues, 'A Cautionary Tale: Spain's solar PV investment bubble' 2014 *The International Institute for Sustainable Development and the Development Research Center of the State Council* https://www.iisd.org/gsi/sites/default/files/rens_ct_spain.pdf.

stability and could not be financially viable for long; in many Member States, such as Czechia, Germany, Greece, Italy and Spain, the feed-in tariffs regimes collapsed: the contracts could not be abided by, and the regimes established needed to abruptly change, for instance through substantial reductions in the fixed tariffs that had been initially agreed with the investors.[27]

The RED II principles react to the foregoing phenomenon and they aim to prevent such situations from happening again. Besides, specific rules add detail to the content of the established principles. In this regard, Article 4(3) of the RED II clarifies that 'with regard to direct price support schemes, support shall be granted in the form of a market premium'. Premia are similar to feed-in tariffs, but they are a more evolved version. They are more market-based and market-responsive, as they do not grant a fixed price, but the market price plus an add-on fee. Thus, they are more flexible and they can better adapt to market price fluctuations. In addition, normally there is no purchase guarantee, but generators bear the burden of selling the electricity in the market. Hence generators are not overly remunerated and electricity markets are better protected from distortion.[28] Therefore, if Member States opt to enact a direct price RESS this must not consist in granting feed-in tariffs, but premia. This requirement transposes into hard law what the Commission had already propounded in soft law since 2013.[29]

Furthermore, Article 4(4) of the RED II also requires that 'support for electricity from renewable sources is granted in an open, transparent, competitive, non-discriminatory and cost-effective manner'. This clause is in harmony with the observed trend that Member States, but third countries too, are more and more resorting to auctions and competitive bidding processes in order to complement the premia with a competitive mechanism that selects the beneficiaries and allocates the support.[30] Such mechanisms aim to increase

---

27 F. Montanaro, '"Ain't No Sunshine": Photovoltaic Energy Policy in Europe at the Crossroads Between EU Law and Energy Charter Treaty Obligations' in G. Adinolfi et al. (eds.), *International Economic Law*, Springer, Cham 2017, pp. 211–230; E. Michalena and J. Maxwell Hills (eds.), *Renewable Energy Governance*, Springer, London, 2013; A. Johnston and G. Block, *EU Energy Law*, Oxford University Press, Oxford 2012. See also Commission, 'European Commission Guidance for the design of renewables support schemes' (Commission Staff Working Document) SWD(2013) 439 final.

28 A. Johnston and G. Block, *EU Energy Law*, Oxford University Press, Oxford 2012; T. Deruytter and W. Geldhof, 'Legal Issues Concerning the Decentralised Energy Production Investment Climate: Subsidies, Tariffs and Priority Access and Dispatch' in B. Delvaux, M. Hunt and K. Talus (eds.), *EU Energy Law and Policy Issues, Vol 4*, Intersentia, Antwerp 2013, pp. 165–188.

29 Commission, 'European Commission Guidance for the design of renewables support schemes' (Commission Staff Working Document) SWD(2013) 439 final, ch 3.1.3.

30 L. Jerrentrup et al., 'Technology-Neutral Auctions for Renewable Energy: EU Law vs. Member State Reality' (2019) 16 *JEEPL (Journal for European Environmental & Planning Law)* 386; M. Haufe and K. Ehrhart, 'Auctions for renewable energy support – Suitability, design, and first lessons learned' (2018) 121 *Energy Policy* 217.

transparency in granting the support, but also to ensure that the RESSs enacted and put into practice will only affect to a minimum extent the functioning of the market. It is believed that a competitive bidding process will make the competitors reveal their true operational costs and only claim the aid that they will truly need in order to be able to make the investment and operate the project.

Given the above, competitive bidding processes combined with premia is the standard model for support schemes for renewable energy sources that national authorities are urged to follow. It is noted that this pathway is more suitable for bigger actors, and not as favourable to smaller actors who can only afford to invest in small-scale projects. Premia that adjust to market fluctuations are more suitable for investors who can afford to be exposed to market risks, while smaller actors might need more profit guarantees and a more secure environment in order to invest in renewable energy projects.[31] In terms of participation in a bidding process and tendering, transaction costs are entailed,[32] as participants need to get acquainted with the procedure that will be followed and with the special laws governing it; they need to draft and submit to the authorities various files and applications; they need to be in constant communication with the authorities, etc. While bigger market actors will normally have specialised departments focused on taking care of such tasks, smaller actors will find it much more difficult to meet the requirements of a competitive bidding process and to take up the burdens entailed just to compete for a contract – and with an uncertain outcome for them, as bigger players are normally in a position to make better offers and be awarded with the contract.[33] Thus, simple feed-in tariffs

---

31 C. Hepburn, 'Carbon Taxes, Emissions Trading and Hybrid Systems' in C. Hepburn and D. Helm (eds.), *The Economics and Politics of Climate Change*, Oxford University Press, Oxford 2009, pp. 365–384; P. Menanteau, D. Finon and M.L. Lamy, 'Prices versus quantities: choosing policies for promoting the development of renewable energy' (2003) 31 *Energy Policy* 799.

32 These are the costs a market transaction necessary entails. According to Ronald Coase, '[i]n order to carry out a market transaction it is necessary to discover who it is that one wishes to deal with, to inform people that one wishes to deal and on what terms, to conduct negotiations leading up to a bargain, to draw up the contract, to undertake the inspection needed to make sure that the terms of the contract are being observed, and so on. These operations are often extremely costly, sufficiently costly at any rate to prevent many transactions that would be carried out in a world in which the pricing system worked without cost'. See R.H. Coase, 'The Problem of Social Cost' (1960) III *J. Law Econ. (The Journal of Law & Economics)* 1, at 15.

33 W. Pizer and B. Prest, 'Prices versus Quantities with Policy Updating' 2016 *NBER Working Papers* Working Paper No. 22379: https://www.nber.org/papers/w22379; C. Hepburn, 'Carbon Taxes, Emissions Trading and Hybrid Systems' in C. Hepburn and D. Helm (eds.), *The Economics and Politics of Climate Change*, Oxford University Press, Oxford 2009, pp. 365–384; F. Baldursson and N. von der Fehr, 'Prices vs. quantities: Public finance and the choice of regulatory instruments' (2008) 52(7) *Eur. Econ. Rev. (European Economic*

regimes, not complemented by bidding processes are more attractive for smaller investors, as they follow a simple logic and they do not entail requirements, or high administrative and transaction costs.

Nevertheless, Article 4(3) and (4) of the RED II clarify that small-scale and demonstration projects might be exempted from the 'market-based and market-responsive' requirements, as well as from competitive bidding procedures for the granting of the support. This leaves an important window open for actively engaging smaller actors in the energy transition. Member States might opt for a feed-in tariffs regime to minimise transaction costs, reduce risk and ensure profitability for a certain time period, exclusively to the benefit of small-scale installations.[34] Indeed, feed-in tariffs can better address the needs and interests of smaller investors, as they guarantee a stream of revenue without imposing on them the burden to actively participate in the market.[35] But the RED II does not *require* Member States to enact such special regimes for smaller market actors; it just *allows* this to happen by way of exception. Member States will decide whether and to which extent they make use of this possibility.

A short mention is worth making to Articles 5 and 6 of the RED II, which are also important for the RESSs design. Article 5 contains a nudge for cross-border support schemes. This provision is linked with the functioning of the internal market. It aims to spur Member States to open their support schemes to generators from other Member States and thus to create a level playing-field for all generators. In this respect, bigger actors are expected to exploit economies of scale and expand their portfolios, but smaller actors might also benefit from more lucrative regimes in other Member States and from trade. In terms of Article 6 of the RED II, it aims to ensure the financial stability of support schemes, which is also beneficial for all actors.

Summarising, Article 4 of the RED II, which is the main article for the RESSs design, leads to RESSs that in principle address bigger market players. But while bigger actors are expected to mostly benefit from the new support framework, there are also exceptions that aim to ensure that RESSs fitting the needs of smaller actors may be also enacted.

Review) 1242; L. Bennear and R. Stavins, 'Second-best theory and the use of multiple policy instrument' (2007) 37 *Environ. Resource Econ. (Environmental and Resource Economics)* 111.

34 See also Commission, 'European Commission Guidance for the design of renewables support schemes' (Commission Staff Working Document) SWD(2013) 439 final, para. 3.1.7.

35 C. Hepburn, 'Carbon Taxes, Emissions Trading and Hybrid Systems' in C. Hepburn and D. Helm (eds.), *The Economics and Politics of Climate Change*, Oxford University Press, Oxford 2009, pp. 365–384; P. Menanteau, D. Finon and M.L. Lamy, 'Prices versus quantities: choosing policies for promoting the development of renewable energy' (2003) 31 *Energy Policy* 799. See also Commission, 'European Commission Guidance for the design of renewables support schemes' (Commission Staff Working Document) SWD(2013) 439 final, para. 3.1.7.

5. SMALLER ACTORS AS DRIVERS OF THE ENERGY TRANSITION: SELF-CONSUMPTION

While Article 4 of the RED II introduces requirements regarding the design of classic RESSs that better fit the profile of bigger actors, the EU has explicitly expressed its willingness to actively involve small actors in the efforts for achieving an energy transition. Indeed, concepts like decentralisation, empowerment of energy consumers, consumer's ownership of the energy transition, renewables self-consumers, prosumers, peer-to-peer transactions, smart grids, etc. have all become central to the modern supranational energy policy.[36] This policy direction has been expressed in the Fourth Electricity Directive,[37] but also in the RED II.

Accordingly, Article 21 of the RED II enshrines the right of consumers to become 'renewables self-consumers', i.e. to 'generate renewable electricity for [their] own consumption, and … store or sell self-generated renewable electricity, provided that … those activities do not constitute [their] primary commercial or professional activity'.[38] Next, Article 22 of the RED II refers to renewable energy communities, which are legal entities that own and develop renewable energy projects and are, *inter alia*, entitled to 'produce, consume, store and sell renewable energy'.[39] As shareholders or members of renewable energy communities are natural persons, small and medium-sized enterprises (SMEs) or local authorities, such as municipalities, their promotion is linked with a paradigm that enables small-scale installations to emerge and play a key role in the energy system.[40]

---

36 Commission, 'United in delivering the Energy Union and Climate Action – Setting the foundations for a successful clean energy transition' (Communication) COM(2019) 285 final; Commission, 'A clean energy for all Europeans' (Communication) COM (2016) 860 final; Commission, 'Delivering a New Deal for Energy Consumers' (Communication) COM(2015) 339 final. See also S. Lavrijssen, 'Power to the Energy Consumers' (2017) 6 *EEELR* 172; S. Lavrijssen, 'The right to participation for consumers in the energy transition' (2016) 5 *EEELR* 152.

37 See Articles 2(8) and 15 of the Directive (EU) 2019/944 of the European Parliament and of the Council of 5 June 2019 on common rules for the internal market for electricity and amending Directive 2012/27/EU [2019] OJ L158/125 (Electricity Directive).

38 Article 2(14) of the RED II. See also Articles 2(8) and 15 of the Electricity Directive on 'active customers'.

39 See Articles 2(16) and 22(2)(a) of the RED II. See also recitals 43–47, Article 2(11) and Article 16 of the Electricity Directive on 'citizen energy communities'.

40 See also T. Iliopoulos, 'The promotion of renewable energy communities in the European Union' in D. Borge-Diez and E. Rosales-Asensio (eds.), *Energy Services Fundamentals and Financing*, Elsevier Science, San Diego 2020, pp. 37–53; J. Lowitzsch, C. Hoicka and F. Van Tulder, 'Renewable energy communities under the 2019 European Clean Energy Package – Governance model for the energy clusters of the future?' (2020) 122 *Renew. Sust. Energ. Rev.* 109489; M. Sokołowski, 'European Law on the Energy Communities: A Long Way to a Direct Legal Framework' (2018) 2 *EEELR* 60.

The furtherance of the involvement of self-consumers and renewable energy communities in the energy transition requires that Member States enact special support schemes that address them. As already noted, the standard design for support schemes under Article 4 of the RED II is suitable rather for bigger actors interested in exploiting larger renewable energy projects, while self-consumers and renewable energy communities are expected normally to invest in small-scale projects. In this regard, the RED II contains special provisions to ensure the right of self-consumers and renewable energy communities to claim participation in support schemes. More specifically, Article 21(2) of the RED II provides a list of self-consumer rights that Member States shall ensure, including: the right to trade electricity in various manners[41] and without discriminatory charges imposed on them; the right to retain their rights and obligations as protected consumers; and the right to 'receive remuneration, including, where applicable, through support schemes, for the self-generated renewable electricity that they feed into the grid'. The same provision also clarifies that the remuneration shall reflect the market value of the self-generated electricity, which may take into account its long-term value to the grid, the environment and society. As far as renewable energy communities are concerned, Article 22 of the RED II does not explicitly enshrine such a right to remuneration, but this should not be interpreted as meaning that they cannot be covered by support schemes. On the contrary, recital 26 of the RED II emphasises that 'Member States should ensure that renewable energy communities can participate in available support schemes on an equal footing with large participants'. Moreover, Article 22(7) of the RED II reads:

> Without prejudice to Articles 107 and 108 TFEU, Member States shall take into account specificities of renewable energy communities when designing support schemes in order to allow them to compete for support on an equal footing with other market participants.[42]

In addition, Article 22(4) of the RED II requires Member States to promote and facilitate the development of renewable energy communities, *inter alia*, through tools to facilitate access to finance.

Member States have indeed enacted support schemes that address self-consumption projects and renewable energy communities. First, as already

In terms of the notion of SMEs, Article 2(8) refers to Article 2 of the Annex to Commission Recommendation 2003/361/EC of 6 May 2003 concerning the definition of micro, small and medium-sized enterprises [2003] OJ L124/36.

41 For instance, through renewables power purchase agreements, electricity suppliers and peer-to-peer trading arrangements.

42 Recital 26 and Article 22(7) of the RED II also show that renewable energy communities are normally distinguished from bigger actors.

mentioned above, Article 4 itself contains exceptions for small-scale installations, on which RESSs that meet the interests and needs of smaller actors can be founded. In this regard, Article 4(3) and (4) of the RED II allows that small-scale installations benefit from feed-in tariffs that might not be granted in a bidding procedure. In many Member States, for instance Germany or Spain, feed-in tariffs have proven effective to incentivise electricity customers to get involved in self-consumption or in renewable energy communities.[43] Apart from such more classic types of RESSs, new forms of support schemes that are inextricably linked with self-consumption, namely net metering and net billing, have been on the rise too. Both net metering and net billing allow self-consumers to feed some of the electricity they produce back into the grid and then offset their electricity purchases from the grid with it. The remuneration they receive does not take a physical form, but appears as a credit on the electricity bill. The difference between these two types of self-consumption support schemes is that under net metering the remuneration granted equals the retail price of electricity, to wit the price at which the self-consumer purchases electricity from the grid. In net billing the remuneration for self-generated electricity fed into the grid has a lower value; the net billing model not only spurs decentralised generation, but gives incentives for actual self-consumption. This is because only self-consumption allows savings at the retail price that will lead to the maximisation of profits for the beneficiaries.[44]

The promotion of self-consumption upgrades the role that smaller actors will have in the attainment of the clean energy transition. Self-consumption relates to a more active involvement of households and final customers in renewable energy projects, and it is founded on instruments that ensure profitability and, hence, allow them to proceed with investments without facing risks and burdens pertaining to actors that generate electricity as their primary

---

43 C. Herbes et al., 'Responding to policy change: New business models for renewable energy cooperatives – Barriers perceived by cooperatives' members' (2017) 109 *Energy Policy* 82; J. Ossenbrink, 'How feed-in remuneration design shapes residential PV prosumer paradigms' (2017) 108 *Energy Policy* 239; C. Romero-Rubio and J. De Andrés Díaz, 'Sustainable energy communities: a study contrasting Spain and Germany' (2015) 85 *Energy Policy* 397.

44 M. Villar Ezcurra and C. Cámara Barroso, 'Tax incentives for photovoltaic power self-consumption: An analysis of the Spanish experience' in T. Zachariadis et al. (eds.), *Economic Instruments for a Low-carbon Future*, Edward Elgar, Cheltenham/Norhampton MA, 2020, pp. 6–31. T. Iliopoulos, M. Fermeglia and B. Vanheusden, 'The EU's 2030 Climate and Energy Policy Framework: How net metering slips through its net' (2020) 29(2) *RECIEL (Review of European, Comparative & International Environmental Law)* 245, https://onlinelibrary.wiley.com/doi/abs/10.1111/reel.12339; S. Jacobs, 'The Energy Prosumer' (2016) 43 *Ecol. Law Q. (Ecology Law Quarterly)* 519; R. Dufo-López and J. Bernal-Agustín, 'A comparative assessment of net metering and net billing policies' (2015) 84 *Energy* 684; A. Butenko, 'Sharing Energy' (2016) 4 *EJRR (European Journal of Risk Regulation)* 701; D. Raskin, 'The Regulatory Challenge of Distributed Generation' (2013) 4 *HBLR Online (Harvard Business Law Review Online)* 38 https://www.hblr.org/2013/12/the-regulatory-challenge-of-distributed-generation/; L. Hughes and J. Bell, 'Compensating customer-generators: a taxonomy describing methods of compensating customer-generators for electricity supplied to the grid' (2006) 34 *Energy Policy* 1532.

commercial or professional activity. Nevertheless, just as the Article 4 RED II instruments might be exceptionally designed in a manner that supports smaller actors, albeit primarily pertinent to favour bigger actors, self-consumption and energy communities might also evolve as trends involving bigger actors. This might lead to problems. RESSs that aim to boost self-consumption often offer a lucrative remuneration in order to be attractive for smaller actors; but since such coverage normally means that only a very small amount of generation benefits from the scheme, its financial stability and viability in principle is not threatened and the electricity markets are not distorted. However, a generalised involvement of bigger actors in self-consumption would entail higher costs and would possibly offer a generous remuneration to players with an already high market concentration, and this *would* distort the functioning of the market. As a safety net, Member States often put a cap that limits the installed capacity per beneficiary that can enter a net metering or a net billing regime.[45]

Lastly, Member States apply network charges and fees, for instance for the excessive use of the central grid or for tax reasons.[46] Depending on the extent to which a Member State makes use of this possibility, the fees imposed may prove an important disincentive for potential self-consumers, and especially for smaller actors that are normally more risk averse.

Before concluding this section, it is interesting to also refer to Articles 15 to 18 of the RED II, which contain certain provisions that may further facilitate investments by smaller actors in renewable energy projects. More specifically, the first paragraph of Article 15 of the RED II as a general rule states that authorisation, certification and licensing rules and procedures applied to plants shall be proportionate and necessary, and elaborates on this rule by specifically requiring that

> (a) administrative procedures are streamlined and expedited at the appropriate administrative level and predictable timeframes are established for the procedures referred to in the first subparagraph;

---

45 This is for instance the model followed by Cyprus, which is one of the first Member States employing net metering. See Articles 4.3, 5.4 and 5.9 of Κυπριακή Δημοκρατία [Republic of Cyprus], 'Ανανεώσιμες Πηγές Ενέργειας (ΑΠΕ) για όλους – Σχέδιο για παραγωγή ηλεκτρικής ενέργειας από Ανανεώσιμες Πηγές Ενέργειας για ίδια κατανάλωση' ['Renewable Energy Sources (RES) for all – Plan for electricity production from Renewable Energy Sources for self-consumption'] March 2019. See also A. Poulikkas, G. Kourtis and I. Hadjipaschalis, 'A review of net metering mechanisms for electricity renewable energy sources' (2013) 6 *IJEE (International Journal of Energy Environment)* 975.

46 Article 15 of the Electricity Directive; Commission, 'Best practices on Renewable Energy Self-consumption' (Communication Staff Working Document) SWD(2015) 141 final. See also M. Villar Ezcurra and C. Cámara Barroso, 'Tax incentives for photovoltaic power self-consumption: An analysis of the Spanish experience' in T. Zachariadis et al. (eds.), *Economic Instruments for a Low-carbon Future*, Edward Elgar, Cheltenham/Norhampton MA, 2020, pp. 6–31; A. Nikolaidis and C. Charalambous, 'Hidden financial implications of the net metering practice in an isolated power system: Critical review and policy insights' (2017) 77 *Renew. Sust. Energ. Rev.* 706.

(b) rules concerning authorisation, certification and licensing are objective, transparent and proportionate, do not discriminate between applicants and take fully into account the particularities of individual renewable energy technologies;
(c) administrative charges paid by consumers, planners, architects, builders and equipment and system installers and suppliers are transparent and cost-related; and
(d) simplified and less burdensome authorisation procedures, including a simple-notification procedure, are established for decentralised devices, and for producing and storing energy from renewable sources.

The above entails that the peculiarities of each project shall be taken into account. And small projects have of course different features comparing to big ones.

Next, Article 16 of the RED II relates to the establishment of contact points that will guide the applicants through the administrative permit application and granting process. Article 16(3) states these contact points 'shall make available a manual of procedures for developers of renewable energy production projects and shall provide that information also online, addressing distinctly also small-scale projects and renewables self-consumers projects'. Therefore, it foresees a distinct treatment for small-scale and self-consumption projects. Similarly, Article 17 of the RED II requires that Member States shall establish a simple-notification procedure for grid connections for 'installations or aggregated production units of renewables self-consumers and demonstration projects, with an electrical capacity of 10,8 kW or less', unless grounds of safety concerns or technical incompatibility of the system components do not allow for such a simplified grid-connection procedure. The second paragraph of the article allows Member States to adopt such a simple-notification procedure 'for installations or aggregated production units with an electrical capacity of above 10,8 kW and up to 50 kW, provided that grid stability, grid reliability and grid safety are maintained.'

Finally, Article 18 of the RED II contains a crucial information requirement, according to which Member States shall ensure that information on support measures is made available to all relevant actors, including renewables self-consumers and renewable energy communities.

6. CONCLUSION

The Clean Energy Package brought important changes in the supranational energy policy. In terms of renewable energy, the RED II and the Energy Union Governance Regulation introduced a new paradigm with a collective target for renewable energy sources, binding for the EU as a whole, which replaced the previous model that was based on different mandatory national targets. This new model might seem like leaving a wider margin of discretion to Member States, as they are not burdened by a mandatory national target anymore; but this is compensated for by a system with more monitoring and intervention powers conferred on the Commission, as well as more concrete rules that determine the elements on which national energy policies shall be founded.

In the field of support for renewable energy sources, such concrete rules can be found in the RED II, particularly Articles 4 to 6, which for the first time set down specific secondary law requirements for the design of the national support schemes. These articles aim to ensure the support granted is not excessive and does not disregard market conditions by relieving investors from market risk and by guaranteeing a fixed price for a long period regardless of market price fluctuations. In addition, it is required that support is granted in a competitive bidding process, so that competition amongst potential beneficiaries lead to bids that will reveal the true costs and needs of renewable energy projects and, thus, the aid granted will be limited to the minimum. These provisions have been enacted in response to the experience gained from the collapse of a number of overly generous RESSs in the early 2010s. The application of such market-responsive instruments is expected to lead to a landscape dominated by bigger market players who can – better – afford income uncertainty and exposure to market risk, as well as the transaction and administrative costs that participation in a bidding process entails. Smaller actors will rather find it harder to be actively engaged in an environment that not only does not guarantee them profitability, but also imposes on them the burden to participate in a bidding process and to compete with stronger competitors.

Nevertheless, the proclaimed supranational objective that consumers take ownership of and have an active role in the low-carbon energy transition has led to the rise of support schemes that better meet the needs of renewable self-consumers and renewable energy communities. Accordingly, the RED II contains exemptions that allow Member States to grant feed-in tariffs, and not necessarily after a competitive bidding procedure, to small-scale installations. In addition, new types of RESSs that specifically relate to self-consumption have emerged, namely net metering and net billing. However, while the RED II requires that Member States facilitate and promote self-consumption, it does not set more clear obligations or targets, and it contains few rules specifically governing the design of support schemes for self-consumption.

In conclusion, the transition to a sustainable future requires a legal framework that ensures bigger and smaller actors can co-exist, so that they can both engage in renewable energy projects and innovations, and contribute to the promotion of renewable energy sources. The EU legal framework allows the Member States to determine who the spearhead of the national efforts will be. Both classic types of RESSs and types of RESSs that relate to self-consumption co-exist, and Member States have a wide margin of discretion as to the extent to which they resort to the one or the other path. In other words, EU law facilitates Member States to adopt the solutions they deem more suitable for serving the process to a sustainable future. Of course, a diversified landscape might emerge, with some Member States mostly relying on large-scale projects and others on small-scale production and self-consumption. Such a mosaic can enhance regulatory competition between Member States and increase the experience and knowledge gained from how laws act in practice, which might prove useful for a future law reform. On the other hand, it might enlarge the existing discrepancies and impede cooperation between Member States. If different national choices prove too diverse to a degree that hampers the attainment of the common target, it will be important that the Commission make use of the new powers conferred on it, so that a more coordinated landscape which can better serve the supranational energy policy will be ensured.

ENERGY RETURN ON ENERGY INVESTMENT (EROI)

Implications for EU Climate and Environmental Law

Matteo FERMEGLIA

1. INTRODUCTION

While the first law of thermodynamics says that the *quantity* of energy remains constant along a given process, the second law says that the energy's *quality* degrades over time. The upshot of these assumptions is that, with the (remarkable) exception of the energy generated from the sun, additional energy inputs and resources are needed to construct and maintain the flourishing of modern society.[1] Achieving effective transition to a sustainable, less carbon- and energy-intensive economy rests, however, on large-scale renewable energy generation, coupled with breakthrough technologies to curb CO_2 and other Greenhouse Gases (GHG) emissions from energy generation and industrial processes.[2]

Against this background, *Energy Return On Energy Investment* (EROI) has been developed to assess the amount of useful energy yielded from each unit of energy input to the process of obtaining energy at the end of the production process.[3] Phrased another way, EROI appraises the geological depletion of natural resources by calculating the ratio of the energy in a given amount of the extracted and delivered fuel to the total primary energy used in the supply chain.[4] EROI provides a useful indication of the societal benefits stemming

---

1 I. Bashmakov, 'Three laws of energy transitions' (2007) 35 *Energy Policy* 3583, 3594.

2 International Energy Agency (IEA) and International Renewable Energy Agency (IRENA), *Perspectives for the energy transition: Investment Needs for a Low-Carbon Energy System*, 2017; Commission Communication COM(2018) 773, A Clean Planet for all – A European strategic long-term vision for a prosperous, modern, competitive and climate neutral economy.

3 C.A. Hall et al., 'What is the Minimum EROI that a sustainable society must have?' (2009) 2 *Energies* 25, 47.

4 C.W. King and C.A. Hall. 'Relating Financial and Energy Return on Investment' (2011) 3 *Sustainability* 1810, 1832; M.W. Gilliland, 'Energy Analysis and Public Policy' (1975) 189 *Science* 1051, 1056.

from the choice of different primary energy exploitation systems in terms of its life-cycle impact on energy fuels and energy balance.[5]

Yet, EROI's implications as a means to support and inform policy-making, and the extent to which it has actually been embedded as a benchmark for regulatory choices remain largely unexplored.[6] This contribution aims to shed light on the legal consequences of embedding EROI as part of the conceptual toolbox in selected EU environmental and energy policies – namely, financing transitional low-carbon technologies through the EU Emission Trading System (EU ETS), and spatial planning under the Strategic Environmental Assessment (SEA) and the Environmental Impact Assessment (EIA) Directives.

2. ENERGY RETURN ON ENERGY INVESTMENT (EROI): AN ENABLING METRIC FOR POLICY-MAKING

2.1. WHAT IS EROI?

EROI's theoretical foundations build on Howard Odum's findings on net-energy analysis, as formally applied to fuels.[7] EROI was eventually endorsed and developed by Charles Hall, professor of biophysical economics at New York State University.[8] Net Energy Analysis (NEA) is specifically concerned with determining how much energy can be delivered to society in the form of a given energy carrier, after subtracting all the energy inputs that are required to support the supply chain of that same energy carrier.[9] EROI can be defined as the following ratio:

$$\text{EROI} = \frac{\text{Energy gained}}{\text{Energy required to get that energy}}$$

The numerator and denominator are usually assessed in the same units so that the ratio so derived is dimensionless, e.g. 30:1 ('thirty to one').[10] The lower an

---

5 C.A. Hall and K. Klitgaard, *Energy and the Wealth of Nations: Understanding the Biophysical Economy*, Springer, New York 2012; C. Hall et al., above n. 3.

6 M. Raugei et al., 'The energy return on energy investment (EROI) of photovoltaics: Methodology and comparisons with fossil fuel life cycles' (2012) 45 *Energy Policy* 576, 582.

7 H.T. Odum, 'Energy, Ecology, and Economics' (1978) 2(6) *Ambio* 220, 227; H.T. Odum, *Environment, Power and Society*, Wiley Interscience, New York 1973.

8 C.A. Hall and C.J. Cleveland, 'Petroleum Drilling and Production in the US: Yield per Effort and Net Energy Analysis' (1981) 211 *Science* 576, 579.

9 International Federation of Institutes for Advanced Studies (IFIAS), 'IFIAS Workshop Report, energy analysis and economics' (1978) 1(2) *Resources & Energy* 151, 204.

10 D.J. Murphy and C.A. Hall, 'C.A.S. Year in Review – EROI or Energy Return on (Energy) Invested' (2010) 1185 *Annals of the New York Academy of Sciences* 102, 118.

energy source's EROI, the more input energy is required to produce the output energy, which results in less net energy available for consumption. For example, if the EROI value is 10:1, this translates into 1 unit of energy (Joule, Kcal, barrel, etc.) invested to yield 10 units of energy, with a net production of 9. If the ratio is equal to 1:1, no return of energy is expected from that process. If the ratio is lower than 1:1, this translates into net energy losses throughout the selected process.

Different components of EROI exist, depending on the calculation methods and system boundaries adopted.[11]

- *Standard EROI* (*$EROI_{ST}$*): the $EROI_{ST}$ approach divides the energy output for a project, region or country by the sum of the direct (i.e., onsite) and indirect (i.e., offsite) energy needed to generate that output. It is applied to fuels at the point where they leave the extraction or production facility (well-head, mine-mouth, farm gate, etc.).[12]
- *Point of Use EROI* (*$EROI_{POU}$*): $EROI_{POU}$ is a more comprehensive EROI, which includes the energy costs associated with fuels' refinement and transportation. As the boundaries of the analysis are expanded, the energy cost of getting it to that point increases, resulting in a reduced EROI.[13]
- *Extended EROI* (*$EROI_{EXT}$*): $EROI_{EXT}$ includes the energy required not only to get, but also to use a unit of energy. In other words, it indicates the energy at the mine-mouth required for that energy to be minimally useful to society – e.g., to drive a truck.[14]
- *Societal EROI* (*$EROI_{SOC}$*): $EROI_{SOC}$ includes the overall EROI that might be derived for all of a nation or society's fuels by summing all gains from fuels and all costs of obtaining them.[15] $EROI_{SOC}$ calculations are at their early stages due to major hurdles in identifying and including all the relevant variables necessary to generate an all-encompassing societal EROI value.[16]

---

11 J.C. Lambert, C.A. Hall and S. Balogh, *EROI of Global Energy Resources: Status, Trends and Social Implications*, Report prepared for the UK Department for International Development, SUNY – Environmental Science & Forestry Next Generation Energy Initiative, Inc. October 2013, 17.

12 D.J. Murphy et al., 'Order from Chaos: A Preliminary Protocol for Determining the EROI of Fuels' (2011) 3(10) *Sustainability* 1888, 1907.

13 C.A. Hall, *Energy Return on Investment: A Unifying Principle for Biology, Economics and Sustainability*, Springer, New York 2017, 127.

14 J.C. Lambert, C.A. Hall and S. Balogh, above n. 11, p. 20.

15 C.A. Hall et al., above n 3. K. Mulder and N.J. Hagens, 'Energy Return on Investment: Toward a Consistent Framework' (2008) 37 *AMBIO: A Journal of the Human Environment* 74, 79.

16 R. Atlason, 'EROI and the Icelandic Society' (2018) 120 *Energy Policy* 52, 57.

2.2. EROI OF DIFFERENT FUELS AND PERSISTENT UNCERTAINTIES

EROI calculations can be applied to all energy sources and carriers with regard to thermal energy and electricity generation, as well as to other energy-intensive industrial processes and technologies. In particular, EROI is proving crucial to determine the degree possible, and the economic consequences, of replacing fossil fuels with renewable energy sources (RESs).[17] All EROI calculations clearly denote a linear, steady decrease of fossil fuels' (oil, coal and gas) EROI over the last decades, as well as very low EROI values for unconventional fossil fuels (e.g., tar sands oil).[18] This trend is countered by increasing EROI values for all renewable energy sources.[19] Recent studies calculate $EROI_{EXT}$ ratios for fossil fuels at the end stage (i.e. electricity, petrol) of around 6:1, thus very close to those for solar PV[20] and wind energy.[21]

Figure 1. Mean EROI values of electric power generation systems from known published assessment

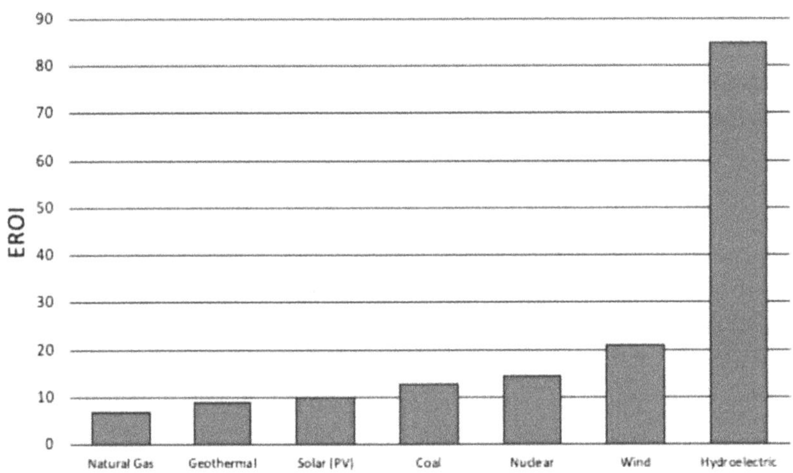

Source: Author's own elaborations based on C.A. Hall, *Energy Return on Investment: A Unifying Principle for Biology, Economics and Sustainability*, Springer, New York 2017.

---

17 M. Raugei et al., above n. 6; M. Raugei and E. Leccisi, 'A comprehensive assessment of the energy performance of the full range of electricity generation technologies deployed in the United Kingdom' (2016) 90 *Energy Policy* 46, 59.

18 J.C. Lambert, C.A. Hall and S. Balogh, 'EROI of different fuels and the implications for society' (2014) 64 *Energy Policy* 141, 152.

19 M. Raugei et al., above n. 6; I. Kubiszewski, C. Cleveland and P. Endres, 'Meta-analysis of net energy return for wind power systems' (2010) 35 *Renewable Energy* 218, 225; R. Atlason and R. Unnthorsson, 'Energy return on investment of hydroelectric power generation calculated using a standardised methodology' (2014) 66 *Renewable Energy* 364, 370; N. Kittner, S.H. Gheewala and D.M. Kammen, 'Energy return on investment (EROI) of mini-hydro and solar PV systems designed for a mini-grid' (2016) 99 *Renewable Energy* 410, 419.

Four drawbacks still hamper EROI analysis as a one-stop-shop indicator for environmental and climate policy-making. First, EROI methods do not include other important considerations such as environmental externalities and social benefits.[22] Second, key discrepancies between EROI calculations remain as to what is considered to be 'energy input'.[23] For example, remarkable differences in EROI values for corn-based ethanol depend on whether residues from alcohol distilling are taken account of as energy input for further processes, such as fertiliser production.[24] Third, some EROI components include only the energy diverted for society, rather than the total energy extracted from natural resources.[25] Energy losses at the point of extraction (such as methane released during coal mining), as well as along the entire supply chain (such as loss of energy content during coal transport and grid losses) are often not adequately factored into $EROI_{ST}$ metrics.[26] Last, major issues relate to the boundaries used in different EROI calculations.[27] EROI figures for thermal fuels are often calculated at the mine-mouth, rather than at the point of use. EROI figures do not fully take into account the high life-cycle GHG emissions from thermal electricity production, and from coal-fired systems in particular.[28] This renders comparison with renewable energy sources – especially solar PV – difficult, as they supply electricity directly.[29]

Furthermore, other factors, such as the energy-intensive Carbon Capture and Storage (CCS) or Carbon Capture and Utilisation (CCU) as applied to fossil fuels and biofuels (in the form of BECCS), while reducing coal, gas and biofuels emissions to levels close to those of wind or solar PV, could also reduce their final EROI value considerably.[30] The same methodological issues, moreover, may water down EROI values when comparing different technologies and site-specific processes for the same energy source and/or carrier. This has been the case for large-scale solar PV installations, whose $EROI_{ST}$ and $EROI_{EXT}$ range from 3:1 to 10:1 depending on the geographical context, and the inclusion of energy used for raw materials extraction, manufacture of panels, storage

20 Solar PV = Solar photovoltaics. The conversion of light into electricity using semi-conducting materials.

21 P.E. Brockway et al., 'Estimation of global final-stage energy-return-on-investment for fossil fuels with comparison to renewable energy sources' (2019) 4(7) *Nature Energy* 612, 621.

22 C.A. Hall, above n. 13.

23 M. Raugei et al., above n. 6.

24 C.A. Hall, B. Dale and D. Pimentel, 'Seeking to understand the reasons for different estimates of the EROI for biofuels' (2011) 3(12) *Sustainability* 2413, 2442.

25 D.J. Murphy et al., above n. 12.

26 Ibid.

27 Ibid.

28 M. Raugei et al., above n. 6.

29 Ibid.

30 S. Sgouridis et al., 'Comparative net energy analysis of renewable electricity and carbon capture and storage' (2019) 4(6) *Nature Energy* 456, 465.

facilities etc.[31] Whilst EROI values for solar PV (and, to a lesser extent, wind) can hardly be universalised, they can rather provide context-specific insights to evaluate similar small- and large-scale projects under different conditions.[32]

Moreover, with specific regard to high-EROI energy sources – more specifically, hydro, wind, and coal – other considerations like generation intermittency and regulatory environments could distort calculations and ultimately downplay the actual energy input needed to get an energy return.[33] For instance, if grids cannot be adjusted to deal with intermittent supply from renewable sources (like wind), that potentially reduces their EROI if a substantial amount of gas-fired power is needed for backup generation.

2.3. EROI AS A TOOL FOR ENERGY AND CLIMATE POLICY-MAKING

Notwithstanding the above inconsistencies and uncertainties, the energy return from different energy sources can play out as a meaningful metric when crafting an energy mix, telling us how much energy to expect from each source and therefore how to efficiently maximise societal needs.[34] As such, EROI is an indicator of public welfare and economic development – similar to GDP.[35] Relevantly, EROI could provide further guidance to strengthen the argument that transition to a low-carbon economy requires energy sources with decreasing EROIs to remain unexploited because they are unworthy to be exploitable from a net-energy perspective.[36] EROI analysis should be undertaken in parallel with other cost-effectiveness indicators (such as the *Levelised Cost of Energy*), in order to fine-tune the economic and energy break-even benefits in order to maximise public welfare.[37] This is primarily the case for oil and coal, while it

---

31 P.A, Prieto and C.A. Hall, *Spain's photovoltaic revolution: the energy return on investment*, Springer, New York 2013, D. Weißbach et al., 'Energy intensities, EROIs (energy returned on invested), and energy payback times of electricity generating power plants' (2013) 52(4) *Energy* 210, 221; M. Raugei et al., above n. 6.

32 G. Palmer and J. Floyd, 'An Exploration of Divergence in EPBT and EROI for Solar Photovoltaics' (2017) 2 *Biophysical Economics & Resource Quality* 15.

33 M. Raugei, 'Net energy analysis should not compare apples and oranges' (2019) 4(3) *Nature Energy* 86, 88.

34 C.A. Hall, above n. 13, 111 ff.

35 D.J. Murphy et al., above n. 12; J.C. Lambert, C.A. Hall, S. Balogh and A. Gupta, 'Energy, EROI and quality of life' (2014) 64 *Energy Policy* 153, 167.

36 C. McGlade and P. Etkins, 'The geographical distribution of fossil fuels unused when limiting global warming to 2°C' (2015) 517 *Nature* 187, 190.

37 Levelised Cost of Energy (LCOE) is equal to the present value of the sum of discounted direct costs divided by the total production of the generating unit (see IEA, *Levelised cost of electricity in the European Union, 2040*, IEA, Paris 2019). Similarly to EROI, LCOE calculations can be integrated to reflect cost-effectiveness of GHG emission reduction projects: see E. Baker,

could be the case for biofuels and biomass under site-specific or technology-specific circumstances.

Yet existing EROI methods (including $EROI_{EXT}$) are generally blind to the overall amount of non-renewable energy consumed per unit of energy output. When two alternatives are compared, the one with the higher EROI may at the same time be the one that leads to the faster depletion of high-quality, non-renewable primary energy stocks; therefore, it might not turn out to be the more desirable from a climate change mitigation perspective.[38] Thus, taken in isolation, EROI (and NEA) unfolds as an arguably rather poor indicator of the long-term sustainability of an energy exploitation system.[39] EROI and net energy science is progressing towards more accurate and comprehensive indicators to embed environmental impacts and GHG emissions. One of them is the recently developed *Energy Return on Carbon* (EROC).[40] EROC takes into account both the net energy potential of a given fuel and its related GHG emissions, to produce a broader picture of fuels' overall utility under climate change policy.

EROC is hence calculated as follows:

$$\text{EROC} = \frac{\left(1 - \dfrac{1}{EROI}\right)}{Carbon\ emission\ factor}$$

EROC comprises climate externalities and net energy costs of fossil fuel energies. It therefore aims to maximise net energy gains from energy fuels within the constraints of the carbon budget. Under EROC calculations, EROI values of both conventional and unconventional fossil fuels fall drastically in light of their high carbon intensity. EROC findings thus support the current prioritisation of fossil fuel phase-out in the order of coal, followed by oil and gas – their net energies per GtCO2 equalling 10.3 EJ, 12.0 EJ and 16.9 EJ, respectively.[41] Accordingly, natural gas provides a significant 64 per cent more net energy/CO_2 than coal, as the lower carbon content overcompensates for the lower EROI. According to EROC values, even greater priority should be given to halting exploitation of unconventional oil. Lastly, CCS should be adequately weighed against its full energy costs to properly assess its prominence in an effectively transitional policy mix.[42]

SN. Khatami, 'The levelized cost of carbon: a practical, if imperfect, method to compare GHG abatement projects' (2019) 19 *Climate Policy* 1132, 1143.

38 See K. Mulder and N.J. Hagens, above n. 15.

39 M. Raugei et al., above n. 6.

40 L.C. King and J. Van den Bergh, 'Implications of net energy-return-on-investment for a low-carbon energy transition' (2018) 3(4) *Nature Energy* 334, 340.

41 Ibid. 1 GtCO2 (gigaton of carbon dioxide) or 1 billion metric tonnes of CO_2. 1EJ (Exajoule of energy) or 10^{18} Joules.

42 The Intergovernmental Panel on Climate Change (IPCC) envisages a prominent role for CCS/CCU technologies in achieving the 1.5° trajectories (see J. Rogelj et al., 'Mitigation

3. EROI IN EU CLIMATE AND ENVIRONMENTAL LAW

Notwithstanding the various relevant insights that EROI calculations can deliver for policy-making, energy balance of different sources and fuels are barely embedded in EU's climate and energy policy documents and regulations. Conversely, economic cost-effectiveness has mainly driven the EU's roadmap towards the 2020 and 2030 Climate and Energy framework.[43] Within this context, integrated economic models have been used, which included technologic and innovation break-through, as well as fuel expenses to achieve the interim emission reductions needed to achieve long-term climate neutrality targets.[44] In the impact assessment of the 2030 Climate and Energy framework, energy aspects of the proposed framework included net energy imports and energy intensity (i.e. primary energy to GDP).[45] These indicators, however, show a lack of comprehensive life cycle assessment thinking, in order to deliver an effective comparative evaluation of energy supply options with regard both to their resource requirements and their health and environmental impacts.[46] In contrast, an overarching policy framework embedding net energy (EROI) as a framework condition might have valuable implications in various relevant EU policy areas, and therefore impact on various regulations. This could mainstream and harmonise the decision-making process across Member States while not impinging on the same Member States' competences in accordance with Articles 192 and 194 TFEU.[47] The following sub-sections will focus on net energy implications for *low carbon innovation* through the EU ETS and *spatial planning* under the Strategic Environmental Assessment (SEA) and EIA.

3.1. LOW-CARBON INNOVATION: THE EU ETS

As a market-based mechanism, the underpinning of the EU ETS is to achieve GHG emissions reductions in energy-intensive sectors in the most

---

Pathways Compatible with 1.5°C in the Context of Sustainable Development' in IPCC, *Global Warming of 1.5°C*, 2018, section 2.4.2.3. at pp. 134–136). Yet increased energy and resources costs have been identified as one of the main setbacks in the uptake of these technologies, see Sgouridis et al., above n. 30; E.S. Rubin et al., 'The cost of CO_2 capture and storage' (2015) 40 *International Journal of Greenhouse Gas Control* 378, 400.

43 T. Van Ierland and S. Vergote, 'How economic analysis shaped EU 2020 and 2030 Target Setting' in P. Vis and J. Delbeke (eds.), *Towards a Climate Neutral Europe: Curbing the Trend*, Routledge, London/New York 2019, pp. 46–66.

44 Commission Staff Working Document SWD(2014) 15 final, accompanying the Communication, A policy framework for climate and energy in the period from 2020 up to 2030.

45 Ibid. pp. 82 ff.

46 K. Fredga and K. Mäler, 'Life Cycle Analyses and Resource Assessments' (2010) 39 *Ambio* 36, 41.

47 See Case C-5/16, *Poland v. Parliament and Council*, ECLI:EU:C:2018:483, para. 150; Case T-370/11, *Poland v. Commission*, ECLI:EU:T:2013:113, para. 18.

cost-effective manner.[48] The EU ETS aims to strengthen the business case for investments in low-carbon technologies by: a) setting monetary incentives, through emission allowances' pricing and allocation, to adopt technologies with an improved rate of return and a reduced payback period compared to more carbon-intensive alternative investments; and b) directly financing innovative, low-carbon projects through *ad hoc* programmes funded through ETS allowances' sale revenues.[49]

EU ETS allowances are allocated to all eligible installations under a two-fold method: auctions (ordinary regime), and free allocation.[50] The ETS Directive mandates that at least half of auctions' revenues be withheld by Member States and used to finance low-carbon and adaptation technologies.[51] In this context, $EROI_{EXT}$ and $EROI_{SOC}$ could both be used to evaluate the mitigation potential and performance of specific projects, alongside GHG intensity (also through integrated metrics, like EROC). In contrast, free allocation of ETS allowances shall be allowed, as long as it enhances competitiveness in economic sectors potentially sensible to carbon leakage. To identify industrial facilities to be allocated free ETS allowances (80 per cent), a set of technological benchmarks has been established (54) under the ETS Directive.[52] These technological benchmark values take account of the average performance of the top 10 per cent most efficient techniques, substitutes and alternative production processes.[53] All benchmarks are calculated on the basis of past production quantities rather than inputs to the production process, with a view to maximising incentives for emissions reductions and energy efficiency savings. The free allocation benchmarks, however, have proved fairly inadequate to reflect structural changes in several economic sectors.[54] Such unfitness has mostly been due to

48 Parliament and Council Directive 2003/87/EC establishing a scheme for greenhouse gas emission allowance trading within the Community [2003] OJ L75/32 (henceforth: ETS Directive).

49 K. Rogge, 'Reviewing the evidence on the innovation impact of the EU Emission Trading System' in S. Weishaar (ed.), *Research Handbook on Emission Trading*, Edward Elgar, Cheltenham 2016, pp. 161–194.

50 Art. 10 ETS Directive. See D. Ellerman et al. 'The EU ETS allocation process: an overview' in A.D. Ellerman, B.K. Buchner and C. Carraro (eds.), *Allocation in the European Emissions trading scheme rights, rents and fairness*, Cambridge University Press, New York 2011, pp. 3–12.

51 Art. 10(3) ETS Directive.

52 Whether a sector is included on the carbon leakage list is determined in general based on a single criterion that reflects both the mathematical outcomes of carbon intensity and trade intensity of the sector. Article 10b of the ETS Directive (as amended by Directive (EU) 2018/410), includes supplemental routes for inclusion.

53 Art. 10a(2) and Annexes ETS Directive.

54 This was also one of the most controversial aspects challenged before the ECJ (and consistently upheld). See, among others, Case C-460/15, *Schaefer Kalk GmbH & Co. KG v. Germany*, ECLI:EU:C:2017:29; Case C-456/15, *BASF SE v. Germany*, ECLI:EU:C:2016:567; Case C-180/15, *Borealis AB and Others v. Naturvårdsverket*, ECLI:EU:C:2016:647. See also

the benchmarks' focus on specific energy use, rather than emission intensity (or overall net energy flows).[55] To address this problem, the newly enacted Free Allocation Regulation (FAR) requires all applicant installations to submit, *inter alia*, a baseline data report on historic activity levels.[56] Reported data must be verified by the FAR national competent authorities.[57] One of the key groups of parameters for data reporting includes the annual installation-wide energy input from fuels (including the respective emissions factor), and – only for installations producing or consuming electricity – the annual balance of imported-exported, produced-consumed electricity.[58] Member States' competent authorities under FAR might well opt for a more stringent regime by mandating for EROI assessment to evaluate installations' eligibility for free allocation.

Importantly, facilities carrying out electricity generation are in principle excluded from free allocation.[59] Yet, derogation from this rule is provided for countries in dire need of modernising their electricity generation systems.[60] Eligible Member States may thus select, through a bidding process, a number of energy generation, transmission and distribution projects to be allocated free ETS allowances.[61] In so doing, Member States can rely on several criteria, which should primarily reflect a cost-benefit analysis and ensure net positive gains in terms of emission reductions.[62] No reference is made here to net energy balances. However, in light of the discretion given to Member States as to the choice of selection criteria – as long as they are transparent, clear and non-discriminatory – EROI and net energy ratios could be used to evaluate and rank RES generation, as well as innovative carbon reduction technologies (such as CCS or CCU) on a context-specific basis.

---

the Commission Report on the Functioning of the European Carbon Market, COM(2019) 557 final.

55 C. Stenqvist and M. Åhman, 'Free allocation in the 3rd EU ETS period: assessing two manufacturing sectors' (2016) 16 *Climate Policy* 125, 144 (showing that this has resulted in misrepresented benchmarks, and ultimately in over-allocation of free allowances in the pulp and paper industry).

56 Commission Delegated Regulation 2019/331/EU determining transitional Union-wide rules for harmonised free allocation of emission allowances pursuant to Article 10a of Directive 2003/87/EC [2019] OJ L59/8 (henceforth: FAR), Art. 4.

57 Art. 15 FAR.

58 Annex IV, 2.4 and 2.5 FAR.

59 Art. 10a(1) ETS Directive.

60 Art. 10c ETS Directive. Only Member States with less than 60% of the EU average GDP in 2013 at market prices are eligible (i.e., Bulgaria, Czech Republic, Croatia, Latvia, Lithuania, Hungary, Poland, Romania and Slovakia).

61 Importantly, these allowances may (in total or partly) be used to support investments under the Modernisation Fund pursuant to Art. 10d ETS Directive to finance small-scale investment projects, to modernise energy systems and improve energy efficiency in relation to generation and use of electricity from renewable sources.

62 Art. 10c(2) ETS Directive.

As for direct fostering of innovation and access to finance for low-carbon technologies, the *Innovation Fund* will replace NER300 as the innovation mechanism in the upcoming ETS fourth phase (2021–2030).[63] The Innovation Fund will include at least 450 million allowances, and up to 500 million by the mid-2020s.[64] The Innovation Fund will be managed directly by the European Commission (with the support of an implementing body) and will provide support to technologies, processes or products that are sufficiently mature and have a significant cost-effectiveness potential to achieve GHG emissions reduction.[65] Potentially funded projects will include all RES generation, CCS and CCU technologies, industrial low-carbon processes in all ETS sectors, and cross-cutting technologies.[66] The Innovation Fund provides for geographical spread as well as specific funding thresholds as to the overall eligibility of projects,[67] and sets general criteria for selection based on: effectiveness as to decarbonisation potential (and scalability); degree of innovation; and economic viability (i.e., bankability and expected performance costs).[68] The Innovation Fund's rationale for financing is thus clearly cost-effectiveness-oriented. Such criteria should ideally be amended so as to include net energy gains – more specifically, through $EROI_{EXT}$, $EROI_{SOC}$ or EROC – under the umbrella of the technological innovation or maturity, as relevant criteria for selection. Thus, Member States authorities could more adequately assess small-size CCS/CCU, renewable energy generation, as well as energy storage projects against their site-specific constraints and lifetime biophysical viability, importantly including the environmental costs of dismantling and decommissioning.[69]

3.2. SPATIAL PLANNING: SEA AND EIA DIRECTIVES

EROI assesses the overall energy balances of different fuels and technologies. In this regard, EROI widely encompasses life-cycle thinking and applies it to

63 Commission Delegated Regulation 2019/856/EU supplementing Directive 2003/87/EC of the European Parliament and of the Council with regard to the operation of the Innovation Fund [2019] OJ L140/6.

64 Art. 10a(8) ETS Directive.

65 Ibid.

66 Commission explanatory memorandum to the Delegated Regulation 2019/856/EU, C(2019) 1492 final, pp. 7 ff. (These technologies may include, *inter alia*, CCS/CCU from industrial plants, transport of CO_2, utilisation and storage, hybrid renewable energy systems, low-carbon hydrogen use and storage, and infrastructure projects.)

67 Art. 10a(8) ETS Directive; Recital (11) and Art. 11(2) Commission Delegated Regulation 2019/856/EU.

68 Art. 11(2) Commission Delegated Regulation 2019/856/EU. Relevantly, the *effectiveness* criteria is to be assessed against the technological benchmarks pursuant to Art. 10a ETS Directive.

69 G. Limpens and H. Jeanmart, 'Electricity storage needs for the energy transition: An EROI based analysis illustrated by the case of Belgium' (2018) 52 *Energy* 960, 973.

energy intensive processes, although limited to energy inputs-outputs.[70] EROI can thus contribute to decision making in spatial planning of infrastructures inasmuch as it contributes assessing impacts of different projects and technologies from a net energy gains standpoint. The Strategic Environmental Assessment (SEA) and Environmental Impact Assessment Directive (EIA) come thus into play. The EIA Directive sets the regulatory framework for taking impacts on the environment into account at the earliest possible stage in all the technical planning and decision-making processes.[71] EROI could serve the EIA Directive's purposes from a two-fold perspective. First, it would contribute to providing high-quality information on environmental impacts through the application of appropriate sub-tools for rigorous assessment. Second, it would lead to more product-oriented and life-cycle-oriented decisions by encompassing projects' up- and downstream impacts.[72] EROI application within the context of EIA can lead to the following four analytical gains:

1. A more explicit focus on embedded product provision;
2. A more rigorous evaluation of life cycle impacts;
3. A more impact-oriented methodology for evaluating resource use;
4. An enhanced framework for quantitative comparison of alternatives.

In other words, EROI could enable the majority of impact assessments to be far-reaching about how a proposed local development represents a component in a larger production system, and whose impacts it is equally important to mitigate. Two further relevant issues have to be pointed out, however. First, EROI analysis may prove unreasonably burdensome on the applicant, and its use might therefore not be legitimised in all EIA contexts.[73] EROI might hence acquire even further relevance when examining cumulative effects through SEA processes – for example for a renewable energy generation plan – rather

---

70 D. Murphy et al., 'Comparing Apples to Apples: Why the Net Energy Analysis Community Needs to Adopt the Life-Cycle Analysis Framework' (2016) 9 *Energies* 917, 932.

71 Parliament and Council Directive 2011/92/EU on the assessment of the effects of certain public and private projects on the environment [2012] OJ L26/1 (henceforth: EIA Directive). See Case C-526/16, *Commission v. Poland*, ECLI:EU:C:2018:356, para. 75; Case C-215/06, *Commission v. Ireland*, ECLI:EU:C:2008:380, para. 58; Case C-411/17, *Inter-Environnement Wallonie and others v. Conseil des ministres*, ECLI:EU:C:2019:622.

72 R. Atlason, above n. 16. Several authors have argued that life cycle assessment as an appropriate analytical tool for application in EIA and SEA. See, *inter alia*, A. Björklund, 'Life cycle assessment as an analytical tool in strategic environmental assessment. Lessons learned from a case study on municipal energy planning in Sweden' (2012) 32 *Environmental Impact Assessment Review* 82, 87; M. Bidstrup et al., 'Life Cycle Assessment in spatial planning – a procedure for addressing systemic impacts' (2015) 91 *Journal of Cleaner Production* 136, 144.

73 A. Björklund, above n. 72.

than impacts of individual projects under EIA.[74] Second, legislators should be wary that EROI as a net energy metric should not be used to rank or assess energy projects alone. A project with a high EROI is not necessarily the project that maximises social welfare in terms of both economic growth and GHG emissions reduction. EROI should therefore operate in combination with life cycle emissions analysis, which encompass the GHG footprint of both direct energy use (i.e., fossil fuels combustion in specific industrial processes such as waste-to-energy, deployment of CCS technologies, etc.) and indirect energy use (i.e., the embodied energy used in manufacturing, construction, maintenance, and deconstruction of the generation plant).[75] If the trade-off between net energy ratio and GHG intensity of the project is deemed adequate, it might be more desirable to opt for a smaller, if less energy efficient project, over a bigger, more energy efficient project. For example, a small-scale natural gas plant would be selected over the plug-in of a CCS technology to a coal power plant. GHG intensity factors can also be directly integrated into EROI calculations, as in the case of EROC.

Climate change aspects are receiving growing international attention in EIA regulation, although their full implementation within EIA practice is still far from being achieved in most developed countries.[76] The EIA Directive explicitly includes climate change as one of the environmental impact factors to be considered in the assessment.[77] Empirical analysis enshrines net-GHG emission as the silver bullet for evaluation of climate change impacts.[78] As discussed above, however, GHG intensity is not a fully comprehensive category, whereby to assess climate change impacts. A project with low GHG emissions at the point of use could in fact generate high GHG emissions at the source, if it requires highly energy-intensive processes to generate, transport and process the fuels and materials necessary to run that process. Hence EIA and SEA Directives should embed net energy balance as a significant environmental effect for the purposes of adopting a plan and programme, as well as for assessing specific

---

74 P. Byer et al., *Climate Change in Impact Assessment: International Best Practice Principles*, Special Publication Series No. 8, International Association for Impact Assessment, Fargo ND 2018.

75 For an example of life cycle analysis as applied to energy generation, see M. Pehl et al., 'Understanding future emissions from low-carbon power systems by integration of life-cycle assessment and integrated energy modelling' (2017) 2(12) *Nature Energy* 939, 945.

76 See S. Agrawala, et al., *Incorporating Climate Change Impacts and Adaptation in Environmental Impact Assessments: Opportunities and Challenges*, OECD Environmental Working Paper No. 24, OECD, Paris 2010.

77 Recital (7) and Art. 3 EIA Directive.

78 Á. Enríquez-de-Salamanca et al., 'Consideration of climate change on environmental impact assessment in Spain' (2016) 57 *Environmental Impact Assessment Review* 31, 39; S. Vammen Larsen, 'Is environmental impact assessment fulfilling its potential? The case of climate change in renewable energy projects' (2014) 32 *Impact Assessment and Project Appraisal* 234, 240.

industrial and energy projects. EROI (alone or combined with GHG intensity) could in turn contribute to adequately assessing climate change impacts with regard to GHG and energy input-output implications of a selected infrastructure if properly included in national SEA/EIA guidelines.[79]

Second, and more specifically, the EIA Directive enlists use of natural resources and the overall intensity of different impacts as the relevant selection criteria of the assessed (or screened) project.[80] To this end, the project's developer must submit accurate information on how the project will deliver on environmental and climate impacts.[81] Resource and energy inputs throughout various life cycle phases under $EROI_{EXT}$ and/or $EROI_{SOC}$ may well fit into this scenario, and therefore be mandated by Member States national authorities in the context of EIA procedures.

Lastly, the project's developer is obliged to describe in the Environmental Impact Assessment Report the main characteristics of the production processes, also with regard to the amount of energy demand and energy used, as well as the quantity and quality of natural resources used.[82] Net energy ratios encompass all these elements (although with specific regard to fuels) to provide a more integrated qualitative appraisal. Moreover, EROI values could be expressly included as a criterion to evaluate the proposed project against 'main alternatives'.[83] EROI should thus be mandated as a set of information to be provided by the developer as to the environmental (and climate) impacts of both the proposed option and all the main alternatives, to ensure that the competent authority is able to carry out a comprehensive assessment that adequately catalogues, describes and assesses the approved project's effects on the environment and climate.[84]

4. CONCLUSION

The selection of enabling energy technologies and resources to be pursued in the transition towards an efficient and low-carbon economy is crucial. Analysis based only on prices, cost-effectiveness, and market trends represents only one side of the coin when it comes to predicting future energy supplies and industrial processes. This contribution has argued that to embed a biophysical perspective, through EROI, in EU policies and legislation on financing of

79 See, with regard to New Zealand's experience, M. Walmsley et al., 'Linking Greenhouse gas emissions footprint and energy return on investment in electricity generation planning' (2018) 200 *Journal of Cleaner Production* 911, 921.

80 Art. 4(3) and Annex III EIA Directive.

81 Art. 4(4) EIA Directive.

82 Art. 5 EIA Directive.

83 Art. 5(3)(d) and Annex IV EIA Directive.

84 Case C-461/17, *Brian Holohan and Others v. An Bord Pleanála*, ECLI:EU:C:2018:883, para. 69.

low-carbon innovation and spatial planning will provide a more comprehensive response to the energy transition dilemma.

Some remarkable shortcomings in EROI calculation methods need yet to be addressed in order to adequately calibrate EROI values and ensure full comparability of data. Nonetheless, EROI could be readily used as a key indicator to foster innovative renewable energy and CCS projects, as well as the modernisation of the energy system and financing of cutting-edge technologies under the EU ETS. Likewise, the adoption of EROI analysis entails the potential to strengthen the EU's environmental and climate objectives in spatial planning and siting of infrastructures while mainstreaming a 'life cycle thinking' in the context of the SEA and EIA Directive. Further research is needed as to net energy's implications for other EU policies, including the existing regime on support to RES generation, siting of CCS facilities, and fuels' emission standards, as well as the upcoming regime on sustainable finance.

Availability and quality of energy will become increasingly important elements affecting the viability of our economy. Yet, a future of declining energy availability need not be an undesirable future. The effectiveness of policies, rules, and actions to achieve a decarbonised, sustainable society will likely depend on the ability to duly take into account the necessary energy and material inputs that allow for our desired standards of living.

RESTORATION BY PRIVATE ENTITIES IN INDONESIA

A Hope in Saving 'Sinks'?

Isna FATIMAH

1. INTRODUCTION

During the time of climate crisis, states throughout the world are expected to come up with noteworthy breakthroughs in achieving ambitious climate change mitigation (mitigation), as well as adaptation targets. In regard to mitigation measures, states are also encouraged to invite private entities to contribute toward the enhancement of mitigation efforts.[1] One of the means to realise mitigation is by enhancing removal of emissions by sinks. The term 'sinks' refers to any kind of component or activity which is capable of sequestering emissions more than it emits.[2] Among other things, it includes forests, peatlands and mangroves, which used to be ubiquitous in Indonesia.[3] Since land-based business activities act as significant drivers of natural sinks' degradation,[4] it is important to ensure that they can equally contribute to restoration as part of the means to enhance emissions removal by sinks.

---

1 Paris Agreement, Paris, 12 December 2015, entry into force 4 November 2016, article 6.4(b) and 6.8(b).

2 See: https://www.ipcc.ch/sr15/chapter/glossary/; R.T. Watson, et al., *Greenhouse Gases: Sources and Sinks*, https://www.ipcc.ch/site/assets/uploads/2018/05/ipcc_wg_I_1992_suppl_report_section_a1.pdf.

3 Indonesian Ministry of National Development Plan, *Indonesian Biodiversity Strategy and Action Plan (IBSAP) 2015–2020*, 2016, pp. 39–55.

4 P. Smith, M. Bustamante, H. Ahammad, H. Clark, H. Dong, E.A. Elsiddig, H. Haberl, R. Harper, J. House, M. Jafari, O. Masera, C. Mbow, N.H. Ravindranath, C.W. Rice, C. Robledo Abad, A. Romanovskaya, F. Sperling, and F. Tubiello, 'Agriculture, Forestry and Other Land Use (AFOLU)' in *Climate Change 2014: Mitigation of Climate Change*, contribution of Working Group III to the Fifth Assessment Report of the Intergovernmental Panel on Climate Change [Edenhofer, O., R. Pichs-Madruga, Y. Sokona, E. Farahani, S. Kadner, K. Seyboth, A. Adler, I. Baum, S. Brunner, P. Eickemeier, B. Kriemann, J. Savolainen, S. Schlömer, C. von Stechow, T. Zwickel and J.C. Minx (eds.)], Cambridge University Press, Cambridge/New York, 2015. https://www.ipcc.ch/site/assets/uploads/2018/02/ipcc_wg3_ar5_chapter11.pdf, pp. 811–922, at pp. 822–829.

There are several discourses relating to legal measures and policies as one of the tools to support climate mitigation from the AFOLU (Agriculture, Forestry and Land-Use) sector,[5] but responsibility-to-restore has never been exclusively addressed. Analysing the possibility of implementing responsibility-to-restore for the enhancement of climate mitigation is essential for, at least, these two reasons: (1) several cases of degraded forests and peatlands in Indonesia are due to the excess of natural-resources exploitation through massive natural-resources concessions; and (2) there is a window which enables responsibility-to-restore to significantly contribute toward the country's effort in enhancing removal by sinks, considering that the breadth of areas which were designated for concessions have contributed, albeit to different extents, to the degradation of the land-based sinks, such as forests and peatlands.[6]

This chapter attempts to explore the possibility of using legal construction of responsibility-to-restore by private entities as one of the instruments which contribute to future climate mitigation measures. In addition, this contribution will assess to what extent that the current international and national legal regimes accommodate the attribution of responsibility to private entities in regard to restoration within mitigation frameworks. The assessment incorporates exploration of law pertaining to restoration and responsibility-to-restore by private entities, as well as the result of interaction of such law with environmental legal principles and the emerging international climate-change law. The phrase 'responsibility-to-restore' will be frequently used in this contribution to address various concepts of responsibility of permit holders in connection with natural resources to restore areas exploited by them, as addressed under the relevant regulation. It is argued that enforcing 'responsibility-to-restore' ensures a direct contribution from environmental law enforcement to mitigation measures. When conducted consistently, it may encourage private entities to make innovations, so as to reduce restoration costs. Indonesia is chosen mainly because of its position as one of the most significant contributors to global greenhouse-gas emissions from the AFOLU sector, aside from Indonesia's active role as a member of the climate change treaties.[7]

The following sections mainly comprise four parts. The second section describes the anatomy of Indonesia's restoration target that is linked to its mitigation target, and analyses whether the responsibility-to-restore exists

---

5 See for instance: A. Wijaya, et. al, 'How Can Indonesia Achieve Its Climate Mitigation Goal? An Analysis of Potential Emissions Reductions from Energy and Land-Use Policies', World Resource Institute, October 2017, https://www.wri.org/publication/how-can-indonesia-achieve-its-climate-goal; T. Cronin et. al., 'Moving consensus and managing expectations: media and REDD+ in Indonesia' (2016) 137 *Climate Change* 57–70.

6 The data will be presented in section 2.

7 See: Climate Action Tracker, 'Indonesia', https://climateactiontracker.org/countries/indonesia/; World Bank et al, *Indonesia and Climate Change: Current Status and Policies*.

within the target or not. The third section addresses the definition of restoration, as well as the legal principles supporting the construction of responsibility-to-restore. The fourth section explains the provisions and mechanisms under the Paris Agreement and other international legal instruments which are relevant to emissions removal by sinks and restoration. The fifth section analyses both the 'responsibility-to-restore' under Indonesia's environmental and natural resources laws, and the shaping of interpretation which allows the use of this approach to enhance removal by sinks through restoration. Finally, the last section concludes the entire analysis.

2. RESPONSIBILITY-TO-RESTORE IN CLIMATE MITIGATION TARGET

In 2009, Indonesia pledged commitment for reduction of emissions by 26 per cent by using the business-as-usual (BAU) approach. Subsequently in 2011, Indonesia raised the commitment to a 41 per cent conditional target (with international support). According to its Third National Communication (TNC) to the UN Framework Convention on Climate Change secretariat, Indonesia pledged to achieve 90 per cent of its target of emissions reduction from the AFOLU sectors.[8] Even with funding from Norway for the operation of Reducing Emissions from Deforestation and Forest Degradation plus (REDD+) since 2010, the latest prediction shows that Indonesia's current climate policy could not afford to meet the target.[9] As a response, in 2019, Indonesia revised its post-2020 target, which aims at 29 per cent reduction from BAU by 2030 and 41 per cent with the conditional situation (which later in the TNC became 38 per cent). Time seemed to be almost running out for Indonesia to achieve its overall target by 2020. However, recently Indonesia's claim of making good progress from REDD+ led to the UN Green Climate Fund's approval of the proposal of REDD+ Results-Based Payment for the period of 2014–2016, which is worth USD 103.8 million in aid.[10] Earlier in 2020, the Rainforest Foundation Norway indicated that it would pay USD 56 million to Indonesia

---

8 According to Indonesia's Third National Communication (TNC), forestry and peatland sectors contribute up to 87%. See: Climate Action Tracker, above n. 7; Government of Indonesia, 'Indonesia Third National Communication under the United Nations Framework Convention on Climate Change', Jakarta, Indonesia, p. 116, http://unfccc.int/national_reports/non-annex_i_natcom/items/10124.php.

9 Climate Action Tracker, above n. 7. https://climateactiontracker.org/countries/indonesia/current-policy-projections/.

10 Government of Indonesia, Indonesia REDD-plus RBP for results period 2014–2016, approved funding proposal by the Green Climate Fund, https://www.greenclimate.fund/document/indonesia-redd-plus-rbp-results-period-2014-2016.

for successfully reducing emissions from deforestation and forest degradation in 2017.[11]

The restoration programme indeed becomes an integral part of Indonesia's mitigation efforts, including being inherent in REDD+'s objectives and activities.[12] In the first Nationally Determined Contribution (NDC), restoration is also mentioned as one of the means of achieving the mitigation target.[13] There are special permits, such as one for conducting ecosystem restoration, which not only allow private engagement in restoring the ecosystem, but also give the right to use a part of the area for tourism or other purposes, which is subject to approval from the authority as a legitimate trade-off.[14] Some enforcement activities in regard to the improvement of the enabling environment for REDD+ and other NDC-related programmes are also mentioned.[15] Past efforts, however, gave more attention to conservation and protection, instead of the enhancement of sinks by employing restoration.

In line with its climate mitigation commitment, Indonesia also pledged to conduct land rehabilitation and peat restoration.[16] In respect of peatland restoration, the President established the Peatland Restoration Agency (*Badan Restorasi Gambut* (BRG)) to accelerate peatland restoration up to 2,103,327 Ha by 2020 – from the total of 6,757,997 Ha of restorable peatland. Such restoration aims to restore the function of the peatland ecosystem to its natural state by regulating the water cycle, rewetting, and maintaining cultivation to align with local wisdom.[17] Limited areas which will be restored by the BRG indicate the urgency for further engagement with other stakeholders to address peatlands which are not covered in the BRG's target.[18]

The National Development Plan for the medium-term 2015–2019 (NDP) has set the restoration target under two primary agenda: (1) Land-and-forest

---

11 The Jakarta Post, *Indonesia to receive $56 million from Norway for reducing emissions*, https://www.thejakartapost.com/news/2020/05/22/indonesia-to-receive-56-million-from-norway for reducing emissions.html.

12 REDD+ Task Force Indonesia, *REDD+ National Strategy*, June 2012, official English version, p. 7, https://www.unredd.net/documents/un-redd-partner-countries-181/national-redd-strategies-1025/15862-indonesia-national-redd-strategy.html?path=un-redd-partner-countries-181/national-redd-strategies-1025.

13 Government of Indonesia, *First Nationally Determined Contribution Republic of Indonesia*, November 2016, p. 2.

14 A. Wijaya et. al., above n. 5, p. 8.

15 For instance, REDD+ Task Force Indonesia, above n 12; Government of Indonesia (TNC), above n 8.

16 Government of Indonesia TNC, above n. 8, p. 15.

17 Article 30 paragraph 3(b) and Article 30A of Government Regulation on Protection and Management of Peatland Ecosystems (Peraturan Pemerintah No. 71 Tahun 2014 jo. Peraturan Pemerintah No. 57 Tahun 2016 tentang Perlindungan dan Pengelolaan Ekosistem Gambut).

18 A. Wijaya et al., above n. 5, p. 12.

Figure 1. Peatland Restoration Target

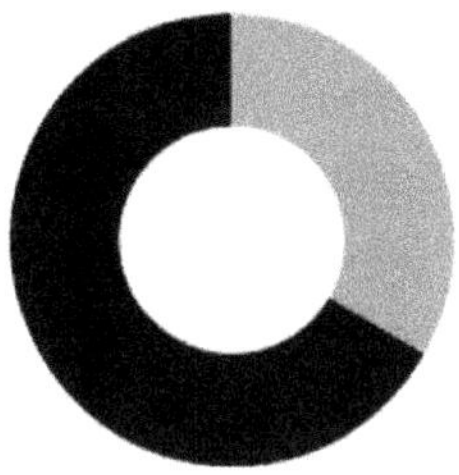

restoration and (2) Social forestry.[19] With respect to land-and-forest restoration, by 2019, the government targeted restoration of 5,000 Ha of City Forest,[20] 100,000 Ha of degraded Conservation Forest,[21] and 5.5 million hectares (MHa) of degraded land within Forest Management Areas (*Kesatuan Pengelolaan Hutan* (KPH)) and Watershed Areas (*Daerah Aliran Sungai* (DAS)).[22] Meanwhile, the restoration target for social forestry was 12.7 million hectares by 2019.[23]

Asides from programmes as previously mentioned, NDP has targeted an additional 500,000 Ha of land to be restored under the ecosystem restoration permit since 2014,[24] which was later decreased to 461,100 Ha in the TNC.[25] Moreover, an additional 100,000 Ha of land was designated for bioenergy in 2019.[26] There was also a commitment to the utilisation of degraded or abandoned land for palm oil plantations, the NDP claiming that such programme can reach the target of 74,530 Gg CO_2e of emissions reduction from this sector.[27] Finally, TNC also mentioned the implementation of REDD+ in two national parks which accounts for 22,500 Ha in total.[28]

In contrast with precise data on the restoration target, the data on the total area of degraded land (including forest and peatland) are quite vague.

19 Ibid.

20 Government of Indonesia, *The National Development Plan – Ministries and Institutions Matrix*, only available in Indonesian, translated informally by author, p. II.M.L.029-12.

21 Ibid. p. I.M.L.029-9.

22 Ibid. p. II.M.L.029-14.

23 Ibid. p. II.M.L.029-19.

24 Ibid. p. II.M.L.029-18.

25 Government of Indonesia (TNC), n 8 above, p. 140. Note: It is uncertain whether the disparity of data is because there are permits which have already been issued for ecosystem restoration after the NDP.

26 Government of Indonesia, above n 20, p. II.M.L.029-17.

27 Government of Indonesia, n 8 above, p. 137. 'Carbon dioxide equivalent' or 'CO2e' is a term for describing different greenhouse gases in a common unit. For any quantity and type of greenhouse gas, CO2e signifies the amount of CO2 which would have the equivalent global warming impact: (Ecometrica, *Greenhouse Gases, CO2, CO2e, and Carbon: What Do All These Terms Mean?* (August 2012)).

28 Ibid. p. 140.

Several prominent research articles argue that the massive decline of Indonesia's forests and peatlands were driven by three major sources of exploitation of natural resources which also fall under the AFOLU category, namely:[29] coal mining, palm-oil plantations and forest-timber utilisation.[30] However, the updated data as provided by the government[31] on total loss of forest cover are scarcely to be found, not to mention that the details on activities which triggered the loss are indeterminate. Surprisingly, TNC is almost entirely silent about those data. The most-accurate information as provided by TNC only explains that around 24.4 million hectares of tree cover were lost during the 2001–2017 period. The table below shows the hectarage of concession areas within forests and peatlands as provided by different institutions.

Despite the discrepancy, the data illustrated below on page 169 are those which are available and most detailed. However, it remains unanswered whether any of those areas overlap with the current restoration target or not. The figures mentioned below have not been included in the restoration target thus far. Nonetheless, it is fair to comment that the area occupied by those concessions within forestry and peatland is significant.

From the explanations above, for analysis purpose in this contribution, we may conclude at least three points. Firstly, restoration has been incorporated as part of the means of achieving Indonesia's climate mitigation target, regardless of its unambitious target if compared to the 90 per cent pledge of emission reduction from the AFOLU sector. Secondly, there are two subjects which may be held responsible in relation to restoration, namely: (1) the state, which is held responsible for restoring degraded land by spending from the state budget or other voluntary funding; and (2) non-state actors, including communities and private parties, which secure permits for activities that may contribute to emission reduction, for instance: social forestry, ecosystem restoration permits or palm-oil plantations within degraded or abandoned land.[32] Thirdly, there is no target for restoration as conducted by private entities operating land-based business activities, even though such activities have significantly contributed to the damage of sinks.

---

29 Ibid. p. 25.

30 Confirmed in Indonesia's first NDC. Theguardian.com, 'Trees covering an area twice the size of Portugal lost in 2014, study finds', 2 September 2015, https://www.theguardian.com/environment/2015/sep/02/trees-covering-an-area-twice-the-size-of-portugal-lost-in-2014-study-finds.

31 What constitute 'data' in this paragraph are research results, published reports or other formal documents which not only give information but also specify areas in number. Statements in the media are excluded.

32 The inclusion of palm-oil plantations is debatable since palm oil is marked as one of the major contributors to forest and peatland degradation.

Figure 2. Major Drivers of Forest and Peatland Degradation[33]

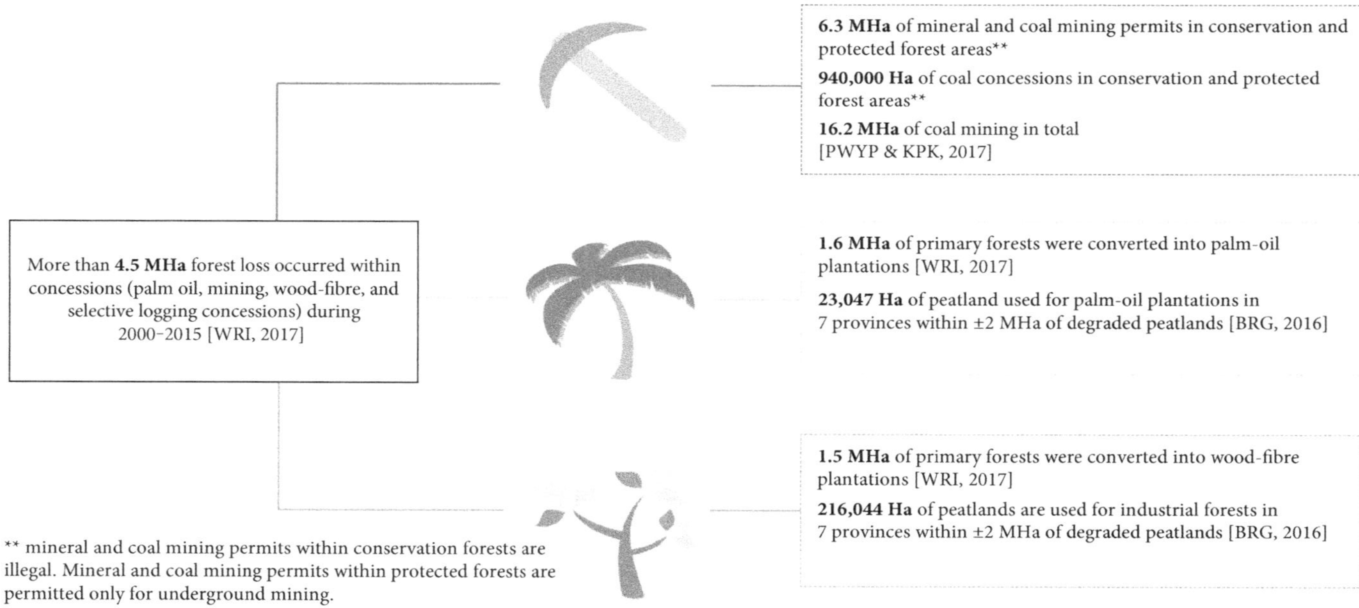

33 Peatland Restoration Agency, *Strategic Plan of Peatland Restoration Agency* (available in Indonesian only: Badan Restorasi Gambut, *Rencana Strategis Badan Restorasi Gambut 2016–2020*), November 2016, pp. 4–38; A. Wijaya, et al., "Drivers of Deforestation in Indonesia, Inside and Outside Concessions Area," World Resource Institute website, https://www.wri.org/blog/2017/07/drivers-deforestation-indonesia-inside-and-outside-concessions-areas; Publish What You Pay Indonesia (PWYP) and KPK, 'Administration of Coal Permit Under Coordination and Supervision of KPK', 1st ed, 2017, p. vii pdf, https://pwypindonesia.org/en/administration-of-coal-permit-under-coordination-and-supervision-of-kpk/.

3. FINDING THE FORM OF RESPONSIBILITY-TO-RESTORE THROUGH THE PRINCIPLES OF INTERNATIONAL ENVIRONMENTAL LAW

Restoration acts as one of the response options which gives immediate impact to enhancing removal by sinks. From the perspective of legal concept, it has been widely addressed under a number of international legal instruments.[34] In connection with international legal documents, they classify restoration into at least two categories.[35] The first category sets out restoration which focuses on reviving certain species or populations of certain species.[36] The second category refers to restoration of a landscape, such as ecosystem restoration and ecological restoration.[37] This contribution focuses on the latter category, but in both concepts the obligation to restore is attributed to the state.

In contrast with the obligation for states to conduct restoration, there is no direct obligation on states to hold private entities responsible for restoring lands or areas which are exploited by them under international legal instruments. However, a number of international environmental law principles are relevant to the adoption and application of responsibility-to-restore on the domestic level. These encompass in particular the precautionary principle, the non-transboundary harm principle, the principle of inter and intra-generational equity, and the polluter pays principle. Several of those principles have been supported by legally-binding norms and adopted into Indonesian law, so that their enforceability is strengthened.

3.1. PRECAUTIONARY PRINCIPLE

The precautionary principle remains a concept with many 'faces', yet it is commonly found in sources of environmental law.[38] Due to its significant implications, it is often constructed using softer wording in legal texts. The UN Framework Convention on Climate Change (UNFCCC) uses the phrase 'precautionary measures' rather than the 'precautionary principle', although the

---

34 See *inter alia*: Legal instruments as mentioned in the Preamble of the UN Decade on Ecosystem Restoration; A. Telesetsky, A. Cliquet and A. Akhtar-Khavari, *Ecological Restoration in International Environmental Law*, Routledge, Abingdon/New York_2017, p. 83.

35 Ibid.; Article 8(f) UN Convention on Biological Diversity (1992).

36 Ibid.

37 Ibid.

38 See the summary in J. Wiener, 'Precaution and Climate Change' in K.R. Gray, R. Tarasofsky, and C. Carlarne (eds.), *The Oxford Handbook of International Climate Change Law*, Oxford University Press, Oxford 2018, pp. 2–6.

scope of both phrases is relatively similar.[39] In Indonesia, this principle has been stipulated as one of the underlying principles of the Environmental Protection and Management Act (EPMA).[40]

UNFCCC requires states to 'take precautionary measures in order to anticipate, prevent or minimize the causes of climate change and mitigate its adverse effects.' The precautionary measures are further explained as:

> where there are threats of serious or irreversible damage, lack of full scientific certainty should not be used as a reason for postponing such measures, taking into account that policies and measures to deal with climate change should be cost-effective so as to ensure global benefits at the lowest possible cost.'[41]

Such provision explicitly denotes that the measures should 'be comprehensively' and 'cover all relevant sources, *sinks* and reservoirs' (emphasis added).

Land-use activities are considered to be a major contributor to emission release.[42] Such activities will most likely degrade the optimal function of natural sinks.[43] For instance, palm-oil plantation activities within peatland areas will dry the peat, while forest utilisation will contribute to forest degradation. Although the environment is capable of self-healing, massive alteration to AFOLU sectors hinders (if not destroys) the self-healing capability of the environment. On the other hand, the contribution from ecosystem restoration to counteracting the threat from AFOLU is yet to be ascertained scientifically. The bottom-line is, the precautionary principle can be construed as a suggestion for the state to ensure that ecosystem restoration is performed despite any uncertainty on whether or not the areas which are damaged by AFOLU activities are able to restore their function as sinks.

3.2. NON-TRANSBOUNDARY HARM PRINCIPLE

The non-transboundary harm principle suggests that states should conduct measures to prevent transboundary harm.[44] As elucidated by Article 2a EPMA, this principle is inherent in the principle of state responsibility. Although the transboundary element is not explicitly mentioned, the principle of state

---

39 See *inter alia*: J. Wiener, 'Precaution and Climate Change' in K.R. Gray, R. Tarasofsky, and C. Carlarne (eds.), *The Oxford Handbook of International Climate Change Law*, Oxford University Press, Oxford 2018.

40 Article 2f Environmental Protection and Management Act (EPMA), Act No. 32 year 2009.

41 Article 3.3 UN Framework Convention on Climate Change (UNFCCC).

42 P. Smith, et al., above n. 4.

43 Ibid.

44 UNFCCC, preamble.

responsibility entails the obligation of the state to prevent utilisation of natural resources to cause environmental pollution and damage.

AFOLU sectors have a tendency to alter the ecosystem's integrity. Since the ecosystem is interrelated regardless of state borders, it is highly possible that AFOLU within one part of the ecosystem deteriorates other components of the ecosystem. For example, the draining of peatland in Indonesia causes its land to be prone to wildfires which trigger transboundary haze pollution. Imposing responsibility-to-restore on every AFOLU business which potentially affects the shared ecosystem or environmental medium may serve as a means to prevent transboundary harm.

3.3. PRINCIPLE OF INTER- AND INTRA-GENERATIONAL EQUITY

Restoration can be deemed one of the means to maintain equity among the present generation as to who bears the cost of the impact from activities that degrade the sinks, as well as equity for future generations to enjoy the ecosystem as much as the generation which enjoys the benefit of preserved sinks. The principle of intra and inter-generational equity under EPMA is addressed in the principle of conservation and sustainability under Article 2b.

Telesetsky et al. link this principle to the concept of corrective justice with a modification to the label of 'connective justice'.[45] Corrective justice in the realms of environmental justice usually demands environmental enforcement against violation and restoration for the harmed.[46] Furthermore, it has close links with the polluter pays principle.[47] Telesetsky et al. argue that the principle of intergenerational equity requires that the damage incurred to date must be repaired in order to ensure environmental justice for future generations.[48] While corrective justice accommodates greater justice among the same and present generation, connective justice is a form of corrective action that connects responsibility-to-restore the present harm with the concerns of generations to come.

3.4. POLLUTER PAYS PRINCIPLE

Although not being a part of climate treaties, it is worth noting that the polluter pays principle remains a principle of environmental law that has

45 A. Telesetsky, A. Cliquet, and A. Akhtar-Khavari, *Ecological Restoration in International Environmental Law*, Routledge, Abingdon 2017, pp. 288–289.

46 R. K. Kuehn, 'A Taxonomy of Environmental Justice' (2000) 30 *Environmental Law Reporter* 10693.

47 See next section.

48 Telesetsky, above n. 45.

direct relevance to the responsibility-to-restore. This principle is widely known as Principle 16 of the Rio Declaration and it also becomes one of the important principles under Indonesia's environmental law.[49] In the context of AFOLU, the principle does not entirely represent the demand for restoration – since restoration demands more than just rehabilitation (repairing the damage/pollution) – but leans more toward the revival of the ecosystem to be in accordance with certain standards which is most likely excluded from reparation.[50] From a conceptual standpoint, it is the most relevant.

The basic concept of the polluter pays principle revolves around the idea that polluters should bear the externality costs which are derived from their activities. The word 'polluter', however, must be stretched to cover damaging the environment not only by polluting, but also through any acts which cause natural depletion.[51] As it has developed, the application of this principle is not limited to internalisation of externality costs but extends also to liabilities, taxes, etc.[52] These inclusions are underpinned by the essence of equality in the polluter pays principle, which ensures that the victim or those harmed do not bear the cost of pollution or damage caused by the polluter/user.[53]

Connecting the principle with the restoration issue raises the problem regarding the restoration cap. Generally, there are two different views in defining the restoration cap.[54] The first view uses an ecosystem reference as restoration cap.[55] Meanwhile, the second view restores an ecosystem to its historical condition.[56]

The obstacle to using the former view lies in the scarcity of ecosystem references, as globalisation and development have continuously altered the environmental conditions significantly. Any changes in one area will likely affect other areas, even in the most pristine ecosystem. Furthermore, not all ecosystems

---

49 Article 2(j) EPMA.

50 Telesetsky et al. (above n. 45) suggest the label 'degrader pays principle' or 'user pays principle'.

51 P.E. Lindhout and B. van den Broek, 'The Polluter Pays Principle: Guidelines for Cost Recovery and Burden Sharing in the Case Law of the European Court of Justice' (2014) 10(2) Utrecht Law Review 46, quoting the Joint Working Party on Trade and Environment, The Polluter Pays Principle as it relates to international trade, OECD, COM/ENV/TD(2001)44/Final, 2002, p. 14; Y. Mossoux, 'Causation in the Polluter Pays Principle' (2010) 19(6) European Environmental Law Review 279, p. 282 in conjunction with M.N. Boeve & G.M. van den Broek, 'The Programmatic Approach: A Flexible and Complex Tool to Achieve Environmental Quality Standards' (2012) 8(3) Utrecht Law Review, pp. 74–85; M.N. Boeve & L. van Middelkoop, 'Sustainable Urban Development, the Dutch Method: Best practice for the European Integrated Approach?' (2010) 7(1) JEEPL, pp. 1–23; see differently: F. Stangl, P. Kaufmann and S. Sagl, Ökonomische Instrumente im Wasserschutz, Manz, Vienna 2012, pp. 39–40.

52 Lindhout and van den Broek, above n. 51.

53 Ibid.

54 Telesetsky et al., above n. 45, pp. 17–18.

55 Ibid.

56 Ibid.

have identical conditions. There is always a chance that using an ecosystem reference might undermine the distinct characteristic of the ecosystem that needs to be restored.

However, the challenge of using the latter view is in deciding the limits of 'historical condition'. The extent of historical condition can be either nearly unrealistic (if it is decided to refer to the natural state of the ecosystem before it was damaged by any anthropocene influences) or too pragmatic (if it is decided to go back only a few years prior to the occurrence of damage).[57] Since there is no explicit legal obligation on restoration yet, it is safe to conclude that it falls within the discretion of the state to determine which construction fits with the domestic law.

4. RESPONSIBILITY-TO-RESTORE UNDER CLIMATE TREATIES

Even though facts show that the contribution of emissions from AFOLU is substantial, the Paris Agreement pays very little attention to removal by sinks,[58] leaving a window of discretion for parties to determine the means for their implementation of climate mitigation. In addition, no explicit reference indicates that restoration should become a part of efforts to conserve and enhance sinks. Generally, it depends on the parties in determining what contribution they wish to make in order to achieve the overarching goal of the agreement through the NDCs.[59] The Paris Agreement undeniably emphasises the aim to perform rapid emissions reduction in bid to achieve a balance between anthropogenic emissions by sources of greenhouse gases and removals of such gases by sinks.[60] Regrettably, it is not incorporated in the forms of strong obligation.

Parties to the Paris Agreement should take action to conserve and enhance sinks and reservoirs of greenhouse gases, including forests.[61] Besides that, they are also obliged to provide incentives to, and facilitate participation by private entities in climate mitigation,[62] and to enhance participation of the private sector in regards to the implementation of the nationally determined contribution.[63] In respect to the existing REDD+ meanwhile, explicit reference to implementing

57 See the elaboration in: Ibid, p. 26–28.
58 P. Sands *et al.*, *Principles of International Environmental Law*, 4th ed., Cambridge University Press, Cambridge 2018, p. 323.
59 Article 4.2 Paris Agreement.
60 Article 4 Paris Agreement.
61 Article 5.1 Paris Agreement.
62 Article 6.4(b) Paris Agreement.
63 Article 6.8(b) Paris Agreement.

and supporting the programme exists under Article 5.2 Paris Agreement, but it doesn't constitute a strong obligation either.[64]

Due to vague provisions under the Paris Agreement, it is plausible to assume that the parties are not prohibited from applying policy to engage private entities within the framework to achieve their climate mitigation targets. It is undoubted that provisions under the Paris Agreement call for an obligation of means which are open for the parties to determine, rather than an obligation of result.[65] Article 6.8(b) Paris Agreement addresses the importance of enhancing public- and private-sector participation for the implementation of NDCs,[66] which allows for a broad interpretation. There are some references to public engagement, as discussed during one of the conferences on outputs from the parties, particularly the proposal on establishing a new mechanism for enhancing engagement of non-party stakeholders in enhancing the implementation of Paris Agreement, including engagement in achieving the NDCs.[67] Although the current discussion still puts more emphasis on transparency, access to information and public participation in developing implementation plans (and NDCs), the report notes the possibility of working towards a mechanism for engaging non-parties in the broader scope of implementation.[68]

Furthermore, the Conference of the Parties serving as the meeting of the Parties to the Paris Agreement (CMA) in Katowice in December 2018 attached the draft decision which provides for the parties to strive for the inclusion of all categories of anthropogenic emissions or removals and that they must explain the reason for excluding specific sources in the NDCs.[69] It could be interpreted that Indonesia must include not only land-based exploitation business as the source of emissions in its national inventory, but also the potential of this sector's contribution to enhancing removal by sinks. This proposal opens the opportunity to encourage a more binding action. Although this remains a subject for discussion, the draft affirms that Paris Agreement does not prohibit its parties from applying their national law to oblige permit holders to restore their concessions or from crediting restoration by private entities as a climate mitigation measure.

In climate summit rounds, a direct link to restoration is not entirely absent either. During the UN Climate Summit 2014, the New York Declaration on

---

64 Article 5.2 Paris Agreement.

65 Telesetksy et al., above n. 45, p. 83.

66 Article 6.8(b) Paris Agreement.

67 Subsidiary Body for Implementation of the UNFCCC, 'Views on opportunities to further enhance the effective engagement of non-Party stakeholders with a view to strengthening the implementation of the provisions of decision 1/CP.21', FCCC/SBI/2017/INF.3, 28 April 2017, paragraph 15.

68 Ibid. paragraph 21. 'The submissions note that low-emission development strategies will need the engagement of non-Party stakeholders during the implementation phase.'

69 CP Kyoto Protocol, 'Decision 4/CMA.1 Further guidance in relation to the mitigation section of decision 1/CP.21', Paragraph 12(c) and (d).

Forests was enacted, endorsing the 2020 Bonn Challenge and extending the target period to 2030. The Bonn Challenge itself is enthroned as the first globally acknowledged document in favour of concrete restoration action.[70] The Bonn Challenge aims to promote extended restoration efforts and set the goal for restoring the ecosystem at 150 MHa in 2020 and 350 MHa by 2030 around the globe.[71] In 2013, 10 principles of landscape restoration were claimed as representing the consensus opinion from a significant number of actors.[72]

The Committee of New York Declaration on Forests tracks the NDCs that incorporate ecosystem restoration as part of the parties' commitment to the Paris Agreement.[73] These instruments underpin the initiative to proactively engage private entities. As an example, one of the biggest companies in Indonesia and globally, i.e. Asia Pulp & Paper, filed and pledged its commitment to the Bonn Challenge, aiming to restore 1 million Ha by 2020.[74]

Recently, in March 2019, the UN Decade of Ecosystem Restoration 2021–2030, as proposed by El Salvador, was announced,[75] marking the emerging commitment to focus on ecosystem restoration which promotes the achievement of existing international commitments, with regard given to sustainable development goals and climate change goals, including the UNFCCC's REDD+.[76] The UN Decade re-emphasises the integration of ecosystem restoration with climate change efforts, especially the REDD+.

Under UNFCCC, the REDD+ framework is still evolving.[77] Nevertheless, the framework in the form of the REDD+ safeguards established in Cancun in 2010 has served as a critical guideline for countries involved in REDD+ project. It potentially credits forest restoration and rehabilitation as part of the scope of incentives.[78] Under the Warsaw Decision in 2013, the forest reference level

---

70 The Bonn Challenge, 'The history of the Challenge', http://www.bonnchallenge.org/content/history-challenge.

71 Ibid.

72 J. Sayer et al., 'Ten principles for a landscape approach to reconciling agriculture, conservation, and other competing land uses', 21 May 2013, (2013) 110(21) *Proceedings of the National Academy of Sciences of the USA* 8349, p. 8351, http://www.cifor.org/publications/pdf_files/articles/ASunderland1302.pdf.

73 Forest Declaration, 'GOAL 5: Restore 150 million hectares of degraded landscapes and forestlands by 2020 and significantly increase the rate of global restoration thereafter, which would restore at least an additional 200 million hectares by 2030', http://forestdeclaration.org/goal/goal-5/.

74 The Bonn Challenge, above n. 70, http://www.bonnchallenge.org/content/asia-pulp-paper.

75 UN Decade of Ecosystem Restoration 2021–2030, https://wedocs.unep.org/bitstream/handle/20.500.11822/26027/Ecosystem_decade_Salvador_Initiative.pdf?sequence=1&isAllowed=y.

76 The Bonn Challenge, above n. 70.

77 K. Austin et al., 'The REDD+ Decision in Cancun,' World Resource Institute, 20 December 2010, https://www.wri.org/blog/2010/12/redd-decision-cancun.

78 B. O'Sullivan and C. Streck, 'Forestry and Agriculture under the UNFCCC: A Jigsaw Waiting to be Assembled?' in K.R. Gray, R. Tarasofsky, and C. Carlarne (eds.), *The Oxford Handbook*

which is set by the host country to the REDD+ project is subject to technical assessment under UNFCCC.[79] It also encourages parties, including the private sector, to take action in reducing the drivers of emissions from the AFOLU sector.[80]

5. RESPONSIBILITY-TO-RESTORE IN INDONESIA

Moving from the international to the domestic level, the obligation for the Indonesian government to enforce the responsibility-to-restore has been stipulated under national law. Article 33 of the Indonesian Constitution (the Constitution)[81] sets out ground rules for acts concerning exploitation of natural resources and environment. The article underpins the importance of legislation pertaining to the national economy and social welfare by stating that natural resources shall be controlled by the state and utilised for the benefit of the people at the utmost. Furthermore, sustainability and environmental perceptions are explicitly mentioned as part of the basis for the national economy. All acts addressing exploitation of natural resources and the environment stipulate reference to sustainability, environmental protection, and conservation in various ways. To some extent, they share a common foundation on imposing responsibility to actively prevent environmental damage, and some of them also add responsibility to actively restore concession areas.

Responsibility-to-restore is usually designated as part of the obligations of holders of permits for natural-resources exploitation activities. However, it has not become a part of corporate social liability or other voluntary measures.[82] It should be noted that the Indonesian government has been making significant efforts to hold some private legal entities responsible for paying compensation toward restoration of forests or peatland areas within their concessions, such as in *Ministry of Environment and Forestry v. PT WAJ*.[83] However, based on the existing law, bringing this case before the civil courts would not be necessary if the authority managed to implement compliance monitoring and detect non-compliance indicators earlier, which would lead to

---

of International Climate Change Law (Online edition: November 2016), accessed online DOI: 10.1093/law/9780199684601.003.0025.

79 UNFCCC sites, 'Warsaw Framework for REDD-plus', available via https://unfccc.int/topics/land-use/resources/warsaw-framework-for-redd-plus, refer to Decision 13/CP.19.

80 Ibid., refer to Decision 15/CP.19.

81 Indonesian Constitution (Undang-Undang Dasar Negara Kesatuan Republik Indonesia tahun 1945), Article 33.

82 See comparison to CSR and voluntary measures in Telesetsky et al., above n. 45, pp. 214–216.

83 W. Soeriaatmadja, 'Firms yet to compensate for Indonesia forest fire', 16 February 2019, *The Straits Times*, https://www.straitstimes.com/asia/se-asia/firms-yet-to-compensate-for-indonesia-forest-fires.

the imposition of administrative enforcement, instead of filing a lawsuit that produces a considerably similar outcome: requiring the corporation to restore the forest/peatland. Such suggestion is derived from the authorisation given to government to impose administrative sanctions on entities which violate their obligation as environmental permit holders and/or natural-resource exploitation permit holders.[84] Conclusively, the enforcement authority is authorised to enforce responsibility-to-restore through administrative law enforcement. The following analysis will describe the legal opportunities and challenges for the government to uphold the responsibility-to-restore.

The concept of responsibility-to-restore exists under several acts concerning environmental protection and exploitation of natural resources. Regulation on exploitation of natural resources falls under the EPMA, as far as environmental protection and management are concerned. Under EPMA, all exploitations of natural resources are required to conduct an Environmental Impact Assessment (EIA) or Environmental Management and Monitoring Programmes (EMMP) (in Indonesia: UKL/UPL) prior to applying for an Environmental Permit (now Environmental Approval), which acts as the prerequisite to applying for a business permit for activity that causes impact to the environment.[85] Activity permits and other regulations relevant to each activity are governed under specific sectoral acts and the Act on Job Creation. As this section will focus on three major sectors, further analysis will shift its focus to the Plantation Act, the Mineral and Coal Mining Act (MCA), and the Forestry Act, with reference to the Job Creation Act.

5.1. ENVIRONMENTAL PROTECTION AND MANAGEMENT ACT

Pursuant to Article 54 EPMA, all polluters shall be held responsible for restoring environmental function.[86] The definition of polluters is confined to those who have been proven to pollute or damage the environment.[87] Such condition indicates that the provision applies only to concession holders

---

84 Article 76 EPMA.

85 By the time this contribution is published, a significant alteration to Indonesia's permit system in general has occurred due to the enactment of the Act on Job Creation No. 11 of 2020. It includes the deletion of the Environmental Permit, now replaced by Environmental Approval.

86 Article 54 EPMA.

87 Anotasi Undang-Undang Nomor 32 Tahun 2009 tentang Perlindungan dan Pengelolaan Lingkungan Hidup. Ed. 1. (Indonesian Center for Environmental Law, 2014), available only in Indonesian. *Annotation on the Act No. 32 year 2009 on Environmental Protection and Management, 1st ed., (Indonesian Center for Environmental Law, 2014).*

whose activities have evidently surpassed environmental pollution and/or destruction caps. In connection with such provision, it is thus premature to conclude that palm-oil, coal-mining and forest-utilisation permit holders may be held responsible for restoration in the absence of evidence showing that their activities have surpassed the environmental pollution and/or destruction caps. Consequently, the enforcement authority has to possess reasonable evidence showing that permit holders have exceeded the ambient cap.

There are two sources of ambient caps which may be used by the authority as a reference point: the ambient cap under ambient-cap regulations, and the assessment of the ambient standard in an EIA. One of the caps that need to be adjusted is the climate change damage cap, comprising the indicators of temperature, sea-level rise, storm and/or drought.[88] However, the first problem which is encountered by the authority is that the caps were adjusted by national government using a top-down method, while the ideal cap should be based on an environmental inventory and a carrying-capacity assessment which should be derived from a bottom-up assessment.[89] Secondly, a handful of EIAs are not reliable, and their quality is far from being adequate.[90] Nevertheless, insofar that the caps are relevant for a particular activity and the authority is able to prove that the activity has exceeded the cap, responsibility-to-restore is enforceable via administrative sanction[91] or a civil-liability mechanism.[92]

Another relevant provision to responsibility-to-restore under EPMA refers to the polluter pays principle.[93] Basically, the principle emphasises the responsibility of polluters to pay the cost of the pollution caused by them.[94] The elucidation of this principle under the EPMA specifically indicates that every responsible entity whose business and/or activities cause environmental pollution and/or degradation shall bear the environmental restoration costs. Both Article 54 EPMA and the polluter pays principle are simultaneously applicable to enforce responsibility-to-restore, but some challenges continue to exist. What about those who comply with the regulation? Will they still be subject to responsibility-to-restore? What if the concession activity is not the sole activity causing the pollution and/or damage? Despite these limitations, this principle may complement and set the ground for strengthening enforcement in favour of environmental protection within other sectors, as will be explained in the next three sub-sections.

---

88 Article 21 para. (4) EPMA.

89 Articles 5, 8, 14(c), 20, 21 EPMA.

90 OECD, *OECD Environmental Performance Reviews OECD Green Growth Policy Review of Indonesia 2019* (OECD, 2019), p. 110.

91 Article 76 EPMA, despite amendment by the Job Creation Act.

92 Indonesian Center for Environmental law, above n. 87.

93 Article 2(j) EPMA.

94 P. Sands, above n. 58, p. 240.

5.2. MINERAL AND COAL MINING ACT

One of the objectives of MCA is to ensure the benefit of sustainable and environmentally-sound mineral and coal mining.[95] Such objective is incorporated in the provision that obliges coal-mining-exploitation permit holders to comply with laws and regulations within the sector of environmental management. The scope of environmental management covers management and monitoring of reclamation of mined lands and post-mining activities,[96] as well as provisions under the EPMA which are applicable to permit holders.

Both MCA and EPMA can be applied in a conjoined manner, allowing the authorities to demand responsibility-to-restore upon two basic rationales. First, the permit holder is responsible for restoring the land by conducting reclamation and post-mining restoration. Second, the quality of restoration must achieve a sustainable and environmentally sound objective. However, this legal construction will only work in favour of the restoration goal, provided that the quality of the cap is adequately determined, and the enforcement works effectively.

Although the legal provisions are clear, hectares of pit mining have been abandoned after over 10 years since the enactment of the MCA.[97] The highlighted legal problem here is claimed to be – setting aside the indication of corruption – the lack of procedural certainty for permit holders to conduct reclamation and post-mining, including guidance on the quality of post-mining restoration which should be achieved by permit holders.[98] Based on the underlying legislative logic of the Act on Legislation Drafting,[99] the objective of the Act must be used as the quality standard to determine the outcome of provisions in its legal text. Thus, the outcome of reclamation and post-mining must achieve sustainable and environmentally-sound conditions. Even though the term 'sustainable and environmentally-sound' remains considerably vague, the regulator (executive authority) is able to adjust the standard to be in favour of restoring forests and peatlands, insofar that the area falls under one or both categories.

---

95 Article 3 Act No. 4 year 2009 as ammended by Act No. 3 year 2020 and Act No. 11 year 2020 (MCA).

96 Article 96b jo. 39 MCA.

97 See for example: https://www.thejakartapost.com/news/2019/02/13/jokowi-saves-forests-but-fails-to-resolve-land-mining-conflicts.html; https://www.insideindonesia.org/samarinda-s-deadly-mining-pits; https://news.mongabay.com/2017/05/who-owns-indonesias-deadly-abandoned-coal-mines/.

98 Publish What You Pay Indonesia (PWYP) and KPK, 'Administration of Coal Permit Under Coordination and Supervision of KPK', 1st ed., 2017.

99 Article 5(a) Act on Legislation Drafting, (Undang-Undang Republik Indonesia Nomor 12 Tahun 2011).

5.3. PLANTATION ACT

In contrast to the MCA, the Plantation Act does not explicitly mention the duty of permit holders in regard to mandatory activities subsequent to the expiration of the permit period. It, nonetheless, provides an umbrella rule to maintain the preservation of the environment in accordance with environmental regulations.[100] In regard to the prerequisites for securing the permit, there was an article re-emphasises the applicant's obligation to be in possession of an approved EIA, risk and management risk assessment (for those who use genetically modified substances), and a statement on the applicant's ability to provide adequate infrastructures to prevent fire.[101] Although the latter has been repealed by the recent amendment, the remaining provisions related to environmental obligation are still connected with environmental regulation. Therefore it must be interpreted in parallel with EPMA.

The polluter pays principle and other relevant provisions under the EPMA should be applicable to plantation activities. Based on Article 21(3) EPMA, the criteria of environmental damage must be addressed to determine the occurrence of environmental damage. Article 21(3)(f) functions as the basis for Government Regulation on Peatland Ecosystem Protection and Management, which further lays out the criteria for environmental damage in peatland, i.e. what level of degradation constitutes the cap for peatland. Every activity which is conducted within peatland areas must adhere to such cap.

This argument has been used as one of the legal bases by the government to impose sanctions on corporations which allegedly cause peatland fire in their concessions.[102] The sanction usually encompasses the duty-to-restore the peatland to meet the cap. This approach can be a way to ensure that permit holders should maintain peatland in accordance with the caps not only during the active planting and harvesting periods, but also near to the expiration of the permit period; thus responsibility-to-restore is upheld.

5.4. FORESTRY ACT

All permit holders which operate within forestry areas are attributed with the duty to keep, maintain, and preserve forestry areas within their concessions.[103]

---

100 Article 67(1), (2) Plantation Act, Act No. 39 year 2014 as partially amended by Act No. 11 year 2020 on Job Creation.

101 Article 67(3) Plantation Act was deleted in Act No. 11 year 2020. On the latest draft of implementing regulations, however, these obligations are still existing.

102 Avit Hidayat, 'Forest Fire: 30 Companies Slapped with Administrative Sanctions', *Tempo.co*, 29 August 2016, https://en.tempo.co/read/799688/forest-fire-30-companies-slapped-with-administrative-sanctions.

103 Article 32 Forestry Act, Act No. 4 year 1999 as amended by Act No. 9 year 2004 and Act No. 11 year 2020.

This provision not only applies to forest-utilisation permit holders, but also to coal-mining permit holders within forestry areas.[104] Moreover, this Act also regulates the duty of mining permit holders to restore forests within their concessions.[105]

Similarly to the arguments outlined in section 5.2 above for the MAC, this provision has the potential to act as a strong basis for authorities to enforce the responsibility of forest-utilisation permit holders to conduct restoration. Since the area of concession was and should remain as a forest, this provision indirectly imposes the duty for permit holders to keep, maintain and preserve the area to remain as 'forest'. Ultimately, it opens a chance to apply reforestation as the cap for restoration.

Despite the legitimate power to enforce responsibility-to-restore degraded land under the four abovementioned acts, there is no direct provision which may link it to the obligation to conduct climate mitigation; hence, it remains within the government's discretion. Considering that the obligation to enforce responsibility-to-restore is quite strong, as supported by the existence of principles of environmental law under the EPMA, it is logical to assume that it is only a matter of political will from the government to incorporate it as part of mitigation measures. The next challenge is to determine to what extent the restoration must be conducted and how to ensure the fair share of responsibility. Both matters are completely beyond the scope of this contribution. In terms of mitigation, the EPMA and the Forestry Act provide the most relevant outcomes. EPMA basically is applicable for the mining, plantation and forestry sectors. The Forestry Act is applicable insofar that the damaging activities were conducted in the areas designated as forest.

6. CONCLUSION

A restoration programme through the enforcement of responsibility-to-restore is yet to be implemented; nor has it been acknowledged as one of the sources of removal by sinks in Indonesia's climate mitigation commitment. However, responsibility-to-restore by private entities addresses the essence of principles of environmental law which have already incorporated under Indonesian law. Among other things, the principles that can be used to shape responsibility-to-restore as part of climate mitigation measures include the precautionary

104 Article 38(3) Forestry Act. Although the phrase 'coal-mining' has been deleted by Act 11 year 2020, practically the provision refers to several activities that include coal-mining activities. Plantation is not allowed in the forest area without initially transforming the status of the forest.

105 Article 45 Forestry Act.

principle, the non-transboundary harm principle, the principle of intra and intergenerational equity, and the polluter pays principle.

International climate legal instruments have acknowledged restoration as part of climate mitigation efforts, such as through REDD+ implementation and the New York Declaration on Forests. Furthermore, the Paris Agreement opens a window for supporting the attribution of a duty of restoration in climate mitigation by providing open provisions and imposing no restriction. Therefore, Indonesia can initiate attribution of private entities' responsibility-to-restore in their climate mitigation effort under the climate treaties' commitment. Not only does this become part of its international commitment, but also national law provides possibility for the implementation of responsibility-to-restore by private entities as part of the country's mitigation measures. In Indonesia, coal-mining, palm-oil-plantation and forest-utilisation permit holders are bound by the responsibility-to-restore their concessions as an inherent consequence of exploiting natural resources according to Indonesian law. The sectoral laws in conjunction with environmental law underpin a strong provision that obliges government to hold permit holders responsible to restore the utilised areas. Although the prevailing Acts do not provide a direct link between responsibility-to-restore and climate change mitigation, a broader interpretation of the restoration cap might be used to draw the link.

PART III

TOOLS FOR HALTING THE LOSS OF BIODIVERSITY

RIGHTS OF NATURE AS AN UNLIKELY SAVIOUR FOR THE EU'S THREATENED SPECIES AND HABITATS

A Critical Introduction to a Revolutionary Idea

Hendrik SCHOUKENS

1. WHAT IF?

Imagine one of the last wild hamsters, an EU protected species, wandering around on an empty and pesticide-ridden piece of cropland in Belgium.[1] Or take the case of a young she-wolf, straddling the borders between Belgium, the Netherlands and Germany. Let us assume a male following her all the way into Belgium and the pair having cubs together in spring. Five months later, the male reportedly stopped bringing food to the den; the she-wolf had disappeared. Rumour has it that some hunters agreed to secretly kill the she-wolf and her cubs in order to rid their hunting grounds of 'invaders'. This leaves the male wolf a 'lone wolf'.[2]

Who should speak up for these 'harmed' species that are strictly protected under Union law? In both instances, our legal order does not allow nature to stand up for its own rights. It is to remain voiceless. Nature does not possess legally enforceable rights, not even moral rights. Although wolves and wild hamsters are protected by the 1992 EU Habitats Directive,[3] they can only be indirectly represented in court by environmental organisations or governmental bodies. Yet can one really be serious about the protection of the intrinsic value

---

1 See more on this: J. O'Brien, 'Saving the common hamster (*Cricetus cricetus*) from extinction in Alsace (France): potential flagship species conservation or an exercise in futility?' (2015) 26(2) *Hystrix (the Italian Journal of Mammalogy)* 89.

2 This is based on actual facts that happened in Flanders. See: *Brussels Times*, 1 October 2019, https://www.brusselstimes.com/all-news/belgium-all-news/70979/flemish-hunters-organisation-accused-of-killing-wolf-naya-to-sue-for-libel/.

3 Council Directive 92/43/EEC on the conservation of natural habitats and of wild fauna and flora [1992] OJ L206/7.

of species without granting them explicit substantive rights?[4] Faced with the underperformance of the existing governance structures,[5] the obscure idea of granting legal rights to nature has garnered more attention lately, with explicit recognition of rights of nature in numerous jurisdictions, such as New-Zealand[6] and Ecuador.[7] With rivers and wider ecosystems being endowed with legal personality and legal rights elsewhere in the world, this chapter critically engages with this novel discourse and explores to what extent it can further the protection of the environment in the European Union. It contemplates the specific role of law in the fundamental transition to a sustainable future, straddling the border between morality, on the one hand, and positive law on the other hand.

2. SYSTEMIC DEFICIENCIES AND RIGHTS OF NATURE AS A NEW NORMATIVE AND MORAL DISCOURSE

The starting point of this analysis is the existing EU environmental legislation, which is the result of many years of growing environmental awareness. Unfortunately, the biodiversity decline in the EU[8] has not yet been stopped in spite of minor successes in terms of the recovery of certain large predators.[9] Poor enforcement and a lack of proper implementation can certainly be singled out as the prominent causes of this glaring underperformance.[10] However, a growing number of authors claim the anthropocentric nature of the existing regulatory schemes lies at the heart of their failure.[11] Many critical observers would automatically agree that even the much heralded 1992 EU

4 S. Emmenegger and A. Tschentscher, 'Taking Nature's Rights Seriously: The Long Way to Biocentrism in Environmental Law' (1994) 6 *Georgetown International Environmental Law Review* 545, 571–572.

5 See more on this: C. Wood, *Nature's Trust. Environmental Law for a New Ecological Age*, Cambridge University Press, Cambridge 2014.

6 A. Hutchison, 'The Whanganui River as a Legal Person' (2014) 39(3) *Alternative Law Journal* 179, https://doi.org/10.1177/1037969X1403900309.

7 L. Kotze and P.V. Caldzadilla, 'Somewhere between Rhetoric and Reality: Environmental Constitutionalism and the Rights of Nature in Ecuador' (2017) 6(3) *Transnational Environmental Law* 401.

8 European Environment Agency, *The European Environment: State and Outlook 2015: Synthesis Report*, 2015.

9 See: G. Chapron et al., 'Recovery of large carnivores in Europe's modern human-dominated landscapes' (2014) 346 *Science* 1517.

10 Milieu Ltd., *Evaluation Study to support the Fitness Check of the Birds and Habitats Directives*, Final Report March 2016.

11 See for instance: C. Cullinan, *Wild Law. A Manifesto for Earth Justice*, Green Books, Cambridge 2011.

Habitats Directive does not explicitly grant legal rights or personhood to endangered species. And although it can have sharp teeth when effectively applied, it appears inherently incapable of halting the exacerbated biodiversity losses in recent times. In part, this is because the 1992 EU Habitats Directive is incapable of reversing the myriad of institutional, legal and policy-related lock-ins that prioritize short-term economic gains over environmental considerations and extinction risks. It still is easier to win elections with the promise of more jobs and economic prosperity than the prospect of saving some species from imminent extinction.

Thus, the question arises who is to speak up for species whose survival is threatened by human actions? As Advocate-General Sharpston put it in the *Trianel* case, 'The fish cannot go to Court.'[12] Action needs to come from stakeholders representing the public interest, such as concerned citizens or, as the case may be, non-governmental organisations (NGOs). Within the framework of the 1998 Aarhus Convention,[13] environmental NGOs are granted standing in environmental cases so as to ensure a better enforcement of environmental legislation. But environmental NGOs also have to make difficult and tough strategic choices, meaning that not every ecological encroachment can be litigated in court.[14] Concerned citizens are often not granted automatic standing in environmental cases, which might generate certain loopholes in environmental protection. It is therefore not surprising to see a growing number of environmentalists becoming increasingly eager to champion or at least contemplate a more rights-based approach to nature conservation and environmental governance as a whole.[15] Under this novel template, the intrinsic value of ecosystems and nature is acknowledged and placed at the centre of the legal order. In furtherance of this approach, ecosystems are granted legal personhood, meaning that appointed guardians can enforce their substantive rights.[16] Likewise, their right to exist is explicitly recognised in positive law and can be enforced through court actions.[17]

---

12 This is a quote from the oral hearing in the Case C-115/09, *Bund für Umwelt und Naturschutz Deutschland, Landesverband Nordrhein-Westfalen eV v Bezirksregierung Arnsberg, Trianel Kohlekraftwerk Lünen (intervening)* Opinion of AG Sharpston, [2011] ECR I-03673 ECLI:EU:C:2010:773.

13 Convention on Access to Information, Public Participation in Decision-making and Access to Justice in Environmental Matters, done at Aarhus, Denmark, 25 July 1998 ('Aarhus Convention') (1999) 2161 UNTS 447.

14 See: Wood, above n. 5, pp. 115–117.

15 See amongst others: D. Boyd, *The Rights of Nature, A Legal Revolution that Could Save The World* (ECW Press, Toronto 2017).

16 For an overview, see: D. Shelton, 'Nature as a legal person' (2015) *Vertigo -La Revue Electronique en Sciences de L'environnement* (Hors-Série 22), https://journals.openedition.org/vertigo/16188.

17 Ibid.

3. WHERE DOES THE IDEA STEM FROM?

Christopher Stone's ground-breaking article 'Should trees have standing?'[18] is to be regarded as one of the catalysts for the rights of nature movements. To quote his own words, Stone was 'quite seriously proposing that we give legal rights to forests, oceans, rivers and other so-called "natural objects" in the environment – indeed, to the natural environment as a whole'.[19] This was no less than a paradigm shift in the legal discourse back in the 1970s. According to Stone, the concept of legal personhood has to be viewed as one end of a continuum granting an entity certain rights based on its intrinsic value rather than its instrumental or economic value to others. However, the often prevailing Cartesian and dualistic thinking is notable for reducing nature to a mere 'commodity' or a 'machine', ready to be explored by scientists and turned to good use for mankind.[20] Even so, it is important to understand that Stone's approach, which was subsequently translated into a plea for 'biotic rights' by Nash,[21] was that of a lawyer, not that of a philosopher. Stone had to come to terms with the decision of the Ninth Circuit Court of Appeals that had ruled that the Sierra Club Legal Defense Fund lacked legal standing to halt the proposed development of the Mineral King Valley in the Sierra Nevada Mountains by Walt Disney Enterprises, Inc.[22] He opined that if the Mineral King Valley had been recognised as a rights holder, it would have been an affected party and the Sierra Club might be authorised to represent it before court.[23]

Ultimately, the U.S. Supreme Court was not swayed by Stone's last-minute plea.[24] However, Stone still managed to convince the Supreme Court Justice William O. Douglas, who paid extensive lip service to this groundbreaking thesis.[25] In turn, Stone further fleshed out his theory. He argued that since streams and species have no rights under the terms of the existing normative framework, they do not have standing. Second, they also lack strict substantive protection in the face of significant destruction. And even if they are indirectly protected through a court ruling, there appears to be no certainty that they will ultimately be the beneficiary of a favourable judicial decision.[26] In order to remedy these inherent flaws of the existing legal system, Stone proposed a radical new guardianship approach, which would not only enable

---

[18] C.D. Stone, 'Should Trees Have Standing? Towards Legal Rights for Natural Objects' (1972) 45 *Southern Californian Law Review* 450.

[19] Ibid. p. 456.

[20] Ibid. pp. 17–18.

[21] J. Nash, 'The case for Biotic Rights' (1993) 18 *Yale Journal of International Law* 235.

[22] *Sierra Club v. Hickel*, 433 F.2d 24 (9th Cir. 1970), aff'd sub nom. *Sierra Club v. Morton*, 405 U.S. 727 (1972).

[23] Stone, above n. 18, pp. 470–475.

[24] *Sierra Club v. Morton*, 405 U.S. 727 (1972).

[25] Ibid., at 741–742 (Douglas, J., dissenting).

[26] Stone, above n. 18, pp. 480–481.

guardians to initiate lawsuits on behalf of threatened species or ecosystems, but also would endow the latter with inherent rights, including the right to exist.[27] As a result, private citizens are also afforded the possibility to enforce the legal protection duties linked to ecosystems.

4. A LOGICAL COUNTERMOVEMENT?

Stone's work draws on previous insights from influential thinkers like Charles Darwin. In his ground-breaking work, Darwin noted that the history of man's moral development is to be regarded as a continued expansion of his 'social instincts and sympathies'.[28] In a similar vein, Charles Darwin observed the difference between humans and other animals to be one 'of degree, not of kind'.[29] Likewise, Aldo Leopold's landmark work 'The Land Ethic', which contemplated 'the right to continued existence' of not only animals and plants but waters and soils as well, clearly impacted Stone's writing.[30] Reference should also be made to the Australian philosopher Tom Regan, who explicitly advocated the granting of certain substantive rights to animals, including the fundamental right to be treated with the respect that, as possessors of inherent value, they are due as a matter of strict justice.[31]

In the past decades we have also noted a sharp rise in the so-called 'Earth Jurisprudence' movement. One of the most vocal champions of this new environmental movement, Thomas Berry, submitted that 'there can be no sustainable future, even for the modern industrial world, unless the ... inherent rights of the natural world are recognized as having legal status'.[32] According to his approach, mankind is merely a part of nature rather than outside of it. This approach was subsequently refined by authors like Cormac Cullinan.[33]

Against this backdrop, it is not surprising to see rights of nature specifically emerge in jurisdictions where indigenous people like the Maori and Native Americans are granted more explicit legal recognition.[34] One of the first laws in which legal personhood was granted to a river was passed in New Zealand, when the New Zealand government decided in 2017 to promulgate a bill recognising

---

27 Ibid. pp. 471–472.

28 C. Darwin, *The Descent of Man and Selection in Relation to Sex*, revised edn. American Publishers Corp, New York 1874, p. 41.

29 Ibid. at 98.

30 A. Leopold, 'The Land Ethic' in Leopold, *A Sand County Almanac*, Oxford University Press, New York 1949, pp. 204–211.

31 T. Regan, *The Case for Animal Rights*, University of California Press, Berkeley CA 1983 (Updated 2004), pp. 328–329.

32 T. Berry, *The Great Work: Our Way into the Future*, Bell Tower, 1999, pp. 60–61.

33 Cullinan, above n. 11, pp. 100–110.

34 E.C. Hsao, 'Whanganui River Agreement – Indigenous Rights and Rights of Nature' (2012) 42(6) *Environmental Policy and Law* 371.

the Whanganui River as holding rights and responsibilities equivalent to a person.[35] In the provisions of the law, the river's ecosystem is recognised as a spiritual living being.[36] A similar evolution has been noted in Ecuador, where from 2008 onwards Article 71 of the redrafted constitution states that Mother Nature not only has the right to exist but also to have the 'maintenance and regeneration of its life cycles, structures, functions, and evolutionary processes' respected.[37] Rights of nature have recently also manifested themselves in the United States and Columbia, where, outside the specific context of the struggle of indigenous peoples for more recognition and political rights,[38] the clear-cut link between rights of nature and non-Western approaches to nature cannot be denied.

5. WHAT DOES IT EXACTLY ENTAIL?

In recent years, Earth Jurisprudence has been translated into positive law in an increasing number of jurisdictions, bridging the gap between moral and legal rights. The new normative framework of granting legal personhood has yielded different manifestations of legal rights of nature, which are succinctly presented below.[39]

5.1. SCOPE OF THE PERSONHOOD?

When lawmakers or judges decide to grant legal personhood to nature, they usually opt to conceptualise nature in a very broad manner. For instance, the Ecuadorian Constitution decided to grant rights to Pacha Mama, 'where life is reproduced and occurs'. No specific delimitation of nature is put forward here.[40] However, in most other jurisdictions, parliaments as well as national courts have opted to grant certain legal rights to specific ecosystems. In New Zealand, for instance, this was the case for the Whanganui River (Te Awa Tupua Act) and the forest Te Urewera (Te Urewera Act).[41] It is notable that none of the recently adopted legislation contemplates an explicit recognition of the rights of particular endangered species, although some lawsuits have already been

---

35 Te Awua Tupua Act 2017, Public Act, no. 71.

36 Ibid, section 12.

37 Ecuadorian Constitution (as revised in 2008). Art. 71.

38 For an overview, see: C.M. Kauffman and P.L. Martin, 'Constructing Rights of Nature Norms in the US, Ecuador, and New Zealand' (2018) 18(4) *Global Environmental Politics* 43, 53–55.

39 Ibid. pp. 48–52.

40 Ibid. 49.

41 E.L. O'Donnell and J. Talbot-Jones, 'Creating legal rights for rivers: lessons from Australia, New Zealand, and India' (2018) 23(1) *Ecology and Society* 7.

initiated on behalf of an endangered species.[42] As for the lawsuits initiated on behalf of captive chimpanzees and killer whales, they have received a non-favourable appraisal by the U.S. courts until now.[43] In Argentina, similar claims related to animals held in captivity received a more positive treatment,[44] and an Indian court recently upheld that 'like humans, animals also have natural rights which ought to be recognized'.[45]

5.2. WHAT TYPE OF LEGAL RIGHTS ARE RECOGNISED?

The next question that arises is which substantive rights are to be granted to nature. As of today, a diverse picture emerges. The Ecuadorian Constitution, for instance, shows a remarkably progressive approach, granting nature the right to exist, to maintain its integrity as an ecosystem, and to regenerate 'its life cycles, structure, functions and evolutionary processes'.[46] In addition, nature also has the right to be restored.[47] Interestingly, some U.S. ordinances go one step further and explicitly recognise the right of nature to flourish,[48] while the legislation in New Zealand basically restricts itself to recognising said ecosystems as legal persons with 'all the rights, powers, duties and liabilities of a legal person'.[49]

5.3. STANDING AND GUARDIANSHIP?

A last point to be addressed is the issue of standing, which was central to Stone's plea for granting rights to nature. In jurisdictions like Ecuador, everyone can and should defend the environment.[50] This could be framed as an '*actio popularis*' approach, while in other jurisdictions specific guardians are appointed, either

---

42 See this case brought by Greenpeace in the Supreme Court of Argentina: https://www.theguardian.com/environment/2019/jul/19/jaguar-argentina-legal-rights-gran-chaco-endangered.

43 For an overview, see: A. Staker, 'Should Chimpanzees Have Standing? The Case for Pursuing Legal Personhood for Non-Human Animals' (2017) 6(3) *Transnational Environmental Law* 485.

44 City Court of Buenos Aires (21 October 2015). 'Argentinian court decides if keeping orangutan in zoo is a human rights violation', *The Independent*, 15 May 2015, https//:www.independent.co.uk/news/world/americas/argentininian-court-decides-if-keeping-oranutan-zoo-human-rights-violation-10252010.html.

45 Islamabad High Court (21 May 2020). https//:www.24newshd.tv/21-May-2020/Elephant-wins-case-in-islamabad-high-court.

46 Ecuadorian Constitution, Article 71.

47 Ibid. Article 72.

48 Kaufmann and Martin, above n. 38, pp. 49–50.

49 Ibid.

50 Ecuadorian Constitution, Article 71.

by the court or the legislation. In New Zealand a mixed guardianship approach prevailed. For instance, the rights of the river Te Awa Tupua are to be defended by representatives both of the Maori communities and of the New Zealand government.[51]

5.4. HIERARCHY OF NORMS AND NATURE?

Recognising the rights of nature does not imply that these rights will automatically prevail. Evidently, the inclusion of rights of nature in the constitutional legal order will enhance its legal relevance. This is the case in Ecuador, where more recent case-law has illustrated the transversal character of the rights of nature, which also allows them to override property rights in some instances. Even so, this jurisprudence is still in flux.[52] At the other end of the spectrum, New Zealand's Te Awa Tupa Act seems to underscore the systemic premise it is based on: the river now enjoys statutory personhood and can no longer be privatised for private economic interests. However, this has not yet led to a transfer of the existing property rights in the riverbed.

6. THE BROADER LEGAL-PHILOSOPHICAL DEBATE

It is fair to say that Stone's ideas did not pass unnoticed. Stone himself proactively anticipated some of the predictable criticism that would befall him.

> Throughout legal history, each successive extension of rights to some new entity has been ... a bit unthinkable. We are inclined to suppose the rightlessness of rightless 'things' to be a decree of Nature, not a legal convention acting in support of some status quo.[53]

Yet how should we appraise the most common and persistent objections?

6.1. A SOCIAL CONTRACT VERSUS CONTRAT NATUREL?

An often recurring argument is that nonhumans are not part of the social contract that is underpinning our society. For instance, when dealing with a claim filed

---

51 See for instance: Te Urewera Act 2014, Public Act, no. 51, section 21.

52 For a detailed analysis see: C.M. Kaufmann and P.M. Martin, 'Can Rights of Nature Make Development More Sustainable? Why some Ecuadorian Lawsuits Succeed and Others Fail' (2017) 92 *World Development* 130.

53 Stone, above n. 18, at 453.

on behalf of a chimpanzee kept in captivity, the New York Supreme Court held that 'legal personhood has consistently been defined in terms of both rights and duties'. The Court finally held that it was the chimpanzee's 'incapability to bear any legal responsibilities and societal duties that renders it inappropriate to confer upon chimpanzees … legal rights'.[54] This train of thought is reminiscent of Rawls' contractarianism, which is famously highlighted in his magnum opus *A Theory of Justice*.[55] As animals are merely 'moral patients', Rawls posited that 'there are no requirements at all with regard to them'.[56]

Although this skeptical stance appears persuasive, it is certainly not flawless either. For instance, human moral patients, such as incompetents, also lack the capacity to express their will.[57] Even if incompetents or, for instance, small children, have no direct duties towards us, this does not entail that they are rightless. Moreover, recent research[58] has given more credit to Lovelock's Gaia theory, which holds that the combined physical, chemical and biological components of the earth system regulate the planet so as to maintain it as a habitat for life.[59] In several studies, it has now been acknowledged that the weak version of the Gaia theory – which states that there are close links between the evolution of life and the environment, and that biology affects the physical and chemical environment – is credible. But on a more fundamental level, one should note that social contract arguments, which were put forward during the Enlightenment by political philosophers like Locke, Hobbes and Rousseau, typically posit that individuals consent, either explicitly or tacitly, to surrender some of their freedoms and to submit to the authority (of the ruler, or to the decision of a majority) in exchange for protection of their remaining individual rights or maintenance of the social order. In a manner similar to the social contract theorists, the French philosopher Michel Serres suggested that mankind should sign a 'natural contract' with the earth to bring balance and reciprocity to our relations with the planet that gives us life.[60] Thus, it remains perfectly possible to rethink the existing social contract theories of emerging ecological insights, which mitigate the anthropocentric underpinnings of our existing normative frameworks and lay more emphasis on the interdependence of humans and nature. Differently put, revisiting Serres' approach, would basically come down to swapping an exclusively human-centred fictitious social contract for a more ecocentric understanding of our interdependence with nature.

---

54 *The Nonhuman Rights Project Inc., on behalf of Tommy v. Patrick C. Lavery*, N.Y. Supp. Ct., Appellate Division, Third Judicial Dept, 4 December 2014.

55 J. Rawls, *A Theory of Justice*, Harvard University Press, Cambridge MA, 1971.

56 Ibid. p. 512.

57 Stone, above n. 18, pp. 451–452.

58 See: I. Enting, 'Gaia theory: is it science yet?', https://theconversation.com/gaia-theory-is-it-science-yet-4901.

59 J.E. Lovelock, 'Gaia as seen through the atmosphere' (1972) 6(8) *Atmospheric Environment* 579.

60 M. Serres, *Le contrat natural*, Champs Essais, Paris 1990 (2020).

6.2. WHY RIGHTS?

As regards the usage of the concept of 'rights', Rolston posited that 'the concept of rights that has worked so well to protect human dignity is a hallmark of recent cultural progress. The rights model, however, proves troublesome when used to protect the biological world'.[61] While powerful at first sight, the criticism does not necessary hold up under scrutiny. Irrespective of the fact that some human beings are 'mere' moral patients, which prevents them from expressing their own desires and beliefs, it is also vital to reiterate that there are two competing theories underlying the concept of subjecthood in law. On the one hand, supporters of the so-called will or choice theories assume that rights are the protection of the rights-holder's free will, freedom of choice or a range of possibilities to make decisions about the self.[62] Yet champions of the so-called interest theories, such as Joseph Raz, approach rights as interests that the lawmakers regard as deserving of legal protection against third parties.[63] So, if we decide to grant legal rights to corporations and incompetents, why not do the same for rivers and animals?

Along similar lines, the notion of rights is closely related to the concept of moral responsibility. The Kantian principle 'ought implies can', presupposes that morality is based upon the premise that you are capable of choosing what to do. Enter the notion of free will. Yuval Noah Harari held that

> [h]umans certainly have a will – but it isn't free. You cannot decide what desires you have. You don't decide to be introvert or extrovert, easy-going or anxious, gay or straight. Humans make choices – but they are never independent choices. Every choice depends on a lot of biological, social and personal conditions that you cannot determine for yourself.[64]

If we accept that our morality is rooted more in our genes than in our rational thought, then we ought to question the human exceptionalism underpinning much of the existing legal schemes.[65] As Mark Rowlands puts it: 'Our (human) morality is rooted in our biology rather than our intellect'.[66] Against this backdrop, the idea of explicitly 'granting' certain rights to nature – instead of human duties towards nature – no longer appears off-chart.

61 H. Rolston, 'Rights and Responsibilities on the Home Planet' (1993) 18 *Yale Journal of International Law* 251.

62 P. Graham, 'The Will Theory of Rights: A Defence' (1996) 15(3) *Law and Philosophy* 257.

63 J. Raz, *The Morality of Freedom*, Clarendon Press, Oxford 1986, pp. 178–182.

64 Y.N. Harari, 'The myth of free will', *The Guardian* (14 September 2018), https://www.theguardian.com/books/2018/sep/14/yuval-noah-harari-the-new-threat-to-liberal-democracy.

65 T. Pietrzykowski, *Personhood Beyond Humanism. Animals, Chimeras, Autonomous Agents and the Law*, Springer, 2018, p. 76.

66 M. Rowlands, 'The kindness of beasts. Dogs rescue their friends and elephants care for injured kin – humans have no monopoly on moral behaviour', https://aeon.co/essays/if-a-lion-did-a-good-deed-would-we-understand-it.

6.3. WHAT IS PRECISELY IN NATURE'S INTEREST?

In line with the above objections, some authors, like Sagoff, mocked Stone's usage of rights by stating that it is simply impossible to know what nature's interest is. 'Why', Sagoff stated, 'wouldn't Mineral King (mountain) want to host a ski resort after doing nothing for a billion years?'.[67] This refutation, even if it appears plausible at first sight, also merits further consideration. For one, when focusing on animals, recent research has indeed underpinned the premise that animals do have certain beliefs and desires. Not only chimpanzees and other primates, but also elephants, killer whales and even octopuses display various signs of some intelligent behaviour.[68] Yet also with respect to ecosystems, our scientific understanding has significantly altered over the past years.[69] Even on a more global scale, such as ecosystems, the growing body of ecological research can be used to understand what nature's interest might exactly be.

6.4. THE ULTIMATE CONQUEST OF NATURE?

In line with John Livingston, one could point out a certain paradox when endowing nature with legal rights: 'To extend or bestow or recognize rights in nature would be, in effect, to domesticate all of nature – to subsume it into the human political apparatus'.[70] Along similar lines, one might contend that the delineation between nature and culture remains blurry and arbitrary at best. Yet this argument only goes so far, as was also highlighted by Peter Burdon.[71] Ultimately, human beings are inevitably limited to using language to describe the reality they are inhabiting. It cannot be contested that 'granting' rights to nature is to be seen as a major step towards a less anthropocentric approach to environmental governance. And in a certain way, it is also a more consequential approach. When NGOs file lawsuits to save protected species, such as wolves or hamsters, what really is at stake is the viewpoint of these animals?[72] In essence, such lawsuits focus on the ecological requirements of the endangered species, not on the statutory objectives or property interests of the NGO at issue.

---

67 M. Sagoff, 'On Preserving the Natural Environment' (1974) 84 *Yale Law Journal* 221, 221–222.

68 For an overview, see: F. De Waal, *Are We Smart Enough to Know How Smart Animals Are?*, W.W. Norton and Company, New York 2017.

69 See: E. Dardenne, 'From Jeremy Bentham to Peter Singer' (2010) 7 *Revue d'études benthamiennes*, DOI: 10.4000/etudes-benthamiennes.204.

70 J. Livingston, *Rogue Primate: Exploration of Human Domestication*, Key Porter Books, Toronto 1994, pp. 159–161.

71 P. Burdon, 'The Rights of Nature: Reconsidered' (2010) 49 *Australian Humanities Review* 69.

72 C.D. Stone, 'Response to commentators' (2012) 3(Special Issue) *Journal of Human Rights and the Environment* 100, 109.

7. DO WE REALLY NEED IT IN THE EU?

As alluded to in the introduction, nature has not been vested with explicit legal rights in the EU legal order. At least, that is the common believe of most scholars. As of today, for instance, no explicit reference to rights of nature can be found in primary EU law. Of course, this does not mean that the EU legal order does not lay down certain human protection duties towards nature. Equally, it might be conceivable to argue that certain implicit legal rights are recognised in the EU legal order. Often the distinction between duties-based protection and rights-based approaches is not clear-cut. For instance, Article 3 of the Treaty on the European Union (TEU) puts 'sustainable development' at the centre of the EU's internal market, specifying that the 'internal market … shall work for the sustainable development of Europe based on balanced economic growth … and a high level of protection and improvement of the quality of the environment'. And although the practical relevance of these norms in lawsuits remains fairly limited,[73] we should certainly not lose sight of the broader picture. This has prompted some scholars, such as Julien Bétaille, to argue that EU environmental law is less anthropocentric than it used to be.[74] In this section, I argue that while this hypothesis indeed has some merits, it should not lead us to dismiss the rights-based approach altogether.

7.1. THE EU AS ENVIRONMENTAL FRONTRUNNER

Not seldomly, the EU prides itself on its remarkable track record of environmental legislation. At first glance, this self-praise seems justified; from the implementation of the first EU environmental action programme to the adoption of several progressive environmental directives like the Wild Birds Directive.[75] Whereas the EU's protected nature has not been explicitly vested with the right to exist, the environmental principles laid down in the TFEU as well as secondary legislation have certainly strengthened environmental protection over the past decades. It is evidently impossible to treat all relevant pieces of EU environmental legislation in the context of this chapter.[76] Reference has to be made to the 2000 EU's Water Framework Directive,[77]

---

73 J. Verschuuren, 'The growing significance of the principle of sustainable development as a legal norm' in D. Fisher (ed.), *Fundamental Concepts of Environmental Law*, Edward Elgar, Cheltenham 2016, pp. 292–293.

74 J. Betaille, 'Rights of Nature: why it might (not) save the world' (2019) 16(1) *JEEPL (Journal for European Environmental and Planning Law)* 35, 43–44.

75 Council Directive 79/409/EEC on the conservation of wild birds [1979] OJ L103/1 (further referred to as the 'Birds Directive').

76 See for a more detailed analysis of the applicable rules in the field of water management: L. Krämer, 'Rights of nature and their implementation' (2020) 17(1) *JEEPL* 47.

77 Directive 2000/60/EC of the European Parliament and of the Council of 23 October 2000 establishing a framework for Community action in the field of water policy [2000] OJ L371/1.

which compelled the Member States to achieve good qualitative and quantitative status of all water bodies (including marine waters up to one nautical mile from shore) by 2015. No legal personhood is granted to rivers, yet the legislation contains several stringent principles, such as a standstill obligation to be observed when granting permits.[78] A recent attempt to apply the 'the polluter pays' principle is offered by the 2014 Environmental Liability Directive, which also requires preventive and remedial action in the context of 'pure' ecological damage,[79] and thus at least partly implements one of Stone's primary suggestions.

Lastly, and perhaps most importantly, the EU has adopted two pieces of legislation explicitly aimed at halting the biodiversity loss within its territory. The aforementioned Birds Directive, which was later complemented by the more cross-cutting Habitats Directive, not only explicitly protected hundreds of endangered species within the EU but also obliged the Member States to designate the most ecologically valuable parts of their territory as protected sites (better known as 'Natura 2000 sites'). Again, these directives do not explicitly grant substantive 'legal rights', such as the right to exist, to certain species or ecosystems; rather, they put forward a more traditional governmental approach, whereby the competent authorities at the national level are tasked to designate the most vulnerable sites on their territory and, subsequently, to implement stricter permitting policies and conservation schemes aimed at the recovery of these sites. A similar approach surfaces with respect to strictly protected species, such as the wolves and hamsters that were mentioned in the introduction to this contribution.

7.2. PROGRESSIVE CASE-LAW DEVELOPMENTS TOWARDS 'EARTH JURISPRUDENCE'?

In the jurisprudence of the CJEU some traces of eco-centrism are also noticeable. Three specific progressive trends can be identified. *First*, since 2008 the CJEU has consistently spawned very progressive jurisprudence when it comes to the standing of environmental NGOs before national courts. This led the CJEU, for instance, to grant standing to a Slovakian NGO that was challenging the legality of hunting regulations regarding protected Brown bears.[80] In doing so, the CJEU highlighted that when appraising the *locus standi* of NGOs, national judges are to also accept claims that are not based on economic or

---

78 Case C-461/13 *Bund für Umwelt und Naturschutz Deutschland e.V. v. Bundesrepublik Deutschland*, ECLI:EU:C:2015:433.

79 Directive 2004/35/CE of the European Parliament and of the Council of 21 April 2004 on environmental liability with regard to the prevention and remedying of environmental damage [2004] OJ L143/56.

80 Case C-240/09, *Lesoochranárske zoskupenie VLK v. Ministerstvo životného prostredia Slovenskej republiky I*, ECLI:EU:C:2011:125, para. 50.

property-related arguments.[81] Of course, these NGOs still need to demonstrate that the legal action squarely falls within the scope of their statutory provisions. Interestingly, NGOs can partly rely on the European Commission, which does not shy away from taking Member States to the EU courts whenever they implement management strategies that blatantly endanger the survival of certain habitats and species, as was recently demonstrated by the halting of the illegal logging in the Bialowieza Forest.[82] As a result, one might submit that both the environmental NGOs and the EU Commission can partly act as guardian of endangered EU protected nature.

Second, the CJEU recently also underlined that the EU protected habitats and species are to be approached as the EU's common heritage, thereby at least implicitly underscoring their intrinsic value.[83] Most prominently, the CJEU rejected the acceptability of destructive forestry practices in the vulnerable Bialowieza Forest in Poland with reference to Article 6(3) of the Habitats Directive, which prevents national authorities from authorising plans and/or projects that put in jeopardy the integrity of the protected site.[84] Irreparable damage cannot be tolerated, unless the strict derogation clause is applied.[85] In recent jurisprudence, the CJEU consistently underlined the prevalence of the precautionary principle in this respect, prompting national authorities to apply the '*in dubio pro natura*' rationale in the context of restorative actions.[86] Regarding protected species, the CJEU has persistently broadened the substantive scope of the protection duties included in Article 12(1) of the Habitats Directive.[87] Bypassing these rules is only possible by way of derogation. And these exceptions are to be interpreted narrowly.[88] Even when applying the derogation clauses, for instance in the specific context of wolf culling, the CJEU has underlined the importance of science-based decision-making.[89] These jurisprudential evolutions all contribute to a more encompassing protection of EU protected species, while also leaving room for taking into consideration the intrinsic value of unique ecosystems or even individual specimens of threatened species, such as Gray wolves.

---

81 Case C-115/09, *Bund für Umwelt und Naturschutz Deutschland, Landesverband Nordrhein-Westfalen eV v Bezirksregierung Arnsberg, Trianel Kohlekraftwerk Lünen (intervening)* [2011] ECR I-03673, ECLI:EU:C:2011:289, para. 46.

82 Case C-441/17R, *Commission v. Poland*, ECLI:EU:C:2017:877.

83 Case C-441/17, *Commission v. Poland*, ECLI:EU:C:2018:255, para. 208.

84 Case C-258/11, *Peter Sweetman and Others v An Bord Pleanála*, ECLI:EU:C:2013:220, para. 46.

85 Ibid.

86 Case C-127/02, *Landelijke Vereniging tot Behoud van de Waddenzee and Nederlandse Vereniging tot Bescherming van Vogels v Staatssecretaris van Landbouw, Natuurbeheer en Visserij* ECLI:EU:C:2004:482, para. 56–59.

87 Case C-183/05 *Commission v. Ireland* [2007] ECR I-137, paras. 15–15.

88 Case C-6/04 *Commission v. United Kingdom* ECLI:EU:C:2005:626, para. 111.

89 Case C-674/17 *Luonnonsuojeluyhdistys Tapiola Pohjois-Savo – Kainuu ry* ECLI:EU:C:2019:851, para. 67.

Third, recent case-law developments have also highlighted the restoration imperative contained in several EU environmental directives, such as the EU Habitats Directive, which also hints towards a more ecocentric understanding of the existing environmental protection statutes. In its recent case-law, for instance, the CJEU seems to prioritise restoration of strictly protected species, such as wild hamsters, whose populations have dwindled over the past decades.[90] Likewise, the CJEU clarified that Member States are equally obliged to designate sites which at present harbour relatively little actual biodiversity but which possess important restoration features.[91] More importantly, the continuation of ongoing and authorised activities in such areas can be challenged through Article 6(2) of the Habitats Directive when it conflicts with the restoration imperative.[92]

7.3. MAJOR SUBSTANTIVE SHORTCOMINGS?

In spite of all the above-mentioned praise and progressive jurisprudence, the EU legal order still falls short of many of the self-evident substantive underpinnings that ought to prevail in a jurisdiction where rights of nature are to be approached as constitutional bedrock. For one, it is a well-known fact that the prevailing case-law of the CJEU with respect to the admissibility requirements for direct actions against EU acts precludes public interest litigation at the EU level.[93] This is not a merely theoretical issue, since many of the EU decisions regarding pesticides, GMOs and fisheries have an important bearing on European ecosystems.[94] One of the more fundamental shortcomings in terms of substantive protection is the apparent lack of an imperative to preserve ecological integrity in the EU treaties, alongside the notable absence of an overarching no-net-loss instrument with binding effects in secondary EU law. It is true that the EU Nature Directives have helped in protecting large swaths of vulnerable habitats and species across the European continent. Even so, the existing protection regime prioritises the most endangered sites and species, leaving several less 'charismatic' species unprotected'. Recent research has revealed that Brown bears, wolves, bitterns and Eurasian lynxes receive

---

90 Case C-383/09, *Commission v. Finland* [2011] ECR I-4713.

91 Case C-281/16, *Vereniging Hoekschewaards Landschapv. Staatssecretaris van Economische Zaken* ECLI:EU:C:2017:774.

92 Case C-399/14, *Grüne Liga Sachsen e.V. and Others v Freistaat Sachsen* ECLI:EU:C:2016:10 paras. 40–46.

93 See more extensively: H. Schoukens, 'Articles 9(3) and 9(4) of the Aarhus Convention and Access to Justice before EU Courts in Environmental Cases: Balancing *On* or *Over* the Edge of Non-Compliance?' (2016) *European Energy and Environmental Law Review* 178.

94 Communication ACCC/C/2008/32 (Part II) (European Union), adopted on 17 March 2017.

almost the same amount as all invertebrates put together.[95] Moreover, the derogation clauses that are present in the majority of the above-mentioned EU environmental directives leave ample room for anthropocentrism to prevail 'via the backdoor'. In addition, endowing all nature in the EU with legal personhood would evidently also require a systemic recalibration of nature protection in terms of territorial scope. Whereas the recognition of the legal rights of certain ecosystems that already have been accorded a legal status under the 1992 EU Habitats Directive, still appears to be in line with a more progressive understanding of EU law, this would imply a genuine paradigm shift in property law when also applied in urban zones and agricultural sites. This conclusion is exacerbated by the lack of an effective integration of ecological integrity as a seminal yardstick in the other sectoral policies of the EU, such as fisheries and agriculture.[96] If the existing environmental protection duties are already poorly applied within the context of, for instance, agricultural policies, what then to expect from a more systemic shift to legal personhood for nature in this context?

8. HOW TO OPERATIONALISE RIGHTS OF NATURE IN THE EU?

As of today, it remains delusional to think that the mere introduction of rights of nature in the EU legal order will fundamentally bring about an 'ecological revolution'. This scepticism is backed up by a recent analysis of the application of rights of nature in Ecuador, which seems to attest that explicitly recognising rights of nature cannot lead to a transformative shift towards more sustainable practices in an economic growth-based society.[97] However, if we are really serious about a shift towards better environmental performance, more systemic changes appear inevitable. Even the European Environment Agency had to recognise that a 'recalibration of the existing policy approaches' is necessary in order to allow a genuinely green economy.[98] And therefore, as the final part of this analysis, I will briefly assess the options left to operationalise a more rights-based approach within the context of the European Union.

---

95 S. Mammola et al. 'Towards a taxonomically unbiased European Union biodiversity strategy for 2030' (2020) *Proc. R. Soc. B.* 2166.

96 See: P. Barkham, 'Europe faces "biodiversity oblivion" after collapse in French birds, experts warn', *The Guardian*, 21 March 2018 (https://www.theguardian.com/environment/2018/mar/21/europe-faces-biodiversity-oblivion-after-collapse-in-french-bird-populations.

97 Kaufmann and Martin, above n. 52.

98 European Environment Agency, *The European Environment: State and Outlook 2015: Synthesis Report, 2015*, p. 155.

8.1. THE TEMPTING YET UNCONVINCING SOLUTION?

At first glance, one of the most obvious pathways to do away with the lack of explicit recognition of nature's rights in the EU is to pass an EU Directive which explicitly recognises the legal rights of all ecosystems within the EU. It is therefore no surprise to see the charitable organisation called 'Nature's Rights' advocating a new directive in this regard.[99] The draft proposal explicitly grants nature substantive and procedural rights. Yet, a more thorough analysis seems to curb the initial enthusiasm. Not only is it very unlikely that this directive will be adopted any time soon by the European Parliament and Council, it also gives rise to some more fundamental legal obstacles that are to be addressed. For one, secondary legislation aimed at revising the dualism between nature and Mankind that is certainly implicitly present in the EU treaties will sooner or later come into conflict with the EU constitutional order. One cannot ponder the recognition of intrinsic rights of nature without revising seminal concepts like the (human) right to property, to give but one example. Likewise, recognising rights of ecosystems would also necessitate the revision of many other EU directives.

8.2. THE LONG YET UNREALISTIC ROAD?

An alternative route, which almost automatically flows from the analysis above, assumes that the operationalisation of rights of nature requires their inclusion in the EU's constitutional order. This taps into the emerging field of environmental constitutionalism, which aims to effectively cure the current problem of fragmentation of environmental law. This approach seems more logical, since it would highlight the interdependency between the internal market, the human values upon which the EU legal order is based and the environment. As of today, however, the cumbersome prospect of initiating a lengthy and complex treaty review to introduce rights of nature within the EU's constitutional order seems to severely diminish the likely success of this 'constitutional' scenario. Even when encompassed in the context of a more general treaty revision, the question remains whether enough political support will be found for the substantive shift towards the recognition of rights of nature. Of course, this leaves the option of an implicit recognition of the legal rights of certain ecosystems by the EU constitutional order unaddressed.

8.3. MORE PRAGMATIC PATHWAYS?

As the two options dealt with above do not present themselves as a realistic pathway, the question remains whether there may be more pragmatic solutions

[99] See https://www.citizensforeurope.eu/organisation/rights-of-nature-europe.

for operationalizing a more rights-based approach to EU environmental law in the short run. And to a certain extent, there are. Especially when taking into account a more Hohfeldian understanding of the concept of 'right's, which focuses more on legal relationships, additional room for recalibration becomes available.[100] In Hohfeldian terms, a nature protection framework may include a duty to refrain from harming a species. Another way to understand this limitation would be to say species have a right to their habitat and a right not to be harmed. As hinted at above, a clear case can be made for the EU Nature Directives to already grant certain habitats and species a 'right', or, as Stone puts it, 'an interest than can be infringed'.[101] Zooming in on the above-mentioned strictly protected species, such as Gray wolves or European hamsters, Article 12(1) of the Habitats Directive basically lays down a list of negative and positive duties towards protected species. This raises the question whether one could not try to reframe these duties as 'rights' owned by species. For instance, the duty not to kill wolves, as put forward in Article 12(1)(a) of the Habitats Directive, might be reframed as a 'right to life' endowed to the species. Similarly, the protection of certain parts of the habitat of protected species, such as the burrows of wild hamsters, grants these species a certain property right.[102] At face value, this reinterpretation of the existing rights appears farfetched. Yet when one puts forward a prohibition on killing certain species, one basically creates a positive duty for the government to protect endangered species from harmful actions by third parties.[103] Likewise, every time authorities decide to protect the burrows or dens of a species, one basically grants it a proto-property right.[104] And even if, as stated above, the rights granted to the said species are not absolute, they still remain very potent precursors of environmental protection. Recognising that certain endangered species possess some kind of property rights would evidently oblige us humans to refrain from deliberate interference with their habitats. But is that not exactly what we are already obliged to do, at least when applying the strict protection schemes included in EU law?[105]

One possible pathway to further the rights-based approach to nature would consist in bringing more cases forward in the interest and on behalf of endangered species under EU law. This is not as novel as it seems: several lawsuits have already been initiated in the United States with endangered

---

[100] W.N. Hohfeld, 'Some Fundamental Concepts as Applied in Legal Reasoning' (1913) *Yale Law Journal* 16.

[101] C.D. Stone, *Should Trees Have Standing? Law, Morality and the Environment*, Oxford University Press, New York 2010, p. 53.

[102] See more broadly on the topic of animal property rights: K. Bradshaw, 'Animal Property Rights' (2018) 89 *University of Colorado Law Review* 810.

[103] Stone, above n. 99, p. 169.

[104] Ibid.

[105] Ibid.

species as plaintiffs, alleging failures to protect their habitat as required under the Endangered Species Act (ESA). In the renowned *Palila case*, the Ninth Circuit Court ruled that the Palila bird 'has legal status and wings its way into the federal court as a plaintiff in its own right'.[106] Similar symbolic victories were scored in subsequent cases, including legal proceedings regarding the Northern Spotted Owl.[107] In all these cases standing was granted for the endangered species. However, it should be pointed out that that in none of these cases was the species the sole plaintiff. And although this case law was subsequently revisited in other jurisprudence,[108] it has certainly hit a nerve amongst US courts.

The afore-mentioned litigation strategy has remained largely unexplored in the EU. As of today, however, the EU treaties do not include an outright prohibition on the vesting of legal personhood in non-human objects. One might thus claim that EU law as such does not necessarily bar lawsuits on behalf of endangered species. In any event, environmental protection is treated as a shared competence within the EU legal framework. In this respect, one might therefore argue that national courts and/or national legislation are still allowed to grant legal rights to nature. Or, at the very least, they might refer the matter to the CJEU through a preliminary reference, which grants the EU judges the opportunity to shed their light on this very topical issue.

9. CONCLUSION

On a concluding note, it needs to be reiterated that, if not accompanied by a comprehensive revision of the existing institutional, political and economic structures, rights of nature will not bring about any short-term fix for the degraded environment. Certainly, this more eco-centric approach is not to be treated as a panacea or a substitute for the enforcement of existing protection statutes. This would be a logical fallacy: there simply is no easy fix for our current environmental predicament if no systemic shift towards a less consumption-based society is implemented in the short run. Even so, the rights of nature narrative puts forward a new language and framework which might be more suitable for dealing with environmental issues in the Anthropocene. This case-study of recent case-law developments of the EU underscored the potential for a more gradual move towards the implicit recognition of certain legal rights for EU protected species, habitats and ecosystems, even when this is not explicitly acknowledged in the existing legal frameworks. In doing so, rights of nature

106 *Palila v. Hawaii Dept. of Land & Natural Resources*, 852 F.2d 1106, 1107 (9th Cir. 1991).
107 *Northern Spotted Owl v. Hodel*, 716 F. Supp. 479 (W.D. Wash. 1988).
108 *Cetacean Community v. Bush*, 386 F. 3d 1169, 1137 (9th Cir. 2004).

would no longer be put forward as a short-term fix, but rather as the result of a incremental ecological understanding and re-interpretation of the existing protection duties towards nature and the wider environment. In this respect, I also want to refer to Thomas Berry, one of the most outspoken modern advocates for the rights of nature. When faced with the multitude of objections, Berry ultimately underlined the pragmatic approach underpinning the rights of nature movement: 'the language of rights answers the legal establishment in its own terms'.[109] As Chapron et al. noted, '[w]hen people and corporations have rights, nature frequently loses .... Rights of nature may help prevent this one-sided outcome'.[110] And this is exactly what also appears to be possible in the EU legal order.

---

109 Thomas Berry as quoted in Burdon, above n. 71.

110 G. Chapron, Y. Epstein and J.V. Lopez-Bao, 'A rights revolution for nature' (2019) 263(6434) *Science* 1392.

A COMPARATIVE ANALYSIS OF THE SELECTION OF SPECIES AND ESTABLISHMENT OF THEIR NATURAL HABITATS IN THE US AND THE EU

Protecting Nature from People

Valerie FOGLEMAN

1. INTRODUCTION

Legislation to conserve biodiversity is notoriously difficult to implement. The legislation tends to be enacted with high ideals and aspirations. As soon as its implementation threatens economic interests, however, opposition begins as people affected by it perceive or experience threats to their livelihoods. The opposition is typically followed by demands that conservation interests should give way to economic interests. In turn, this is followed by a weakening of the legislation.

This contribution illustrates the above sequence of events by examining the Endangered Species Act (ESA)[1] in the United States (US) and the Birds Directive[2] and the Habitats Directive[3] in the European Union (EU). The examination shows that whereas the Directives have withstood most of the challenges to them, the ESA has been less successful in doing so. The chapter analyses one key reason for this difference in effectiveness: differences in the processes for selecting species to be protected by the legislation and the way in which their natural habitats are established.

Finally, the chapter briefly examines the future of the ESA and the Directives. Whereas the European Commission published a plan in May 2020 to improve the effectiveness of the Directives, revisions to the regulations under the ESA in 2019 reduced its effectiveness, although the revisions may well be reversed.

---

1 16 USC ss. 1531 *et seq.*

2 Directive 2009/147/EC on the conservation of wild birds [2009] OJ L20/7.

3 Council Directive 92/43/EEC on the conservation of natural habitats and of wild fauna and flora [1992] OJ L206/7. A consolidated version was issued on 1 January 2007.

2. ADOPTION OF CONSERVATION LEGISLATION

The US is a world leader in enacting legislation to protect endangered species,[4] in particular the ESA in 1973. The ESA was followed by the EU about six years later.[5] The legislation in both jurisdictions was idealistic and aspirational; measures to protect threatened and endangered species and the prohibition of actions that could lead to their extinction were to be carried out regardless of their socio-economic effects. In short, the legislation was enacted to protect nature from people.

The ESA became law on 28 December 1973 when it was signed by President Nixon following a 356 to four vote in the US House of Representatives and a unanimous vote in the US Senate.[6] The ESA differed from other federal environmental laws that were enacted during the 'Environmental Decade' of the 1970s. The primary purpose of major laws such as the Clean Water Act,[7] the Clean Air Act[8] and the Resource Conservation and Recovery Act[9] was to protect human health from water pollution, air pollution, and hazardous and non-hazardous waste, respectively.

In striking contrast, the primary purpose of the ESA was to prevent animals and plants that were to be listed under it from becoming extinct due to human influence on the ecosystems that make up their natural habitats and to recover them to the '"point where they are valuable components of their ecosystems"'.[10] The protection of human health was not an issue, although the ESA had an anthropocentric element in that species were to be protected because of their 'esthetic, ecological, educational, historical, recreational, and scientific value to the Nation and its people',[11] and to conserve the 'natural heritage' of the American people.[12]

The priority of the ESA and its implementation by the US Fish and Wildlife Service (FWS), which administers the ESA for terrestrial and freshwater

---

4 See, e.g., Migratory Bird Treaty Act of 1918, 16 USC ss. 703–712; Bald Eagle Protection Act of 1940, 16 USC ss. 668–668d.

5 Some Member States had already enacted nature conservation legislation. See, e.g., Reich Conservation Act of 1935 (*Reichsnaturschutzgesetz*) (Germany).

6 See B.E. Gray, 'The Endangered Species Act: Reform or Refutation?' (2007) 13 *Hastings West-Northwest Journal of Environmental Law and Policy* 1, 1; H. Doremus, 'The Endangered Species Act: Static Law Meets Dynamic World' (2010) 32 *Washington University Journal of Law and Policy* 175, 177.

7 33 USC ss. 1251 *et seq.*

8 42 USC ss. 7401 *et seq.*

9 Ibid. ss. 6901 *et seq.*

10 See F.F. Skillern, *Environmental Protection Deskbook* (2nd ed., Shepard's/McGraw-Hill, New York 1995), 506 (quoting H.R. Rep. No. 1625, 95th Cong. 2d Sess. 5 (1978), *reprinted in* 1978 US Code Congressional and Administrative News 2989, 2990).

11 16 USC s. 1531(a)(3).

12 US Fish & Wildlife Service, 'Endangered Species Act; Overview'; https://www.fws.gov/endangered/laws-policies/index.html.

animals and plants,[13] is the conservation of threatened and endangered species. Designation of their natural habitat is secondary.[14]

In 1979, the EU adopted the Birds Directive. Similarly to the ESA, its primary focus is the protection of species (of birds) although, like the ESA, the Directive includes provisions to protect their natural habitats.[15]

In 1992, the EU substantially broadened its approach with the adoption of the Habitats Directive which specifically protects natural habitat types as well as species. In addition, the Directive provides for a 'coherent European ecological network of special areas of conservation [SACs]';[16] that is, the Habitats Directive specifically directed the establishment of a network of areas, called Natura 2000, to protect the natural habitats of endangered and other vulnerable species of birds, animals and plants across the EU. No such network exists in the US, although substantial areas of land are conserved under other legislation.[17]

3. SELECTION OF SPECIES AND DESIGNATION OF NATURAL HABITATS IN THE EU

The Birds Directive protects all species of wild birds that naturally occur in the EU.[18] In addition, Member States must take special protection measures, including the classification of special protection areas (SPAs),[19] for species and sub-species listed in annex I.[20] The Habitats Directive also includes annexes that

---

13 The National Marine Fisheries Service (NMFS) administers the ESA for marine wildlife including whales and other mammals and salmon and other anadromous fish. See US Fish & Wildlife Services, 'ESA Basics; 40 Years of Conserving Endangered Species'; https://www.fws.gov/endangered/esa-library/pdf/ESA_basics.pdf. The Services share responsibility for species such as sea turtles that live on land and in the ocean. See US Government Accountability Office, 'Report to the Ranking Member, Committee on Natural Resources, House of Representatives; Environmental Litigation; Information on Endangered Species Act Deadline Suits' (GAO-17-304, 02.2017), p. 1 fn. 2.

14 US Fish & Wildlife Service, 'Flood of Court Orders Preclude New Listings of Threatened and Endangered Species in FY2001' (22.11.2000): https://www.fws.gov/news/ShowNews.cfm?ID=-516062208; see also M. Rosso Grossman, 'Habitat and Species Conservation in the European Union and the United States' (1997) 45 *Drake Law Review* 19, 48 fn 233; J.L. Sax, 'Nature and Habitat Conservation and Protection in the United States' (1993) 20 *Ecology Law Quarterly* 47, 52.

15 Birds Directive, art. 3.

16 Habitats Directive, art. 3.

17 See, e.g., Sax (above n 14); R.L. Fischman, 'The National Wildlife Refuge System and the Hallmarks of Modern Organic Legislation' (2002) 29 *Ecology Law Quarterly* 457; R.L. Glicksman, 'Wilderness Management by the Multiple Use Agencies: What makes the Forest Service and the Bureau of Land Management Different?' (2014) 44 *Environmental Law* 447.

18 Birds Directive, art. 1.

19 Ibid. art. 4(1).

20 Ibid. art. 2.

list species of animals and plants protected by it,[21] as well as natural habitat types.[22] The predominant means of protecting natural habitats is to include SPAs and SACs in Natura 2000.[23] As a result of amendments to both Directives, especially when new States have acceded to the EU, the annexes now list over 1,200 species and sub-species as well as 231 habitat types.[24]

Species and natural habitat types in the annexes are selected by experts and are added to the Directives by Decisions of the European Commission. Whilst the annexes are over inclusive as well as under inclusive[25] by not, for example, fully including all taxonomic groups, the selection of species and natural habitat types has not tended to be controversial. Further, overall omissions from them are not considered to be 'a serious obstacle to achieving [their] general objectives'.[26]

The procedure for classifying SPAs is relatively simple. Member States classify the most suitable areas in their territories in number and size on the basis of ornithological criteria, taking into account, among other things, species in danger of extinction, those vulnerable to specific changes in their habitats, and rare species.[27] During the classification process, Member States may not consider socio-economic criteria.[28] In the second stage, each Member State submits the relevant information to the Commission to enable it to 'take appropriate initiatives ... to ensure that the areas ... form a coherent whole which meets the protection requirements of [the] species' in the EU.[29]

The procedure for designating SACs under the Habitats Directive is more elaborate. Member States carry out comprehensive assessments of species and habitat types in their territories in the context of the EU and its biogeographical

21 Habitats Directive, annexes II and IV.

22 Ibid. annex I.

23 Habitats Directive, art. 3.

24 Commission Staff Working Document, Fitness Check of the EU Nature Legislation (Birds and Habitats Directives); Directive 2009/147/EC of the European Parliament and of the Council of 30 November 2009 on the conservation of wild birds and Council Directive 92/43/EEC of 21 May 1992 on the conservation of natural habitats and of wild fauna and flora (SWD(2016) 472 final), 62 (Fitness Check): https://ec.europa.eu/environment/nature/legislation/fitness_check/docs/nature_fitness_check.pdf.

25 See D. Maes and others, 'Not the Right Time to Amend the Annexes of the European Habitats Directive' (2013) 6 *Conservation Letters* 468, 468–469; A. Hochkirch and others, 'How Much Biodiversity does Natura 2000 Cover?' (2013) 6 *Conservation Letters* 470, 471.

26 Fitness Check (above n. 24), 63; see also ibid. 92.

27 Birds Directive, art. 4(1). Article 4(2) also directs Member States to take similar measures to protect regularly occurring migratory species not listed in annex 1.

28 Case C-355/90, *Commission v. Spain* [1993] ECR I-4221, para. 45; Case C-44/95, *R v. Secretary of State for the Environment ex parte Royal Society for the Protection of Birds* [1996] ECR I-3805, paras. 39–42.

29 Birds Directive, art. 4(3).

regions according to criteria in the Directive.[30] Based on the assessments, they then submit proposed lists of sites to the European Commission.[31] The Commission evaluates each proposed list, prepares a draft list of sites of Community importance (SCIs) in agreement with each Member State, and issues Decisions to adopt them.[32] In issuing the Decisions, the Commission assesses whether a Member State had proposed sufficient sites and whether the Natura 2000 network is complete for the relevant biogeographical region. Member States then designate the SCIs as SACs,[33] following which they should establish conservation measures and prepare management plans to avoid the deterioration of species and natural habitats in the SACs.[34]

NGOs may informally suggest sites to be included in Natura 2000.[35] They do not, however, submit petitions to the European Commission or any other governmental entity to list species or sites under either Directive.

4. SELECTION OF SPECIES AND DESIGNATION OF NATURAL HABITATS IN THE US

In contrast to the approach taken in the EU, the ESA does not contain any provisions to establish a network of protected areas in the US. This does not mean that the ESA does not protect the 'critical habitat' of species listed as threatened or endangered under it. For most of its history, however, the FWS 'has made designating critical habitat for species a low priority because [the FWS] believed it was more important to devote limited resources to listing threatened and endangered species'.[36]

Further, the ESA does not include any annexes that list species to be protected by it. Instead, the FWS may propose species for listing.[37] The predominant method of listing species, however, is for non-governmental organisations (NGOs), as 'interested persons' under the Administrative Procedure Act (APA),[38] to petition the FWS to list species.

---

30 Habitats Directive art. 4(1).
31 Ibid.
32 Ibid. art. 4(2).
33 Ibid. art. 4(4).
34 Ibid. art. 6(2). The Habitats Directive does not specifically require Member States to prepare management plans for SACs or SPAs.
35 See Case C-3/96 *Commission v. Netherlands* [1998] ECR I-3031, paras. 40–41, 68 (referring to list of 70 sites that the International Council of Bird Preservation had concluded met the classification criteria for SPAs compared with 53 sites proposed by the Netherlands).
36 Flood of Court Orders (above n. 14).
37 16 USC s. 1533(a)(2)(A).
38 5 USC s. 553(e). Section 553(e) states that ('Each agency shall give an interested person the right to petition for the issuance, amendment, or repeal of a rule').

After an NGO or another person petitions the FWS to list one or more species, the FWS makes an initial determination whether the species is endangered or threatened. An 'endangered' species is one that is 'in danger of extinction throughout all or a significant portion of its range'.[39] A 'threatened' species is one that is 'likely to become an endangered species within the foreseeable future throughout all or a significant portion of its range'.[40]

The FWS bases its determination on the following factors:

- the present or threatened destruction, modification or curtailment of its habitat or range;
- overutilization for commercial, recreational, scientific or educational purposes;
- disease or predation;
- the inadequacy of existing regulatory mechanisms; or
- other natural or manmade factors that affect its continued existence.[41]

In making the determination, the FWS must consider only 'the best scientific and commercial information available';[42] economic and social implications of the listing may not be considered.

If the FWS concludes that the petition contains 'substantial scientific or commercial information' to support the action requested in it,[43] it makes a determination that the requested action may be warranted. The FWS makes this determination '[t]o the maximum extent practicable' within 90 days after receiving the petition.[44] The FWS then has 12 months from the date that it received the petition to make a finding that the action is warranted, not warranted, or warranted but precluded.[45]

A warranted but precluded finding means that the FWS has determined that listing the species is precluded by the need to address other actions concerning listing species that have a higher priority.[46] Such findings are controversial and

39 16 USC s. 1532(6). There is an exception for insects determined to 'present an overwhelming and overriding risk to man'. Ibid.

40 Ibid. s. 1532(20).

41 Ibid. s. 1533(a).

42 Ibid. s. 1533(b)(1)(A).

43 Ibid. s. 1533(b)(3)(A).

44 Ibid.

45 Ibid. s. 1533(b)(3)(B).

46 See, e.g., FWS, Endangered and Threatened Wildlife and Plants; Five Species Not Warranted for Listing as Endangered or Threatened Species, 84 Fed Reg 69,707, 69,707 (19.12.2019) (describing warranted but precluded findings as (a) the petitioned action is warranted but the immediate proposal of a regulation to implement it is precluded by other pending proposals, and (b) 'expeditious progress is being made to add qualified species to the Lists of Endangered and Threatened Wildlife Plants … and to remove [other species from those lists'); https://www.govinfo.gov/content/pkg/FR-2019-12-19/pdf/2019-27334.pdf.

have been referred to as a 'black hole' from which petitions do not emerge,[47] leading to a substantial number of challenges by NGOs against the FWS.[48]

If the FWS makes a warranted finding, it issues a proposed rule to list the species in the *Federal Register*,[49] the US Government's daily publication that includes proposed and final rules for all federal administrative agencies.[50] Proposal of the list and all other procedures involved in listing – or declining to list – a species are governed by the APA. The FWS then has one year, with up to a six-month extension for scientific uncertainty, to issue a final rule to list the species or to withdraw the proposal.[51]

At the same time that the FWS lists a species, it must concurrently 'to the maximum extent prudent and determinable' designate the species' 'critical habitat.'[52] As at 24 December 2020, 1,666 species of plants and animals were listed as threatened or endangered in the US.[53] Critical habitat had not been designated for all of them.[54]

A species' critical habitat is defined as the area that contains the physical or biological features essential to conserve it.[55] The FWS must make the designation 'on the basis of the best scientific data available' after considering the economic impact, the impact on national security and any other relevant impacts of the designation.[56] The FWS may exclude an area of critical habitat if the benefits of excluding it outweigh those of including it, unless the FWS determines, again on the basis of 'the best scientific and commercial data available', that the failure to designate it would result in the species becoming extinct.[57]

As with proposals for listing species, etc., the designation of critical habitat is also governed by the APA. The FWS publishes a proposed rule in the *Federal Register* to designate the critical habitat, receives public comments to

---

47 See J.J. Tutchton, 'Getting Species on Board the Ark One Lawsuit at a Time: How the Failure to List Deserving Species has Undercut the Effectiveness of the Endangered Species Act' (2014) 20 *Animal Law* 401, 418–420.

48 See, e.g., *Wildwest Institute; Alliance for the Wild Rockies v. Kurth*, 855 F3d 995 (9th Cir, 28.04.2017).

49 16 USC s. 1533(b)(5)(A).

50 5 USC s, 552. The *Federal Register* also includes advanced notices of proposed rulemaking, notices of hearings, etc. Final regulations are codified in the *Code of Federal Regulations* (CFR), which is updated annually. The key regulations to implement the ESA are: (1) endangered and threatened wildlife and plants, 50 CFR part 17; (2) interagency co-operation regulations, 50 CFR part 402; and (3) listing regulations, 50 CFR part 424.

51 16 USC s. 1533(b)(6)(A)–(B).

52 Ibid. s. 1533(a)(3)(A).

53 See ECOS Environmental Conservation Online System; Listed Species Summary (Boxscore); https://ecos.fws.gov/ecp0/reports/box-score-report. Fourteen species in the US are counted more than once. Ibid.

54 The list of designated critical habitats is at 50 CFR ss. 17.94–17.99.

55 16 USC s. 1532(5)(A).

56 Ibid. s. 1533(b)(2).

57 Ibid.; see M.L. Corn and A.M. Wyatt, 'The Endangered Species Act: A Primer' (Congressional Research Service, RL31654, updated 08.09.2016), 15 https://fas.org/sgp/crs/misc/RL31654.pdf.

the proposal, and after considering them, publishes a final rule that includes the boundaries of the critical habitat.

After a species is listed, the FWS should develop a recovery plan,[58] with the caveat that the plans are non-binding.[59] As of 24 December 2020 the FSW, either separately or jointly with the NMFS, had generated 609 draft and final recovery plans for 495 animal and 723 plant species in the US, for a total of 1,218 recovery plans.[60]

5. WEAKENING OF THE ENDANGERED SPECIES ACT

The designation of species regardless of the economic effects of doing so came to an abrupt end in the US in 1978 when the US Supreme Court granted a permanent injunction to ban the Tennessee Valley Authority from continuing to build the then 80 per cent complete Tellico Dam on the Little Tennessee River on which US$78 million (EUR 64,014,600) had been spent because opening the dam gates would result in the extinction of the snail darter (*Percina tanasi*), a fish about seven centimetres long.[61] Chief Justice Burger stated that

> [t]he plain intent of Congress in enacting [the ESA] was to halt and reverse the trend toward species extinction, whatever the cost. This is reflected not only in the stated policies of the Act, but in literally every section of the statute.[62]

Following the judgment, the ESA was amended 'to introduce "some flexibility" to the act'[63] by an exemption to it.[64] If the Secretary of the Interior concludes that a proposed action would adversely affect the continued existence of a listed species or its critical habitat, the federal agency, the governor of a State in which the action is taking place, or the applicant for a relevant permit may submit an application to the Endangered Species Act Committee,[65] commonly called the 'God Squad', for an exemption. The Committee may grant an exemption if it determines that there are no reasonable and prudent alternatives to the agency action, subject to specified requirements that include carrying out 'reasonable mitigation and enhancement measures' to minimise the adverse effects of the

58 16 USC s. 1533(f).
59 See Corn and Wyatt (above n. 57) 17–18.
60 Boxscore (above n. 53).
61 *Tennessee Valley Authority v. Hill*, 437 US 153 (1978).
62 Ibid. 184.
63 See Skillern (above n. 10), 506 (quoting H.R. Rep. No. 1625, 95th Cong. 2d Sess. 5 (1978), *reprinted in* 1978 US Code Congressional and Administrative News 9453, 9455).
64 16 USC s. 1536(g)–(h).
65 The 1979 amendments originally created a review board prior to review by the Endangered Species Act Committee. The 1982 amendments to the ESA eliminated the review board.

agency action.[66] Exemption orders (which are rarely issued), are subject to judicial review.[67]

The ESA thus includes a mechanism by which measures that adversely affect the continued existence of a listed species may proceed provided that specified measures are taken to minimise their effects on the species.

6. IMPLEMENTATION OF THE LEGISLATION

Implementation of the ESA in the US and the Birds and Habitats Directives in the EU means that the rights of persons that own or otherwise use areas affected by the legislation are curtailed. Designating critical habitats of species listed under the ESA can result in restrictions on the use of the designated areas[68] as well as on activities that are harmful to the species,[69] although it does not affect ownership of the land, allow governmental authorities to access private land, or require non-federal landowners to implement restoration, recovery or enhanced measures.[70] Similarly, classifying and designating SPAs and SACs, respectively, under the Birds and Habitats Directives results in restrictions on their use[71] as well as on activities that are harmful to the species, although, as in the US, it does not affect ownership of the sites or require the owners to carry out measures to protect natural habitats or species on them. Although both the ESA[72] and the Birds and Habitats Directives[73] have exceptions, threatened and actual restrictions as a result of designating areas under them have resulted in opposition to their implementation.

The Birds Directive directed Member States to classify SPAs by 1981[74] with a continuing duty to classify further sites that meet the requisite criteria.[75]

66 16 USC s. 1536(h), (l).

67 Ibid. s. 1536(g).

68 16 USC s. 1536(a)(2).

69 Ibid. s. 1538(a)(1)(b); see ibid. s. 1532(19); *Babbitt v. Sweet Home Chapter of Communities for a Great Oregon*, 515 US 687, 708 (1995).

70 See FWS, 'Endangered and Threatened Wildlife and Plants; Designation of Critical Habitat for Yellow Lance, Proposed Rule', 85 Fed Reg 6856, 6858 (06.02.2020). The ESA is more effective in reducing habitat loss on federal, compared to private, land. A.J. Eichenwald, M.J. Evans and J.W. Malcom, 'US imperilled species are most vulnerable to habitat loss on private lands' (2020) *Frontiers in Ecology and the Environment* 1–8 https://esajournals.onlinelibrary.wiley.com/doi/epdf/10.1002/fee.2177.

71 Habitats Directive, art. 6(4); see Case C-127/02, *Landelijke Vereniging tot Behoud van de Waddenzee v. Staatssecretaris van Landbouw, Natuurbeheer en Visserij* [2004] ECR I-7405, para. 43 (appropriate assessment required if there is a 'probability or a risk' that a plan or project will have significant effects on the site).

72 16 USC ss. 1539(a)(1)–(2).

73 Birds Directive, art. 9; Habitats Directive, art. 16.

74 Birds Directive, art. 12(1).

75 Case C-209/04, *Commission v. Austria* [2006] ECR I-2755, para. 43.

The Habitats Directive also established a timetable for Member States to submit lists of proposed sites to the Commission, for the Commission to review and adopt lists of SCIs, and for Member States to designate SCIs as SACs.[76]

The timetables were not met. By 2008, the Commission was pursuing 16 infraction proceedings against Member States under the Birds Directive[77] and 17 under the Habitats Directive.[78] The CJEU eventually ruled against 19 Member States for breaching the Birds Directive[79] and four Member States for proposing incomplete lists of SCIs.[80]

A major reason for the failure of Member States to classify or propose adequate lists of SPAs and SCIs was strong opposition by persons that owned or otherwise used the sites. This resulted in the Commission failing to meet its target to complete the lists of SCIs for all biogeographical regions in the then EU-15 by the end of 2002.[81] Since that time, however, completion of the Natura 2000 network has progressed more rapidly. By the middle of 2020, the network covered over 18 per cent of the land area in the EU[82] and eight per cent of its marine area.[83]

Progress in completion of Natura 2000 means that many, if not most, of the formal challenges to the designation of species and establishment of natural habitats in the EU have ceased. The focus of recent challenges has instead been on plans or projects that may have a significant effect on an SPA or an SAC.[84]

---

76 Habitats Directive, art. 4.

77 See Commission Staff Working Document accompanying document to the Communication from the Commission to the Council, the European Parliament, the European Economic and Social Committee and the Committee of the Regions, A mid-term assessment of implementing the EC biodiversity action plan, Consolidated Profile, p. 7 (SEC(2008) 3044, 16.12.2008) https://ec.europa.eu/environment/nature/biodiversity/comm2006/pdf/consolidated_profile.pdf. The proceedings were against Austria, Bulgaria, the Czech Republic, Estonia, Germany, Greece, Hungary, Ireland, Italy, Latvia, Lithuania, Luxembourg, Poland, Slovakia, Spain and the UK. Ibid. p. 7, fn. 6.

78 The proceedings were against Austria, Bulgaria, the Czech Republic, Denmark, Estonia, France, Germany, Greece, Ireland, Lithuania, Malta, the Netherlands, Poland, Slovakia, Slovenia, Spain and the UK. Ibid.

79 The Member States were Austria, Bulgaria, Cyprus, the Czech Republic, Denmark, Finland, Greece, Hungary, Ireland, Latvia, Lithuania, Malta, Poland, Portugal, Romania, Slovakia, Slovenia, Spain and the UK. Ibid. p. 8, fn. 7.

80 The Member States were Austria, Ireland, Poland and the UK. Ibid.

81 See e.g., Communication from the Commission to the Council and the European Parliament – Biodiversity Action Plan for the Conservation of Natural Resources vol. 2, 6, para. 16 (COM(2001) 162 final, 27.03.2001), 7–8, para. 21.

82 See 'Natura 2000 Barometer' (February 2020) 47 Natura 2000, 8–9; https://ec.europa.eu/environment/nature/info/pubs/docs/nat2000newsl/ENG%20Nat2k47%20WEB.pdf.

83 European Commission, 'EU Biodiversity Strategy for 2030: Bringing nature back into our lives' (July 2020) Natura 2000, 3 https://ec.europa.eu/environment/nature/info/pubs/docs/nat2000newsl/EN%20Natura%202000%2048%20WEB.pdf.

84 See, e.g., Case C-521/12, *Briels v. Minister van Infrastructuur en Milieu*, ECLI:EU:C:2014:330; Joined Cases C-387/15, C-388/15, *Orleans v. Vlaams Gewest; Malcorps v. Vlaams Gewest*, ECLI:EU:C:2016:593.

In contrast, challenges in the US to species proposed for listing, and the closely related issue of the establishment of their critical habitats, continue. The challenges are assisted by the following provisions in the ESA, neither of which exist in the Birds or Habitats Directives:

- a 'citizen suit' provision that authorises a private person (including an NGO) to bring an action against any person alleged to be in breach of the ESA or any regulations issued under it;[85] and
- a provision that authorises an action against the FWS for failing to carry out 'any act or duty under [the ESA] which is not discretionary',[86] including meeting a deadline mandated by it.

Challenges to the FWS' decisions, including decisions to list, reclassify, or de-list a species, are brought under the APA,[87] which waives the sovereign immunity of the US to allow a person to sue the federal government for non-monetary relief based on unlawful agency action. The APA establishes the general mechanisms for judicial review of the final action of a federal agency;[88] with the applicable standard being whether the action is 'arbitrary, capricious, an abuse of discretion, or otherwise not in accordance with law'.[89]

The challenges are further assisted by provisions that reimburse legal fees incurred by NGOs and other challengers. Not only does the ESA authorise the recovery of fees in citizen suits,[90] but the Equal Access to Justice Act (EAJA) authorises a federal court to make an award of attorney fees and costs to an individual or organisation that prevails in a judicial review action against the FWS in respect of its implementation and enforcement of the ESA.[91] A court

85 16 USC s. 1540(g)(1)(A). The person bringing the action must provide 60 days' notice to the FWS before it may bring the action. Ibid. s. 1540(g)(2)(A).

86 Ibid. s. 1540(g)(1)(C). A third provision that authorises an action against the FWS to compel it 'to apply [specified sections of the ESA] with respect to the taking of any resident endangered species or threatened species within any State', ibid. s. 1540(g)(1)(B), is used less frequently.

87 Ibid. s. 1533(b)(6)(B)(ii); see 5 USC s. 706(2)(A). The APA also applies, among other things, to a decision that action in a petition is warranted, not warranted or warranted but precluded, and the designation of critical habitat, etc.

88 5 USC ss. 702, 706.

89 Ibid. s. 706(2)(A). Other grounds are that it is '(B) contrary to constitutional right, power, privilege, or immunity; (C) in excess of statutory jurisdiction, authority, or limitations, or short of statutory right; (D) without observance of procedure required by law; (E) unsupported by substantial evidence in a case subject to sections 556 and 557 of [title 5] or otherwise reviewed on the record of an agency hearing provided by statute; or (F) unwarranted by the facts to the extent that the facts are subject to trial de novo by the reviewing court'.

90 16 USC s. 1540(g)(4).

91 28 USC s. 2412(b) ('[u]nless expressly prohibited by statute, a court may award reasonable fees and expenses of attorneys, in addition to the costs which may be awarded pursuant to subsection (a), to the prevailing party in any civil action brought by or against the

may make such an award if the FWS fails to demonstrate that its position was 'substantially justified',[92] which has been construed to mean that it did not have a reasonable basis in law and fact.[93]

A substantial part of the litigation under the ESA involves challenges to the FWS's delay in listing species. This is not necessarily the fault of the FWS. Rather, the FWS has long had a backlog of petitions to list species and has often had inadequate funding to list them expeditiously. As indicated above, listing is subject to the APA's rule-making procedures and is necessarily a lengthy process that includes public participation and, frequently, litigation.

The backlog of listing decisions began soon after the ESA was enacted. At that time, there was already a list of 78 species that had been published by the FWS on 11 March 1967 under the Endangered Species Preservation Act of 1966.[94] Soon, however, there were over 3,000 additional plant species for the FWS to consider adding to the list due to the ESA directing the Smithsonian Institution to carry out a review of plants that were, or might become, endangered or threatened, together with methods adequately to conserve them.[95] The FWS treated the list in the Smithsonian's report to Congress as a petition,[96] requiring it to commence rulemaking on listing the species.

The ESA has been highly politicised, with moves by the Administration and the US Congress to reduce or enhance its implementation and enforcement depending on the politics of the time. For example, in 1982, as a reaction to what it viewed as the then Administration's failure to implement the Act, Congress amended the ESA to introduce judicially enforceable deadlines[97] and (as noted above) to authorise actions by NGOs and others against the FWS for failing to comply with deadlines in the ESA.[98]

United States or any agency or any official of the United States acting in his or her official capacity'). As indicated here, the EAJA is not limited to the ESA; it applies to judicial review actions under the APA against federal agencies, which includes the FWS.

92 Ibid. s. 2412(d)(1)(A).

93 See H.J. Krent, 'Fee Shifting Under the Equal Access to Justice Act – A Qualified Success' (1993) 11 *Yale Law and Policy Review* 458, 459.

94 See M.J. Bean, 'The Endangered Species Act; Science, Policy and Politics' (2009) 1162(1) *The Year in Ecology and Conservation Biology, Annals of the New York Academy of Sciences*, 369, 370.

95 16 USC s. 1541; see B. Jesup, 'Endless War or End this War? This History of Deadline Litigation under Section 4 of the Endangered Species Act and the Multi-District Litigation Settlements' (2013) 14 *Vermont Journal of Environmental Law* 327, 341 (referring to the Smithsonian Institution, 'Report on Endangered and Threatened Plants of the United States' (1975)).

96 See 81 Fed Reg 69,425, 69,431 (06.10.2016) (referring to 40 Fed Reg 27,824 (01.07.1975)).

97 See Jason M. Patlis, 'The Endangered Species Act: Thirty Years of Politics, Money, and Science: Riders on the Storm, or Navigating the Crosswinds of Appropriations and Administration of the Endangered Species Act: A Play in Five Acts' (2003) 16 *Tulane Environmental Law Journal* 257, 282.

98 Endangered Species Act Amendments of 1982, Pub L No 97-304, 96 Stat 1411 (1982); 16 USC s. 1540(g)(1)(C). The ESA was amended in 1976, 1977, 1978, 1979, 1980, 1982, 1988,

In 1992, President George H.W. Bush imposed a moratorium on new regulations including those under the ESA.[99] In 1995, Congress reduced funding for the ESA and imposed a moratorium on final listing decisions.[100] As a result, the FWS did not list any species in over a year, resulting in a backlog of 243 proposed listings.[101]

In addition to litigation concerning listing deadlines, States and landowners have brought actions to challenge the FWS's designation of critical habitat that affects their land.[102] Conversely, NGOs have brought actions to request courts to order the FWS to implement the Act. The FWS has been caught in the middle.[103]

In 2007, the backlog of petition findings and critical habitat designations was reduced due to an increase in funding by Congress for the listing programme.[104] In that year, however, the number of species to be considered for listing increased substantially when an NGO called WildEarth Guardians filed two mega-petitions: one for 475 species in southwest US and one for 206 species in the west.[105] On 20 April 2010, they increased again when the Center for Biological Diversity filed another mega-petition of 1,145 pages to list 404 aquatic species in the southeast US.[106]

The ability of NGOs and others to petition the FWS to require it to consider listing substantial numbers of species for protection under the ESA means that the ESA could, in theory at least, provide protection for a much greater number of species than the Birds and Habitats Directives. As discussed above, however, this does not necessarily occur as a practical matter due, especially, to the length

and 2003. Congress has not authorised funding under the ESA since authorisation expired on 1 October 1992. Since that time, funding has been provided by annual appropriations by Congress. See Corn and Wyatt (above n. 57), 1. The deadline for designations of critical habitat was introduced in 1978. See Bean (above n. 94), 377. The ESA had by then listed 236 species but had designated critical habitat only for 33, with proposals for a further 73 designations. Ibid.

99 See Jesup (above n. 95) 342. The moratorium was challenged by NGOs on the basis that it did not apply to statutory deadlines. The challenge resulted in a settlement. See ibid. 343 (citing *Fund for Animals, Inc v. Lujan* No 92-800 (DDC 1992)). A further action by the Fund for Animals resulted in a settlement in December 1992 to resolve the status of all 401 candidate species and future warranted but precluded species. See ibid. 343–44.

100 Congress reduced funding for the ESA by US$1.5 million in the fiscal year 1995 budget. Emergency Supplemental Appropriations and Rescissions for the Department of Defense to Preserve and Enhance Military Readiness Act of 1995, Pub L No 104-6, 109 Stat 73, 86 (1995).

101 FWS, Endangered and Threatened Wildlife and Plants; Restarting the Listing Program and Final Listing Priority Guidance, 61 Fed Reg 24,722, 24,722–23 (16.05.1996) https://www.govinfo.gov/content/pkg/FR-1996-05-16/pdf/FR-1996-05-16.pdf.

102 See Jesup (above n. 95) 359–360.

103 See, e.g., Flood of Court Orders (above n. 14).

104 See Jesup (above n. 95) 362–363.

105 See ibid. 363.

106 Center for Biological Diversity, Petition to list 404 aquatic, riparian and wetland species from the Southeastern United States as Threatened or Endangered under the Endangered Species Act (20 April 2010); https://www.fws.gov/southeast/pdf/petition/404-aquatic.pdf.

of time taken to list a species and to designate its critical habitat, and opposition to listings.

An example of the length of time that it takes to list a species and to designate its critical habitat is the case of the yellow lance (*Elliptio lanceolate*), a species of freshwater mussel. The yellow lance was included in the 20 April 2010 petition filed by the Center for Biological Diversity. On 27 September 2011, the FWS announced that listing the yellow lance as a threatened species might be warranted. On 5 April 2017, the FWS published a proposed rule to list it as a threatened species.[107] On 3 April 2018, the FWS published a final rule to list it as a threatened species.[108] On 6 February 2020, the FWS published a proposed rule to list its critical habitat as approximately 319 miles (514 km) of rivers in North Carolina, Virginia and Maryland.[109]

7. FUTURE OF THE LEGISLATION

In 2016, the REFIT evaluation of the Birds and Habitats Directives[110] concluded that they remained 'highly relevant' and 'fit for purpose'.[111] In May 2020, the European Commission published a plan to address the main causes of biodiversity loss in the EU, including enforcing the Birds and Habitats Directives to 'focus on completing the Natura 2000 network, the effective management of all sites, species-protection provisions, and species and habitats that show declining trends'.[112]

In the US, despite the failure of congressional Bills to revise the ESA,[113] the ESA has fared less well. For example, in *Weyerhaeuser Co. v. US Fish & Wildlife*

107 Fish and Wildlife Service, Endangered and Threatened Wildlife and Plants; Threatened Species Status for Yellow Lance; Proposed rule, 82 Fed Reg 16,599 (05.04.2017); https://www.govinfo.gov/content/pkg/FR-2017-04-05/pdf/2017-06783.pdf.

108 Fish and Wildlife Service, Endangered and Threatened Wildlife and Plants; Threatened Species Status for Yellow Lance; Final Rule, 83 Fed Reg 14,189 (03.04.2018); https://thefederalregister.org/83-FR/14189.

109 Fish and Wildlife Service, Endangered and Threatened Wildlife and Plants; Designation of Critical Habitat for Yellow Lance; Proposed Rule, 85 Fed Reg 6856, 6858 (06.02.2020); https://www.fws.gov/policy/library/2020/2020-02294.pdf.

110 Fitness Check (above n. 24).

111 Ibid. 96, 8.

112 Communication from the Commission to the European Parliament, the Council, the European Economic and Social Committee and the Committee of the Regions, EU Biodiversity Strategy for 2030; Bringing nature back into our lives (COM(2020) 380 final, 20.05.2020), s. 3.2, p. 16; https://eur-lex.europa.eu/legal-content/EN/TXT/?qid=1590574123338&uri=CELEX:52020DC0380.

113 See, e.g., S 1863, 115th Cong (2017–2018), which would have prohibited the ESA to protect species whose range was entirely within a State; https://www.congress.gov/bill/115th-congress/senate-bill/1863; HR 2098, 114th Congress (2015–2016), which would have required the Secretary of the Interior to publish and make available for public comment

Service,[114] a large timber company challenged the FWS' designation of 1,544 acres of land in Louisiana, called Unit 1, as critical habitat for the dusty gopher frog (*Rana sevosa*), an endangered species. Unit 1, on which the company harvested timber, was over 50 miles from the ephemeral pond in Mississippi inhabited by the frogs. The frogs had not lived in Unit 1 for many decades, but it had rare, high-quality ephemeral ponds (although it needed some modification to be critical habitat for the frogs). The FWS had concluded that Unit 1 met the statutory definition of unoccupied critical habitat and commissioned a report on the probable economic impact of the designation. The report concluded that the designation might bar future development of the site, depriving Weyerhaeuser and the other owner of US$33,900,000 (EUR 27,794,610). The FWS concluded, however, that the potential costs were not disproportionate to the conservation benefits. The US Supreme Court upheld the challenge, ruling that an area could not be 'critical habitat' unless it was currently 'habitat'; that is, inhabited by an endangered species.

The most significant weakening of the ESA occurred on 27 August 2019 when the FWS and the NMFS published revised final rules under the ESA. Among other things, the regulations codified *Weyerhaeuser*, stating that areas currently unoccupied by a listed species should be considered for designation as critical habitat only after occupied areas have first been considered and deemed inadequate to ensure that the species will be conserved and only if there is 'reasonable certainty' that the area will contribute to the conservation of the species.[115]

A further revision to the ESA removed language that required the FWS and the NMFS to make listing decisions 'without reference to possible economic or other impacts of such determination'; the Services must now list economic impacts even though they do not refer to them in their determinations.[116] Yet another revision limits the designation of species as threatened based on long-term predictions of the impact of climate change within the foreseeable future. Under the new rule, the foreseeable future 'extends only so far into the future as the Services can reasonably determine that both the future threats and the species' responses to those threats are likely'.[117]

a draft economic analysis when a proposed rule to designate critical habitat is published; https://www.govtrack.us/congress/bills/114/hr2098.

[114] 586 US xxx, 139 S Ct 361 (2018) https://www.supremecourt.gov/opinions/18pdf/17-71_omjp.pdf.

[115] Fish and Wildlife Service, Endangered and Threatened Wildlife and Plants; Regulations for Listing Species and Designating Critical Habitat, 84 Fed Reg 45,020, 45,021–22, 45,043 (27.08.2019) https://www.govinfo.gov/content/pkg/FR-2019-08-27/pdf/2019-17518.pdf (to be codified at 50 CFR s. 424.12(b)(2)).

[116] Ibid. 45,025.

[117] Ibid. 45,028 (to be codified at 50 CFR s. 424.11(d)).

8. CONCLUSION

The ESA's approach to selecting species to protect, whilst it arguably has the potential to include more vulnerable and endangered species than the approach of the Birds and Habitats Directives, has not proven to be resilient. It has been too easy to counter petitions to list species by a reduction in funding to the FWS preventing it from considering them expeditiously. In addition, the rules under the ESA are much more easily revised than provisions of the Directives themselves.

Whereas the European Commission is taking measures to preserve and restore ecosystems and biodiversity in the fundamental transition to a sustainable future in the EU,[118] revisions to the rules under the ESA during the Trump Administration have reduced its effectiveness. As a result nature is currently much less protected from people in the US than in the EU. Whether this will change in the future due to the highly politicised nature of the ESA remains to be seen. This may well change, however. On 20 January 2021, the Biden Administration announced that it would review the Trump Administration's revisions to those rules.[119]

118 See Communication from the Commission to the European Parliament, the European Council, the Council, the European Economic and Social Committee and the Committee of the Regions, The European Green Deal (COM(2019) 640 final, 11.12.2019), pp. 13–14. s. 2.1.7, https://ec.europa.eu/info/sites/info/files/european-green-deal-communication_en.pdf.

119 See Sierra Club, 'On Day One, President Biden Announces Review of Endangered Species Act Rollbacks' (20 January 2021), https://www.sierraclub.org/press-releases/2021/01/day-one-president-biden-announces-review-endangered-species-act-rollbacks.

THE IMPACT OF NATIONAL AND EU CRIMINAL LAW ON THE PROTECTION OF BIODIVERSITY

Robert Esser

1. ENVIRONMENTAL CRIMINAL LAW IN THE PROCESS TO A SUSTAINABLE FUTURE

The UN Organisation IPBES[1] recently issued a 'Global Assessment Report Biodiversity'[2] which was introduced to representatives of the then 132 IPBES Member States during a conference in Paris from 29 April to 4 May 2019. The report sets out a 1.5 degree-moment of protection of biodiversity. It states that '[e]ven for global warming of 1.5°C to 2°C, the majority of terrestrial species ranges are projected to shrink dramatically'.[3] Scientists are warning of the sixth greatest mass extinction in history which is mostly human-made. Every year tens of thousands of plants and animals are disappearing from earth. The report identifies land use by humans as one of the drivers of biodiversity loss.

The human being is born from nature and depends upon nature and its resources. Especially while the human population is growing bigger and bigger and human wishes and expectations become more ambitious and demanding, the line is becoming thinner and thinner between 'using' nature as an original resource for human life and 'overusing' or even 'abusing' natural resources.

---

1 The Intergovernmental Science-Policy Platform on Biodiversity and Ecosystem Services (IPBES) is an intergovernmental body of currently 136 Member States, with Italy and Uzbekistan joining the organisation in January/February 2020. Its self-imposed task is to provide scientific information and research to international players in order to improve the scientific basis for political decisions.

2 The Global Assessment Report on Biodiversity and Ecosystem Services is the result of three years of scientific research by 150 experts from 50 countries, supported by 310 further authors. The report numbers 1000 pages and examines 15,000 sources. The summary for policy-makers is available on: https://ipbes.net/global-assessment-report-biodiversity-ecosystem-services.

3 Summary for policy-makers of the global assessment report on biodiversity and ecosystem services of the IPBES, Addendum to the Report of the Plenary of the IPBES on the work of its seventh session, Paris, 29 April to 4 May 2019, 45 pages, available on: https://ipbes.net/global-assessment-report-biodiversity-ecosystem-services, p. 8.

The (so-called) 'human development', including major human achievements in the field of human rights, such as the general freedom of action, is currently taking its toll.[4]

The tension between *exploitation* and *protection* of the environment has always existed. But especially in the current model of modern industrial society, damage to the environment has become inevitable, as humans put their interests above the preservation of nature. In addition to biodiversity[5] loss caused by *legal* (land use) action as mentioned in the IPBES-report we face a large amount of biodiversity loss caused by *illegal* actions as well (the number and development of which unfortunately has not been officially evaluated yet). Most of these actions can be considered environmental crimes, such as illegal logging, fishing and the capture and trade of species.

Since a UNEP Study[6] warns states of an increasing number of cases of environmental crimes, the question arises of *how* to protect the environment *by law*, and more specifically biodiversity, in a sustainable and effective way. In this regard, *criminal law* and its estimated deterrent effects ('general prevention') might offer important tools for the preservation of natural biodiversity in the long run.

However, within our modern industrial society and our way of living, environmental criminal law merely has a secondary, flanking function. The reason for this is the following: Traditionally, environmental regulations have been assigned primarily to administrative law. For reasons of uniformity of the legal system and certainty of law, it is still a common principle that certain human conduct cannot be allowed (by administrative law) on the one hand, but forbidden (by criminal law) on the other hand. This principle is also called the principle of accessoriness of criminal law to administrative law, and it governs almost all fields of environmental criminal law.[7]

The following lines try to analyse if this traditional approach of *national, in this case German*, criminal law is able to deliver a fruitful contribution to the transition processes needed for a sustainable future development. In case it turns out that the *national* scope of biodiversity protection by criminal law is rather limited in its positive effects, and even rather hampers sustainable solutions, *European* criminal law comes into focus as a possible tool to save the natural basis of mankind.

---

4 Compare: M. Pfohl, *Artenschutz – Strafrecht 2017*, NuR (2017), 812.

5 Biodiversity describes the variety and variability of all living organisms on Earth.

6 C. Nellemann (ed. in chief), R. Henriksen, A. Kreilhuber, D. Stewart, M. Kotsovou, P. Raxter, E. Mrema and S. Barrat (eds.), *The Rise of Environmental Crime – A Growing Threat To Natural Resources, Peace, Development and Security. A UNEP-INTERPOL Rapid Response Assessment*, United Nations Environment Programme and RHIPTO Rapid Response-Norwegian Center for Global Analyses, 2016.

7 P. Krell, *Umweltstrafrecht*, C.F. Müller, Heidelberg 2017, paras. 20 et seq.; F. Saliger, *Umweltstrafrecht*, Vahlen, Munich 2012, paras. 63 et seq.

2. CRIMINAL LIABILITY IN THE FIELD OF BIODIVERSITY: LIMITATIONS OF THE NATIONAL APPROACH (GERMANY)

In 2014 the German government issued warnings that the country would in the future still serve as a destination for organised criminal activities in the area of environmental crime.[8] Therefore, on a *political* level, several initiatives by Germany to fight environmental crime were started. During the German G20-Presidency in 2016/2017 new priorities for the G20 Anti-Corruption Working Group (ACWG)[9] were established. In particular, High-Level Principles were formulated and developed in order to fight corruption, especially in connection with illegal wildlife trade. Those principles contain recommendations for action and concern effective prevention and prosecution of corruption along the entire trade chain. They were approved at the G20-summit in Hamburg in July 2017.

Furthermore, the German Corporation for International Cooperation (GIZ) was asked to implement a global plan with the goal of enhancing the cross-continental combat of poaching and illegal trade in ivory and rhinoceros horn. Therefore, the German Federal Ministry for Economic Cooperation and Development[10] has founded a Partnership against Poaching and Illegal Wildlife Trade in Africa and Asia.[11] Along the whole trade chain, that is from the producing country (in Africa) to the consuming country (in Asia), this agreement seeks to influence demand and supply of illegal wildlife products and provides for short-term intervention as well as for long-term development measures.

Additionally, the government maintains bilateral agreements[12] in order to develop alternative means of livelihood, to improve the management of protected areas and to advise partner countries on laws, regulations and the improvement of legal enforcement. It furthermore supports both the Wildlife

---

8 Compare C. Weerth, *Das neue europäische Artenschutzrecht – CITES und die Umsetzung durch die Zollverwaltung in Deutschland*, Umweltstiftung WWF-Deutschland und TRAFFIC Europe-Germany, 5th ed. Frankfurt am Main 2014.

9 The ACWG were established by G20 Leaders during the Canadian Presidency at the Toronto Summit in 2010.

10 Bundesministerium für Wirtschaftliche Zusammenarbeit und Entwicklung (BMZ).

11 See for example the publication of the Federal Ministry for Economic Cooperation and Development, *Stopping poaching – safeguarding natural livelihoods, The role and contribution of German development cooperation* (2018): https://www.bmz.de/en/publications/type_of_publication/information_flyer/flyer/Stopping_poaching.pdf.

12 See the list of bilateral nature conservation agreements at https://www.bfn.de/themen/internationaler-naturschutz/bilaterale-zusammenarbeit.html.

Crime Interpol Work Group[13] and the Interpol Anti Corruption & Financial Crime Unit regarding the illegal timber trade in South East Asia.

Germany also supported a World Bank study for the reappraisal of projects to combat illegal wildlife trafficking, as well as assisting the UN Office on Drugs and Crime (UNODC) in issuing a Wildlife Crime Report. The UN(GA) Resolutions to Combat Illegal Wildlife Trafficking[14] were initiated by Germany. Generally, the country also enforces the Basel Convention[15] and cooperates with EnviCrimeNet,[16] i.e. the informal police EU network to combat environmental crime.

Specific initiatives to combat illegal, unregulated and unreported fishing (IUU-Fishing) consist in the cooperation with the European Fisheries Control Agency and the development of a European IT system to control fishery products. Moreover, Germany enforces the IUU Regulation 1005/2008[17] that entered into force on 1 January 2010 and seeks to prevent the import of illegal fishery products by requiring a certificate of legal origin of product. The Regulation calls for a complete and seamless traceability system by means of establishing stricter controls, as well as deterrent sanctions. The impact of the Regulation is that 70 per cent of the Atlantic is now sustainably cultivated and that the biomass in the North and Baltic Sea has recovered since 2013.

Despite all these multifaceted *political* initiatives, on a *legal level*, environmental criminal law, and in particular, biodiversity criminal law is a relatively new, even undiscovered area of law in Germany.[18] The origin of national biodiversity criminal law (*Artenschutzstrafrecht*) lies in the 1960s, 1970s and 1980s. In the 1960s, administrative laws for the protection of biodiversity were passed. In order to ensure and facilitate their enforcement, corresponding

---

13 https://www.interpol.int/en/Crimes/Environmental-crime/Wildlife-crime.

14 UN Resolution A/RES/69/314 adopted by the General Assembly on 30 July 2015 and A/71/L.88 of 5 September 2017, both on Tackling illicit trafficking in wildlife.

15 Basel Convention on the Control of Transboundary Movements of Hazardous Wastes and Their Disposal.

16 European Network for Environmental Crime.

17 Council Regulation (EC) 1005/2008 of 29 September 2008 establishing a community system to prevent, deter and eliminate illegal, unreported and unregulated fishing, amending Regulations (EEC) No. 2847/93, (EC) 1936/2001 and (EC) No. 601/2004 and repealing Regulations (EC) 1093/9 and (EC) No. 1447/1999 [2008] OJ L286/1. See also: Commission Regulation (EC) 1010/2009 of 22 October 2009 laying down detailed rules for the implementation of Council Regulation (EC) 1005/2008, [2009] OJ L280/5; Regulation (EU) 2017/2403 of the European Parliament and of the Council of 12 December 2017 on the sustainable management of external fishing fleets, and repealing Council Regulation (EC) 1006/2008, [2017] OJ L347/81.

18 Fundamental: B. Gütschow, *Der Artenschutz im Umweltstrafrecht – Strafrechtlicher Schutz der Tier- und Pflanzenarten de lege lata und de lege ferenda*, Nomos, Baden-Baden 1998; F. Stegman, *Artenschutz-Strafrecht – Der strafrechtliche Schutz wildlebender Tïer- und Pflanzenarten im nationalen und internationalen Recht*, Hartung-Gorre, 2000; M. Pfohl, *Artenschutz – Strafrecht 2017*, NuR (2017), 812, 813.

criminal legislation was introduced at the same time, albeit outside the central German Criminal Code in the 'final' part of Bills governing questions of environmental law or at least administrative law in relation to environmental law aspects (so-called *Nebenstrafrecht*).[19]

Under the first law to fight environmental crime in 1980,[20] several of those criminalising provisions were transferred into the Criminal Code (*Strafgesetzbuch / StGB*), thereby obtaining the symbolic weight of a position within the core of the German criminal law, and a stronger dissuasive character that goes along with this position. The second law to fight environmental crime[21] came into force in 1994 and was designed to fill those gaps of criminal liability that had not yet been covered.[22] There is no denying the fact that the '1990s' were the era showing the most striking criminal law initiatives for the protection of the environment, not only in Germany but in the whole of Europe.

Nevertheless, current legislative initiatives in Germany point in the opposite direction: A German law of 10 November 2016 led to an outsourcing of parts of Section 326(2) StGB into provisions outside the Criminal Code.[23] This development, inter alia,[24] contradicts the path initially embarked upon of including environmental criminal provisions in the core of German Criminal law in order to strengthen their symbolic position and the awareness of people.

Statistical data on environmental crime in general show that in Germany the total number of environmental crimes recorded by the police fell by 32 per cent between 2004 and 2016, from 29,117 in 2004 to 19,704 in 2016, despite those changes in substantive criminal law mentioned above that have extended the scope of several of the relevant provisions in the Criminal Code.[25] The reason for this development is to be found in a reduction in the capacity of authorities to inspect, control, investigate and institute criminal prosecution rather than

---

19 See for example Section 71 Gesetz über Naturschutz und Landschaftspflege (BNatSchG) (introduced in 1986).

20 Erstes Gesetz zur Bekämpfung der Umweltkriminalität (1. UKG, 18. Strafrechtsänderungsgesetz, BGBl. I 1980, pp. 373 ff), entry into force on 1 July 1980.

21 Zweites Gesetz zur Bekämpfung der Umweltkriminalität (2. UKG, 31. Strafrechtsänderungsgesetz, BGBl. I 1994, pp. 1440 ff), entry into force on 1 November 1994.

22 It introduced, for example, a new provision that criminalises soil contamination, see Section 324a StGB. It also solved the dispute about authorisation which was acquired by abuse of rights by the amendment of Section 330d StGB: P. Krell, *Umweltstrafrecht*, Heidelberg 2017, paras. 52 ff; F. Saliger, *Umweltstrafrecht*, Vahlen, Munich 2012, paras. 101 ff et seq.

23 Article 2 of the Gesetz zur Änderung abfallverbringungsrechtlicher Vorschriften, BGBl. I 2016, p. 2452 (Sections 18a, 18b Abfallverbringungsgesetz (AbfVerbrG)); compare B. Hecker and M. Lorenz, *Systematische Übersicht der Rechtsprechung zum Umweltstrafrecht*, NStZ-RR 2017, 33.

24 The outsourcing of those provisions also leads to problems of logical distinction within the national law.

25 J. Tröltzsch, C. Gerstetter and L. Mederake (eds.), on behalf of the German Environment Agency (Umweltbundesamt), *Environmental offences in Germany 2016: a statistical analysis (short version)*, p. 5.

in improved compliance by those actors potentially endangering natural resources.[26]

Besides, crime statistics do always contain a misleading element, naturally portraying only those crimes that have come to the knowledge of public officials. There is also a 'structural deficiency' in environmental crimes that has to be taken account of: Traditionally, provisions of environmental criminal law only cover criminal offences sanctioning the *direct* threat to endangered species. However, biodiversity loss is a complex phenomenon, being influenced by direct and indirect risk factors likewise. The main reason is the structural change in natural habitats caused by pollution and the steady expansion of human habitat. Significantly, these and other indirect hazards usually take place within the national legal framework, i.e. these actions are not illegal as such. Yet, they contribute to an increasing danger for biodiversity.

The question therefore arises whether and how criminal law may or even must set a limit to such behaviour, *far in advance* of the actual attack on or loss of the protected legal and natural interest.

3. PREVENTING INDIRECT THREATS BY CRIMINAL LAW?!

Following the *ultima ratio* principle, i.e. the principle that criminal law serves merely as a last resort, criminal liability in the field of biodiversity so far usually starts where an existing threat to an already vulnerable species is being further aggravated. To put it in other words, the protection of species by criminal law only combats the *direct* threat of illegal picking, hunting or trade. Accordingly, Section 304 of the German Criminal Code, for example, stipulates that whosoever unlawfully damages or destroys – inter alia – natural monuments[27] or objects which serve a public need[28] shall be liable to imprisonment for not exceeding three years or a fine.

---

26 See J. Tröltzsch, C. Gerstetter and L. Mederake (above n. 25), p 5.; P. Krell, *Umweltstrafrecht*, Heidelberg 2017, para. 17.

27 Whereby the notion of a 'natural monument' for the purpose of Section 304 StGB is to be understood as defined by Section 28 BNatSchG (see BT-Drs. 8/2382, pp. 12 f):

> 'Natural monuments are unique creations of nature, or corresponding areas of up to 5 ha, that have been designated in a legally binding manner and that require special protection for the following reasons:
>
> 1. for reasons of science, natural history or national heritage, or
> 2. because of their rarity, special characteristics or beauty.'

28 For the purpose of Section 304 StGB, the interest the public has in the object must originate directly from the object.

But is it at all possible to detect and define precisely – as demanded by the Constitution and the international human rights framework (*nullum crimen, nulla poena sine lege*) – certain patterns of behaviour (indirect threats), for example by means of so-called *Gefährdungsdelikte*,[29] i.e. criminal provisions tackling dangerous activities far beyond or in advance of the direct threat?[30]

At the moment biodiversity criminal law is rather focusing on crimes concentrating on 'environmental media' (objects to be protected), instead of crimes concentrating on 'environmental multimedia' (abstract dangerous behaviour).

For example, Section 326 of the German Criminal Code provides that whosoever unlawfully stores, dumps, disposes of or commercialises – inter alia – waste which 'because of its nature, composition or quantity is *capable of endangering* an existing population of animals or plants shall be liable to imprisonment not exceeding five years or a fine' (emphasis added).

Whilst this provision criminalises potentially dangerous behaviour (*Gefährdungsdelikt*), it still focuses on objects to be protected, i.e. in this case 'animals or plants', so that it does not yet tackle dangerous activities '*far* beyond' and '*far* in advance' of a direct threat.

Accepting the need to criminalise abstract dangerous behaviour for the protection of the environment as such, we have to shift the perspective from an anthropometrical focus to a more ecological focus.[31] As a core obstacle to this shift of movement we detect the accessory function of criminal law. In the future the administrative (dis-/non-) approval of a certain behaviour should no longer be regarded as a (de-)criminalising factor.

An example of a national provision that displaces criminal liability in order to impose liability far in advance of an actual attack of legal interests may be Section 329 of the German Criminal Code. Hereby, one *may be criminally liable for operating facilities* within certain areas which require special protection.[32] Its *objective is to protect* endangered areas *and to take preventive action.*

However, the provision does not (yet) call into question the fundamental principle of accessoriness of criminal law to administrative law, as Section 329 of the German Criminal Code still holds on to public ordinances in order to determine criminal liability. In particular, Section 329 subsection 4 of the German Criminal Code provides that whosoever, in violation of duties under

---

29 See on the dimension of Gefährdungsdelikte in environmental criminal law: F. Saliger, *Umweltstrafrecht*, Vahlen, Munich 2012, para. 51 ff.

30 See intensively: B. Gütschow, *Der Artenschutz im Umweltstrafrecht – Strafrechtlicher Schutz der Tier- und Pflanzenarten de lege lata und de lege ferenda*, Nomos, Baden-Baden 1998, pp. 28 et seq., 88 et seq.

31 P. Krell, *Umweltstrafrecht*, Heidelberg 2017, para. 9; F. Saliger, *Umweltstrafrecht*, Vahlen, Munich 2012, para. 27 et seq.

32 Subsections 1 to 4 each define specific areas that are to be protected.

administrative law, causes substantial damage in a Natura 2000 Area to the habitat of especially listed species or to an especially listed habitat which is of relevance to the conservation and protective aims of such an area, shall be liable to imprisonment not exceeding five years or a fine.

There again, criminal liability depends upon whether the act in question is administratively forbidden and the subsection criminalises only direct threats to the protected area ('whosoever causes substantial damage'). Yet, Section 329 of the German Criminal Code criminalises not only intentional conduct, but provides also for negligence and gross negligence, so that the provision is at any rate comprehensive in this regard.

Seen from a more practical perspective and with regard to the statistics mentioned before, environmental criminality is classical 'control-criminality', i.e. the number of cases correlate with the number and qualification of deployed personnel controlling a potential misbehaviour. One goal therefore has to be that environmental crimes should be interpreted as 'economic crimes' and investigated by specially trained units of police departments and public prosecutor's offices. At least for public officials a duty to report such crimes to these criminal branches should be regulated by law.

At the same time, the provisions on forfeiture and confiscation of proceeds of crime[33] need to be applied in an efficient way in order to enhance their dissuasive effect. Regularly, real businesses are developed that cause environmental pollution and breach environmental laws. Where such businesses bring financial profit to their operators, this profit needs to be confiscated.

To sum up, it has turned out that, taking the German system as an example, *national* criminal law needs to undergo significant adaptations and changes in order to serve the goal of sustainability. In its traditional form and mode of operation the scope of biodiversity protection of national criminal law is rather limited. However, it is easy to predict that 'overcoming' these traditional structures of criminal law 'from the inside' – i.e by people serving the well-proven system they are used to – is almost impossible, or at least would mean a marathon effort.

The necessary changes to criminal law provisions protecting the environment in general and particularly biodiversity may therefore be much more encouraged by the idea of a modern *European* environmental criminal law harmonising the criminal structures and standards needed in at least all Member States and being equally executed by centralised institutions of the Union.

---

33 See Sections 73–76b of the German Criminal Code on the forfeiture of proceeds of crime from the principal or a secondary participant.

4. EUROPEANISATION OF ENVIRONMENTAL CRIMINAL LAW AS A TOOL OF SUSTAINABILITY?

The 'Europeanisation' of environmental criminal law as a suitable measure to meet the challenges mentioned already started around 15 years ago.[34] In its judgment of 13 September 2005[35] the European Court of Justice (ECJ) developed an annex-competence of the (former) European Communities according to the old legal framework ('three-pillars') – a competence which had been debated controversially before. The ECJ made it clear that the EC should define minimum standards and instruct Member States to issue criminal provisions. That initiative of the Court resulted in Directive 2008/99/EG of 19 November 2008 for protection of the environment through criminal law – a criminal initiative and legal instrument located in the former 'first pillar'.[36]

By the Treaty of Lisbon which entered into force on 1 December 2009 this competence was expressly anchored in primary legislation: Article 83 paragraph 2 TFEU states:

> If the approximation of criminal laws and regulations of the Member States proves essential to ensure the effective implementation of a Union policy in an area which has been subject to harmonisation measures, directives may establish minimum rules with regard to the definition of criminal offences and sanctions in the area concerned.

5. NEED FOR A NEW DIRECTIVE ON CRIMINAL LAW PROTECTION OF THE ENVIRONMENT

A first attempt to protect the environment through criminal law consisted in the framework decision 2003/80/JHA[37] which was later nullified by the ECJ.[38]

The problem of environmental crime had been discussed in many international and European fora for many years until the European Commission adopted a proposal for a directive aiming to ensure the protection of the environment through criminal law. After lengthy institutional discussions and two judgments

---

34 Compare: S. Ruhs, 'Europäisierung des Umweltstrafrechts' *ZJS (Zeitschrift für das Juristische Studium)* 2011/1, 13.

35 Case C-176/03, *Commission v. Council* [2005] ECR I-7879, paras. 47, 48.

36 As implemented into German national law by the *45. Stafrechtsänderungsgesetz*, BGBl. I 2011, p. 2557.

37 Council Framework Decision 2003/80/JHA of 27 January 2003 on the protection of the environment through criminal law [2003] OJ L29/5.

38 By Case C-176/03, *Commission v. Council* [2005] ECR I-7879.

of the ECJ[39] on the extent of the Community's competence ('first-pillar') in the area of criminal law, the Council and the European Parliament agreed on the text of the directive on the protection of the environment through criminal law.[40]

Directive 2008/99/EC of the European Parliament and of the Council of 19 November 2008 obliges Member States to provide for criminal penalties in their national legislation in respect of serious infringements of provisions of Union law on the protection of the environment. It requires Member States to attach to these existing prohibitions sanctions which have to act as effective, proportionate and 'dissuasive penalties for environmentally harmful activities'.

Under the Directive, the Member States shall determine as offences, for example, the

> discharge, emission or introduction of a quantity of materials or ionising radiation into air, soil or water, which causes or is likely to cause death or serious injury to any person or substantial damage to the quality of air, the quality of soil or the quality of water, or to animals or plants.[41]

According to Article 3(b) of the Directive, the Member States must criminalise as well

> the collection, transport, recovery or disposal of waste, including the supervision of such operations and the aftercare of disposal sites, and including action taken as a dealer or a broker (waste management), which causes or is likely to cause death or serious injury to any person or substantial damage to the quality of air, the quality of soil or the quality of water, or to animals or plants.

The Directive furthermore requires Member States to impose sanctions upon whosoever ships waste, or operates a plant in which a dangerous activity is carried out or in which dangerous substances are stored, or upon whosoever handles nuclear materials, takes specimens of protected wild fauna or flora species or trades in those specimens. It requires Member States to punish any conduct causing significant deterioration of a habitat within a protected site and the production or use of ozone-depleting substances.[42]

---

39 Case C-176/03, *Commission v. Council* [2005] ECR I-7879 and Case 440/05, *Commission v. Council* [2007] ECR I-9097.

40 S. Ruhs, 'Europäisierung des Umweltstrafrechts', *ZJS* 2011/1, 13, 15; S. Kingston, V. Heyvaert and A. Čavoski, *European Environmental Law*, Cambridge University Press, Cambridge 2017, p. 213.

41 Article 3(a) of Directive 2008/99/EC.

42 Offences required under Article 3(c)-(i) of Directive 2008/99/EC.

Inciting, aiding and abetting these offences must also be punishable as criminal offences.[43] While it must be possible for legal persons to be held liable for offences committed for their benefit, it is not mandatory that their responsibility be of a criminal nature; see Article 6 of the Directive.

The Directive also stresses the fact that 'in order to achieve effective protection of the environment, there is a particular need for more dissuasive penalties for environmentally harmful activities, which typically cause or are likely to cause substantial damage to the air, including the stratosphere, to soil, water, animals or plants, including to the *conservation of species* (emphasis added)'.[44] It therefore shows a direct link to biodiversity law.

Yet, the Directive only sets *minimum* standards of environmental protection through criminal law to be adopted by the Member States. It does not define any measures concerning the procedural part of criminal law; nor does it touch upon the powers of prosecutors and judges. It creates no obligation regarding the *application* of such penalties, or any other available system of law enforcement. Therefore, a 'new' EU directive on environmental and biodiversity criminal law, at least covering *all* branches of environmental criminal law and forming more precise duties for the EU Member States, is desirable and presumed to be in line with Article 5(3) TEU, i.e. the principle of subsidiarity.

Since environmental criminal law is not mentioned in the list of areas of crime where the European Parliament and the Council may, by means of directives adopted in accordance with the ordinary legislative procedure, establish minimum rules concerning the definition of criminal offences and sanctions, such an initiative can only be based on Article 83 paragraph 2 TFEU (set out in section 4 above).

Directive (EU) 2017/1371[45] on the fight against fraud to the Union's financial interests may serve as a model in this regard. The so-called 'PIF Directive' was proposed by the Commission in July 2012, and adopted by the Council in April 2017, with Article 83 paragraph 2 TFEU serving as a legal basis. The overall aim of this Directive is to harmonise the definition of fraud throughout the Member States and the provisions on misappropriation and corruption when committed to the detriment of the Union's financial interests. Furthermore, the Directive especially harmonises the sanctions for PIF offences which are provided for by the national legal systems.

---

43 Article 4 of Directive 2008/99/EC.

44 See the fifth recital of Directive 2008/99/EC of the European Parliament and of the Council of 19 November 2008 on the protection of the environment through criminal law [2008] OJ L328/28.

45 Directive (EU) 2017/1371 of the European Parliament and of the Council of 5 July 2017 on the fight against fraud to the Union's financial interests by means of criminal law [2017] OJ L198/29.

Additionally, Article 12 of the PIF Directive also requires the Member States to take necessary measures to provide for a limitation period that enables an effective investigation, prosecution, trial and judicial decision in the field of the protection of the Union's financial interests. Accordingly, the Member States have to provide for the law to apply over a sufficient period of time to ensure that infringements can be addressed in an efficient way. This was the first time an instrument of EU criminal law touched upon national provisions concerning limitation periods.

Finally, Article 15 of the Directive stipulates an obligation for the Member States, the Commission, the agencies and the Court of Auditors to cooperate with each other. The PIF Directive will serve as a legal basis for the powers of the European Public Prosecutor's Office (EPPO) and it defines its competences precisely.

6. EVALUATION OF DIRECTIVE 2008/99/EC

In October 2019, the EU Commission launched an evaluation of Directive 2008/99/EC on the protection of the environment through criminal law. Between then and January 2020, public administrations and authorities at national, regional and local level, non-governmental organisations and experts in the field of the protection of the environmental, business associations, scientists, lawyers and law firms, advocacy groups and private individuals were called upon to communicate their thoughts for improvement.

With this survey, the Commission intends to analyse whether the Member States have implemented the Directive sufficiently,[46] for example in terms of specialisation and training, the allocation of sufficient resources for police and judicial authorities, cooperation between all competent national authorities and elements of cross-border cooperation.

New challenges in environmental crime will also be explored, such as the increased engagement of criminal organisations and the need to promote structures for cross-border cooperation. The results of this consultation were expected in the first half of 2020.

---

46 See also: N. Torres Rosell and M. Marquès Banqué, Study on the implementation of Directive 2008/99/ec on the Protection of the Environment Through Criminal Law, https://www.eufje.org/images/docPDF/Study-on-the-implementation-of-Directive-2008_99_ENEC_SEO_BirdLife_May2016.pdf.

7. EUROPEAN INVESTIGATION 2.0: EPPO, EUROPOL AND EUROJUST

Another important aspect of environmental crimes is the fact that most criminal acts endangering biodiversity loss are not confined to a particular territory. Offences often have an international background or at least a cross-border dimension. Illegal deforestation, poaching and illegal disposal of waste are worldwide phenomena. Damage of USD 216.5 billion is caused annually by illegal trafficking of wildlife as well as by illegal, unregistered and unregulated fisheries.

Correspondingly, on the level of the European Union, several networks have been created specifically in order to supervise, detect and investigate into environmental crimes.[47] Other EU initiatives have not been designed specifically for the enforcement of environmental law, but also deal with it as a part of their competence and responsibility.

Agencies like Europol (European Union Agency for Law Enforcement Cooperation) and Eurojust (European Union Agency for Criminal Justice Cooperation) already deal with serious, organised forms of environmental crimes, but unfortunately do not have enough financial resources and personal support to concentrate on this branch of crime more intensively. These control deficiencies are complicating the combat of environmental crime on an EU-level. Initiatives to foster the structures and competences of the Union's criminal law agencies are needed.

As the EU Serious and Organised Crime Threat Assessment (SOCTA) underlines, there is an urgent call for active and effective combatting of crimes against the nature and our environment. Correspondingly, Germany cooperates with and participates in the operative Europol cooperation within the framework of the new 'Priority Environmental Crime' area of the European Multidisciplinary Platform Against Criminal Threats (EMPACT).

At the same time, German national agencies, such as the German Federal Criminal Office (*Bundeskriminalamt*), the Customs Criminal Office (*Zollkriminalamt*) and the Federal Agency for Agriculture and Food (*Bundesanstalt für Landwirtschaft und Ernährung*) participate in working groups of the Interpol Environmental Security Programme. Examples of such working groups are the Wildlife Crime Interpol Work Group as well as the Interpol Anti-Corruption & Financial Crime Unit.

---

47 IMPEL (EU Network for Implementation and Enforcement of Environmental Law); ENPE (EU Network of Prosecutors for the Environment); EnviCrimeNet (EU Network of Police Officers focusing on tackling environmental crime); IPEC (Intelligence Project on Environmental Crime by EnviCrimeNet and Europol).

According to Article 85 paragraph 1 TFEU Eurojust's mission shall be to support and strengthen coordination and cooperation between national investigating and prosecuting authorities in relation to serious crime affecting two or more Member States or requiring a prosecution on common bases, on the basis of operations conducted and information supplied by the Member States' authorities and by Europol.

Formerly, under the 'three-pillar' regime of the Union, Eurojust was simply charged with duties of coordination. Currently, however, Article 85 TFEU has strengthened the agency's position: it may now obtain the competence to initiate criminal investigations as well as the competence to propose the initiation of prosecutions conducted by competent national authorities, particularly those relating to offences against the financial interests of the Union – Article 85 paragraph 1(a) TFEU. Apart from that, Eurojust's task still is to coordinate investigations and prosecutions and to strengthen judicial cooperation, e.g. by cooperating closely with the European Judicial Network.

Regulation (EU) 2018/1727 of 14 November 2018 on the European Union Agency for Criminal Justice Cooperation (Eurojust),[48] which is based on Article 85 TFEU, offers a procedural 'scope of protection' in this regard that can also be used for the protection of the environment and biodiversity. According to Article 4 paragraph 2(a) of the Regulation, Eurojust may ask the competent authorities of the Member States concerned, giving its reasons, to undertake an investigation or prosecution of specific acts, including crimes against the environment falling under its competence (Article 3 of the Regulation).

According to Article 86 paragraph 1 TFEU the Council and the European Parliament may establish a European Public Prosecutor's Office (EPPO) – emerging from Eurojust – whose intended function is to combat crimes affecting the Union's financial interests.[49] Similarly, Eurojust is already seen as the EPPO's 'germ cell' as it helps to coordinate national prosecutions in the affected Member States. However, it implies by its nature the fragmentation of prosecution on a national and a supranational level. The main additional value of establishing an EPPO would therefore consist in establishing a coherent European response to certain 'EU crimes', so that obstacles deriving from the current fragmentation of criminal law and procedures in the EU may be overcome.

The EPPO shall be responsible for *investigating, prosecuting and bringing to judgment*, where appropriate in liaison with Europol, the perpetrators of, and accomplices in, offences against the Union's financial interests.

48 Regulation (EU) 2018/1727 of the European Parliament and of the Council of 14 November 2018 on the European Union Agency for Criminal Justice Cooperation (Eurojust), and replacing and repealing Council Decision 2002/187/JHA, [2018] OJ L295/138.

49 See Article 86 para. 1 TFEU.

The 'Union's financial interests' are defined by Article 2 of the already mentioned Directive (EU) 2017/1371 as containing 'all revenues, expenditure and assets covered by, acquired through, or due to the Union budget or the budget of the Union institutions, bodies, offices and agencies.' It comprises serious infringements of the common VAT systems linked to the territory of two or more Member States and any losses totalling at least EUR 10 million.

In order to establish the EPPO, the Council shall act unanimously and adopt Regulations in accordance with a special legislative procedure set out in Article 86 TFEU. According to Article 86 paragraph 2 TFEU, the EPPO shall exercise the functions of prosecutor in the competent courts of the Member States in relation to such offences.[50] That means that, within the limits of its competence, the EPPO will supersede the national public prosecutor's offices.

On 12 October 2017, Regulation (EU) 2017/1939 establishing the EPPO[51] was adopted by those Member States which are part of the EPPO enhanced cooperation. So far, 22 Member States have joined the enhanced cooperation. The EPPO central office will be based in Luxembourg. The date on which the EPPO will assume its investigative and prosecutorial tasks will be set by the Commission on the basis of a proposal from the European Chief Prosecutor once the EPPO has been set up, but not earlier than three years after the entry into force of the regulation.

In theory, the EPPO's competence and field of function are expandable by means of a unanimous European Council decision and the consent of the European Parliament – Article 86 paragraph 4 TFEU. The establishment of a European Public Prosecutor's Office will be a major innovation in EU criminal law, as it will transfer powers of investigation and prosecution from the national to the supranational level.

Finally, it has turned out to be a rather *political* question whether the competence of the European Public Prosecutors Office (EPPO) will be extended to environmental crimes having a cross-border dimension, according to Article 86 paragraph 4 TFEU, covering also the field of biodiversity criminal law. The *legal* framework of the EPPO – Council Regulation (EU) 2017/1939 – is almost ready to cover environmental crimes: For the time being, the EPPO's primary mandate consists of the investigation and prosecution of offences related to fraud against the Union's financial interests. However, there are two possible ways by which one might find a competence of the EPPO to deal with environmental crimes as well.

---

[50] See also Directive (EU) 2017/1371.

[51] Council Regulation (EU) 2017/1939 of 12 October 2017 implementing enhanced cooperation on the establishment of the European Public Prosecutor's Office ('the EPPO') [2017] OJ L283/1.

On the one hand, environmental crimes may be included within the scope of the EPPO if they are considered to be 'ancillary offences' related to fraud; yet, the exact definition and scope of the term 'ancillary offence' are currently under debate.

On the other hand, Article 86 paragraph 4 TFEU expressly allows an extension of the EPPO's mandate to include serious crimes having a cross-border dimension. If this provision is used, environmental crime will most likely fall expressly within the mandate of the European Public Prosecutor's Office.

8. CONCLUSION

Low risk, high profit – that is the current situation of environmental crimes.[52] We have to state an annual rise of cases due to lack of resources to combat environmental crime. A further reduction of resources must be feared, although the impact of environmental crime on global ecosystems is hardly measurable. If natural resources and biodiversity are destroyed irretrievably, we will see consequences also for human coexistence.

Article 37 of the Charter on Fundamental Rights of the European Union ('Environmental protection') demands that a high level of environmental protection and improvement of the quality of the environment must be integrated into the policies of the Union and ensured, in accordance with the principle of sustainable development.

This provision is also addressed to the *national* criminal law systems and its actors when 'implementing Union [environmental] law' (Article 51 paragraph 1 Charter). These systems have to direct their focus more closely on *serious* crimes against the environment, in addition to administrative protective measures. For sustainable species protection, however, this form of protection should no longer concentrate on the actual ('direct') endangerment of concrete individual objects or landscapes, but rather the endangerment of underlying natural resources must be examined more intensively.

This necessary change of the shape of national environmental criminal law will hardly be achievable by actors involved in the system itself, but by a revision

---

52 Compare C. Nellemann (ed. in chief), R. Henriksen, R. Pravettoni, D. Stewart, M. Kotsovou, M. Schlingemann, M. Shaw and T. Reitano (eds.), *World Atlas of Illicit Flows. A RHIPTO-INTERPOL-GI Assessment*. RHIPTO-Norwegian Center for Global Analyses, INTERPOL and the Global Initiative Against Transnational Organized crime (2018), p. 15; UmweltBundesamt (ed.), *Status quo und Weiterentwicklung des Umweltstrafrechts und anderer Sanktionen: Instrumente zur Verbesserung der Befolgung von Umweltrecht (Compliance) Abschlussbericht*, June 2019, pp. 74 et seq.

of Directive 2008/99/EC based on Article 83 paragraph 2 TFEU. In addition, the competence of the European Public Prosecutor's Office (EPPO) should be extended to environmental crimes having a cross-border dimension.

Criminal law itself cannot, however, consider the interrelations for this *indirect* protective approach, i.e. as to which behaviour will have long-term effects on species population. The interdependencies as to the endangerment of legal goods have to be explained by other sciences – in so far as criminal law remains *naturally* limited to the accompanying protection of the society as a means of *ultima ratio*.

OVERABUNDANT UNGULATES CAUSING BIODIVERSITY LOSS AND HUMAN-WILDLIFE CONFLICTS

The Role of the National Law and Governance Structure in the Italian Jurisprudence

Stefano Giacomelli and Michael Gibbert

1. INTRODUCTION

Overabundant ungulates (such as the white-tailed deer (*Odocoileus virginianus*) in the United States and the wild boar (*Sus scrofa*) in Europe) occupy an awkward space halfway between fair game and pest, and pose a number of management challenges both for anthropic activities and for legislators. A series of judgments[1] delivered by the Italian *Corte Costituzionale* (Constitutional Court, the highest judicial body in Italy) in recent years provide a case in point. They may appear – at first glance – relatively simple decisions about the allocation of legislative power between the central State and the Regions on an environmental subject, specifically on wildlife management. However the analysis in this contribution suggests that they actually represent a symptom of rising social pressures (in Italy and elsewhere). In particular, these pressures arise from a situation where: (a) a national wildlife governance system dates from a period where the ungulates were scarce (rather than abundant as they are now) and where the management credo was 'conservation', and as such is ill-suited to respond to new local necessities in a timely fashion; (b) biological evidence internationally is highly ambiguous when it comes to the most effective measures to take in the first place. Last-but-not-least, the analysis here provides insights into the peculiar law on property of wildlife in Italy compared to other European countries, and into reimbursement procedures for wildlife-related damage

1 Corte Costituzionale nr. 44 of 2019 (*Presidente del Consiglio dei ministri vs. Regione Liguria*); Corte Costituzionale nr. 139 of 2017 (*Presidente del Consiglio dei ministri vs. Regione Liguria*); Corte Costituzionale nr. 107 of 2014 (*Presidente del Consiglio dei ministri vs. Regione Veneto*).

so as to stress some idiosyncrasies of the Italian system with the European Directives, while at the same time offering lessons learnt for other countries which treat game as public property (*res publica* or *res communis*, e.g. in the United States). All these points give ground to the idea that law when not updated and when it makes use of atypical constructs, gives birth to social tensions and hampers innovative solutions for the management and conservation of the environment.

Environmental literature emphasises the importance of a healthy environment, with an obligation to preserve the environment's integrity for future generations. Many pieces of legislation around the world embrace this view, to the extent of constitutionalising it.[2] In terms of wildlife, literature recognises human interdependency with the natural environment, but acknowledges that wildlife conservation and biodiversity may actually be losing ground.[3] Indeed, many countries have fallen short of the Strategic Plan for Biodiversity 2011–2020 and its Aichi targets, adopted under the auspices of the Convention on Biological Diversity (CBD), so that today a new global biodiversity framework for the post-2020 era is far from clear. In order to guarantee more efficient wildlife protection, scholars propose several methodologies, such as 'good governance' principles,[4] the 'public trust thinking and doctrine',[5] or the 'adaptive governance'[6] structure, hoping for shared rules and policies at a global level. Following the experience of relocating authority in global climate governance, some authors suggest that polycentric systems of governance should be implemented also for the management of wildlife.[7] However, because of the specific challenges posed to economic, social and environmental interests by their proliferation, overabundant ungulates require a targeted and far more local approach to framing a suitable legal structure for their management. Even though comparable legal principles for wildlife conservation can be found in different national laws,[8] legal markers of individual countries remain imperative to study since wildlife management sometimes constitutes a regional and even

---

2 e.g.: C. Soyapi, 'Environmental Protection in Kenya's Environment and Land Court' (2019) 31(1) *JEL (Journal for Environmental Law)* 151.

3 D. Decker, C. Smith, A. Forstchen, D. Hare, E. Pomeranz, C. Doyle-Capitman, K. Schuler and J. Organ, 'Governance principles for wildlife conservation in the 21st century' (2016) *Conservation Letters* 290: doi: 10.1111/conl.12211.

4 Ibid. [3].

5 D. Hare and B. Blossey, 'Principles of Public Trust Thinking' (2014) 19(5) *Human Dimensions of Wildlife* 397.

6 B. Chaffin, H. Gosnell and B. Cosens, 'A decade of adaptive governance scholarship: synthesis and future directions' (2014) 19(3) *Ecology and Society* 56.

7 P. Pattberg, O. Widerberg and M. Kok, 'Towards a Global Biodiversity Action Agenda' (2019) 10(3) *Global Policy* 385.

8 S. Giacomelli, D. Hare, M. Gibbert and, B. Blossey, 'Public trust thinking and public ownership of wildlife in Italy and the United States' (2019) 29(3) *Environmental Policy and Governance* 209.

local matter. What at the international or national level may appear feasible, in practice may be not applicable locally. In the past, scholars have focused predominantly on studying endangered and vulnerable species, and ways to counter illegal human activities directed toward them.[9] Overabundant species, by contrast, have attracted less scholarly attention, also in the legal field. This is a significant *lacuna*, because of their serious impact on biodiversity (such as destroying habitats, harming other species, preventing forests' regrowth) and on anthropic activities (such as devastating agricultural fields, spreading diseases among farmed animals, involvement in vehicle collisions).

The wild boar provides a case-in-point, representing a systemic challenge on economic, social and environmental levels. It is by a large margin the most overabundant ungulate, whose population has grown exponentially during the last decades in the whole of Europe[10] and the United States.[11] It causes considerable damage to agriculture, spreads diseases such as swine fever, negatively impacts local habitats (e.g. by raiding birds' nests), can be found scavenging in major metropolitan areas from Berlin to Barcelona, and due to its significant body mass, is particularly problematic when involved in car accidents. Many reasons have contributed to its proliferation, such as its exponential reproductive rate, its adaptability to different habitats, a highly diversified diet and, in Europe, a lack of natural predators apart from the (only recently re-emerging) wolf (*Canis lupus*). Moreover, even humans contribute to its proliferation, through the illegal act of releasing boars bred on farms for recreational hunting purposes.[12] Importantly, for our purposes here, biologists are far from unanimous on how to manage wild boar populations effectively. For example, scholars have found that a traditional method such as hunting, which comes with significant history and social significance,[13] has the counterintuitive side-effect of actually increasing the population by enhancing the reproductive

---

[9] E. Bennett, 'Another inconvenient truth: the failure of enforcement systems to save charismatic species' (2011) 45(4) *Oryx* 476. K. Dhanjal-Adams, K. Mustin, H. Possingham and R. A. Fuller, 'Optimizing disturbance management for wildlife protection: the enforcement allocation problem' (2016) 53(4) *Journal of Applied Ecology* 1215.

[10] G. Massei, J. Kindberg, A. Licoppe, D. Gačić, N. Šprem, J. Kamler, E. Baubet, U. Hohmann, A. Monaco, J. Ozoliņš, S. Cellina, T. Podgórski, C. Fonseca, N. Markov, B. Pokorny, C. Rosell and A. Náhlik, 'Wild boar populations up, numbers of hunters down? A review of trends and implications for Europe' (2015) 71(4) *Pest Management Science* 492.

[11] N. Snow, M. Jarzyna and K. VerCauteren, 'Interpreting and predicting the spread of invasive wild pigs' (2017) 54(6) *Journal of Applied Ecology* 2022.

[12] S. Giacomelli, M. Gibbert and R. Viganò, 'Community empowerment for managing wild boar: a longitudinal case study of northern Italy 2001–2018' (2018) 23(4) *Ecology and Society* 12.

[13] S. Giacomelli and M. Gibbert, '"He likes playing the hero – I let her have fun shooting". Gender games in the Italian forest during the hunting season' (2018) 62 *Journal of Rural Studies* 164.

rate of the species as a natural response to a threat.[14] Others conclude that hunting remains the most effective instrument for reducing damage to crops, followed by fencing.[15] Still others studied the use of supplementary feeding and poisoning, but found that they have marginal effects.[16]

The resulting uncertainty on how to control the overabundance of wild boar leaves legislators around the world wondering about the most effective legal frameworks to guide management strategies for the species. Due to the interference of the species with many human activities, there is great social pressure to resolve the issue, but the difficulty of such a task is increased by conflicting stakeholder demands (for instance, hunters vs. farmers), further complicating legislative practices.

2. THE CASE

Judgment nr. 139 of 2017 of the Italian Constitutional Court (*Presidente del Consiglio dei ministri vs. Regione Liguria*) determines (*inter alia*) the attribution of legislative power between the Italian central State and the Regions on a specific aspect of wildlife management. It builds on previous decisions of the same Court (e.g. Corte Costituzionale nr. 107 of 2014 – *Presidente del Consiglio dei ministri vs. Regione Veneto*) and it has become the basis for new decisions (e.g. Corte Costituzionale nr. 44 of 2019 – *Presidente del Consiglio dei ministri vs. Regione Liguria*).

More specifically, the Court was asked to pronounce on whether the Liguria Region indeed has the legislative power to extend the list of people authorised by article 19.2 of national law nr. 157 of 1992 to be part of culling plans approved by the Region itself. Article 19.2 of national law 157/1992 provides that:

> For the best management of the livestock, for the protection of the soil, for health reasons, for biological selection, for the protection of the historical-artistic heritage, for the protection of the zoo-agro-forestry and fish production, Regions control wildlife species even in areas prohibited for hunting. This control, done selectively, is normally practised through the use of ecological methods based on the opinion

14 S. Servanty, J.M. Gaillard, F. Ronchi, S. Focardi, É. Baubet and O. Gimenez, 'Influence of harvesting pressure on demographic tactics: implications for wildlife management' (2011) 48(4) *Journal of Applied Ecology* 835.

15 H. Geisser and H.-U. Reyer, 'Efficacy of hunting, feeding, and fencing to reduce crop damage by wild boars' (2004) 68(4) *Journal of Wildlife Management* 939.

16 G. Massei, S. Roy and R. Bunting, 'Too many hogs? A review of methods to mitigate impact by wild boar and feral hogs' (2011) 5(1) *Human-Wildlife Interactions* 79.

> of the National Institute for Wildlife. If the Institute verifies the ineffectiveness of the aforementioned methods, *Regions can authorise culling plans. These plans are implemented by guards employed by Provinces. The latter will also be able to avail themselves of the owners or conductors of the lands on which these plans are to be implemented, provided they have a licence for hunting, as well as forest guards and Municipal guards licensed for hunting purposes* (emphasis added).[17]

By regional law nr. 29 of 2015, at article 93, the Liguria Region ruled that also 'hunters gathered in teams' were allowed to implement culling plans approved by the Region inside its territory.

The plaintiff (represented in the person of the Prime Minister) argued that it was not within the legislative power of a Region to extend the list of people authorised to implement culling plans, in view of article 19.2 of national law 157/1992 being grounded in article 117.s. of the Constitution, for which 'the central State has exclusive legislative powers in the ... protection of the environment, the ecosystem and cultural heritage'.[18] The defendant (Liguria Region) claimed that the national process of reorganising the functions attributed to Provinces has significantly reduced the staff of the provincial police assigned to the wildlife management.[19] It was therefore necessary to introduce new categories of people authorised to effectively implement the culling plans.

In its decision (point 7 of the motivation), the Court declared that the list of people indicated in article 19.2 as authorised to implement culling plans, is in fact not flexible. Additions by Regional laws would diminish the minimum and uniform level of protection of the environment decided by the national law 157/1992, with the central State maintaining exclusive legislative power on the topic.

Even if the case – at first glance– may appear a relatively simple issue about legislative power attribution and the Court decided in favour of the plaintiff, there are two antecedents (which are discussed subsequently below) to consider which can help in understanding why the defendant tried to push national legislative boundaries, probably even with the awareness that its law would be found unconstitutional.

---

17 Authors' own translation.

18 See http://www.senato.it/1025?sezione=136&articolo_numero_articolo=117.

19 Title V of the Constitution has been in the last decades the object of many reforms. One of the last laws that directly impacted on national governing Bodies was law nr. 54 of 2014 about the role, functions and budget of Provinces. Spurred by a necessity of 'making cash' through cutting expenses, the central State cut the financing of many provincial activities. Whereas these activities were transferred to Regions, the same did not happen with the financing, so that Regions did not have the funds to run properly all their new tasks and had to cut resources. This happened with the Provincial police force, which in some cases had to find creative solutions to make up for the lack of staff. See for example: ibid. [12].

3. ANALYSIS: THE ANTECEDENTS

In order to grasp the setting surrounding judgment nr. 139 of 2017 of the Italian Constitutional Court, two main antecedent circumstances need to be considered: one related to Italy's wildlife governance structure as set by law, and one related to the concept of wildlife property from which originates civil liability and its implications at the international and national level.

As for the first of these circumstances, Italian wildlife governance follows a top-down hierarchical structure: article 117.s. of the Constitution provides that the central State has exclusive legislation on environmental subjects. Law 157/1992 titled 'Rules for the protection of warm-blooded wild animals and hunting'[20] sets (in accordance with international treaties) the national overall framework for the management of those 'species of mammals and birds living in conditions of freedom in the national territory'.[21] Within this framework, some legislative powers and administrative responsibilities are transferred to the Regions,[22] such as the approval of culling plans or the reimbursement for damage caused by wild animals. Importantly, regional laws can only be more stringent than national rules, but cannot contradict or relax laws made at the national level.[23] So for example, the national law provides a list of weapons that can be used during hunting, i.e. rifles, bows and the use of hawks.[24] Regional laws cannot reform this list through adding e.g. crossbows, but they can be more stringent by forbidding, for example, the use of bows. Regions are then allowed to delegate part of their executive powers to Provinces and metropolitan cities, which in turn cannot contradict national and regional provisions.[25] So for example, the police force of the Provinces is generally entrusted with the implementation of culling plans, to be performed in adherence to the Regional law that authorised them.[26]

Some scholars consider such a top-down governance structure ill-suited for the modern management of ecosystems, because a) it easily causes conflicts among institutions, b) it does not well define responsibilities vis-à-vis citizens, and c) it does not provide enough flexibility to respond fast enough to new local needs. Decentralised legal and governance structures (as in the United States for instance) are largely preferred in recent literature,[27] which also points to

20 Ibid. [17].
21 Article 2 of national law 157/1992. Authors' own translation.
22 In Italy there are 20 Regions: 15 are 'regular', 5 have 'special' legislative powers that render them less constrained by national laws.
23 E.g. Judgment of the Constitutional Court nr. 101 of 2010.
24 Article 13 of national law 157/1992.
25 Ibid. [8].
26 E.g. Piedmont Regional Law 19 June 2018, nr. 5.
27 Ibid. [8]. D. Decker, S. Riley and W. Siemer, *Human Dimensions of Wildlife Management*, 2nd ed., Johns Hopkins University Press, Baltimore 2012.

the experience of relocating authority in an era of global climate change via polycentric systems.[28]

The second antecedent circumstance to consider requires consideration of article 1 of national law 157/1992 which establishes that warm-blooded wild animals are non-disposable public property (*res publica*) protected in the interest of the national and international community, so that they are bounded to a public use destination. This legal classification was originally introduced with law nr. 968 in 1977, taking the place of royal decree nr. 1016 of 1939, under which wildlife was considered property of no one (*res nullius*). It has been a peculiar re-categorisation of wild animals, in contrast with the ancient roman tradition,[29] and which by some commentators has been partially attributed to the country's communist party's great political influence in that period.[30] As such, Italy is today one of a minority of European countries[31] in which wildlife is clearly defined as property of the State.

From an international perspective, this aspect has implications in terms of civil liability for damage caused by wildlife, a topic on which both the doctrine and the jurisprudence have long debated and that has been considered for various purposes. Referring to damage caused by wild boar to agriculture, a sector that is highly affected by this species in the amount of millions of Euros each year, Italy asked a Parliamentary question[32] about reimbursements provided by the Regions to farmers, and in particular whether the European Regulation nr. 1408 of 2013 about the '*de minimis*' aid in the agricultural sector applies. The question was raised precisely because wild boar constitutes public property in Italy, and as such the State has an obligation to reimburse all damage caused by

---

28 Ibid. [7].

29 On this aspect some scholars (e.g. M. Blumm and A. Paulsen, 'The public trust in wildlife' (2013) *Utah Law Review* 1437) consider that modern North American rules about the State sovereign ownership of wildlife have been inherited by the Roman law. In fact, having no owner, wild animals were deemed to belong to the public in common (*res communis*). The source of this interpretation is the Latin text dated 2nd century A.D.: Gaius 2, 66–67, *Institutionum comentarius secundus*, in which the commentator said that wild animals are *res nullius*, and when hunted they become property of the hunter (*res alicuius*). [Latin text: '66. *Nec tamen ea tantum, quae traditione nostra fiunt, naturali nobis ratione adquiruntur, sed etiam quae occupando ideo adepti erimus, quia antea nullius essent, qualia sunt omnia, quae terra mari caelo capiuntur. 67. Itaque si feram bestiam aut uolucrem aut piscem ceperimus, simul atque captum fuerit hoc animal, statim nostrum fit, et eo usque nostrum esse intellegitur, donec nostra custodia coerceatur; cum uero custodiam nostram euaserit et in naturalem se libertatem receperit, rursus occupantis fit, quia nostrum esse desinit: naturalem autem libertatem recipere uidetur, cum aut oculos nostros euaserit, aut licet in conspectu sit nostro, difficilis tamen eius persecutio sit.*'].

30 A. Manfredini, *'Chi caccia e chi è cacciato ...' Cacciatore e preda nella storia del diritto* (Giappichelli Editore, Torino 2006).

31 R. Putman, 'A review of various legal and administrative systems governing management of large herbivores in Europe' in R. Putman, M. Appolonio and R. Andersen (eds.), *Ungulate Management in Europe*, Cambridge University Press, Cambridge 2011.

32 Parliamentary Question E-013563/2015.

its own property. Note that under the national perspective, these funds can be categorised as 'reimbursements' and not 'aids' to farmers, so that articles 107 and 108 of the Treaty on the Functioning of the European Union seemed not to be applicable. The direct implication was that reimbursements should not be computed within the maximum amount of 15,000 Euros over a period of three years that a state can provide to single undertakings.[33]

The intention behind this request to compute such compensations outside the '*de minimis*' aid was to balance claims of farmers asking the Regions to strongly reduce wild boar overabundance. Yet, it is in the opinion of the European Commission that the categorisation of a compensation as an aid or reimbursement has relevance at the national level only, whereas in a European outlook the categorisation of 'aid' is made from the beneficiary's perspective. Thus, funds provided by the Regions to farmers for wild boar damage – a species not protected by the Habitats Directive (92/43/EEC) and considered of 'least concern' in the IUNC red list of threatened species – enter the maximum of 15,000 Euros that the State can provide over 3 years, whereas it is the duty of each Region to manage the species so to avoid or minimise its negative impacts.

On the national level, the national Supreme Court (*Corte di Cassazione*) similarly had to decide which rules apply regarding damage caused by ungulates in a vehicle collision.[34] Motorists hoped for the application of the same norm relating to private owners of pet animals (article nr. 2052 of the Civil Code), in which it is incumbent upon the owner of the animal to demonstrate that s/he did their best to avoid the harmful event. However, judgments recognise that the Regions and Provinces have a non-contractual liability toward the community (article nr. 2043 of the Civil Code, inherited from the Roman *lex acquilia de damno*) and it is the individual person who concretely suffered the damage who has to demonstrate the negligent conduct of the public entity. The claimant has thus to demonstrate the traceability of the harmful event – based on the principles of omission causation – to the failure of the public entity (the Region or Province) to effectively manage local wildlife (a burden of proof that in the opinion of some commentators is most of the time impossible to meet – so called *probatio diabolica*).

---

33 The European Parliament Commission in E-000241-14 answered: 'The wild boar is not a species of European interest protected by the Habitats Directive and its management is normally not linked with environmental objectives. It is therefore a competence for the Member States to ensure that wild boar populations are managed so as to avoid or minimize negative impacts on agricultural land'. The compensation for damage caused by wild boar has to be considered State aid independently from the legal category under which the compensation is granted by the State.

34 E.g. Corte di Cassazione, VI Sezione Civile, ordinanza nr. 13488, of 29 May 2018.

Overall, the effect of State property of wild animals is *de facto* mitigated by a favourable civil liability for Institutions, moving the burden of proof to citizens. Recognising that the burden of proof lied with Institutions would have partially softened claims of citizens who complain about the danger of driving on certain roads, especially at night, and alleviated the social pressure (motivated by health and economical concerns) against the Regions for more effective management.

4. CONCLUSION

Judgment nr. 139 of 2017 of the Italian Constitutional Court provides a decision (point 5) which was in fact highly predictable based on previous national (and international) jurisprudence. At the same time, it is remarkable that a Region, regardless of the unlikely success of the manoeuver, tried to push legal boundaries in order to press for a national change on the issue of the overabundance of certain wild species. The Regions (local level) feel social pressure because they are perceived as the 'true' owners and directly responsible for the management – including damage-reimbursements – of (*res publica*) wildlife, and regional politicians feel the need to demonstrate they are doing their very best against the central rules (national level) to respond to local stakeholders' needs. The judgment we analysed can best be seen as a symbolic attempt by one Region to publicly blame the central State for its failure to deliver an effective legal framework for the management of a pest species, thereby leading to a kind of public exoneration of the Region. The Liguria Region aimed for a modification of the article of the national law, unchanged from 1992, and embraced the idea of culling as a solution to reduce wild boar numbers. Because of financial limitations and in particular the insufficient number of Provincial police officials, the possibility to prevail on private hunters willing to volunteer looked compelling as an easy solution to a complex problem. Nevertheless, it is important to recall that biological scientists are not at all aligned when it comes to the most effective measures to control wild boar numbers. This doubt seems supported by the central State, which maintains unchanged article nr. 19.2 of law 157/1992, and by the Constitutional Courts that apply a principle of prudence. Limiting the list of people who can be involved in culling plans appears to provide a much-needed compromise between the necessities of controlling wildlife, balancing competing stakeholder demands, and the required strict control by police forces to tackle poaching and guarantee conservation.

It is important to observe, then, that following this judgment and in view of the impossibility to challenge the national law, some Regions (e.g. Piedmont Region, for the hunting season 2019–2020) have decided instead to extend the hunting period of wild boar. Since setting the hunting calendar is within the legislative power of the Regions, the extension of the hunting season bypasses the impossibility for hunters to take part in official culling plans and guarantees a bigger number of kills. Yet, this aspect denotes a rift between central State and the Regions about the management of overabundant wildlife, with Regions pushing for a relocation of authority, willing to take a clear cut position even on unsure scientific ground (and in the opinion of some, to the advantage the hunters' lobby), and the central State looking for a management compromise.

Considering that a conclusive solution for controlling wild boar numbers is still very much missing, the judgment can be an opportunity for Italy (and other countries with similar *res publica* and top-down governance systems[35]) to rethink the idea of State ownership of wildlife and to change the wildlife governance structure though a transition to a more decentralised management. This approach has several advantages:

- it will provide the country with a more updated and uniform regulation compared to the majority of European countries;
- it will be consistent with the vision of the post-2020 global biodiversity framework that is (currently) negotiated under the CBD and for which subnational actors will be expected to 'generate resources, political coalitions, and institutional structures that could not emerge from traditional state-to-state multilateralism';[36]
- it will also restructure currently misplaced social pressure from Regions, avoiding maneuvers such as the one discussed here.

In a broader perspective, we believe that the law hampers innovative solutions for better management of the ecosystems when it is too rigid. Legislation that is not updated despite the many reasons to do so, and that uses peculiar legal classifications abandoned by other countries, are the two concrete examples we bring forth here. The result we present is a misplaced tension in the society that then fosters a suboptimal management of wildlife. We have no doubt that, since ecosystems can be easily compromised and humans have obligations of preservation toward future generations, the support of the scientific evidence should always guide all laws that implement environmental management strategies. At the same time, we want to stress that the legal apparatus should be sufficiently flexible to allow for such evidence to guide human behaviour, so that to follow a principle of prudence is desirable but at the same time it must not become an excuse for inertness. In any event, managing overabundant species, such as the one discussed here, constitutes an integral part in environmental sustainability.

35 Ibid. [31].
36 T. Hale and D. Held, 'Breaking the Cycle of Gridlock' (2018) 9(1) *Global Policy* 129, 134.

LEGISLATION TO MANAGE INVASIVE ALIEN PLANTS IN ENGLAND

What is the Meaning of 'Landowner Responsibility'?

Kenji KAMIGAWARA, Shin-ya HIEDA and Trevor RENALS

1. INTRODUCTION

Invasive alien species (IAS) are a major cause of biodiversity loss.[1] However, IAS management is a relatively young policy area for nature conservation although not for agricultural, forestry and pastoral protection. Many countries have introduced legislation to manage IAS for nature conservation since 2000 when the International Union for Conservation of Nature (IUCN) adopted Guidelines,[2] and especially after the adoption of 'Guiding principles for the prevention, introduction and mitigation of impacts of alien species that threaten ecosystems, habitats or species' by the sixth Conference of the Parties to the Convention on Biological Diversity (CBD) in 2002.[3] Therefore legislation to manage IAS for nature conservation has been in an early developing stage.

The above-mentioned IUCN Guidelines and CBD guiding principles adopted the so called three-stage approach; prevention, early response and long-term containment. However, it was pointed out that 'national frameworks tend to be much stronger on preventing introductions than on mitigating their impacts'.[4] It seems that basically the situation has not changed. Prohibition

---

1 IUCN (2000) IUNC Guidelines for the Prevention of Biodiversity Loss Caused by Alien Invasive Species; Díaz et al. (2019) Summary for policymakers of the global assessment report on biodiversity and ecosystem services by the Intergovernmental Science-Policy Platform on Biodiversity and Ecosystem Services, p. 5.

2 IUCN (2000), above n. 1.

3 CBD (2002) COP 6 Decision VI/23.

4 C. Shine, N. Williams, and F, Burhenne-Guilmin, 'Legal and Institutional Frameworks for Invasive Alien Species' in H.A. Mooney et al. (eds.), *Invasive Alien Species: A New Synthesis* SCOPE Series No. 63, Island Press, Washington DC/London 2005, p. 271.

of trade and release into the wild could reduce risk of intentional dispersion. However, plants can disperse through watercourses and by wild animals such as birds.[5] Therefore, prohibition of trade, intended release and transportation is not enough to stop dispersion of invasive alien plants. It is necessary also to manage established invasive alien plant populations on sites.

England, France and Japan have already introduced legislation to prohibit sale and release into wild after 2000. Japan enacted the Invasive Alien Species Act in 2004; however, nobody is explicitly responsible for managing invasive alien plants on sites.[6] In France in 2007 legislation was enacted, which prohibited the introduction of designated IAS into the environment even by negligence or imprudence.[7] It implies that landowners must manage invasive alien species on their land to prevent escape even by negligence or imprudence. However, this responsibility has not been well-known by land managers and many believed that nobody was responsible for managing designated invasive alien plants on sites. Landowners were managing those plants on a voluntary basis at least until 2018.[8] Without a positive response by landowners, rapid response does not seem to work well. Among the above-mentioned three countries, only England has explicitly referred to the concept of 'landowner responsibility' to manage sites invaded by invasive alien plants. In this context, 'landowner' means the owner, occupier or manager of land. In addition, in May 2019, the Swiss federal government proposed amendments to the Environment Protection Law to manage IAS. It includes a proposal (Article 29*f*^{bis}) that 'owners of buildings, facilities or objects that are or may be infested with invasive alien organisms shall monitor, isolate, treat or destroy these organisms in collaboration with competent authorities, or tolerate these measures.'[9]

---

5 J. Haury and J.P. Damien, 'De Nouvelles Mauvaise Herbes en Zones Humides: Les Forms Terrestres des Jussies Invasives sur Prairies' (2014) 15 *Science, Eaux Territoires* 16–21, available at https://hal.archives-ouvertes.fr/hal-01145331; A. García-Álvarez et al., 'Internal Transport of Alien and Native Plants by Geese and Ducks: An Experimental Study' (2015) 60 *Freshwater Biology* 1316–1329.

6 English translation of the text can be seen at: http://www.env.go.jp/en/nature/as/040427.pdf. One can urge that public land managers have general responsibility to manage their lands in an environmentally sound manner. However, in Japan at this moment it seems that they have discretion to carry out or not to carry out IAS management projects, in considering their priorities within the limits of financial and human resources. So, invasive alien plants have not been treated in many rivers and lakes in Japan. Many public land (river) managers in Japan have been heard to say that 'if the situation would become serious, we will control those plants', which is in contradiction to the principle of rapid response.

7 Article L 411-5, Code de l'environnement. Also see K. Kamigawara et al., 'What kind of legislation can contribute to on-site management?: Comparative case studies on legislative developments in managing aquatic invasive alien plants in France, England and Japan' (2020) 23(2) *Journal of international wildlife law and policy* 83–108.

8 Interview and personal communications with public land managers in France.

9 Confederation Suisse. (2019) Loi fédérale sur la protection de l'environnement (Loi sur la protection de l'environnement, LPE) Modification du … available at: https://www.newsd.admin.ch/newsd/message/attachments/56929.pdf.

The UK had been a Member State of the EU until the end of January 2020, during which period the EU regulation applied. In 2014 EU introduced the Regulation on the prevention and management of the introduction and spread of invasive alien species.[10] It established the list of invasive alien species of Union concern. It has restricted the importation, keeping, trade, release, etc., of the species listed. It also has provided provisions for early detection, rapid eradication and management of widely spread species. For example, Article 7, paragraph 2 of the EU Regulation stipulates that 'Member States shall take all necessary steps to prevent the unintentional introduction or spread, including, where applicable, by gross negligence, of invasive alien species of Union concern.' Provisions for early detection, rapid eradication and so on are so general that those allow wide discretion by member states. Also, the regulation does not include any explicit reference to 'landowner responsibility'. The UK enacted the Invasive Alien Species (Enforce and Permitting) Order 2019, to comply with the duty by providing enforcement provisions, prescribing the offences and penalties and introducing permitting and licensing provisions.[11] This legislation and the EU Regulation (1143/2014) continues to operate effectively after the UK leaves the EU.[12]

2. THE THREE ELEMENTS OF 'LANDOWNER RESPONSIBILITY' TO MANAGE IAS

In England, the concept of 'landowner responsibility' to manage invasive alien plants has three elements.

The first is the UK government's interpretation of section 14 of the Wildlife and Countryside Act 1981, the second is the community protection notice served under the Anti-social Behaviour, Crime and Policing Act 2014 and the third are the 'species control provisions' of the Wildlife and Countryside Act 1981 which were introduced by the Infrastructure Act 2015.

2.1. THE UK GOVERNMENT'S INTERPRETATION

The first element is the UK government's interpretation of section 14 of the Wildlife and Countryside Act 1981 which argues that 'responsibility

---

10 EU Regulation 1143/2014 of 22 October 2014 on the prevention and management of the introduction and spread of invasive alien species.

11 The order is available at http://www.legislation.gov.uk/uksi/2019/527/made/data.pdf. Also see Defra (2019), Explanatory Memorandum to the Invasive Alien Species (Enforcement and Permitting) Order 2019 (SI 2019/527).

12 The Animal Health, Invasive Alien Species, Plant Breeders' Rights and Seeds (Amendment etc.) (EU Exit) Regulations 2019 (SI 2019/1220).

for dealing with invasive alien plants rest with individual landowners'.[13] Section 14(2) states:

> (2) Subject to the provisions of this Part, if any person plants or otherwise causes to grow in the wild any plant which is included in Part II of Schedule 9, he shall be guilty of an offence.[14]

The Guidance by Defra recognises that section 14 does not impose an explicit obligation to manage designated species not introduced onto the land by the landowner's actions. However, based on indications in case law, it says that

> it may be possible to argue that a landowner who knowingly allows a Schedule 9 species that he did not introduce, to accumulate on his land and create a problem as it spreads to other areas of the wild, and who makes a conscious decision to do nothing about it, is 'causing it to grow'.[15]

This interpretation, first published in 2009, has been repeated in the government's pamphlet that 'responsibility for dealing with invasive weeds rests with individual landowners'.[16]

2.2. THE COMMUNITY PROTECTION NOTICE

The second element of landowner responsibility is the 'community protection notice' served under the Anti-social Behaviour, Crime and Policing Act 2014, gives power to local councils and the police to issue notices for invasive alien species like Japanese knotweed (*Reynoutria japonica*).

Section 43(1) states:

> An authorised person may issue a community protection notice to an individual aged 16 or over, or a body, if satisfied on reasonable grounds that-
>
> (a) the conduct of the individual or body is having a detrimental effect, of a persistent or continuing nature, on the quality of life of those in the locality, and
> (b) the conduct is unreasonable.

---

13 Defra (2009, amended 2010) Guidance on Section 14 of the Wildlife and Countryside Act, 1981, p. 8, available at: https://assets.publishing.service.gov.uk/government/uploads/system/uploads/attachment_data/file/69205/wildlife-countryside-act.pdf.

14 Part II no longer includes invasive plants that are on the IAS European Regulation list as these are covered by the 2019 Order which creates a similar offence to s. 14(2) WCA 1981.

15 Ibid.

16 Environment Agency (2010), Managing invasive non-native plants, p. 5.

The Home Office published a guidance document that said local councils and the police 'will have the power to issue notices for invasive non-native species like Japanese knotweed', if an individual, or organisation, is not controlling it and could be reasonably expected to do so.[17] In December 2018, the court fined a property firm which allowed Japanese knotweed to grow for 10 years in a housing area in Bristol and ignored a community protection notice issued by the city council in 2017.[18]

2.3 SPECIES CONTROL PROVISIONS

The third element of landowner responsibility is the 'species control provisions', which were introduced by the Infrastructure Act 2015. Section 23 of the Act amended the Wildlife and Countryside Act 1981 by inserting a new Schedule 9A. 'Species control provisions' introduced by the Infrastructure Act 2015 give powers to environmental authorities to ask a landowner to conclude an agreement to manage 'invasive non-native species', and to issue an order to manage the species if the landowner refuses to conclude an agreement or fails to comply with it.

Before this legislation, 'in contrast to powers available under animal and plant health legislation to combat disease and pests, the network bodies (of Defra and the Welsh Government) had no powers to require landowners to act; nor did they have powers of entry for surveillance or to carry out work themselves in respect of invasive non-native species.'[19] In 2014 the Law Commission (LAW COM No. 342) proposed the concept of this legislation to Parliament, referring to the Scottish legislation. In Scotland non-native species control provisions had been introduced by the Wildlife and Natural Environment (Scotland) Act 2011 which amended the Wildlife and Countryside Act 1981.[20] The Explanatory Notes prepared by the UK government for the Infrastructure Act 2015 described

---

17 Home Office (December 2014) Reform of anti-social behaviour powers; Japanese Knotweed and other invasive non-native plants. Available at: japanese knotweed (nationalarchives.gov.uk).

18 BBC, 'Japanese knotweed: Property firm fined £18k over "forest"', 6 December 2018, available at: https://www.bbc.com/news/uk-england-bristol-46470898.

19 The Department for Transport et al. (n.d.) Explanatory Notes to the Infrastructure Act 2015, paragraph 88, available at: http://www.legislation.gov.uk/ukpga/2015/7/notes/data.pdf.

20 The Law Commission, (LAW COM No 342) (2014) Wildlife Law: Control of Invasive Non-native Species, available at: https://assets.publishing.service.gov.uk/government/uploads/system/uploads/attachment_data/file/286638/1039.pdf. This report referred the opinion of the Hampshire and Isle of Wight Wildlife Trust (New Forest Non-Native Plants Project) that 'the ability of a landowner to refuse to cooperate with an eradication programme and difficulties in tracing landowners have jeopardized the effectiveness of control programmes.' (pp. 14–15).

the reason to introduce 'species control provisions' as being that 'whilst most landowners are willing to enter into voluntary agreements, experience has shown that a small minority (around 5%) are not.'[21]

Although there is no list of 'Invasive non-native species', the UK government interprets that the scope of the provisions include those listed in Part I (animals) and Part II (plants) of Schedule 9 (animals and plants to which Section 14 applies) to the Wildlife and Countryside Act 1981.[22,23] The code of practice stipulates that 'these provisions should be used primarily to remove newly arrived invasive non-native species or species that currently have a relatively restricted distribution but have the potential to become more widely spread', taking into account the limit of administrative resources.[24] However, Schedule 4 of the Invasive Alien Species (Enforcement and Permitting) Order 2019 amended Schedule 9A of the Wildlife and Countryside Act 1981 to ensure that these can be applied for all species of Union concern including widely-spread invasive species.[25]

In addition, the environmental authorities (the Secretary of State, Natural England, the Environment Agency and the Forestry Commission) may request a landowner to enter into a 'species control agreement', which requires an owner to carry out control operations against IAS (including water primrose). The agreement may also allow the environmental authorities to carry out the control operations themselves.[26] The agreement may include a provision for payments from the government to the landowner.[27] Where an agreement cannot be reached, or is breached, the environmental authority can make a 'species control order'. Failure to comply with the order is a criminal offence, and breach of it allows the authority to enter the land and carry out operations.[28]

3. APPLICATION OF 'LANDOWNER RESPONSIBILITY' TO MANAGING IAS

We chose management of water primrose *Ludwigia grandiflora* as the subject of case studies on the application of 'landowner responsibility' to manage IAS

---

21 The Department for Transport et al. (n.d.) paragraph 88, above n. 19.

22 Ibid. paragraph 94.

23 These Parts have effectively been replaced by the EU Regulation list referred to in the 2019 Order.

24 Defra (July 2017) Species Control Provisions: Code of Practice for England, p. 5, available at: www.nonnativespecies.org/ downloadDocument.cfm?id=1567.

25 Defra (2019) above n. 11, p. 4.

26 Paragraph 7(1), Part 1 of Schedule 9A of the Act says 'A species control agreement must provide for– … (b) the party who is to carry [the species control operations] out.'

27 Paragraph 7(3), Part 1 of Schedule 9A of the Act says 'That [a species control agreement] may include provision as to– … (b) payment to be made by either party to the other, or to another person, in respect of the species control operations to be carried out.'

28 Defra (2017) above n. 24.

on sites. Water primrose is an aquatic plant of South American origin, which is regarded as 'among the most aggressive, aquatic, invasive plants in the world'.[29]

Figure 1. Water primrose in Stowmarket, Suffolk. (photo by K. Kamigawara, 3 September 2019)

In summer it can form dense mats on the water surface and causes serious social and ecological problems, constraining navigation, inhibiting leisure activities, and outcompeting indigenous aquatic plants in USA, France and other countries.[30] In England it was first recorded in the wild in the Wildfowl & Wetlands Trust's London Wetland Centre (LWC) in 1998.[31,32] In England naturalists and policy-makers have drawn special attention to this species.[33] For example in August 2010 the Non-native Species Secretariat published 'the Invasive Species Action Plan against water primrose, *Ludwigia grandiflora*',[34] which was the first of six invasive species action plans that had been published as of January 2020.[35]

Before describing the result of case studies on the application of 'landowner responsibility' to manage water primrose on sites, reference should be made to the restriction in trade, and release into the wild, of water primrose as

---

29 B.J. Grewell, M.D. Netherland and M.J.S. Thomason, 'Establishing Research and Management Priorities for Invasive Water Primroses (*Ludwigia* spp.)' (ERDC Aquatic Plant Control Research Program, February 2016) p. 2.

30 L. Thouvenot, J. Haury and G. Thiebaut, 'A success story: water primrose, aquatic plant pests' (2013) 23(5) *Aquatic Conservation: Marine and Freshwater Ecosystems* 790–803.

31 R. Bullrock, 'The End of a Golden Era … and a Good Thing Too' (2011) 53 *Biodiversity News* 32–33.

32 Water primrose was eradicated in the LWC in 2010.

33 They noticed serious problems caused by this species in France. See e.g. R.M. Burton, 'Botanical records for 1998' (1999) 78 *The London Naturalist* 199–204; Defra et al. (2008) The Invasive Non-Native Species Framework Strategy for Great Britain, pp. 5–6.

34 Available at: https://secure.fera.defra.gov.uk/nonnativespecies/downloadDocument.cfm?id=460.

35 See http://www.nonnativespecies.org/index.cfm?sectionid=92.

the prerequisite of on-site management. In March 2010 England listed water primrose as a species prohibited from release into the wild. The listing was done under the Wildlife and Countryside Act 1981 (Variation of Schedule 9) (England and Wales) Order 2010, which amended the schedule pertaining to invasive species in the Wildlife and Countryside Act 1981. Section 14(2) of the Wildlife and Countryside Act 1981 stated that 'if any person plants or otherwise causes to grow in the wild any plant which is included in Part II of Schedule 9, he shall be guilty of an offence'.[36] The listing came into force in April 2010. The Government also released the 'be plant wise' communications campaign in cooperation with the horticultural industry to raise awareness regarding invasive alien aquatic plants and to encourage gardeners and pond owners to dispose of their plant material carefully and avoid spread into the wild. In March 2014, England listed creeping water primrose and water primrose as species that were prohibited from sale. This was passed under the Wildlife and Countryside Act 1981 (Prohibition on Sale etc. of Invasive Non-native Plants) (England) Order 2014,[37] and the listing came into force in April, 2014.[38]

3.1. WATER PRIMROSE ON-SITE MANAGEMENT CASES

The UK government has flexibly applied 'landowner responsibility' based on a case-by-case basis, as shown by the following five cases.[39] The Environment Agency always seeks to cooperate with landowners, and as of the end of 2019, 'species control provisions' have not been necessary for water primrose on-site management.[40]

3.1.1. An Artificial Pond Owned by a Sports Club

In 1999 a naturalist found water primrose in an artificial pond in a sports facility owned by a sports club at Barton-on-Sea, Hampshire. At that time two ponds were completely covered with the species, and the club had tried to remove

---

36 See above n. 14.

37 http://www.legislation.gov.uk/uksi/2014/538/made.

38 In Scotland, the sale, etc. of *Ludwigia grandiflora* has been prohibited since April 2019 by the Wildlife and Countryside Act 1981 (Prohibition on Sale etc. of Invasive Animal and Plant Species) (Scotland) Order 2019, available at: http://www.legislation.gov.uk/ssi/2019/38/made/data.pdf.

39 Those cases were chosen from relatively large cases in which the species was not yet eradicated as of September 2019. Those do not include the LWC case in which the species had already been almost nearly eradicated before the government's interpretation on 'landowner responsibility' first published in December 2009.

40 T. Renals, 'The GB Water Primrose *Ludwigia grandiflora* eradication programme: 2017 progress report' (2018).

the plant.[41] The Environment Agency started to commit to the management of the species there in 2009. As of the end of 2018, the club had carried out a combination of herbicide application and manual removal on 12 occasions under the supervision of the Environment Agency.[42] In 2017 the club also carried out mechanical excavation in another pond. The club and the Environment Agency have shared the cost of managing the species.[43] In September 2017, only a few isolated plants were observed in two ponds.[44]

3.1.2. A Pond Owned by a Farmer

In 2008 a naturalist found water primrose at a pond owned by a farmer in Newport, the Isle of Wight. The pond (60m×20m) was completely covered by water primrose. The Environment Agency had applied herbicide by hiring contractors from 2008 until 2014[45] (the costs were paid by the Agency). Since 2015 a member of staff from the Environment Agency has visited the pond and manually removed residual individuals of the species several times a year. The farmer permitted the management but did not contribute towards it.[46] Small residual areas of regrowth continue to be chemically treated by the Environment Agency.

3.1.3. A Marsh Owned by a Private Company

In 2009 a botanist who was then Chairman of the New Forest National Park Authority and had been working for Hampshire & Isle of Wight Wildlife Trust (HIWWT) found water primrose at a pond in Breamore marsh in the New Forest District of Hampshire, during his annual survey of a rare plant.[47] The marsh has been designated as a Site of Special Scientific Interest (SSSI) since 1978,[48] requiring the landowner, a real estate company,[49] to keep it in favourable

---

41 E.J. Clement, '*Ludwigia grandiflora* Established at Barton-on-Sea (V.C. 11, S. HANTS)' (2001) 87 *BSBI News* 52–53.

42 T. Renals, 'The GB Water Primrose *Ludwigia grandiflora* eradication programme: 2019 progress report' (2019).

43 Staff member of the Environment Agency, interview, 6 September 2017.

44 Field survey by Kenji Kamigawara guided by staff member of the Environment Agency, 6 September 2017.

45 T. Renals, Water Primrose *Ludwigia grandiflora:* A Management Guide for Landowners (2016).

46 Staff member of the Environment Agency, personal communication, 10 October 2019.

47 J. Gore, 'Control of creeping water primrose *Ludwigia grandiflora* at Breamore Marsh, in New Forest District, Hampshire, UK' (April 2013), available at: https://www.hiwwt.org.uk/sites/default/files/2018-06/Control%20of%20creeping%20water%20primrose%20at%20Breamore%20Marsh.pdf, p. 9.

48 Natural England (n.d.) Designated Site citation file, https://designatedsites.naturalengland.org.uk/PDFsForWeb/Citation/1003799.pdf.

49 J. Gore, personal communication, dated 25 September 2017.

condition. HIWWT was asked by Natural England to manage the water primrose site because HIWWT had an existing project to manage invasive alien plants in the Avon Valley (the New Forest Non-native Plants Project).[50] HIWWT first tried hand-pulling and herbicide application, then carried out mechanical excavation in 2014. HIWWT received technical advice from staff of the Environment Agency and Natural England and other experts, and financial support from the Environment Agency and Natural England.[51] HIWWT has continued regular monitoring and hand-pulling of isolated water primrose plants[52] On 13 September 2018, it was difficult to observe any remaining individuals, although a small amount of regrowth was found later.[53]

3.1.4. A Ditch Owned by a Local Government Body

In 2009 a member of the public found water primrose in an urban ditch near a port in West Bay, Dorset. Since 2010, West Dorset District Council, which owns the ditch, has managed water primrose by mechanical excavation, chemical treatment (25 times) and manual removal as of the end of 2018,[54] and has borne the cost of hiring an environmental contractor. Also the Environment Agency did mechanical excavation in March 2011.[55] In September 2018, there remained only a small amount of regrowth which is being manually removed.[56] This site has received the most management intervention of the whole UK water primrose control programme to date.

3.1.5 A Retention Pond Owned by a Real Estate Developer

In 2018 water primrose was found at a retention pond in a housing development project area owned by a large real estate developer in Stowmarket, Suffolk. In 2018 the contractor hired by the developer mechanically excavated the invaded part of the pond and removed 2500m^2 of water primrose.[57] In 2019, water primrose grew again, so the contractor applied herbicide. The developer paid all

---

50 J. Gore (2013), above n. 47; J. Gore, personal communication, dated 18 December 2018.

51 J. Gore (2013), above n. 47, at pp. 12–31.

52 J. Gore (2018), 'Update on Creeping Water Primrose – Round Pond – Breamore Marsh – the battle continues', available at: https://secure.fera.defra.gov.uk/nonnativespecies/downloadDocument.cfm?id=1807.

53 Field survey by K. Kamigawara and S. Hieda on 13 September 2018.

54 T. Renals (2019), above n. 42.

55 A. Fraser, S. Moors, R. Clarke and B. Murray, (n.d.) 'Treatment of water primrose *Ludwigia* in an urban ditch'; T. Renals (2019).

56 Field survey by K. Kamigawara and S. Hieda, guided by S. Rice, Kingcombs Stonbury Ltd., on 10 September 2018.

57 T. Renals (2019), above n. 42.

of the management costs.[58] However, in September 2019, considerable regrowth was observed there.[59]

3.1.6 Conclusions of the Five Case Studies

The above-mentioned five cases show that 'landowner responsibility' does not mean the landowner must carry out control operations only by himself. The UK government has flexibly applied this, e.g. the government agencies have provided financial support (see 3.1.1; 3.13 above), and technical advice. In some situations the staff of the Environment Agency have managed the species instead of the owner of the waterbody (see 3.1.2). A number of factors determine how costs are shared, including willingness to pay by the landowner, whether the landowner introduced the water primrose and the risk the site presents to the surrounding environment.

3.2. COMMITMENT BY THE UK GOVERNMENT

'Landowner responsibility' is supported by the UK government's strong commitment to managing invasive alien plants. The Great Britain Non-native Species Programme Board was established in 2005 and its secretariat (Great Britain Non-native Species Secretariat), established in 2006, has coordinated invasive alien species policies in Great Britain. The first Great Britain Invasive Non-native Species Strategy was published in 2008 and revised in 2015.[60] The Strategy published in 2008 already stressed the importance of a 'partnership approach', that 'success will involve, for example, the combined results of control efforts by landowners, the surveillance and monitoring work of conservation bodies and operation of the high-level mechanisms set in place by the governments.' The UK government has committed to the management of water primrose by commissioning a research project, 'Eradication strategies for invasive non-native Ludwigia species – PH0422',[61] published in 2007, and instigating an eradication campaign in 2009, coordinated by the Environment Agency. In addition in August 2010 the Non-native Species Secretariat published 'the Invasive Species Action Plan against water primrose, *Ludwigia*

58 Ibid.

59 Field survey by K. Kamigawara and S, Hieda guided by a staff member of the Environment Agency, 3 September 2019.

60 Defra, the Scottish Government & the Welsh Government (2015), The Great Britain Invasive Non-native Species Strategy.

61 See Centre for Ecology and Hydrology, 'Eradication strategies for invasive non-native Ludwigia species – PH0422', http://randd.defra.gov.uk/Default.aspx?Module=More&Location=None&ProjectID=14763.

grandiflora,'[62] which was the first of six invasive species action plans that had been published as of January 2020.[63] The action plan tasked the coordination to the Environment Agency. Each new detected site is allocated to a site coordinator, who is an official of the Environment Agency or a project manager of NGOs.[64] To support this programme and facilitate engagement with landowners, the Environment Agency published a management guide for landowners in 2016.[65]

3.3. MANAGEMENT PERFORMANCE

So far England has shown good performance with on-site management of water primrose. By the end of 2018, England had detected 38 sites invaded by water primrose (an additional one site had been recorded in Wales). 'Nine sites have been confirmed as eradicated', and 'a further six sites are believed to be eradicated and in their five-year inspection period' (Figure 2 below).[66] The rate of eradicated sites is very high compared with France and Japan where local eradication cases have been rarely reported.[67]

4. CONCLUSION

England has developed 'landowner responsibility' by three stages: firstly in 2010 Defra published its interpretation of section 14 of the Wildlife and Countryside Act 1981, which argues that 'responsibility for dealing with invasive alien plants rests with individual landowners'; secondly in 2014 the Anti-social Behaviour, Crime and Policing Act introduced the 'community protection notice', which gives power to local councils and the police to serve notices for invasive alien species like Japanese knotweed; thirdly in 2015 Infrastructure Act introduced 'species control provisions' into the Wildlife and Countryside Act 1981. which give powers to environmental authorities to ask a landowner to conclude an agreement to manage an invasive alien species.

'Landowner responsibility' does not require landowners to do everything by themselves concerning management of designated invasive alien plants in their area. The UK government, namely the Environment Agency, has flexibly

62 Available at: https://secure.fera.defra.gov.uk/nonnativespecies/downloadDocument.cfm?id=460.
63 See http://www.nonnativespecies.org/index.cfm?sectionid=92.
64 T. Renals (2018), above n. 40.
65 Ibid.
66 T. Renals (2019), above n. 42.
67 The authors have carried out a joint research on *Ludwigia grandiflora* management with experts in France, England and Japan. Until October 2019, no local eradication case has reported in France and Japan.

applied 'landowner responsibility' based on case-by-case consideration, as shown by case studies on water primrose on-site management (see section 3.1 above). Usually the UK government has supported landowners by providing technical advice and in some cases providing financial support. In one case, the UK government asked an environmental NGO to manage an invaded marsh designated as a SSSI owned by a private company. In addition, the UK government itself managed an invaded pond owned by a farmer on an island. The UK government is strongly committed to water primrose management, for example in publishing the national action plan which tasked the coordination to the Environment Agency, and each new detected site is allocated to a site coordinator. Therefore 'landowner responsibility' is an important element of the process for collaboration among stakeholders in managing invasive alien plants in England.[68] These authors believe that 'landowner responsibility' combined with awareness raising, clear provisions to order landowners to take necessary measures, and strong commitment by the government, can contribute to strengthening collaborative management on sites in other countries. This could improve effectiveness of the law to manage invasive alien plants, which are a major threat to our environment and economy (biodiversity), and could thus also contribute to a transition to sustainability.[69]

Figure 2. The progress achieved during the first 10 years of the water primrose eradication programme in Great Britain

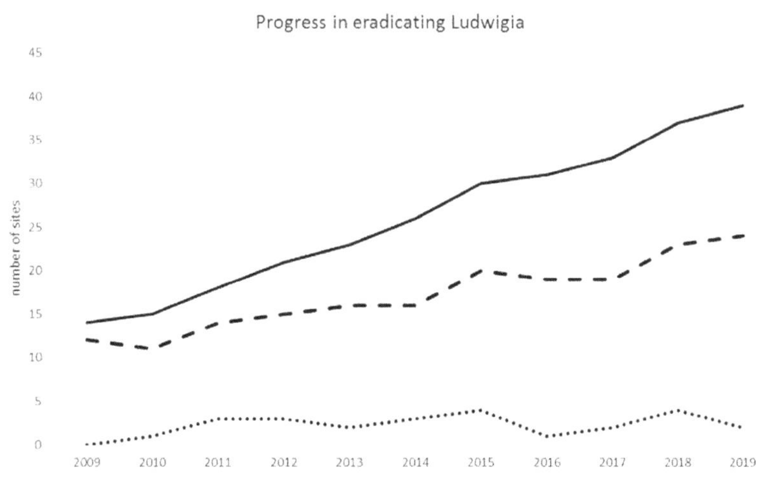

68 C. Chatters and J. Gore, stressed 'partnership working between NFNNPP (New Forest Non-Native Plants Project) land owners, land managers, volunteers and contractors is proving to be the key to successful control of invasive non-native plants.' C. Chatters and J. Gore, 'The New Forest Non-Native Plants Project: Effective Partnership Working at the Catchment Scale' (2017) 2 *New Forest Waternews* pp. 3–49.

69 We would like to thank the many people who supported this study, especially J. Gore and C. Chatters.

- 'Total recorded sites' is the combined number of confirmed sites, both existing sites and those believed eradicated. 'New sites' refers to the new confirmed records for that particular year.
- 'Actual sites' refers to the sites either in management, or prior to management, that have yet to be eradicated.

PART IV

TOOLS FOR ACHIEVING WATER SECURITY

REPORTING MECHANISM UNDER THE WATER CONVENTION

Innovation in the Sustainable Management of Transboundary Water Resources?

Alistair Rieu-Clarke

1. INTRODUCTION

Reflexive environmental law has been increasingly recognised as an important means by which to, 'establish internal evaluative procedures and patters of decision making within institutions to think critically, creatively and continually about how their activities affect the environment and how they improve their environmental performance'.[1] In so doing, such an approach offers the potential for law to more effectively support the most promising pathways to sustainability. However, the adoption of reflexive approaches to water resources governance is largely lacking at a transboundary level.[2] Few watercourse treaty arrangements contain any comprehensive mechanisms that can 'critically, creatively and continually' evaluate their environmental performance.

One promising development, however, is the establishment, in November 2015, of a reporting mechanism[3] to monitor the implementation of the Convention on the Protection and Use of Transboundary Watercourses and International Lakes (Water Convention).[4] In some respects, the decision for the Parties to the

---

1 E.W. Orts, 'A Reflexive Model of Environmental Regulation' (1995) 5(4) *Business Ethics Quarterly* 779.

2 Efforts to adopt such an approach can be seen at the national and EU level. See for example, L. Carvalho et al., 'Protecting and restoring Europe's Waters: An analysis of future development needs of the Water Framework Directive' (2019) 658 *Science of the Total Environment* 1228, 1229.

3 Economic Commission for Europe (ECE), Decision VII/2 Reporting under the Convention, in ECE, Report of Meeting of the Parties on its seventh session, 7 July 2016, UN Doc. ECE/MP.WAT/49/Add.2, 2–15.

4 Convention on the Protection and Use of Transboundary Watercourses and International Lakes, adopted 17 March 1992, entered into force 6 October 1996 (1936 UNTS 269).

Water Convention to introduce a reporting mechanism capable of monitoring the extent to which the Convention's commitments have been implemented by the Parties might be seen as unsurprising. Recent decades have witnessed the introduction of reporting into multilateral environmental agreements at such levels that some commentators suggest that, 'most environmental conventions [provide] for contracting Parties to transmit regularly to the Secretariat information on the measures adopted by them in the implementation of the convention to which they are Parties'.[5]

However, a number of factors make reporting under the Water Convention significant; and, combined, they have the potential to ensure that transboundary watercourse agreements make a more effective contribution to the drive towards sustainability. Firstly, while the Water Convention was originally conceived as a framework instrument covering the pan-European region, as of March 2016 an amendment to it has meant that it is now open to all UN Member States.[6] Since then Chad and Senegal have become the first Parties from outside the UNECE regional to become Parties to the Convention, and other countries have expressed an interest in joining.[7] Secondly, the introduction of reporting under the Water Convention coincided with the introduction of the Sustainable Development Goals (SDGs), and their associated targets and indicators.[8] What is particularly notable about the SDGs for the purposes of this contribution is that they include an explicit target and two indicators that recognise the critical importance of transboundary water cooperation; an overarching indicator (SDG 6.5.1) seeks to monitor the implementation of integrated water resources management (IWRM) at all levels, including transboundary; whereas a more specific indicator (SDG 6.5.2) measures the proportion of a transboundary basin area (river, lake or aquifer system) with an operational arrangement for water cooperation in place.[9] Thirdly, while hundreds of bilateral and multilateral agreements have been adopted by countries sharing rivers, lakes and aquifers, the introduction of reporting under the Water Convention marks the first time that a transboundary water-related instrument has adopted such a mechanism.

These developments suggest that the introduction of reporting under the Water Convention might be quite significant. The opening of the Water

5 UN Environment Programme, *UNEP Training Manual on International Environmental Law*, Nairobi 2006, https://wedocs.unep.org/handle/20.500.11822/20599.

6 See ECE, The Water Convention: responding to global water challenges, June 2018, UN Doc. ECE/MP.WAT/52.

7 ECE, 'More than 15 countries express their interest to join the Water Convention at historic eighth Meeting of the Parties in Astana', https://www.unece.org/?id=50143.

8 UN General Assembly, Transforming our world: the 2030 Agenda for Sustainable Development, 21 October 2015, UN Doc. A/RES/70/1; and UN General Assembly, Work of the Statistical Commission pertaining to the 2030 Agenda for Sustainable Development, 20 July 2017, UN Doc. A/RES/71/313.

9 Ibid.

Convention suggests that reporting may have a broader and potentially global reach. Moreover, the introduction of SDG indicator 6.5.2 and its co-ordination with reporting under the Water Convention also heightens the possibilities for a reporting mechanism to operate at a global level to support better transboundary water cooperation and sustainable development. At the same time, reporting for the purpose of reporting's sake is unlikely to gain much traction. For reporting under the Water Convention to play a significant role at the global level, countries must see the value of reporting. The purpose of this contribution is therefore to evaluate the reporting under the Water Convention following its introduction, and following the experiences of the first reporting exercise, which took place in 2017–18.

Firstly, the chapter will explore the reasons why the Water Convention introduced a reporting mechanism. Secondly, the pilot reporting exercise, which took place in 2017–18 will be evaluated in order to assess the process and its outcomes. Thirdly, following a review of the pilot exercise, the chapter considers whether there are any lessons that can be learned from that process, and whether any improvements to the mechanism might be made to strengthen subsequent reporting exercises. In conclusion, the chapter considers the future prospects for the reporting mechanism under the Water Convention in light of its initial rationale and the experience of the first exercise. A key focus of the chapter is therefore on the reporting mechanism under the Water Convention specifically. While recognising important linkages to the reporting process under the SDGs, and in particular SDG indicator 6.5.2, the chapter will focus on the value of reporting primarily for Parties to the Water Convention. An analysis of the value of reporting under SDG indicator 6.5.2 has been considered elsewhere.[10]

2. BACKGROUND TO THE REPORTING MECHANISM UNDER THE WATER CONVENTION

2.1. THE WATER CONVENTION

The Water Convention was negotiated by Member States of the UN European Economic Commission for Europe (ECE) between 1991 and 1992, and adopted on 17 March 1992.[11] The Convention entered into force in October 1996.

[10] A. Rieu-Clarke, 'Can reporting enhance transboundary water cooperation? Early insights from the Water Convention and the Sustainable Development Goals reporting exercise', *Review of European, Comparative and International Environmental Law*, https://doi.org/10.1111/reel.12344.

[11] A. Rieu-Clarke, 'Remarks on the Drafting History of the Convention' in A. Tanzi *et al.* (eds.), *The UNECE Convention on the Protection and Use of Transboundary Watercourses and International Lakes – Its Contribution to International Water Cooperation*, Brill, The Hague 2015, pp. 1–14.

However, as noted above, the Convention was then amended in 2003 to allow for membership of it by all UN Member States. There are currently 43 Parties to the Convention, mainly from across Europe, Central Asia and the Caucasus, as well as more recently, Chad and Senegal.[12]

The primary aim of the Water Convention is to foster cooperation between Parties in order to ensure their transboundary waters are governed in a way that prevents, reduces and controls transboundary impact. Central to achieving this aim is the requirement under the Water Convention for riparian Parties to establish, adopt or revise agreements or other arrangements for their shared transboundary waters, and to ensure that joint institutional bodies are in place to support the implementation of those arrangements.[13]

A number of substantive requirements are contained in the Water Convention, the main overarching one being, to 'take all appropriate measures to prevent, control and reduce any transboundary impact'.[14] In determining what might be deemed appropriate, Parties must take into account the need 'to ensure that transboundary waters are used in a reasonable and equitable way', and ensure the 'conservation and, where necessary, restoration of ecosystems'.[15]

The Water Convention also contains a series of provisions concerning procedural aspects of transboundary water cooperation, including the obligation to exchange information, elaborate joint monitoring programmes, set up early warning and alarm systems for critical situations that may have a transboundary impact, ensure that information on transboundary waters is available to the public, elaborate joint water-quality objectives and criteria, and develop concerted action programmes for the reduction of pollution.[16] These should be contained in and implemented through the agreements and arrangements mentioned above.

An additional element of the Water Convention, which has proven to be fundamental to its development, is its institutional framework. This institutional framework consists of meetings of the Parties (at three-year intervals), a secretariat, and various institutional bodies, including the Working Group on IWRM, the Working Group on Monitoring and Assessment, a Task Force on Water and Climate, a Task Force on Water-Food-Energy-Ecosystems Nexus, and an Implementation Committee.[17] Through these bodies the Parties to the Water Convention have been able to develop guides, handbooks, recommendations

12 See UN Treaty Collection, https://treaties.un.org/Pages/ViewDetails.aspx?src=TREATY&mtdsg_no=XXVII-5&chapter=27&clang=_en.

13 See Art. 9 of the Water Convention.

14 Art. 2(1). 'Transboundary impact' is defined as 'any significant adverse effect on the environment resulting from a change in the conditions of transboundary waters caused by a human activity, the physical origin of which is situated wholly or in part within an area under the jurisdiction of a Party, within an area under the jurisdiction of another Party' (Art. 1(2)).

15 Art. 2(2) of the Water Convention.

16 See Articles 9–16 of the Water Convention.

17 See ECE (No. 4).

and other soft-law instruments on a range of topics that fall within the purview of the Convention, as well as to develop protocols related to Water and Health, and Industrial Accidents.[18] Such activities are agreed upon and implemented through the Convention's three-yearly programme of work.[19]

2.2. INTRODUCTION OF THE REPORTING MECHANISM

The Parties adopted the reporting mechanism at the seventh session of the Meeting of the Parties, which took place in Budapest, Hungary in November 2015.[20] At that time it was decided to start with a pilot reporting exercise in 2016–17. As noted above, reporting was introduced at the same time as the SDGs were being adopted, and their associated targets and indicators developed. Given their complementarity, it was decided that both reporting under the Water Convention and reporting under SDG indicator 6.5.2 (transboundary water cooperation) should be conducted in parallel.[21] The reporting template or questionnaire had been developed in 2014–15 by a consultative process that involved both Parties and non-Parties of the Water Convention. Originally, the template included questions that were arranged into three main sections, which closely aligned to the commitments under the Water Convention.[22] The first section asked countries to report on the measures that they had taken at the national level to implement the Convention. Such measures included the national laws, policies, plans and strategies in place to prevent transboundary impact; any national licensing or permitting system to prevent, control and/or reduce pollution (from both point and non-point sources[23]); and the laws and procedures in place for transboundary environmental impact assessment. The second section concentrated on individual transboundary rivers, lakes and aquifers, and asked Parties to report on the agreements and other arrangements in place, any joint institutional bodies that had been established, and the level

---

18 Protocol on Civil Liability and Compensation for Damage Caused by the Transboundary Effects of Industrial Accidents, adopted 21 May 2003; and Protocol on Water and Health, adopted 17 June 1999, entered into force 4 August 2005.

19 See ECE, Water Convention Programme of Work 2019–2021, https://www.unece.org/fileadmin/DAM/env/water/publications/WAT_NONE_14_PoW/UNECE-Transboundary-cooperation-15-19-FINAL-WEB2.pdf.

20 Ibid.

21 ECE and UNESCO, were designated custodian agencies for SDG indicator 6.5.2, which meant that they had the overall responsibility for developing the methodology for monitoring the indicator, as well as gathering and analysing the data collected from countries sharing transboundary waters.

22 ECE, Proposal for a reporting mechanism by the core group on reporting, 14 April 2015, UN Doc. ECE/MP.WAT/WG.1/2015/5.

23 Point source pollution is emitted from a discrete identifiable source, e.g. a sewage treatment plant, whereas non-point source pollution arises from a combination of pollutants from a wide area, e.g. runoff.

of implementation on matters related to any joint action plans or strategies; measures to protect ecosystems; data exchange; joint monitoring and assessment; joint water-quality standards; accidental pollution and extreme weather events; procedures for mutual assistance; and stakeholder participation. The third and final section invited Parties to report on the main challenges and achievements in implementing the Water Convention, as well as provide information on the process of completing the questionnaire.

Prior to inviting Parties to report, and in light of the SDGs, the Working Group on IWRM under the Water Convention took the decision to revise the template in order to also incorporate questions related to the calculation of SDG indicator 6.5.2 value. SDG indicator 6.5.2 measures the proportion of a transboundary basin area (river, lake or aquifer) covered by an operational arrangement. The 'operationality' of an arrangement rests on certain criteria, namely whether an arrangement is in force and a joint institutional body established; whether states meet at least once per year; whether they exchange data and information at least once per year; and whether they have established any joint or co-ordinated plans or joint objectives.[24]

Given that these criteria were similar to some of the questions covered in the reporting template under the Water Convention, Parties to the Water Convention were invited to complete a reporting template that included the aforementioned sections together with an additional section concerning the calculation of the SDG indicator 6.5.2.[25] As many of the questions concerning the Water Convention also proved relevant to the SDG indicator 6.5.2 calculation – such as whether any arrangements and joint bodies were in place, data was exchanged and/or plans or objectives had been agreed – non-Parties were encouraged to complete a similar reporting template to that developed under the Water Convention.[26] This allowed non-Parties to substantiate their calculation of SDG indicator 6.5.2, while also allowing them to provide supplementary information on their national and international efforts to advance transboundary water cooperation.

3. THE PILOT REPORTING EXERCISE

3.1. THE REPORTING PROCESS

Countries were formally invited to report under the Water Convention and SDG indicator 6.5.2 in January 2017.[27] A deadline for Parties to the Water Convention

---

24 UN-Water, ECE and UNESCO, Progress on Transboundary Water Cooperation – Global baseline for SDG indicator 6.5.2, UN Doc. ECE/MP.WAT/57.

25 ECE, Reporting under the Convention on Sustainable Development Goal indicator 6.5.2, 28 June 2018, UN Doc. ECE/MP.WAT/WG.1/2017/3.

26 Ibid.

27 Ibid.

to report was set at 15 May 2017.[28] An initial challenge faced in the reporting exercise was that only 13 out of the 40 Parties who were asked to report, submitted reports by the 15 May deadline.[29] An additional 17 were received by 26 June 2017, with the last reports being submitted in October 2017.[30] n total 38 out of 40 riparian Parties submitted reports.[31]

While the number of Parties participating in the pilot reporting exercise might be seen as encouraging, the late submission of reports proved problematic for both the Implementation Committee[32] and the Secretariat of the Water Convention – both bodies were responsible for analysing the national reports prior to the eighth session of the Meeting of the Parties, which took place from 10–12 October 2018 in Kazakhstan. Additionally, while the Secretariat played a limited role in checking the content of the national reports, there were occasions where they requested countries to submit a revised report because, for example, the report had not been signed or key data was missing. This process of resubmission led to additional delays in analysing national reports.[33]

Pursuant to the Decision establishing the reporting mechanism, and despite the delays in the submission of national reports, the Secretariat of the Water Convention produced a synthesis report, 'summarising the progress made and identifying significant trends, challenges and solutions' prior to the eighth session of the Meeting of the Parties.[34] As per the original decision, the reporting template and reporting procedures were also reviewed in light of the pilot reporting exercise (see discussion below). In addition to the analysis produced by the Secretariat and the Implementation Committee, the national reports in their original form, were posted on the UNECE Water Convention website.[35]

3.2. RESULTS

In general, the results of the pilot reporting exercise under the Water Convention suggest that the Parties have made significant progress in the implementation of

---

28 Ibid.

29 Ibid. 12.

30 ECE, Progress on Transboundary Water Cooperation under the Water Convention, UN Doc. ECE/MP.WAT/51, 58.

31 The only Parties not to report were Denmark and Lichtenstein, ibid.

32 The Implementation Committee of the Water Convention was established at the 6th session of the Meeting of the Parties to the Convention in Rome, 28–30 November 2012, with the primary objectives of facilitating, promoting and safeguarding, 'the implementation and application of and compliance with' the Water Convention (see ECE, Decision VI/1 Support to Implementation and Compliance, in ECE, Report of the Meeting of the Parties on its sixth session, 19 September 2013, UN Doc. ECE/MAP.WAT/37/Add.2, 2–11).

33 Ibid. 3.

34 ECE (above n. 3).

35 See Reporting under the Water Convention and Sustainable Development Goal 6.5.2, https://www.unece.org/water/transboundary_water_cooperation_reporting.html.

the Convention since its entry into force in 1996.[36] However, as discussed below, the results also suggest areas where the Convention might be enhanced.[37] While such a finding might point to where efforts can be focused in future years, it also demonstrates that the Parties were willing to report on both the achievements and difficulties they face in the implementation of the Convention.

Another general point to note concerns the compatibility of the national reports. In some instance, one country may have reported on a particular basin, while another country sharing that basin may have chosen not to. In other instances, one country may have reported on the tributary or sub-basin of a particular river basin, whereas another country may have reported on the basin as a whole. Countries party to the same arrangement have also answered questions concerning the scope, function and content of that arrangement, as well as its level of implementation, differently.[38] In some instances, countries may have responded differently due to differing interpretations concerning the content of an arrangement, or due to a different perspective on how successfully an arrangement has been implemented. These differences are therefore an important part of the analysis of national reports and may in themselves highlight important differences of opinion between countries party to the same arrangement. However, there may also be significant opportunities in subsequent reporting exercises to improve the consistency of reporting between countries. For instance, some countries sought to co-ordinate their responses with those of their riparian neighbours via the joint institutional bodies that they have in place. Hungary, for example, used the bilateral commissions that it has established with all its neighbours in order to discuss draft versions of their national reports, and seek to come up with common responses, where appropriate.[39] Such a practice should be encouraged in future reporting exercises in order to improve co-ordination amongst Parties sharing the same rivers, lakes and aquifers, which in turn might offer a means by which Parties can develop a shared understanding of transboundary water cooperation within a particular river, lake or aquifer system, and therefore enhance their cooperation.

As noted previously, the first section of the reporting template asked countries to report on progress in implementing the Water Convention at the national level. The importance of having national measures in place to prevent, control and reduce transboundary impact is well reflected in the provisions of the Water Convention, and in Articles 2 and 3 in particular.[40] All reporting

36 ECE (above n. 30), viii–x.
37 Ibid.
38 Ibid.
39 ECE, Guide to reporting under the Water Convention and as a contribution to Sustainable Development Goal indicator 6.5.2, UN Doc. ECE/MP.WAT/WG.1/2019/INF.4, 7–8, available at https://unece.org/sites/default/files/2021-02/ece_mp.wat_60_eng_web.pdf.
40 See ECE, Guide to Implementing the Water Convention, September 2013, UN Doc. ECE/MP.WAT/39.

Parties confirmed that they have national laws, policies, plans and strategies in place to prevent, control and reduce transboundary impact.[41] More specifically, all reporting Parties confirmed that they have licensing or permitting systems in place to prevent, control and reduce pollution from a range of point and non-point sources, with most countries also setting emission limits for licensing systems on best available technology.[42] The record of adopting national laws and procedures for environmental impact assessment (EIA) was also reported as high, with 37 out of 38 reporting Parties confirming that transboundary EIA was a requirement at the national level.[43] Such a finding is perhaps unsurprising, given that almost all of the reporting Parties are also party to the 1991 Convention on the Environmental Impact Assessment in a Transboundary Context (Espoo Convention), which obliges its Parties to have transboundary EIA laws and procedures in place.[44]

The second section of the reporting template asked countries to report on their progress in the adoption and implementation of specific arrangements for the transboundary waters they share. As noted above, a key obligation under Article 9 of the Water Convention is for the Parties to established agreements or other arrangements for the transboundary waters that they share. There is considerable flexibility concerning the form that such arrangements might take.[45] The national reports showed that riparian Parties have taken the Article 9 commitment seriously, with only a few instances where a basin-wide arrangement had not been concluded by Parties sharing the same transboundary waters.[46] This also reflects a concerted effort on behalf of the Water Convention and its institutional framework to support the negotiation and adoption of arrangements in river basins such as the Chu-Talas, Kura, Drin and Dniester.[47] Moreover, the Water Convention's Programme of Work 2019–2021 commits the Parties to supporting the development of arrangements and the establishment of joint bodies.[48]

---

41 ECE (above n. 30), 13–14.

42 Ibid. 14.

43 Ibid. 16.

44 Convention on the Environmental Impact Assessment in a Transboundary Context, adopted 25 February 1991, entered into force 10 September 1997 (1989 UNTS 309). Out of the reporting Parties, only the Russian Federation and Uzbekistan are not party to the Espoo Convention. Additionally, EU Member States are obliged to follow Directive 85/337/EEC on the assessment of the effects of certain public and private projects on the environment, as amended by Directive 97/11/EC of 3 March 1997; Directive 2003/35/EC of 26 May 2003, and Directive 2014/52/EU of 16 April 2014.

45 See ECE (n. 39), 13–15.

46 ECE (above n. 30), 20.

47 B. Libert, 'The UNECE Water Convention and the development of transboundary cooperation in the Chu-Talas, Kura, Drin and Dniester River Basins' (2015) 40(1) *Water International* 168.

48 ECE, Water Convention Programme of Work 2019–2021: Responding to global water challenges in transboundary basins, https://www.unece.org/fileadmin/DAM/env/water/publications/WAT_NONE_14_PoW/UNECE-Transboundary-cooperation-15-19-FINAL-WEB2.pdf, 7.

In relation to joint bodies, a similar finding can be made, with Parties demonstrating a strong track record in the establishment of such bodies in order to implement their commitments under their basin and sub-basin arrangements.[49] The national reports also demonstrate considerable dynamism within the evolution of joint bodies, which have developed subsidiary bodies to respond to a wide range of topics including accidental pollution, data and information management, hydraulic engineering, hydrogeology/ groundwater, economics, ecosystem protection, the EU Water Framework Directive, floods, legal issues, monitoring, navigation, nutrients management, public participation, river basin management, thermal water, water quality issues and water allocation.[50] However, it should be noted that in some basins, there is still a need to establish joint bodies.[51]

Article 9 of the Water Convention requires that arrangements be consistent with, 'the basic principles' of the Convention, and that they 'embrace relevant issues covered by [the] Convention'. The national reports demonstrate that the main procedural and institutional requirements of the Water Convention, such as provisions related to water quality and quantity, monitoring and data exchange, are reflected in the content of existing arrangements. However, the reports also suggest that certain topics are not so well reflected, including the elaboration of joint water-quality objectives and criteria (Article 9(2)(e)), the maintenance of joint pollution inventories (Article 9(2)(c)), and provisions on mutual assistance (Article 15).

The remaining part of section two of the reporting template asked Parties to go beyond providing information on what arrangements and joint bodies are in place, and rather asked what activities the Parties have put in place to support the implementation of their arrangements within *specific* rivers, lakes and aquifers. In this regard, the completed reports suggested that the level of implementation of several key areas of the Water Convention is high, including the adoption of joint or co-ordinated water management plans and measures to protect the ecosystems of transboundary waters; the exchange of data and information; and the joint monitoring and assessment of transboundary waters.[52] Less well implemented activities, according to the national reports, relate to the prevention of accidental pollution, mutual assistance in light of extreme events, and public participation in transboundary water management.[53] Again, additional analysis might reveal the significance of these less well implemented areas of the Convention. However, with the growing potential impacts of extreme events, it is perhaps surprising to see that activities related to such subjects are limited. Similarly, it

---

49 ECE (above n. 30), 32–33.

50 Ibid. 32.

51 Ibid.

52 Ibid. 40–45.

53 Ibid. 46–49.

might also be expected that stakeholder participation in decision-making might be reported as higher across the basins of the pan-European region, given that almost all the Parties to the Water Convention are also party to the Convention on Access to Information, Participation in Decision-making and Access to Justice in Environmental Matters (Arhus Convention).[54]

The final section of the reporting template concerned, in part, the main achievements and challenges faced by countries in progressing their transboundary water cooperation with their neighbours. Common challenges included the difficulty in negotiating arrangements, a lack of harmonised governance and management systems concerning transboundary waters, a lack of resources, how better to engage stakeholders, and climate-change-related issues.[55]

4. LESSONS LEARNED AND NEXT STEPS

The aforementioned results of the reporting exercise fed into the eighth Meeting of the Parties to the Water Convention in two different ways. As noted previously, the Secretariat of the Water Convention conducted their own analysis and produced a report entitled *Progress on Transboundary Water Cooperation under the Water Convention*; and the reports were also reviewed by the Convention's Implementation Committee.[56]

The Implementation Committee's analysis of the reports fed into its report to the Meeting of the Parties, and decision VII/1 on general issues of implementation.[57] In its report, the Implementation Committee recognised a strong correlation between its work and the reporting mechanism, which it described as being, 'an essential tool for fulfilment of its mandate'.[58]

Upon reviewing the work of the Implementation Committee, as well as the aforementioned analysis undertaken by the Secretariat, a decision 'on general issues of implementation' was adopted at the eighth session of the Meeting of the Parties, which *inter alia* noted, 'concern that certain common challenges to implementation and compliance remain and that some Parties appear to face specific challenges in implementation and compliance'.[59]

---

54 Convention on Access to Information, Participation in Decision-making and Access to Justice in Environmental Matters, adopted 25 June 1998, entered into force 30 October 2001 (2161 UNTS 447).

55 ECE (above n. 30).

56 Ibid.

57 ECE, Report of the Implementation Committee to the Meeting of the Parties and draft decision on implementation, 30 July 2018, UN Doc. ECE/MP.WAT/2018/8.

58 Ibid. 7.

59 ECE, 'Decision VIII/3 – General issues of implementation', in Report of the Meeting of the Parties on its eighth session, 30 January 2019, UN Doc. ECE/MP.WAT/54/Add.2, 58.

The Implementation Committee was established, *inter alia*, to advise Parties in the implementation and application of the Convention, and, at the request of the Meeting of the Parties, to consider specific issues of implementation and compliance. They are therefore well placed to respond to these implementation and compliance challenges that have been highlighted in the national reports, and therefore support countries generally, and where specific assistance is needed at a country or basin level. While it remains early days, reporting might therefore offer an opportunity to realise the full potential of the Implementation Committee, which since its adoption in 2012, has dealt with only one specific issue of implementation.[60]

In addition to the activities of the Implementation Committee and the decision on general issues of implementation, the Parties also adopted a specific decision at the eighth session of the Meeting of the Parties, on 'Reporting under the Water Convention'.[61] This decision related both to the outcomes of the analysis of the national reports, as well as to the reporting process. In terms of the outcomes, the decision is consistent with the decision on general issues of implementation in encouraging Parties to make use of the reports, 'in order to improve their transboundary cooperation, for example by setting national and basin-wide targets'.[62] It will be interesting to see how far this suggestion is taken forward by Parties. The use of targets might also be a useful means by which the Implementation Committee might monitor progress and fulfil its mandate.

In relation to the reporting process itself, the decision on reporting adopted a revised template for reporting; set the frequency of reporting at three-yearly intervals with a deadline of 30 June; requested the Working Group on IWRM, with support from the Convention Secretariat, to develop a guide to reporting which would assist countries in completing the reporting template; encouraged Parties to cooperate when preparing reports; and requested the Secretariat to carry out capacity-building activities to improve the quality of the reports.[63] This decision therefore responded to some of the key lessons learned during the first reporting exercise.

For instance, some countries, together with the Implementation Committee and the Secretariat, recognised that some of the questions in the reporting template were unclear or overlapping with one another, countries faced difficulties in answering some of the more open questions, and the meaning of key terminology was at times unclear or not consistently applied, for example, 'agreement'

60 See the issue related to the Irtysh and Ili River Basins, ibid, 6.
61 ECE, 'Decision VIII/1 – Reporting under the Water Convention', in Report of the Meeting of the Parties on its eighth session, 30 January 2019, UN Doc. ECE/MP.WAT/54/Add.2, 34.
62 Ibid.
63 Ibid. 34–35.

vis-à-vis 'arrangement', or 'river basin' *vis-à-vis* 'transboundary waters'.[64] A technical meeting, which brought together 36 countries from all regions of the world, therefore took place in Budapest (16–17 January 2018) to review the original template.[65] Generally, the countries recognised that making any major changes to the reporting template would be counter-productive.[66] Major revisions would mean that countries would not be able to base their second report on the data provided for the initial exercise. Additionally, it was felt that while some tweaks to the template would be useful, on the whole the reporting template had proved robust enough to capture progress in implementing the Water Convention across the array of contexts represented by the Parties.[67] Revisions to the template were therefore limited to refining some of the questions that appeared to overlap or were unclear; avoiding the use of open questions and including more 'tick box' answers; and ensuring that terminology was consistently applied throughout the template.[68] No doubt these improvements to the template will strengthen the quality of national reports submitted in subsequent exercises.

Developing a guide to reporting was also recognised as an important means by which to improve the quality of national reports. Following the decision of the Meeting of the Parties, a drafting group of Parties and non-Parties was established to develop the guide. The drafting group met twice in 2019 (9–10 May 2019 and 3–4 September 2019) before finalising their work in time for the fourteenth Meeting of the IWRM Working Group in Geneva in October 2019.[69] The guide will likely assist countries in the completion of national reports for subsequent reporting in a number of ways, including clarifying key terminology; explaining how certain questions should be completed and what data might be relevant; illustrating how the report might be structured; and providing examples from countries that highlight the type of information that might be included in response to certain questions.[70]

A further challenge highlighted above was the inconsistencies in responses given by countries that are party to the same agreement and/or share the same

---

64 ECE, 'Overview of comments received on the template for reporting under SDG indicator 6.5.2 and the Water Convention and how such comments have been reflected in the revised template', https://www.unece.org/fileadmin/DAM/env/documents/2018/WAT/01Jan_16-17_Budapest/Inf4_Comments_template.pdf.

65 ECE, Technical meeting on the template for reporting on SDG indicator 6.5.2 and under the Water Convention, https://www.unece.org/index.php?id=47476.

66 Ibid.

67 Ibid.

68 Ibid.

69 ECE, Fourteenth meeting of the Working Group on IWRM, https://www.unece.org/index.php?id=50208.

70 ECE, Guide to Reporting under the Water Convention and as a Contribution to SDG indicator 6.5.2, UN Doc. ECE/MP.WAT/60 (February 2020), https://www.unece.org/index.php?id=53745.

river, lake or aquifer. During the first exercise, there were certain examples of countries co-ordinating with their neighbours in the submission of their national reports, sometimes through a pre-existing joint institutional structure.[71] However, the decision to organise additional capacity-building activities in support of the next reporting exercise, might also assist in this regard.

5. CONCLUSION

Given the significance of transboundary waters globally, transparent reporting, monitoring and evaluation measures are critical to ensuring that transboundary watercourse agreements support the transition towards a sustainable future. The introduction of reporting under the Water Convention can generally be seen as an important milestone towards this endeavour. This is particularly significant at a time when countries are focused on the implementation of the SDG framework and the target of achieving IWRM at all levels by 2030, as well as the decision to open the Water Convention to accession by all UN Member States.

The results of the first reporting exercise demonstrate that the Parties to the Water Convention have made significant progress towards its implementation, but gaps do still remain. It will therefore be interesting to see how the Parties respond to those gaps, and use the reporting exercise to support implementation, specifically at the national and basin level, and more generally at the Convention level. A key component in this regard will be the future programmes of work, which are adopted triennially at each Meeting of the Parties. While the last Meeting of the Parties focused more on the reporting process than the results, it will be important for the success of reporting, for the future programmes to respond to the results of the reporting exercise. Similarly, there is certainly a strong correlation between the Implementation Committee and the reporting under the Water Convention. How the Implementation Committee is utilised to support areas in need of implementation support will also have an important impact on the success of reporting.

The second reporting exercise requires countries to submit their national reports by June 2020. As almost all the Parties to the Water Convention have submitted reports, this will provide an opportunity to enhance the quality of the national reports and learn from the experience of the first reporting exercise. As the first mechanism of its kind concerning transboundary waters, reporting under the Water Convention, and the progress made so far in its application, offers significant innovation within the transboundary water context. In particular, it is hoped that this reflexive approach will lead to greater transparency both in terms of the arrangements that countries have entered into with their riparian neighbours, and the challenges that they face in their implementation.

---

71 Ibid. 5–7.

THE CONCEPT OF ENVIRONMENTAL DAMAGE ACCORDING TO DIRECTIVE 2004/35 AND THE DEROGATION UNDER ARTICLE 4(7) OF DIRECTIVE 2000/60

How to Effectively Remedy Water Damage*

Mariusz BARAN

1. INTRODUCTION

Under the responsibility mechanism introduced by Directive 2004/35 on environmental liability with regard to the prevention and remedying of environmental damage[1] in order to establish a framework of this liability based on the 'polluter pays' principle,[2] the EU legislator formulated the normative definitions of 'damage' and 'environmental damage'. Accordingly, 'damage' means 'a measurable adverse change in natural resources or measurable impairment of a natural resource service which may occur directly or indirectly' (Article 2(2) of Directive 2004/35). In accordance with Article 2(1)(b)(i), 'environmental damage' includes, but is not limited to,

> 'water damage', which is any damage that significantly adversely affects:
>
> (i) the ecological, chemical and/or quantitative status and/or ecological potential, as defined in Directive 2000/60, of the waters concerned, with the exception of adverse effects where Article 4(7) of that Directive applies ...

---

* This contribution was prepared as part of the scientific project carried out under the contract concluded with the National Science Centre in Kraków, Poland on the basis of agreement no. UMO-2016/21/D/HS5/03841 (Research project registration number 2016/21/D/HS5/03841).

1 Directive 2004/35/CE of the European Parliament and of the Council of 21 April 2004 on environmental liability with regard to the prevention and remedying of environmental damage, [2004] OJ L143/56.

2 See Article 1 of Directive 2004/35.

Recital 5 of Directive 2004/35 emphasises the need for the uniform use of the same definitions of terms in legislation in order to use common criteria and promote their uniform application (the so-called cohesion objective of the Directive).[3] To determine the scope of the term 'water damage', reference should be made to the definitions, criteria and objectives of the Water Framework Directive.

From the perspective of the effectiveness of Directive 2004/35's enforcement, there arises a question of whether the above definition of water damage is an effective tool to prevent and remedy such damage. This problem is relevant in relation to the derogation from the adverse effects of 'environmental damage' where Article 4(7) of Directive 2000/60/EC[4] applies. This leads to the question of whether the concept of environmental damage within the meaning of Directive 2004/35 and in the derogation in Article 4(7) of Directive 2000/60 has fulfilled its expectations and whether it has substantially contributed to achieving a sustainable and good status for all EU waters. If not, can the Directive 2004/35 be improved, or do we need a completely different instrument?

Directive 2000/60 is a framework directive adopted on the basis of Article 175(1) of the Treaty establishing the European Community (now Article 192(1) TFEU) as a legal instrument of environmental policy. It established a general, common and long-term framework for measures to protect waters in the European Union, which were to be subsequently developed and adopted by the Member States within the terms set out in the Directive.[5] The Water Framework Directive, being a directive issued as part of environmental policy, does not harmonise in a full (integral) way the laws of the Member States in the field of water (Article 193 TFEU).[6]

The primary purpose of Directive 2000/60, in accordance with Article 1(a), is to establish a framework for the protection of various water categories that will

---

3 Advocate General Bobek also uses this term to describe the relation of Directive 2004/35/EC to the relevant environmental legislation in his Opinion in Case C-529/15, ECLI:EU:C:2017:1, para. 58.

4 Directive 2000/60/EC of the European Parliament and of the Council of 23 October 2000 establishing a framework for Community action in the field of water policy, [2000] OJ L327/1.

5 See judgments in Case C-32/05, *Commission v. Luxembourg* [2006] ECR I-11349, para. 41; Case C-525/12, *Commission v. Germany*, ECLI:EU:C:2014:2202, para. 50.

6 Case C-461/13, *Bund für Umwelt und Naturschutz Deutschland e.V. v. Bundesrepublik Deutschland (Weser case)*, ECLI: EU:C:2015:433, para. 34; see: C. Keskitalo and M. Pettersson, 'Implementing Multi-level Governance? The Legal Basis and Implementation of the EU Water Framework Directive' (2012) 22 *Environmental Policy and Governance* 90; C.W. Backes and H.F.M.W. van Rijswick, 'Ground Breaking Landmark Case on Environmental Quality Standards? The Consequences of the CJEU "Weser-judgment" (C-461/13) for Water Policy and Law and Quality Standards in EU Environmental Law' (2015) 12 *JEEPL (Journal for European Environmental & Planning Law)* 363; A. Keessen and others, 'European River Basin Districts: Are They Swimming in the Same Implementation Pool?' (2010) 22 *JEL (Journal of Environmental Law)* 197; L. Baaner, 'Programmes of Measures under the Water Framework Directive – A Comparative Case Study' (2011) 1 *NELJ (Nordic Environmental Law Journal)* 31; T. Paloniitty, 'The Weser Case: Case C-461/13 *Bund v Germany*' (2016) 28 *JEL* 151.

prevent their further deterioration, protect them and ensure the improvement of the status of aquatic ecosystems.[7] Ultimately, the objective of Directive 2000/60 was to achieve, through coordinated action, 'good status' for all surface waters in the European Union as a rule by 2015.[8] The environmental objectives – whose achievement is meant to lead to the objectives of the Directive being achieved – are specified in Article 4(1) of Directive 2000/60.[9]

In order to answer the above question, it is necessary to analyse the provisions of Directive 2000/60/EC and the previous case law of the EU Court of Justice (CoJ) interpreting its provisions. This will allow an evaluation of the EU legislator's cohesive approach in the scope of defining 'environmental damage' (as regards water damage) in Article 2(5) of Directive 2004/35 with reference to the Water Framework Directive.

2. CAN DAMAGE COVERED BY A PERMIT ISSUED UNDER NATIONAL LAW STILL BE 'WATER DAMAGE'?

In Case C-529/15 *Folk*,[10] the subject of the Court of Justice's judgment was, *inter alia*, whether the exclusion of damage covered by an authorisation issued in accordance with the provisions of national law from the scope of the definition of 'environmental damage' caused to waters is in compliance with Article 2(1)(b) of Directive 2004/35. According to the definition set out in Article 2(1)(b)(i) of Directive 2004/35, environmental damage means, *inter alia*, 'water damage', with the exception of adverse effects where Article 4(7) of the Water Framework Directive applies.

---

7 The other objectives of Directive 2000/60 are listed in Article 1(b)–(e); see also C-461/13, above n. 6 at paras. 35–39.

8 C-461/13, above n. 6 at para. 37.

9 C-461/13, above n. 6 at para. 38.

10 C-529/15 *Gert Folk*, ECLI:EU:C:2017:419, para. 26; see also: L. Bergkamp and B. Goldsmit (eds.), *The Environmental Liability Directive. A Commentary*, Oxford University Press, Oxford 2013; G. Roller, 'Liability' in R. Macrory (eds.), *Principles of European Environmental Law*, Europa Law Publishing, Groningen 2006, pp. 134 et seq.; G. Winter, J.H. Jans, R. Macrory and L. Krämer, 'Weighing up the EC Environmental Liability Directive' (2008) 20 *JEL* 163–191; S. Casotta, *Environmental Damage and Liability Problems in a Multilevel Context: The Case of the Environmental Liability Directive*, Kluwer Law International, Alphen aan den Rijn 2012, pp. 141–216; N. de Sadeleer, 'Case Note. Preliminary Reference on Environmental Liability and the Polluter Pays Principle: Case C-534/13, "Fipa"' (2015) 24(2) *RECIEL (Review of European, Comparative & International Environmental Law)* 232, 237; G. Betlem and E.H.P. Brans (eds.), *Environmental Liability in the EU. The 2004 Directive compared with U.S. and Member State Law*, Cameron May, London 2006; E.H.P. Brans, 'Liability for Damage to Public Natural Resources under the 2004 EC Environmental Liability Directive – Standing and Assessment of Damages' (2005) 7(2) *Environmental Law Review* 90, 91 et seq.; B. Pozzo, 'Liability for environmental harm in Europe: towards a harmonised regime?' (2016) 44 *Hitotsubashi Journal of Law and Politics* 43, 65.

In interpreting the above provision of Directive 2004/35, the CoJ highlighted that Article 2 paragraph 1(b) of the Directive (defining water damage) does not provide for general derogation, in meaning that the damage is not covered by the concept of 'environmental damage'.[11] The exemption (derogation) provided for in the above provision applies *only to the (identified) adverse effects* to which Article 4 paragraph 7 of Directive 2000/60 applies.[12]

To determine the exclusion of the application of Directive 2004/35 to water damage, it is necessary to meet the conditions of the derogation indicated in Article 4(7) of Directive 2000/60. This provision provides that Member States will not be in breach of the provisions of the Water Framework Directive in terms of environmental objectives when:

- failure to achieve good groundwater status, good ecological status or, where relevant, good ecological potential or to prevent the deterioration of the status of a body of surface water or groundwater is the result of *new modifications* to the physical characteristics of a surface water body or alterations to the level of bodies of groundwater, or
- failure to prevent the deterioration from high status to good status of a body of surface water is the result of *new sustainable forms of human economic activity*[13] [subject to further requirements] (emphasis added).

To determine the scope of the possible exclusion from Directive 2004/35 for water damage (and to answer to the question about the effectiveness of the liability mechanism with the concept of water damage defined in this way), the nature of the derogation referred to in Article 4(7) of Directive 2000/60/EC must be analysed. This first requires a short description of the environmental objectives of Directive 2000/60 (which constitute the obligation of result[14] imposed on Member States), from which Article 4(7) is excepted (as one of the possible exceptions).

3. ENVIRONMENTAL OBJECTIVES OF DIRECTIVE 2000/60 – OBLIGATIONS OF RESULT

Directive 2000/60 introduced a transitional period during which, despite the expiration of the implementation deadline, Member States are not obliged to

[11] C-529/15, above n. 10 at para. 28.
[12] C-529/15, above n. 10 at para. 28.
[13] C-529/15, above n. 10 at para. 29.
[14] See J.J.H. van Kempen, 'Countering the Obscurity of Obligations in European Environmental Law: An Analysis of Article 4 of the European Water Framework Directive' (2012) 24 *Journal of Environmental Law* 499.

undertake all the measures envisaged by it. According to the first subparagraph of Article 24(1) of Directive 2000/60, Member States had to bring into force the laws, regulations and administrative provisions necessary to comply with that Directive by 22 December 2003 at the latest, and river basin management plans had to be published, at the latest, nine years after the date of entry into force of the Directive (Article 13(6) of the Directive), i.e. 22 December 2009. As the CoJ explained in Case C-43/10 *Nomarchiaki*, this provision

> does not concern the time-limit for the transposition of that Directive into national law, but merely sets a deadline for the implementation of *one of the measures that Member States must take in applying that Directive after its transposition.* (emphasis added)[15]

However, the existence of the transitional period does not mean full discretion on the part of Member States. During this period, the Member States had a commitment (Article 4(3) TEU in conjunction with Article 288(3) TFEU) to refrain, first, from adopting provisions that could seriously jeopardise the attainment of the objectives set out in that Directive[16] and, second, from the application of national provisions incompatible with the Directive.[17]

Article 4 of Directive 2000/60 is entitled 'Environmental objectives'. Article 4(1) lists the operational objectives to be achieved for surface waters, groundwater and protected areas,[18] collectively called 'environmental goals'. The most extensive objectives are for surface waters (paragraph 1(a)) and groundwater (paragraph 1(b)). As regards the environmental objectives for protected areas, the Directive refers to EU law as the basis for setting them (paragraph 1(c)).[19] To characterise the environmental objectives for the types of water, their classifications, as introduced by the Water Framework Directive, should be presented (Article 2 of Directive 2000/60).

---

15 Case C-43/10, *Nomarchiaki Aftodioikisi Aitoloakarnanias and Others v. Ypourgos Perivallontos and Others*, ECLI:EU:C: 2012:560, para. 45.

16 C-43/10, above n. 15 at para. 57; see judgments: Case C-129/96, *Inter-Environnement Wallonie ASBL v. Région wallonne*, ECLI:EU:C:1997:628, para. 45; Joined Cases C-165/09 to C-167/09, *Stichting Natuur en Milieu and Others v College van Gedeputeerde Staten van Groningen and Others*, ECLI:EU:C: 2011:348, para. 78 and the case-law cited therein.

17 C-43/10, above n. 15 at para. 58; see Cases C-165/09 to C-167/09, above n. 16 para. 79 and the case-law cited therein.

18 See e.g. Opinion of Advocate General Jääskinen in Case C-461/13, *Bund für Umwelt und Naturschutz Deutschland e.V. v. Bundesrepulik Deutschland*, ECLI:EU:C:2014:2324, para. 41; and also C-43/10, above n. 15 at para. 51.

19 Member States shall comply with all standards and objectives, at the latest, 15 years after the date of entry into force of this Directive, unless otherwise specified in Community legislation under which individual protected areas have been established – Art. 4(1)(a)(ii) and (iii) and 4(1)(b)(ii) of Directive 2000/60.

Waters are divided into surface waters and groundwater. Surface waters are all inland waters except for groundwater, as well as transitional waters and coastal waters.[20] Inland waters are all standing or flowing waters on the surface of the land and all groundwater on the landward side of the baseline from which the breadth of territorial waters is measured (Article 2(1) of the Directive). Underground waters are all waters below the surface of the earth in the saturation zone and in direct contact with the ground or subsoil (Article 2(2) of the Directive).

The environmental objectives that Member States are required to attain are stipulated in Article 4(1) of Directive 2000/60. The Court of Justice in the *Bund für Umwelt und Naturschutz Deutschland* case, interpreting this provision, pointed out that 'it provides for two different objectives, though in fact inseparable from each other':[21]

- firstly, *the obligation to prevent the deterioration of the status of waters* (in accordance with Article 4(1)(a)(i), Member States shall implement the necessary measures to prevent the deterioration of the status of all bodies of surface water),
- secondly, *the obligation to enhance the status of waters* (in accordance with Article 4(1)(a)(ii) and (iii), Member States shall protect, enhance and restore all bodies of surface water with the aim of achieving good surface water status by 2015 at the latest).[22]

The environmental objectives indicated above are common for surface waters (subject to modifications of the objectives for artificial and heavily modified bodies of water[23]) and groundwater.[24]

Such an interpretation of Article 4(1) of the Water Framework Directive – which indicates how two objectives that are equal and complementary to each other, both the obligation to enhance and the obligation to prevent the deterioration of bodies of water – is justified by the need to ensure the implementation of the quality objectives of the Directive (i.e. the protection and restoration of the good status, good ecological potential and good chemical status of surface waters[25]), because it avoids the risk that 'a part of a body of

20 In exceptional circumstances, surface waters can also include territorial sea waters due to their chemical status (Article 2(1) *in fine* of Directive 2000/60).

21 C-461/13, above n. 6 at paras. 38–39.

22 C-461/13, above n. 6 at para. 39.

23 See Article 4(1)(a)(iii) of Directive 2000/60.

24 See Opinion of Advocate General Hogan in Case C-535/18, *IL and others v. Land Nordrhein-Westfalen*, ECLI:EU:C:2019:957, paras. 55–58.

25 C-461/13, above n. 6 at para. 41.

water classified in the category higher than the category "good status" could be degraded to the category "good status"'.[26]

To ensure that Member States implement the environmental objectives, the various provisions of Directive 2000/60/EC (in particular Articles 3, 5, 8, 11 and 13 and Annex V) – through their constructions (wording), as well as the obligations imposed on Member States in the form of clearly defined steps – are designed to enable them to implement the necessary measures appropriate to the specificity and characteristics of waters occurring in their respective territories.[27]

Of the two possible directions of interpretation of the provisions of Directive 2000/60[28] – firstly, the minimalist approach[29] that would treat the Directive only as a tool for planning water management on a large scale; and secondly, a maximalist approach that detaches the Water Framework Directive from the planning level and sees it as an instrument to achieve binding environmental objectives, expressed in the adoption of specific measures with the aim of achieving good water status and avoiding the deterioration of water status[30] – the CoJ opted for the second (maximalist) approach in Case C-461/13 *Bund für Umwelt und Naturschutz Deutschland.* The confirmation of this interpretation of the provisions of Directive 2000/60 is the CoJ's statement that the wording 'Member States implement the necessary measures to prevent the deterioration of all bodies of surface water', implies:

- firstly, that the *adoption of such measures by these States is mandatory*, and
- secondly, that *permission for a specific project should be seen 'as such an implementation*' in the meaning of Article 4(1) of the Directive.[31]

This – as the CoJ states – leads to the conclusion that Article 4(1)(a) of Directive 2000/60 should be understood as obliging Member States – subject to a possible derogation (as described in more detail below) – 'to refuse a specific project' if it may cause the deterioration of water status or when it threatens achieving good water status.[32]

26 C-461/13, above n. 6 at para. 40.
27 See C-461/13, above n. 6 at para. 42.
28 Advocate General Jääskinen noted the above-mentioned two possible directions of interpretation of the provisions of Directive 2000/60 in his Opinion in Case C-461/13, above n. 18 at paras. 4–5.
29 Concept proposed by Advocate General Jääskinen in his Opinion in Case C-461/13, above n. 18 at para. 4.
30 Ibid.
31 C-461/13, above n. 6 at paras. 31, 32, 35.
32 C-461/13, above n. 6 at para. 51.

Such an interpretation of Article 4(1) of Directive 2000/60 – which gives this provision a normative character and, moreover, programmatic character with regard to the objectives of water management planning – leads to the conclusion of *a binding effect*, 'at each stage of the procedure provided for by this Directive',[33] *upon the obligations of Member States* (above all, the prohibition of the deterioration of water status and the obligation to enhance water status) *as soon as the ecological status (class) of a given body of water is determined.*[34] Finally, the need, or even the possibility, to balance negative impacts on waters, on the one hand, and economic interests related to waters and the use of them, on the other, in the framework of assessing compliance with the obligations to prevent deterioration and to enhance the status of water cannot be inferred from Article 4(1) of Directive 2000/60.[35] The wording of Article 4(1) imposes on Member States *only environmental obligations* (targets) *that cannot be associated with economic interests. Only within* the framework of the prerequisites of applying *derogation under Article 4(7)* (the Water Framework Directive) *is there a place for weighing the conflicting interests*: environmental objectives under Article 4(1) of the Directive and economic interests (reasons related to human activity).

4. DEROGATIONS FROM THE ENVIRONMENTAL OBJECTIVES IN DIRECTIVE 2000/60

As regards the environmental objectives of Directive 2000/60, as emphasised by the Court of Justice in the *Nomarchiaki* case, in accordance with Article 4 paragraph 1(a)(ii),

> Member States are to 'protect, enhance and restore all bodies of surface water … with the aim of achieving good surface water status at the latest 15 years after the date of entry into force of this Directive, in accordance with the provisions laid down in Annex V, subject to the application of extensions determined in accordance with paragraph 4 and to the application of paragraphs 5, 6 and 7, without prejudice to paragraph 8'.[36]

33 C-461/13, above n. 6 at para. 43.

34 Ibid. This conclusion is further supported by recital 25 of Directive 2000/60 (C-461/13, above n. 6 at para. 35); see also Opinion of Advocate General Hogan in Case C-535/18, above n. 24 at paras. 55–67.

35 See C-461/13, above n. 6 at para. 68.

36 C-43/10 *Nomarchiaki*, above n. 15 at para. 61.

The above – due to the common objectives and the wording of subsequent paragraphs of Article 4 of Directive 2000/60 – should also refer to groundwater.[37]

The provisions pointed out by the CoJ concerning derogations from the environmental objectives set out in Article 4(1) of Directive 2000/60 can be categorised – as proposed by Jerzy Rotko[38] – as follows:

- derogation allowing the obligation to achieve (restore) good water status to be postponed[39] (Article 4(4)),
- derogation allowing less stringent environmental objectives to be established for specific bodies of water when they are so affected by human activity that it would be infeasible or disproportionately expensive to achieve these objectives and if specific additional conditions are met (Article 4(5)),
- derogation allowing a temporary (transient) deterioration of the status of water due to circumstances of natural cause, due to the unforeseeable action of an accident or force majeure (Article 4(6)),
- derogation 'relating to human activity'[40] (*external cause*), justified by: a) the occurrence of new changes in the physical characteristics of surface water bodies or changes in the level of groundwater; or b) the need to apply new sustainable forms of human economic activity,[41] subject to further conditions (which will be discussed in more detail below) (Article 4(7)).

Moreover, in Article 4(8) and (9) of the Directive, it is stipulated in respect of each of the above derogations that:

- firstly, the application of the derogation cannot exclude or compromise the attainment of the objectives of the Directive in other bodies of water in the same river basin district and must be consistent with the implementation of other Community legislation on environmental protection, and
- secondly, the application of a derogation must ensure at least the same level of protection as the existing Community legislation.

---

37 See Opinion of Advocate General Hogan in Case C-535/18, above n. 24 at para. 55.

38 J. Rotko, *Ramowa Dyrektywa Wodna – analiza prawna [Water Framework Directive – legal analysis]*, Wydwnictwo Naukowe Wyższej Szkoły Pedagogiki i Administracji im. Mieszka I, Poznań 2013, pp. 155 and 156.

39 As Advocate General Kokott aptly points out, in her view, this derogation concerns the obligation to repair (restore) water status and cannot apply to a measure deteriorating water status, so this prohibition cannot be relativised in a temporal aspect – see Opinion of Advocate General Kokott in Case C-43/10, *Nomarchiaki Aftodioikisi Aitoloakarnanias*, ECLI:EU:C:2011:651, para. 69.

40 The term aptly characterising the kind of possible deviation from the environmental objectives, used by J. Rotko, *Water Framework Directive*, above, n. 38 at p. 156.

41 Ibid.

5. DEROGATION UNDER ARTICLE 4(7) OF DIRECTIVE 2000/60: NATURE AND CONDITIONS

The derogation stipulated in Article 4(7) of the Water Framework Directive, being the result of human activities (man-made projects), regulates the possibility of justifying derogation from the environmental objectives set out in Article 4(1) of Directive 2000/60 for new projects *due to overriding interests*. The justification for derogation from the environmental objectives on the above basis results either from 'new modifications to the physical characteristics of surface water body or alterations to the level of groundwater' (*the first indent*) or 'the need for new sustainable forms of human development activities' (*the second indent*) – this is *the first condition of derogation*. Moreover, the subsequent wording of Article 4(7)(a)–(d) of Directive 2000/60 clarifies that, by way of derogation, a specific project may be approved when *all* of the following further conditions are satisfied (together, *the second condition of derogation*):

- all practicable steps are taken to mitigate the adverse impact on the status of the body of water;
- reasons for the modification (e.g. implementation of a given project) are specifically set out and explained in detail in the river basin management plan required under Article 13 of the Directive, and the objectives are reviewed every six years;[42]
- reasons for those modifications or alterations (e.g. the implementation of a specific project) are of overriding public interest (which may include, for example, water supply, electricity production or irrigation[43]) and/or the benefits to the environment and to society of achieving the objectives set out in Article 4(1) are outweighed by the benefits to human health, to the maintenance of human safety or to sustainable development; and
- beneficial objectives served by the project cannot, for reasons of technical feasibility or disproportionate costs, be achieved by other means, which are a significantly better environmental option.[44]

The criterion of cause (the first condition of derogation, which is external: related to human activity) is not worded in the same way in each of the two indents of Article 4(7) of the Water Framework Directive: *the first indent indicates the effect*,

[42] See judgment in Case C-43/10, above n. 15 at paras. 67 and 69. An analogous view was expressed by Advocate General Kokott in the Opinion in case C-43/10 *Nomarchiaki*, above n. 39 at para. 80.

[43] The CoJ in Case C-43/10, above n. 15 at paras. 67 and 68.

[44] In Case C-529/15, the CoJ explicitly stated that 'the application of this derogation presupposes fulfillment of the conditions laid down in Article 4 para. 7(a)–(d) of the same directive' (above n. 10 at para. 30); see also C-43/10 *Nomarchiaki*, above n. 15 at para. 67, and also Case C-346/14, *Commission v. Austria* (*Schwarze Sulm case*), ECLI:EU:C:2016:322, paras. 65–66.

and *the second indent refers to the reason*. In the first case, the failure to achieve environmental objectives is the result of new modifications to the physical characteristics of waters, but in fact these '*new modifications*' – as aptly pointed out by Rotko[45] – *are not the cause but the effect (result) of the modifications*. This means that, in this aspect, no explicit reason is expressed; only the effects of such an external cause, i.e. 'new modifications', are pointed out. In the alternative, referring to the second indent, it can be pointed out that the *new modifications* mentioned in this part of the provision *may (but need not) result, inter alia, from new sustainable forms of activity*.[46]

In the second case, this external cause influencing the breach of the environmental objectives of the Directive is 'new sustainable human development activities', and it may affect all water characteristics (physical and chemical).

In cases where the implementation of a project may cause a breach of the environmental objectives through deterioration or by their failure to achieve good status for bodies of water, Member States are obliged to refuse authorisation for a project unless the above-mentioned conditions to grant a derogation set out in Article 4(7) of Directive 2000/60[47] are satisfied. Moreover, as the CoJ explains in Case C-529/15 *Folk*, the derogation in Article 4(7) of Directive 2000/60 not only applies to projects requiring permission, but includes in its scope 'any deterioration of the status of a body of water caused or not caused by an installation'.[48] This, in turn, means that the provisions of Article 4(7) of Directive 2000/60 – as a condition, by way of derogation from environmental objectives, of permission for a specific project – are of no importance for possible water damage.[49] It remains a separate issue whether such damage to the aquatic environment will be subject to the liability regime under Directive 2004/35 because the concept of environmental damage will not include adverse effects on the aquatic environment where derogation under Article 4(7) of Directive 2000/60 applies.

6. THE CRITERION OF EFFECT ON WATER CHARACTERISTICS/CLASSIFICATIONS

In the context of the application of derogation under Article 4(7) of Directive 2000/60 and the envisaged cases of the effect of such derogation on water characteristics/classification,[50] it is necessary to decide *how to understand*

---

45 J. Rotko, *Water Framework Directive*, above n. 38 at p. 171.

46 J. Rotko, *Water Framework Directive*, above n. 38 at p. 171.

47 C-529/15, above, n. 10 at para. 31; similarly, see C-461/13, above, n. 6 at para. 50.

48 C-529/15, above, n. 10 at para. 32.

49 C-529/15, above, n. 10 at para. 32.

50 First, failure to achieve good groundwater status, good ecological status or, where appropriate, good ecological potential, or to prevent the deterioration of a surface water body

the term 'deterioration of the status' of waters. This concept is not defined in Directive 2000/60 itself,[51] and thus reconstruction of its meaning is required, taking into account both the aim and the context of the legislation in which it occurs.[52] When considering how to understand the concept of 'deterioration of the status' of waters, two approaches can be adopted, as pointed out by the CoJ in the case *Bund für Umwelt und Naturschutz Deutschland*:

- 'status classes theory' – according to which 'deterioration of the status' covers *only* adverse modifications resulting in classification to a lower status in accordance with Annex V to that Directive,[53] or
- '*status quo* theory' – according to which 'deterioration of the status' means *any deterioration* of a body of water concerned; however, a question then arises as to which criteria should be used to assess the occurrence of the deterioration of the status of waters.

In the case *Bund für Umwelt und Naturschutz Deutschland*, the CoJ – sharing the views of Advocate General Niilo Jääskinen[54] and the European Commission[55] – pointed out that

> there is 'deterioration of the status' of a body of surface water (…) as soon as the status of at least one of the quality elements, within the meaning of Annex V to the directive, falls by one class, even if that fall does not result in a fall in classification of the body of surface water as a whole. However, if the quality element concerned, within the meaning of that annex, is already in the lowest class, any deterioration of that element constitutes a 'deterioration of the status' of a body of surface water (…).[56]

In order to justify such an understanding of the term 'deterioration of the status', at least the following arguments can be given:

- first, the wording of Article 4(1)(a)(i) and (1)(b)(i) of Directive 2000/60 shows that the deterioration of all bodies of surface water and groundwater should be prevented, which also includes deterioration events that do not lead to the classification of the body of water concerned to a lower class;

---

or groundwater, and second, failure to prevent the deterioration of a body of surface water from very good status to good status (Art. 4(7) first and second indents.

51 C-461/13, above n. 6 at para. 53.

52 See e.g. the following judgments: Case C-317/12, *Lundberg v. Sweden*, ECLI:EU:C:2013:631, para. 19; Case C-187/12 to C-189/12, *SFIR v. AGEA*, ECLI:EU:C:2013:737, para. 24; Case C-114/13, *Bouman v. Rijksdienst voor Pensioenen*, ECLI:EU:C:2015:81, para. 31.

53 C-461/13, above n. 6 at para. 52 and 65.

54 See Opinion of Advocate General Jääskinen in Case C-461/13, above, n. 18 at paras. 100–105.

55 See the European Commission's arguments in the Opinion of Advocate General Jääskinen in Case C-461/13, above, n. 18 at paras. 87 and 88.

56 C-461/13, above n. 6 at para. 69.

- second, Article 4(1)(a)(i) and (b)(i) of Directive 2000/60 provide in principle for the obligation to prevent a deterioration of the status of surface waters[57] and groundwater[58] without mentioning a possible change of class, because Article 4(1)(a)(ii) and (iii) and (1)(b)(ii) of that Directive refer to Annex V in that Directive only in relation to the obligation to enhance the status of bodies of surface water and groundwater; therefore, it should not raise doubts that a 'deterioration of the status' of a body of water is a general concept, and therefore Article 4(1)(a)(i) and (1)(b)(i) do not refer to Annex V;[59]
- third, the interpretation referred to above is fully justified in the context and given the purpose of Directive 2000/60, since a different interpretation of the term 'deterioration of the status' would discourage Member States from preventing a deterioration of the status of surface water bodies or groundwater within a status class ('one-out-all-out' principle); if a different interpretation was adopted, this would lead to the conclusion that 'classification of a body of surface water depends on the poorest value of the applicable parameters, all the other values could be reduced without that having legal consequences';[60] the same applies to groundwater, which would be in contradiction to the objectives of Directive 2000/60;
- fourth, 'application of the status classes theory would result in a weakening of the protection of waters falling within the highest classes", the more so as 'the classification of waters is determined by the poorest value of the applicable parameters, clear deterioration of other elements would not change the classification of the body of water concerned at all as long as it did not result in classification in a lower class';[61]
- fifth, the additional interpretation indicated is justified by the provision of 'Article 4 para. 5(c) of Directive 2000/60, which expressly provides for a prohibition on the further deterioration of the status of a body of water with regard to heavily modified surface water bodies, for which Member States may pursue less stringent environmental objectives';[62]
- sixth, only if 'the term 'deterioration' is interpreted by reference to an element of quality or substance, is the obligation to prevent deterioration fully

57 As defined in Art. 2(17) of Directive 2000/60, the status of surface waters is a general expression of the status of a body of surface water, determined by the poorer of its ecological status and chemical status.

58 As defined in Art. 2(19) of Directive 2000/60, the status of groundwater is a general expression of the status of a body of groundwater, determined by the poorer of its quantitative and chemical status.

59 C-461/13, above n. 6 at para. 61.

60 C-461/13, above n. 6 at para. 62.

61 C-461/13, above n. 6 at para. 65.

62 C-461/13, above n. 6 at para. 64 and 66.

effective, since it covers any modifications that may jeopardise the primary purpose of Directive 2000/60';[63] and

- seventh, the wording of Article 4 of Directive 2000/60/EC, in particular paragraph 6 and 7, clearly shows that a 'deterioration of the status of bodies of water, even transitory, is permitted only under strict conditions', which leads to the conclusion that 'the threshold above which there is a breach of the obligation to prevent deterioration of the status of water bodies must be defined low'.[64]

7. ARE THE PROVISIONS OF ARTICLE 4(7) OF DIRECTIVE 2000/60 DIRECTLY EFFECTIVE?[65]

In the *Folk* case, one of the questions asked of the CoJ by the Austrian court concerned the following issue: if permission to pollute is issued under national law without examining the fulfilment of the conditions set out in Article 4(7) of Directive 2000/60, is it the task of the national court alone to verify that the conditions laid down in that provision are satisfied in order to determine whether environmental damage has been caused within the meaning of Article 2(1)(b) of Directive 2004/35? In essence, this is a question about the direct effectiveness of derogation under Article 4(7) of Directive 2000/60.[66] The CoJ replied in the negative, stating that 'EU law in no way obliges the national courts to take the place of the competent authority by itself examining those conditions when that authority has granted the authorisation without having carried out that examination'.[67]

The priority *obligation to verify* whether the conditions set out in Article 4(7)(a)–(d) of Directive 2000/60 are satisfied with regard to a specific project (adverse modification) *lies with national authorities* and *through appropriate procedures* (the institutional aspect of the implementation of Directive 2000/60/EC), in accordance with the principle of procedural autonomy

63 C-461/13, above n. 6 at para. 66 and the Opinion of Advocate General Jääskinen in Case C-461/13, above, n. 18 at para. 105.

64 C-461/13, above n. 6 at para. 67. See Ch.W. Backes and H.F.M.W. van Rijswick, above n. 6 at 369–377.

65 In Case C-664/15, *Protect Natur-, Arten- und Landschaftsschutz Umweltorganisation v. Bezirkshauptmannschaft Gmünd*, ECLI:EU:C:2017:987, the CoJ interpreted the environmental objectives of Article 4 of Directive 2000/60 as having a direct effect, however it did not clarify whether this concerned the whole of Article 4 (para. 34 of judgment); see also J. Söderasp and M. Pettersson, 'Before and After the *Weser* Case: Legal Application of the Water Framework Directive Environmental Objectives in Sweden' (2019) 31 *JEL* 265, 290.

66 The question of the national court is similarly understood by Advocate General Bobek – see Opinion in Case C-529/15, above, n. 3 at paras. 54 and 56.

67 C-529/15, above n. 10 at para. 39.

(Article 2(3) of the Directive), without prejudice to possible judicial review, and by the decisions of competent national authorities.[68]

The possibility to invoke the exemption provided for in Article 2(1)(b) of Directive 2004/35 depends on whether Article 4(7) of Directive 2000/60[69] applies. This application proceeds, as indicated above, in accordance with national institutional provisions and procedures set out in national legislation implementing Article 4(7) of the Water Framework Directive. These circumstances seem to have led the CoJ in the *Folk* case to the conclusion that 'water damage' as defined in Article 2(1)(b) of Directive 2004/35, by reference to Article 4(7) of Directive 2000/60, does not require the national court to leave out national procedural and institutional arrangements envisaged for the implementation of the obligations under the Water Framework Directive in order to determine whether the exemption from the definition of 'water damage' is in fact effective.[70]

As regards the problem of the direct effectiveness of Article 4(7) of Directive 2000/60, regardless of doubts as to whether this provision is sufficiently unequivocal and precise, it is certainly not unconditional. For this reason, in Case C-664/15 *Protect Natur*, the CoJ – interpreting the environmental objectives of Article 4 of Directive 2000/60 – highlighted that

> the effectiveness of Directive 2000/60 and its aim of protecting the environment ... require that individuals or, where appropriate, a duly constituted environmental organisation be able to rely on it in legal proceedings and that the national courts be able to take that directive into consideration as an element of EU law in order, inter alia, to review whether a national authority that has granted a permit for a project that may have an effect on the water status has complied with its obligations under Article 4 of the directive, in particular preventing the deterioration of bodies of water, and has thus kept within the limits of the discretion granted to the competent national authorities by that provision.[71]

In light of the conditions of the application of derogation listed in Article 4(7) (a)–(d), it is clear that 'its application is spread over several successive steps and requires a series of qualitative verifications, in which Member States probably have considerable discretion'.[72] Such an assessment of the nature of Article 4(7) of

---

68 C-529/15, above n. 10 at para. 39; see also the Opinion of Advocate General Bobek in Case C-529/15, above n. 3 at para. 60.

69 See Opinion of Advocate General Bobek in Case C-529/15, above, n. 3 at para. 62.

70 See C-529/15, above n. 10 at para. 39 and Opinion of Advocate General Bobek in Case C-529/15, above n. 3 at para. 62 and the judgment in C-664/15, above, n. 65 at para. 34.

71 C-664/15, above n. 65 at para. 34; see, by analogy, Case C-237/07, *Dieter Janecek v. Freistaat*, ECLI:EU:C:2008:447, para. 37 and Case C-243/15, *Lesoochranárske zoskupenie VLK v. Obvodný úrad Trenčín*, ECLI:EU:C:2016:838, para. 44.

72 See Opinion of Advocate General Bobek in Case C-529/15, above, n. 3 at para. 56.

Directive 2000/60 also determines the assessment of reference to this provision contained in Article 2(1)(b) of Directive 2004/35.

8. CONCLUSION

Directive 2004/35, as already indicated, functions in close connection with other Union environmental instruments. An example of such a link is stipulated in Article 2(5) of Directive 2004/35, which defines the concept of 'water' and 'environmental damage' in relation to waters. The definition of water damage refers to specific definitions of terms introduced in the Water Framework Directive (e.g. 'quantitative status' or 'ecological status'). The definition of 'water damage' (Article 2(1)(b) of Directive 2004/35) excludes the 'adverse effect referred to in Art. 4 para. 7' of Directive 2000/60.

The possibility of invoking the exemption provided for in Directive 2004/35 depends on whether Article 4(7) of Directive 2000/60[73] applies. The purpose of the exclusion is to take into account specific derogations permitted under Article 4(7) of Directive 2000/60. The derogation applies to new modifications or alterations, or new sustainable human development activities, provided that certain criteria and conditions (indicated in Article 4(7)(a)–(d) of the Directive) are satisfied.

The very fact of the exclusion from the concept of 'environmental damage' (in the scope of water damage) of adverse effects falling within the scope of Article 4(7) of Directive 2000/60 does not jeopardise the effective enforcement of the liability mechanism introduced by Directive 2004/35, i.e. the prevention and remedying of water damage. First, this is because the derogation under Article 4(7) of the Water Framework Directive is an exception from binding obligations of Member States to prevent deterioration and to enhance water status. Second, although Member States have a certain amount of discretion in weighing the conflicting interests of environmental goals and economic interests when assessing the fulfilment of the conditions for derogation, the exemption provided for in Directive 2004/35 will take place only when the authorisation issued, based on national law (modifications made), satisfies the stringent criteria for derogation under Article 4(7)(a)–(d) of Directive 2000/60.[74]

From the perspective of the effectiveness of the enforcement of Directive 2004/35, there are doubts concerning the opinion expressed by the CoJ in the *Folk* case, which states that when the permit is issued under national law without examining the fulfilment of the conditions set out in Article 4(7)(a)–(d) of Directive 2000/60, the national court is not obliged itself to verify whether

---

[73] See Opinion of Advocate General Bobek in Case C-529/15, above, n. 3 at para. 62.

[74] See Case C-346/14, above n. 44 paras. 64–82.

the conditions laid down in that provision are satisfied. However, it should be emphasised that the above interpretation of Article 4(7) of the Water Framework Directive – as interpreted by the CoJ in the *Protect Natur* case – does not affect the competence of national courts to examine the compliance with EU law of decisions adopted by competent national authorities responsible for ensuring the compliance of implemented projects (modifications made) with the criteria contained in Article 4(7)(a)–(d) of Directive 2000/60.

CHALLENGES AND PROSPECTS ON THE APPLICATION OF DIRECTIVE 92/43/EEC ON MARINE ECOSYSTEMS

Need for a New Legal Framework?

Georgios Kalogerakis and Sofia Fotopoulou

1. INTRODUCTION

The conservation of marine biodiversity plays a central role in environmental protection. The main piece of EU legislation for the conservation of biodiversity remains the Directive 92/43/EEC[1] – known as the Habitats Directive (HD).[2] The rest of the legal framework consists of certain legal texts aiming at the transition to a sustainable marine environmental management model. This contribution attempts to address the question whether the current EU legal framework is sufficient for the protection of the marine environment. More specifically, given the deficiencies of the HD, it will be examined whether a higher – or at least equal – level of marine environmental protection can be achieved through other EU legislative acts mainly oriented toward sustainable management of marine resources. In this direction, the examples of some basic EU legal tools aiming to the consolidation of a sustainable development model in the marine environment will be studied. This question is often neglected in legal theory, which seems to be almost exclusively focused on the role of the HD in the EU biodiversity conservation system. To this end, the section 2 of the chapter will assess how the HD is implemented in the protection of the marine environment in general. A brief analysis will then follow (section 3) on the rest of the pieces of the EU legal framework on marine environmental protection and their potential for attaining biodiversity targets and filling in the gaps of the HD. In the final

1 Council Directive 92/43/EEC of 21 May 1992 on the conservation of natural habitats and of wild fauna and flora [1992] OJ L206/7.

2 V. Frank, *The European Community and Marine Environmental Protection in the International Law of the Sea – Implementing Global Obligations at the Regional Level*, Martinus Nijhoff Publishers, Leiden 2007, p. 383.

section (section 4), conclusive remarks on the adequacy of the current legal framework and the perspectives of its possible amendment in the future are presented.

2. THE IMPLEMENTATION OF THE HD FOR THE PROTECTION OF THE MARINE ENVIRONMENT

2.1. THE SCOPE OF THE DIRECTIVE AND THE CURRENT SITUATION OF MARINE ECOSYSTEMS

The HD is based on two pillars. Firstly, the Directive requires Member States to establish a site-based protection system of a coherent European ecological network of Sites of Community Importance (SCIs) known as Natura 2000 (Articles 3–10). In this network the Special Areas of Conservation (SACs) are included as well as the Special Protection Areas (SPAs) under Directive 2009/147/EC[3] (the so-called Birds Directive (BD)).[4] Secondly, Member States are required to establish a direct species-based protection system for animal and plant species listed in Annexes IV–V (Articles 12–16). Central to the Directive's protection system is the concept of the 'natural habitat'. According to the definition in Article 1(b), 'natural habitats' means 'terrestrial or aquatic areas distinguished by geographic, abiotic and biotic features, whether entirely natural or semi-natural'. The 'aquatic areas' cover both marine areas and wetlands. For the very first time the conservation of marine ecosystems is explicitly included in the scope of a European legislative act. Concerning marine areas, the HD can be applied to coastal areas as well as areas without coastal parts, such as the open sea or sea bottom. A long disputed question is whether the provisions of the HD are applicable beyond Member States' territorial waters. In 2005, the European Court of Justice judged that SACs can also be designated in the Exclusive Economic Zone of the Member States.[5]

The HD provides an autonomous protection system for marine ecosystems, where Member States play a crucial role for the completion of the Natura 2000 network since they are responsible for proposing the relevant list of SACs (Article 4). Nevertheless, the marine Natura 2000 network covers a relatively small number of marine ecosystems. Almost two decades after the HD was

---

3 Council Directive 2009/147/EC of 30 November 2009 on the conservation of wild birds [2010] OJ L20/7.

4 The SPAs are important for the purposes of this chapter as long as they are established in marine areas (Article 4 BD), given that various species of seabirds are protected according to the Annexes to BD [see The United Nations, *The First Global Integrated Marine Assessment: World Ocean Assessment I* (report), Cambridge University Press, Cambridge 2017, p. 527].

5 Case C-6/04, *Commission v. United Kingdom* [2005] ECR I-9017, 9084 paras. 115–120.

adopted, the network covered more than 18 per cent of the EU terrestrial land area and only four per cent of European seas.[6] The European Commission had already foreseen the inherent problems of implementing the HD in marine ecosystems and issued, in May 2007, the first Guidelines for the establishment of the Natura 2000 network in the marine environment. However the trends still remain unsatisfactory. That led to the EU setting a specific target in its Biodiversity Strategy for 2020 to complete the marine Natura network (Target 1),[7] with the inclusion of areas representing 10 per cent of European seas, in order to meet Target 11 of the Aichi Convention on Biological Diversity – which requires 10 per cent of EU waters to be within marine protected areas (MPAs) or other effective area-based management measures to be taken by 2020.[8] Currently, according to the latest official data published (end 2018), it seems that the target has been achieved: more than 3,150 marine areas have been designated as Natura 2000 sites, covering approximately 9.5 per cent of the total EU marine area (over 551,898 km^2), doubling the percentage of marine Natura 2000 coverage since 2012.[9]

2.2. THE MAIN CHALLENGES OF IMPLEMENTING THE HD IN MARINE ECOSYSTEMS

In terms of mere area coverage the trends are positive. However, various legal and physical factors make the application of the HD in marine ecosystems a complex issue yet. The Directive itself has various legal gaps and impediments which inhibit the effective protection of marine ecosystems. Firstly, it places greater emphasis on terrestrial ecosystems, as may be ascertained by its tone and wording. The use of terms such as 'land-use planning' or 'landscape' is very characteristic [Article 3(3), 10], whilst there is no reference to 'marine spatial planning' and 'seascapes'.[10] Likewise, the various Annexes of the Directive have been dominated by terrestrial species and habitats: only 7 marine mammals,

---

6 European Environment Agency, *State of Nature in the EU – Results from reporting under the nature directives 2007–2012*, Technical Report no 2/2015, Luxembourg 2015, p. 119.

7 See European Commission, *Our life insurance, our natural capital: an EU biodiversity strategy to 2020*, COM(2011) 244 final, Brussels 3.5.2011, pp. 5, 11.

8 R. Long, 'Evolutionary Character of International and European Law: Linking Sustainability with Environmental Responsibility and Marine Ecosystem Restoration under the European Union's Ocean Governance Agenda' in M. Nordquist, J. Norton Moore and R. Long (eds.), *Legal Order in the World's Oceans: UN Convention on the Law of the Sea*, Brill Nijhof, Leiden 2018, pp. 27, 41–42.

9 See also European Commission, *Mid-term review of the EU biodiversity strategy to 2020*, COM(2015) 478 final, Brussels 2.10.2015, pp. 5–6.

10 R. Caddel, 'The Maritime Dimensions of the Habitats Directive: Past Challenges and Future Opportunities' in G. Jones (ed.), *The Habitats Directive – A Developer's Obstacle Course?*, Hart Publishing, Oxford 2012, pp. 183, 186.

19 fish species, 1 marine invertebrate, 2 sea turtles, 66 seabird species and 9 marine habitats are protected, limiting the designation of SACs to a relatively small and unrepresentative list of marine species and habitats compared to their terrestrial counterparts. Especially, regarding cetaceans, only two species (bottlenose dolphin and harbour porpoise) are included in Annex II of the Directive, whilst the Bern Convention on the Conservation of European Wildlife and Natural Habitats (1979) covers almost 30 species.[11]

Secondly, the HD sets very high thresholds for the designation of marine SACs. In particular, Article 4(1) of the Directive provides that in case of aquatic species which range over wide areas, SACs can be proposed only where there is a clearly identifiable area representing the physical and biological factors essential to their life and reproduction. This means that Member States are more sceptical about proposing the relevant list; only that part of a wide area can be proposed as SAC where the species under protection live and additionally reproduce. In particular, various impediments make the requirement for a clearly identifiable area of living and reproduction difficult to determine:

- Enlarged marine ecosystems. In many cases of marine species (especially of cetaceans), a single area of reproduction is difficult to locate,[12] as some of them migrate throughout the seasons, expanding their area of living and reproduction.
- Instability of marine ecosystems. The sensitivity of these ecosystems to marine pollution, the change in numbers of endemic species and migration of species to and from them (see Lessepsian migrants) significantly change the biotic and abiotic characteristics of these ecosystems.
- Lack of data. For the designation of SACs, accurate scientific data on the criteria set out in Annex III to the HD is required, such as the size and density of the population of the species, the degree of isolation of the present population on the site, etc. Often, this data is very difficult to collect, given the physiology of these types of ecosystems, which are generally less accessible than terrestrial areas,[13] imposing practical and financial difficulties in gathering data.

The physical characteristics of marine ecosystems and the aforementioned stringent requirements for the designation of marine SACs act as a further obstacle

[11] S. Luk and S. Gregerson, 'Marine species protection and management in the European Union: Who will save our dolphins?' in C-H. Born, A. Cliquet, H. Schoukens, D. Misonne and G. Van Hoorick (eds.), *The Habitats Directive in its EU Environmental Law Context: European Nature's Best Hope?*, Routledge, London and New York 2014, pp. 399, 405.

[12] Ibid. at pp. 407–408, 417.

[13] Caddel (above n. 10), p. 190.

to the protection of the already unrepresentative number of marine species and habitats in the HD. However, various political factors also highlight the HD's impediments in these types of ecosystems. The Member States' conflicting interests – especially in enclosed seas (such as the Mediterranean Sea)[14] – inhibit cooperation for the common designation of SCAs. Unfortunately, it is an inescapable truth that marine ecosystems are often treated as an exploitable natural resource (fishing, hydrocarbons exploitation, etc.) by Member States – further deepening the conflict between Member States and giving rise to their unwillingness to cooperate. Moreover, there are truly inherent difficulties in controlling and reporting on marine spatial zones by the competent State Authorities which cannot be ignored. All these obstacles show that although the HD has been utilised in marine areas during the last decade, it seems to have reached its limits in terms of area coverage. The crucial question that EU policy-makers will face for the years to come is not a matter of a mere increase in coverage rates but a matter of a more qualitative coverage of the protected species and habitats.

3. AN ATTEMPT AT A HARMONISED APPROACH: DIRECTIVE 92/43/EEC IN RELATION TO OTHER EU LEGISLATION

Regardless of the fact that the HD is the single piece of EU legislation specifically aimed at the protection and conservation of vulnerable species and habitats both in the terrestrial and marine environment, its underlying deficiencies as analysed above undermine its overall effectiveness in the conservation of the marine ecosystems. It is undeniable that nature conservation is essential for the safeguarding of present and future generations; hence any limitations in the existing legislation impeding the achievement of this goal must be overcome. The first step in dealing with these deficiencies is to examine whether other parts of the EU legal framework can be effectively employed to complement the HD. It is interesting that the remaining pieces of EU legislation offer legal tools aiming at a more sustainable management of the marine environment; as a result these instruments do not include directly in their scope the conservation of marine biodiversity, as they are focused on the sustainable exploitation of marine resources. That gives rise to the question whether all these legal texts can provide an efficient biodiversity conservation model in the EU.

---

14 See the rates of coverage per regional sea by the European Environmental Agency https://www.eea.europa.eu/data-and-maps/daviz/coverage-of-natura-2000-n2k#tab-chart_1.

3.1. ASSESSING THE EFFICACY OF DIRECTIVE 2004/35/EC IN THE CONSERVATION OF MARINE ECOSYSTEMS

Another piece of EU legislation which also aims at protecting biodiversity – as a restitutive mechanism, however – is Directive 2004/35/EC, the so-called European Liability Directive (ELD).[15] In fact, liability under the ELD is tightly linked to the HD and the protection of species and natural habitats. Specifically the very first definition of environmental damage under the ELD, pursuant to Article 2(1), is 'damage to protected species and natural habitats, which is any damage that has significant adverse effects on reaching or maintaining the favourable conservation status of such habitats or species'.

Protected species, according to Article 2(3) of the ELD, include, first of all, the species and their habitats mentioned in Article 4(2) or in Annex I to Directive 79/409/EEC (formerly BD) or listed in Annexes II and IV to the HD. Additionally, its scope covers any other habitat or species, not listed in those Annexes, which the Member State designates for equivalent purposes to those laid down in those two Directives. Despite the fact that the definition of protected species under the ELD is tailored to the HD, the scope of the ELD is not restricted to the Natura 2000 network, but covers all fauna and flora in the EU, whether part of a designated SAC under the HD (or SPA under the BD), an area designated by any Member State which does not qualify as a SAC (or SPA) or an area which meets the criteria for their designation of SACs (or SPAs) but which Members States have failed to designate.[16] At a first glance it appears remarkable that there is a general piece of EU legislation which does *not* specifically address the conservation of specific habitats and species, but offers protection for the conservation of all possible habitats and animal and plant species in the EU. Could one therefore assert that the ELD is the one piece of legislation that can complement the HD and effectively contribute to limiting biodiversity loss?

A closer look at the definition of environmental damage provides the answer. As stipulated in Article 2(1) of the ELD, environmental damage covered under the ELD is only 'damage to protected species and natural habitats … that has significant adverse effects on reaching or maintaining the favourable conservation status of such habitats or species.' Thus, the threshold for the protection of habitats and species is rather high and it is evident that the ELD does not cover all harmful incidents to habitats or species. To be more specific, it relates only those which have a *significant* adverse effect – in relation to the

15 Council Directive 2004/35/CE of 21 April 2004 on environmental liability with regard to the prevention and remedying of environmental damage [2004] OJ L143/56.

16 G.M. Van den Broek, 'Environmental liability and nature protection areas – Will the EU Environmental Liability Directive actually lead to the restoration of damaged natural resources?' (2009) 5 *Utrecht Law Review* 117, 118–119.

baseline condition at the time of the damage [Article 2(14)] – on reaching or maintaining the favourable conservation status of the affected habitats or species.[17] Therefore, anything which has an adverse effect below significant is by definition excluded from the scope of the ELD. One must follow two steps in order to ascertain the aforementioned:

- Identify the current condition of the species and habitats affected in comparison with their hypothetical condition that would have existed if the harmful incident had not occurred (baseline condition);[18] and
- Measure the adverse change which occurred to the affected species and habitats after the harmful incident so as to assess the significance of the damage. The significance of the damage will be determined in relation to its effects on reaching or maintaining the favourable conservation status of the specific habitat or species.

All of the above show that the ELD aims at achieving environmental protection primarily through a restitutive mechanism, rather than a preventive one. The provisions of the ELD provide greater emphasis on this aspect of the biodiversity protection, despite the fact that the ELD includes also a few provisions that oblige operators to take preventive measures: biodiversity conservation is not included under the ELD's goals. Article 5 provides an exception to the ELD's protection system, but is only activated when the threat of a significant damage to an ecosystem is imminent. An imminent threat to a marine ecosystem is, however, difficult to ascertain, given that such damage may take a long time to show its negative consequences. Also the area that the preventive measures should relate to remains often unidentifiable due to plenty of factors that can influence the spread of damage (sea currents, winds etc.). Last but not least the aforementioned measures are not required to be constant but are time bound until the threat ceases. Consequently, Member States have no obligation under the ELD to take *a priori* conservation measures aimed at reaching a favourable conservation status for habitats and species. That makes the biodiversity conservation system of the ELD inefficient.

Furthermore the ELD, in case of biodiversity damage, seems to have defects also as restitutive mechanism. Assessing the significance of the damage requires accurate data both for determining the conservation status and measuring the adverse change. Specifically, a Member State must collect data not only on the condition of the species and habitats affected after the harmful incident but also on their condition before the incident (baseline condition) in order to determine the significance of the damage. Collecting data on marine ecosystems remains

[17] Ibid.
[18] Van den Broek (above n. 16), pp. 118–120.

a difficult task for the Member States due to their inherent inaccessibility, as mentioned above. Moreover, the problem deepens regarding marine areas outside the Natura 2000 network. Unless there is an obligation under the law of a Member State to establish management plans or monitoring reports for areas not designated as SACs, the information available on the baseline condition and the conservation status of such an area is limited. This unavailability of information essentially means that the significant damage threshold set by the ELD is not likely to be exceeded in many cases, not because the harmful incidents occurring are classified as insignificant, but because the lack of data and the challenges in obtaining it leave many incidents unclassified. In this light, the ELD does not seem like an instrument efficient in complementing the HD in the conservation of marine species and habitats either in its preventive or restitutive aspects.

3.2. DIRECTIVES 2000/60/EC AND 2008/56/EC: COMPLEMENTARY TOOLS FOR CONSERVING MARINE ECOSYSTEMS

The overall objective of Directive 2000/60/EC, the so-called Water Framework Directive (WFD)[19] is to promote sustainable water policy and management. In particular, the WFD aims *inter alia* at protecting and enhancing the status of aquatic ecosystems, preventing their further deterioration, promoting the sustainable use of water and obliging Member States to take specific measures on the progressive reduction of pollution in the aquatic environment (Article 1). The achievement of the targets set by the WFD could of course lead to the achievement of the conservation objectives under the HD, given that reaching a good ecological water status positively affects every habitat.[20] The quality of water and the conservation of a habitat are physically interconnected. Nevertheless, the fact that the conservation of the marine environment is not one of the direct goals of the WFD plays a crucial role in the context of Article 4(2) of the WFD, namely in case of conflicting aims.

Despite the broader objective of the WFD, its scope regarding marine environmental protection is narrower than that of the HD. Specifically, the WFD does not apply to every aquatic ecosystem that the HD applies to. On the contrary the WFD aims to establish a legal framework exclusively for the

19 Council Directive 2000/60/EC of 23 October 2000 establishing a framework for Community action in the field of water policy [2000] OJ L327/1.

20 G. Janauer, J. Albrecht and L. Stratmann, 'Synergies and Conflicts between Water Framework Directive and Natura 2000: Legal Requirements, Technical Guidance and Experiences from Practice' in S. Ignar and M. Grygoruk (eds.), *Wetlands and Water Framework Directive: Protection, Management and Climate Change*, Springer Open, Cham 2015, pp. 9, 13.

protection of inland surface waters, transitional waters, coastal waters and groundwater against land-based pollution [Articles 1(a) and 2].[21] Central to the WFD's protection system is the concept of the river basin districts. Consequently, the WFD does not include within its scope marine areas, the only exception being marine ecosystems in coastal waters. Moreover, the definition of 'coastal waters' further restricts the implementation of the WFD. In contrast to the International Law of the Sea, 'coastal water' pursuant to Article 2(7) extends only to one – not twelve – nautical miles from the nearest point of the baseline (except for transitional waters) as far as this area can be identified and assigned to the nearest or most appropriate river basin district [Article 3(1)].

Concerning the protected areas under the HD and the BD, their status as SCIs is not affected by the WFD, but seems to be enhanced, as can be ascertained from Articles 4(1)(c), 6 and 8(1). In fact, the river-basin-based water management measures under the WFD must always consider the conservation status of coastal habitats under the HD, given that taking such measures means, in essence, management of a SAC.[22] However, the objectives of the two Directives may sometimes be contradictory, as the WFD allows for derogations from its objectives in cases of new modifications to physical characteristics or in the case of new sustainable human activities [Article 4(7)], which also applies to protected areas according to the European Commission in the Guidelines for the application of the WFD.[23] All the above clearly demonstrate that the WFD is not oriented to achieving the conservation objectives of the HD: the balance tips – most of the time – towards the sustainable development model; hence its value in the conservation of marine life is rather limited.

Another important piece of the EU legislation in the field of marine environmental protection is Directive 2008/56/EC, known as the Marine Strategy Framework Directive (MSFD).[24] The MSFD aims to achieve the full economic potential of oceans and seas in harmony with the marine environment: a sustainable use of marine resources through development of a

---

21 A. Hildering, A.M. Keessen and H.F.M.W. van Rijswick, 'Tackling pollution of the Mediterranean Sea from land-based sources by an integrated ecosystem approach and the use of the combined international and European legal regimes' (2009) 5 *Utrecht Law Review* 80, 90.

22 That is stated in the European Commission's *Guidelines for the establishment of the Natura 2000 network in the marine environment*, 2007, p. 14. See also P. De Smedt and H.F.M.W. Van Rijswick, 'Nature conservation and water management: one battle?' in C-H. Born, A. Cliquet, H. Schoukens, D. Misonne and G. Van Hoorick (eds.), *The Habitats Directive in its EU Environmental Law Context: European Nature's Best Hope?*, Routledge, London and New York 2014, pp. 417, 419.

23 Janauer, Albrecht and Stratmann (above n. 20), pp. 15–16; De Smedt and Van Rijswick (above n. 22), pp. 421 *et seq.*

24 Council Directive 2008/56/EC of 17 June 2008 establishing a framework for community action in the field of marine environmental policy [2008] OJ L164/19.

marine strategy plan by the Member States.[25] Specifically, Article 1(2)(a) names as a goal of the aforementioned strategy the protection and preservation of the marine environment from deterioration or, where practicable, the restoration of marine ecosystems in areas which have been adversely affected. Central to the MSFD is the meaning of 'good environmental status' to which every protective measure taken by the Member States must aim [Articles 1(3) and (3), 3(5), 5(2) and (3) and 9]. This concept is determined in each individual case through a set of characteristics based on qualitative descriptors [Article 9(1)]. Among these descriptors of 'good environmental status' referenced in Annex I the maintenance of biodiversity with reference to protection of marine habitats and species is included.

The MSFD has a wider scope than all the other Directives applicable to every marine zone and area, protected or not (Articles 2 and 3).[26] The designation and the management of MPAs under the HD and the BD remain intact under the MSFD. Moreover, the MSFD recognises that the further designation of SACs and the extension of the Natura 2000 network contribute to the achievement of its targets, as is proclaimed in its Recitals no 5–6 and 18. It must be noted that implementing protective measures can also include spatial protection measures that contribute to coherent and representative networks of MPAs, adequately covering the diversity of the constituent ecosystems, such as SACs [Article 13(4)].[27] However, no specific protection measures for the protected areas are defined in the MSFD, with the exception of Article 13(5).[28]

However, just like the WFD, the MSFD focuses on attaining sustainable development instead of the preservation of threatened and vulnerable marine habitats and species, opting for a much broader, ecosystemic approach in relation to the marine environment. Despite the reference to the establishment of a coherent MPAs network (Recital no 18) and the potential importance of certain provisions,[29] this Directive does not impose any obligation on Member States; nor does it provide new legal tools or fill the gaps of the conservation system of marine ecosystems. Thus its contribution in terms of complementing the HD is deemed limited.[30]

---

25 H. Schoukens and H. Dotinga, 'Natura 2000 and fisheries – A question of competence or willingness?' in C-H. Born, A. Cliquet, H. Schoukens, D. Misonne and G. Van Hoorick (eds.), *The Habitats Directive in its EU Environmental Law Context: European Nature's Best Hope?*, Routledge, London and New York 2014, pp. 375, 379.

26 Hildering, Keessen and van Rijswick (above n. 21), p. 92.

27 D. Braun, 'Marine Protected Areas as Spatial Protection Measures under the Marine Strategy Framework Directive' in P. Goriup (ed.), *Management of Marine Protected Areas: A Network Perspective*, Wiley Blackwell, Chichester 2017, pp. 89, 94–95.

28 See Hildering, Keessen and van Rijswick (above n. 21), p. 96.

29 For example, Descriptor 11 of Annex 1 can benefit mainly the cetaceans. See Luk and Gregerson (above n. 11), p. 401, fn. 11.

30 Caddel (above n. 10), p. 185.

3.3. PREVENTING THE DANGERS OF FISHING: FILLING THE GAPS THROUGH THE FISHERIES REGULATIONS?

Fishing remains the main danger for marine ecosystems. Since the EU retains exclusive competence in 'the conservation of marine biological resources under the common fisheries policy' [Article 3(1)(d) TFEU], plenty of Regulations have been issued with certain aspects of them also referring to the protection of marine species and habitats. It is not within the scope of this contribution to analyse the complex EU fisheries policy in relation to the conservation of marine habitats, but certain key references will be made. The main piece of EU legislation in this field is the Regulation 1380/2015 on the Common Fisheries Policy (CFPR),[31] while there are also specific Regulations which apply to fishing in different regional seas such as the Mediterranean (Regulation 1967/2006)[32] or the Northeastern Atlantic Ocean (Regulation 2016/2336). In the Recitals of all the Regulations it is explicitly stated that they do not aim to affect the specific status of MPAs. The legal framework on fisheries and biodiversity conservation work in parallel: for the first, competency lies with the EU; whereas for the second, with the Member States. This already shows a significant deficiency of the current legal framework, as it gives rise to conflict of powers, concerning who is competent to take restrictive measures on fishing within MPAs.

Article 11 of the CFPR attempts to resolve this conflict.[33] Pursuant to paragraph 1, Member States are empowered to adopt conservation measures (not affecting fishing vessels of other Member States) that are applicable to waters under their jurisdiction and that are necessary for the purpose of complying with their obligations under Article 6 of the HD, provided that those measures are also compatible with the objectives set out in Article 2 of the said Regulation, meet the objectives of the EU legislation that they intend to implement, and are at least as stringent as measures under the EU law. However, if the initiating Member State considers that other Member States also have a direct management interest in the fishery affected by the aforementioned measures it must ask the European Commission to adopt such measures. As a result, it must be examined *ad hoc* whether the conservation measure that is going to be taken by the Member State in its SACs affects fishing by fishing vessels of other Member States; if it does

---

31 Council Regulation 1380/2013 of 11 December 2013 on the Common Fisheries Policy [2013] OJ L354/22.

32 Council Regulation 1967/2006 of 21 December 2006 concerning management measures for the sustainable exploitation of fishery resources in the Mediterranean Sea [2006] OJ L409/9.

33 See M.C. Ribeiro, 'The Protection of Biodiversity in the Framework of the Common Fisheries Policy: What Room for the Shared Competence?' in G. Andreone (ed.), *The Future of the Law of the Sea – Bridging Gaps Between National, Individual and Common Interests*, Springer Open, Cham 2017, pp. 65, 71 *et seq*.

not affect their fishing, the Member State is competent to take it. The CFPR also provides for a procedure regarding temporary emergency measures taken by the European Commission (Article 12) or the Member State (Article 13), in case of a serious threat to the conservation of marine biological resources.

The relationship between the EU Regulations of 'regional' application and the HD is of greater interest. For the purposes of this contribution, reference will be made to the Regulation 1967/2006 on fishing in the Mediterranean Sea. This particular Regulation has plenty of references to the HD and the protected species thereunder – to such a large extent that one could argue that it also aims to reinforce the HD's protection system.[34] Furthermore, this Regulation recites provisions of the HD in great detail on the prohibition of capturing and killing marine species or deteriorating and destroying the marine habitats. As far as protected marine species are concerned, the Regulation refers to Annex IV to HD (Article 3). Article 4(4) provides for special conservation measures on all Mediterranean marine Natura 2000 sites, prohibiting over five fishing methods that are *per se* dangerous to marine life other than the targeted fish, such as fishing with trawl nets, dredges, purse seines, etc.

In summary, the EU legislation on fishing offers greater protection and is more specialised concerning the conservation of the environmental status of marine areas. This is evidently due to the imminent dangers that marine ecosystems may face due to fishing. However it remains fragmentary, since some of its main and more effective pieces are implemented exclusively in certain marine regions.

4. A NEW LEGAL FRAMEWORK? CONCLUDING REMARKS ON THE NEED FOR MORE EFFECTIVE PROTECTION

The trends of marine coverage rates under the Natura 2000 network in the last decade have been positive in terms of area coverage. However, these trends seem to have reached their peak. The Member States may be unwilling to designate more SCIs in the years to come or to expand the already existing ones, mainly due to their conflicting interests regarding marine exploitation. Besides, Article 4(1) of the HD is an inhibiting factor for the inclusion of wider areas. No one expects marine coverage rates to go beyond – or even approach – the coverage rates of terrestrial areas, for the reasons addressed in this chapter. The challenges of protecting the marine environment show that the goals of the current biodiversity conservation system must change in general. The EU should

---

34 R. Churchill and D. Owen, *The EC Common Fisheries Policy*, Oxford University Press, Oxford 2010, p. 253.

aim at a more qualitative model of protection rather than mere increase of area coverage rates.

On the other hand, the EU legal framework seems to have some important flaws that prevent the further utilisation of the already known legal tools. The EU legislation on this issue synthesises a complicated, quite technical and – sometimes – contradictory legal framework, resulting in the need for a harmonised approach. Furthermore, the heteronomy of the aims of all these legal texts means that each of these should be interpreted according to its main targets, which most of the time differ from those of the HD. The most interesting fact is that the pieces of EU law aiming at a model of sustainable environmental management and development in the marine environment do not provide sufficient and efficient legal tools to meet the growing needs of marine biodiversity protection. Given the HD's deficiencies in marine biodiversity conservation, we conclude that the EU needs a new legal framework oriented exclusively at attaining biodiversity conservation. The biodiversity goals in marine ecosystems cannot be fully and adequately achieved through a legal framework aimed at promoting sustainable development.

The ambiguity regarding the competences between the EU and Member States, the lack of an efficient control system on implementing measures of EU legislation in marine areas, and the lack of cooperation of Member States with third countries all reduce the effectiveness of the current protection system.[35] Consequently, EU legislation should focus on creating a harmonised legal framework that will serve the following purposes:

- Single legal treatment of all MPAs, providing a minimum level of protection. This leads to a single legal framework for all regional seas which will set basic rules regarding the protective measures that the Member States must take in every case (such as the prohibition of specific types of fishing, degradation, environmental pollution, etc.).
- Wider protection of marine species and habitats. The Annexes to the HD include an unrepresentative number of marine species and habitats. The European legislator should amend them so as to increase the number of marine species recognised as in need of protection. Furthermore, special attention must be paid to migratory species and cetaceans, through a special legal framework that will be adopted especially for them – perhaps according to the BD's model.[36]
- Potential cooperation between Member States. Due to the vulnerability of marine ecosystems, the impact of their possible degradation cannot easily be geographically contained and may affect neighbouring areas. One of the

35 Schoukens and Dotinga (above n. 25), p. 398.
36 Luk and Gregerson (above n. 11), pp. 414–415.

major shortcomings of the current legal framework is the lack of an explicit and effective co-operation system between Member States on this issue. It is the EU's duty to oblige coastal states of the region concerned to cooperate on carrying out studies and collecting data on the marine environment, pursuant to the model of Article 11 of the MSFD. The lack of scientific data is one of the main impediments to effective marine conservation. Cooperation amongst Member States in the adoption of protective measures (in particular in case of marine pollution) as well as joint monitoring reports on the application of the legislation in MPAs should also be provided for. An important reform could also be the joint planning and designation of cross-border MPAs in cases of marine areas extending into the waters of several Member States. This could cease their reluctance in designating large MPAs (especially in narrow enclosed seas), since each neighbouring coastal state would contribute in an analogous way to the designation and operation of the common MPA.

- Delegation of powers to the EU. Fisheries regulation and marine biodiversity preservation are like the two faces of Janus. The regulation of the first belongs to the exclusive competence of the EU, which must always consider its impact on marine biodiversity [Articles 2(3) and 7 of CFPR]. However, this does not suffice. The decentralised protection system under the HD (in which the Member States have exclusive competence – with the exception of Article 5 of the HD – in designating SACs and taking protective measures) cannot provide adequate guarantees for stricter protection. It is time for the EU to amend this system to a more centralised one without neglecting the jurisdiction of the coastal Member States in their marine zones. Consequently, in order for the negative effects of fishing to be counteracted, the EU must have decisive authority on the protective measures taken in MPAs. This would lead to a more effective coordination of the initiatives that are taken by the EU and better spatial design and organisation of MPAs. More specifically, the EU should, firstly, acquire the power to take protective measures regardless of the requirements of Article 11 of the CFPR, pursuant to its general exclusive competence [Article 3(1)(d) of TFEU]. Secondly, if a Member State fails to take effective measures to achieve the specific conservation objectives of each MPA, then it must be replaced in that function by the EU, since the latter retains its competence [Articles 3(1)(d) and 4(2)(d) of TFEU].

FEES FOR WATER SERVICES IN THE NEW POLISH WATER LAW ACT

A Step Towards Transition to Sustainability?

Martyna ROBAKOWSKA

1. INTRODUCTION

On 1 January 2018, a new Polish Water Law Act[1] entered into force. The voluminous bill, comprising more than 550 articles, introduced significant changes to the Polish water resources management system. It was adopted to ensure the full implementation of the Water Framework Directive[2] ('WFD') into the national legal system.

The crucial idea behind the Water Law Act was to achieve a major improvement of water resources management.[3] The bill was meant to resolve the most severe problems Poland now faces in, *inter alia*, ensuring good water quality, determination of effective drought and flood prevention measures and deciding how best to use particular water resources.[4] The expectation of the legislator was also that the new rules would constitute an important factor encouraging businesses to apply more sustainable operation models.

Therefore, the new Water Law Act envisaged many new legal instruments aimed at achieving these purposes. One of the most controversial and debatable of the solutions introduced by this Act concerns fees for water services. For this reason, this contribution analyses these regulations, with a particular focus on fees for water abstraction and waste-water discharge, as

1 Water Law Act of 20 July 2017, consolidated text: Journal of Laws of 2020 pos. 310.

2 Directive 2000/60/EC of the European Parliament and of the Council of 23 October 2000 establishing a framework for Community action in the field of water policy [2000] OJ L327/1.

3 Justification of the governmental draft of the Water Law Act, document no. 1529 p. 1, http://www.sejm.gov.pl/sejm8.nsf/druk.xsp?nr=1529.

4 Ibid. pp. 1–4.

these water services are most widely provided.[5] Thus, this chapter will answer the following questions:

1) Do the new rules on fees for water abstraction and waste-water discharge adopted by the Polish legislator constitute a proper implementation of the WFD, in particular do they respond adequately to the principle of recovery of costs of water services?
2) Does the Polish water services' fee system encourage businesses to adopt more sustainable operation solutions, enabling them to save water or generate less waste-water?

2. FORMER RULES REGULATING WATER FEES IN POLAND

Assessing whether the new Polish rules on water fees constitute proper implementation of the WFD should be preceded by a brief description of former rules relating to incurring fees for certain forms of water use, in order to emphasise the scope and significance of changes introduced by the new Water Law Act. Also, comparing the former and currently applicable regulations in this field from the perspective of the WFD requirements will be crucial in finally assessing the amendments introduced into the Polish legal system in 2018.

Before the new Water Law Act entered into force, fees for water abstraction and waste-water discharge to water or soil[6] were regulated by the Environmental Protection Law Act[7] (EPL) pursuant to article 273 section 1 points 3 and 4 of the EPL.[8] The fees were calculated according to the 'polluter pays' principle.[9] Thus, the level of fees reflected the actual extent of exploitation of the environment.

5 It should be noted that 'providing' water services within the meaning of the Water Law Act means not only providing such services for third parties but also for a given entity's own needs – e.g. abstraction of groundwater from the entity's land for the purposes of conducting production activity.

6 Note that waste-water discharge to the municipal mains was not considered an action covered by the obligation to incur fees (*a contrario* article 273 section 1 point 2, read with article 3 point 46 EPL). This rule was upheld by the Water Law Act (article 268 section 1 point 2, read with article 35 section 3 point 5 of this bill).

7 Environmental Protection Law Act of 27 April 2001, consolidated text: Journal of Laws of 2020, pos. 1219.

8 It should be noted that the term 'principle of recovery of costs of water services' was introduced to article 1 of the former Water Law Act by the bill dated 5 January 2011. More on the meaning of this principle in the former Water Law Act – S. Urban, 'Wdrożenie zasady zwrotu kosztów usług wodnych w świetle doświadczeń polskich i nowego Prawa wodnego' in M. Pchałek (ed.), *Gospodarowanie wodami. Kluczowe wyzwania w ramach nowego cyklu planistycznego*, Wolters Kluwer, Warsaw 2020 pp. 261–262, 265.

9 W. Radecki 'Komentarz do artykułu 272 ustawy Prawo ochrony środowiska' in M. Górski, M. Pchałek, W. Radecki, J. Jerzmański, M. Bar, S. Urban, J. Jendrośka (eds.), *Prawo ochrony*

In relation to fees for water abstraction, the due amount depended mainly on the volume of water abstracted and whether it was ground water or surface water. Its place of abstraction, quality and designation were factors which also had impact on the fee rates applied. Calculation of respective fees for waste-water discharge required determination of the type of waste-water (domestic, municipal, industrial), temperature of the waste-water, manner of discharge (into water or soil) and its composition (quantity of particular substances present in the discharged waste-water[10]).[11] It should also be noted that articles 294 and 296 of the EPL listed 12 activities where water fees were not charged. These included, *inter alia*, abstraction of water for hydroelectric power generation purposes, abstraction of surface water for irrigation of farmland and forests, and discharge of waste-water into the soil for agricultural use, provided that the entity obtained a relevant water permit.

The obligation to pay fees for exploitation of the environment burdened the 'entities exploiting the environment'.[12] This category covered mainly professional undertakings – individuals or companies that used water and/or produced waste-water in operating their business. This specific allocation of obligation also resulted from the polluter pays principle.

The obliged entities were required to present an annual report on the scope of their use of the environment to the relevant authority – marshal of the province. The report covered data necessary to calculate due fees and information on obtained water permits.[13] The entities were required to calculate due environmental exploitation fees themselves and pay them by 31 March each year, to the authority's bank account.

środowiska. Komentarz, C.H. Beck, Warsaw 2011 p. 978, B.A. Draniewicz, 'Problem konstytucyjności opłat za korzystanie ze środowiska' (2007) 9 *Państwo i Prawo* p. 78.

10 The substances were: 5-day biochemical oxygen demand (BOD_5), dichromate chemical oxygen demand (COD_{Cr}), total suspended solids, sum of chlorides and sulphates ($Cl + SO_4$), volatile phenols, hexachlorocyclohexane (HCH), tetrachloromethane (CCl_4), pentachlorophenol (PCP), aldrin, dieldrin, endrin, isodrin, hexachlorobenzene (HCB), hexachlorobutadiene (HCBD), trichloromethane ($CHCl_3$), 1,2-dichloroethane (EDC), trichloroethylene (TRI), tetrachloroethylene (PERC), trichlorobenzene (TCB), mercury, cadmium, zinc, copper, nickel, chromium, lead, arsenic, vanadium and silver.

11 The detailed manner of fees calculation was regulated by Regulation of the Council of Ministers of 12 October 2015 on fees for exploitation of the environment, Journal of Laws of 2015, pos. 1875.

12 According to article 3 point 20 EPL, the following entities constitute entities exploiting the environment:

- businesses and foreign businesses within the meaning of respective Polish laws, as well as farmers conducting agriculture production activity, including arable crops, livestock rearing, gardening, vegetable growing, forestry and inland fishing,
- an organisational entity not qualified as a business as described above,
- a natural person not qualified as a business as described above, who exploits the environment in such a way that it is obliged to obtain a respective environmental permit.

13 Or permits under the Pollution Prevention and Control Directive – IPPC permits, if obtained.

Of course, the law envisaged a mechanism enabling the authority to question the correctness of either the fees calculation or data provided in the report and, based on its own findings or the results of environmental inspection, impose a fee for exploitation of the environment by issuing an administrative decision. The authority was granted the same powers, if an obliged entity failed to submit the report within the statutory deadline.[14]

After the new Water Law Act entered into force, the scope of the fees for exploitation of the environment was significantly narrowed. Nowadays, this obligation applies only to waste storage and introducing gases and dust into the atmosphere, including also emission of greenhouse gases covered by allocated emission allowances (EU ETS).

3. PROVISIONS OF THE WFD

Pursuant to the WFD, the principle of recovery of costs of water services (cost recovery principle) is one of the crucial factors to be taken into account when establishing economic measures. This conclusion, among others, arises from the wording of recital no. 38 of the WFD, which places this rule alongside the fundamental 'polluter pays' principle.

Analysis of the importance of the cost recovery principle for establishing economic measures should commence by citing the legal definition of the term 'water services' included in article 2 point 38 of the WFD. These services constitute

> all services which provide, for households, public institutions or any economic activity:
>
> (a) abstraction, impoundment, storage, treatment and distribution of surface water or groundwater,
>
> (b) waste-water collection and treatment facilities which subsequently discharge into surface water.

In the next clause, the WFD states that water services constitute one of the forms of water use.

Further, pursuant to article 9 paragraph 1 of the WFD, Member States are obliged to ensure firstly that their water-pricing policies provide adequate incentives for users to use water resources effectively. While establishing pricing policies, Member States have to take into account both of the abovementioned principles – the cost recovery principle and the polluter pays principle.

---

[14] Article 288 section 1 EPL.

The interpretation of these provisions was extensively discussed by legal scholars,[15] in particular with respect to the actual scope of water services subject to the cost recovery principle. According to the narrow interpretation, the notion of 'water services' in this context should be generally limited only to water supply and waste-water disposal services,[16] whereas the wider interpretation assumes that all activities listed in article 2 point 38 of the WFD must be covered by this principle to effectuate the environmental objectives of the WFD.[17] Also the Court of Justice of the European Union ('CJEU') analysed the above-cited provisions of WFD in several cases. Three of them should be described, as they are relevant in answering the questions raised in the introduction to this contribution.

In the first and most important[18] case, the CJEU had to establish whether Germany, by excluding services such as impoundment (reservoir storage) for the purposes of hydroelectric power generation, navigation and flood protection, abstraction for irrigation and industrial purposes, and personal consumption from the category of water services and, consequently, excluding these actions from the obligations to incur fees, had failed to implement the concept of 'water services' into its national law. While reviewing this case, the court emphasised that the WFD is a framework directive and therefore, its aim is not to completely harmonise the rules regarding water management in all Member States.[19] Then, it underlined the major objective of the WFD – maintaining and improving the aquatic environment – and the need to formulate pricing mechanisms locally, so the Member States could, by establishing these mechanisms, having regard for regional conditions and problems, achieve this objective effectively.[20] Finally, the CJEU noted that although exclusion of some activities from the obligation to incur fees for water services may impact on the achievement of the objectives, it does not automatically mean that such action jeopardises attainment of these objectives. The Court concluded that 'the Member States may, subject to certain conditions, opt not to proceed with the recovery of costs for a given water-use

---

15 See e.g. W. Howarth, 'Cost recovery for water services and the polluter pays principle' (2009) 10 *ERA Forum* pp. 565–587, P.E. Lindhout and B. van der Broek, 'The Polluter Pays Principle: Guidelines for Cost Recovery and Burden Sharing in the Case Law of the European Court of Justice' (2014) 10(2) *Utrecht Law Review* pp. 46–59.

16 The argumentation is wider discussed e.g. in: M. Reese, 'Cost Recovery and Water Pricing in Water Services and Water Uses in Germany' (2013) 10(4) *JEEPL (Journal for European Environmental & Planning Law)* pp. 361–364, J. Rotko, 'Zasada zwrotu kosztów usług wodnych i jej znaczenie prawne' (2016) 2 *Studia Prawnicze* p. 133.

17 The argumentation is wider discussed e.g. in: P.E. Lindhout, 'Application of Cost Recovery Principle on Water Services in the Netherlands' (2013) 10(4) *JEEPL* pp. 327, 332.

18 S. Hendry, 'The EU Water Framework Directive – Challenges, Gaps and Potential for the Future' (2017) 14 *JEEPL* pp. 259–261.

19 Case C-525/12, *European Commission v. Federal Republic of Germany*, ECLI:EU:C:2014:2202, para. 50.

20 Ibid. paras. 51–53.

activity, where this does not compromise the purposes and the achievement of the objectives of the directive [WFD]'.[21]

It needs to be noted that this judgment was widely criticised by legal scholars, who rightly pointed out that the Court did not clarify the notion of 'water services'.[22] Lindhout and van Rijswick underlined that the CJEU positioned cost recovery as a practically voluntary tool for Member States, and as a result, limited the potential effectiveness of this principle.[23] Gawel, sharing this point of view, stressed that the judgment enables the Commission to initiate further infringement proceedings upon re-adjustment of the claim and extending the arguments in line with the CJEU remarks.[24]

The judgment in the next case was issued in relation to a dispute between a consumer and a company responsible for supplying water to several municipalities in Croatia. The consumer claimed that it should pay only the variable component of the price for the supplied water, corresponding to the actual use of water in a given period, whereas the price set by the company also included a fixed component, independent of the volume of water actually used. While resolving this case, the CJEU re-emphasised the framework character of the WFD, its main objectives and the need to set water-pricing policies so that they contribute to achieving these aims. Therefore, the choice of measures applied in this respect was left to the discretion of Member States.[25] Then the Court explained that in order to comply with the obligation to recover the costs of the services connected with water use, the Member States may adopt water-pricing methods which enable recovery of, *inter alia*, costs borne by water distribution services in making it available to users in sufficient quantity and of sufficient quality, irrespective of their actual consumption of that water.[26] In conclusion, the CJEU held that the requirements of article 9 paragraph 1 of the WFD are not breached if a Member State establishes a policy according to which the price for water charged to users includes two components: a variable one, related to the volume of water actually consumed and a fixed one, unconnected with it.[27]

21 Ibid. para. 57.

22 E. Gawel, 'ECJ on Cost Recovery for Water Services under Article 9 of the Water Framework Directive: Camera Locuta Causa non Finita' (2015) 12 *JEEPL* 71, pp. 73–74, 77–79, P.E. Lindhout and H.F.M.W. van Rijswick, 'The Effectiveness of the Principle of Recovery of the Costs of Water Services Jeopardized by the European Court of Justice – Annotations on the Judgment in C-525/12 – European Commission v Federal Republic of Germany of 11 September 2014' (2015) 12 *JEEPL* 78, pp. 84–85, A.A. Seuser, 'Die Entscheidung des EuGH zu Wasserdienstleistungen' (2014) 36 *Natur und Recht* 847, p. 849.

23 P.E. Lindhout and H.F.M.W. van Rijswick, n. 22 above, pp. 80–94.

24 E. Gawel, above n. 22, pp. 71–79, cf. A.A. Seuser, above n. 22, pp. 849–850.

25 Case C-686/15, *Vodoopskrba i odvodnja d.o.o. v. Željka Klafurić* ECLI:EU:C:2016 paras. 18–21.

26 Ibid. para. 22.

27 Ibid. para. 24.

It also noted that such determination of water-pricing policy is a common practice in Member States.[28]

In the last case the CJEU had to resolve, *inter alia*, whether the Spanish tax on the use of inland waters for the production of electricity was established in compliance with article 9 paragraph 1 of the WFD. The hydroelectricity producers tried to demonstrate that regulations imposing this tax neither incentivised the efficient use of water nor established mechanisms for the preservation and protection of public water resources, as the obligation to pay the tax was 'totally unconnected' to the capacity to cause damage to the public water resources.[29] The claimants argued that the tax focused exclusively on their capacity to generate income and thus infringed the WFD. The Court clarified that the cited provision of the WFD obliges Member States to consider the cost recovery principle and the polluter pays principle while establishing water-pricing policies in general. Therefore, a single measure such as the present tax cannot be assessed independently of the system of water fees.[30] In conclusion, the CJEU stated that article 9 paragraph 1 of the WFD does not require that each tax on water, taken in isolation from the overall water-pricing policy, should be established in order to fulfil either the cost recovery principle or the polluter pays principle.[31]

Summarising these judgments, the CJEU ruled that the WFD does not prevent Member States from:

1) excluding some water-related activities from the definition of 'water services' and, consequently, from the obligation to pay fees for their provision,
2) establishing water-pricing policies dependent not only on the extent of actual use of water, but also on other factors, such as for example costs of distribution of water in sufficient quantity and of sufficient quality,
3) imposing tax on water use which, assessed separately from the system of water fees, does not reflect the cost recovery principle or the polluter pays principle, as these principles should be considered when determining the water-pricing policy as a whole.

It needs to be emphasised that the matter of 'water services' and the scope of required application of the cost recovery principle while establishing water-pricing policies still needs to be clarified, especially due to different approaches presented by Member States and views described in the legal literature.

---

28 Ibid. para. 25.

29 Joined cases C-105/18 to C-113/18, *Asociación Espanola de la Industria Eléctrica and Others v. Administración General del Estado*, ECLI:EU:C:2019:935, para. 25.

30 Ibid. paras. 32–35.

31 Ibid. paras. 43–45.

4. NEW POLISH RULES ON WATER SERVICES FEES

The central element of the water fee system introduced by the new Water Law Act is the concept of water services. These consist of providing households, public institutions or economic entities with the possibility of using water in excess of common and ordinary use, or special use of water.[32] Such services include, for example, abstraction of surface and groundwater, discharge of waste-water into water or soil (including discharge of waste-water into water facilities), release of rainwater or melt from a storm sewer system into water or water facilities, etc.[33]

The obligation to incur fees for water services is much wider than formerly. It concerns not only abstraction of water and discharge of waste-water into water or soil, but also, for example, decreased natural terrain water retention as a consequence of construction work. For each type of listed activity,[34] the legislator provided different rules for calculating the fees.[35] Considering the scope and aim of this chapter, only the regulations regarding water abstraction and waste-water discharge are further analysed.

There are two types of fees for such water services: a variable fee and a fixed fee. The former is calculated similarly to that under previous regulations. The latter is a completely new solution, as the due fee amount depends on the wording of the water permit.[36]

In case of water abstraction, the amount of the variable fee depends on the volume of abstracted water. This volume should be multiplied by a unit rate established based on factors such as the purpose of the water abstraction and the kind of abstracted water (whether it is surface or groundwater). With respect to abstraction of surface water, the location of its abstraction affects the applied fee rate. Similarly, when abstracting groundwater, the water treatment processes performed have an impact on the unit rate. The amount of the fixed fee relies on the wording of the water permit, specifically on the duration and the maximum quantity of water abstracted, determined on the basis of the water permit. The unit rate necessary to calculate the fixed fee for *groundwater* abstraction is connected to the ratio of the volume of water that may be abstracted on the

---

32 It should be noted that the WFD treats 'water services' as one of the forms of water use, whereas the Polish legislator explicitly states, that 'water services' constitute activities beyond water use. Pursuant to the opinions of Szuwalski, Grabarczyk and Chojnacki, this discrepancy may be relevant to assess whether the WFD was correctly implemented to the Polish legal system – P. Szuwalski, 'Komentarz do artykułu 35 Prawa wodnego' in P. Szuwalski (ed.), *Prawo wodne. Komentarz do wybranych przepisów*, LEX/el 2019, T. Grabarczyk and D. Chojnacki, 'Pozycja usług wodnych w systemie prawa' in M. Białek, T. Grabarczyk and D. Chojnacki (eds.), *Opłaty za usługi wodne w nowym Prawie wodnym*, C.H. Beck, Warsaw 2018, p. 18.

33 The catalogue of water services is listed in article 35 section 3 of the Water Law Act.

34 The list of water services subject to the obligation to incur fees is determined in articles 268 and 269 of the Water Law Act.

35 For details refer to M. Białek, T. Grabarczyk, D. Chojnacki, n. 32 above, pp. 21–94.

36 Or IPPC permits covering water abstraction or waste-water discharge, if obtained.

basis of the permit, to the available groundwater resources. The unit rate applied to determine the fixed fee for *surface water* abstraction depends on the ratio of surface water to the low average long-term annual level of flow.[37]

When it comes to calculating a variable fee for waste-water discharge, the actual volume of particular chemical substances present in discharged waste-water is relevant.[38] Application of the appropriate unit rate relies on the kind of waste-water (whether it is domestic, industrial or municipal). The amount of the fixed fee depends on the content of the water permit, specifically on the highest volume of waste-water to be discharged and the duration of such discharge.[39]

The Water Law Act does not explicitly specify which entities are obliged to incur such fees, however, it exempts certain persons, for example maritime offices, churches and other religious associations, from the obligation to pay these fees.[40] Hence, this obligation generally burdens entities actually providing water services subject to fees payment.

Another significant rule introduced by the new Water Law Act is that the amount of fees due for water services is to be determined not by the entity providing water services, but by the water authority, who is to notify the obliged entity. In addition, the fees are to be paid quarterly rather than annually.

The Water Law Act does not envisage exemptions from the obligation to incur fees for water services in general, in contrast to previous regulations. However, certain activities are excluded from the obligation to pay a fixed fee.[41] The Polish legislator explained that abolishing complete exemptions from the obligation to incur fees for water services was necessary to fulfil the requirements stemming from article 9 paragraph 1 of the WFD.[42]

5. PRACTICAL PROBLEMS WITH THE NEW RULES ON WATER SERVICES FEES

One of the most severe difficulties in applying the new regulations was associated with empowering the water authority to impose fees. The problems occurred for three major reasons.

37 Pursuant to article 271 sections 2 and 3, read with article 272 section 1 of the Water Law Act, read with paragraph 5 sections 3 and 7 of the Regulation of the Council of Ministers of 22 December 2017, Journal of Laws of 2017 pos. 2502.

38 The list of chemical substances is identical to those in previous regulations – see above n. 10.

39 Pursuant to article 271 section 5, read with article 272 section 6 of the Water Law Act, read with paragraph 10 of the Regulation of the Council of Ministers of 22 December 2017.

40 Article 269 sections 3 and 4 of the Water Law Act.

41 E.g. abstraction of water: for irrigation of farmland, fish-breeding or for operation of hydroelectric power plants – article 270 section 2 of the Water Law Act.

42 Justification of the governmental draft of the Water Law Act, document no. 1529 pp. 33–34, http://www.sejm.gov.pl/sejm8.nsf/druk.xsp?nr=1529. See also: S. Urban, above n. 8, p. 272.

Firstly, the new Water Law Act completely transformed the structure of the water authorities by establishing a State Water Enterprise 'Polish Waters'. The three-tier structure (central – regional – local authorities) was replaced by a four-tier one (central – regional authorities competent for river basin management – regional authorities competent for sub-basin management – local authorities) to better exercise much wider powers granted by the new law.[43] The right to impose fees was conferred on the lowest tier of Polish Waters – water supervisory bodies – which did not exist before 1 January 2018. As a consequence, the first few months of their operations were, to say the least, not very effective.[44] Secondly, the number of entities obliged to pay the fees was significantly greater than previously, as the obligation related not only to water abstraction and waste-water discharge, but also to other specific kinds of water services. Thirdly, the method of fees calculation is more complex than formerly.

As a result, calculating due fees and notifying entities providing water services within the statutory deadlines proved to be impossible. Hence, the legislator was compelled to amend the interim rules on calculating fees for water services. According to these, entities obliged to pay fees for water services are required to report the scope of provided water services by submitting relevant data on official forms by 31 December 2026.[45] These declarations currently constitute the main basis for Polish Waters to impose due fees for water services.[46]

However, proper completion of the abovementioned forms often poses a serious challenge. For example, the entity abstracting water is required to specify the purpose of water abstraction, whereas the law differentiates between more than 40 goals.[47] In the event of abstraction of water for more than one purpose,

---

43 Pursuant to article 240 of the Water Law Act, Polish Waters not only issue administrative decisions and orders but may also conduct inspections and execute certain investment projects. They are also in charge of the execution of the State's ownership rights with respect to waters, grounds under the waters and water facilities.

44 The organisational chaos was widely reported in the press, see examples: https://www.money.pl/gospodarka/wiadomosci/artykul/wody-polskie-chaos-kompetencje-prezes-wyplaty,114,0,2397298.html, https://biznes.gazetaprawna.pl/artykuly/1101690,nowe-prawo-wodne-podwojna-oplata.html.

45 See article 552 of the Water Law Act, which was amended twice: by Act of 20 July 2018 amending the Water Law Act and certain other Acts, Journal of Laws of 2018 pos. 1722 and by Act of 11 September 2019, Journal of Laws of 2019, pos. 2170. The latter Act extended the duration of this obligation – initially it was applicable until the end of 2020.

46 Other factors involve: the purpose and scope of water use specified in the water permit, measurements made by administrative bodies as part of water management control or findings from reviews of water permits, and readings from measuring devices made during water management inspections.

47 In previous regulations the purpose of abstraction also had an impact on the unit rate applied to calculate the fee, but the law differentiated only 3 purposes – see paragraph 9 sections 1–3 of Regulation of the Council of Ministers of 12 October 2015 on fees for exploitation of the environment.

the entity has to determine the amount of water abstracted for each purpose. Neither the legislator nor Polish Waters have provided guidance to entities on how to properly fulfil this obligation. Furthermore, such entities are required to ensure separate measurements of water abstracted for particular purposes. Before the new Water Law Act entered into force, there was no such obligation. Thus, the entities do not generally possess devices enabling them to carry out measurements of this kind. It should be noted, however, that Polish Waters are required to provide the entities with relevant measuring devices at their own cost by 1 January 2027.[48]

The above-described problems constitute only selected examples of practical difficulties which arose as a result of the entry into force of the new Water Law Act.[49] However, even such a limited description of these difficulties allows the conclusion that the Polish water law reform was not properly drafted. New regulations are very complex and ambiguous (and, to a certain extent, still raise considerable doubts with respect to their effectiveness as well as compliance with WFD); the water authorities were not able to properly fulfil their new obligations; and, most importantly, the entities affected by the new obligations were not given sufficient time to adapt their business to the new laws.[50]

6. DO THE NEW POLISH RULES ON WATER SERVICES FEES CONFORM WITH THE WFD?

This assessment should be preceded with a mention of the judgment of CJEU in Case C-648/13, in which the Court ruled that Poland had failed to properly implement provisions of the WFD, including also provisions effectuating the cost recovery principle, in its national law – mainly in the former Water Law Act. The CJEU did not, however, assess whether the system of fees for exploitation of the environment is compliant with this principle. The scope of the Court's adjudication was limited only to determining whether the provision requiring that Member States report in their river basin management plans on the intended steps towards implementing the cost recovery principle had been

48 Article 36 section 4, read with article 574 point 6 of the Water Law Act. It should be noted that this term was extended – initially it was 1 January 2021.

49 More of them are described in the article – M. Robakowska and D. Wałkowski, 'Further amendments to the Water Law', 20 September 2018, *In Principle*, http://www.codozasady.pl/en/further-amendments-to-the-water-law/.

50 The Water Law Act was published in the Journal of Laws on 23 August 2017, the majority of provisions entered into force on 1 January 2018.

duly implemented. Therefore, this judgment cannot be seen as proof, that the former rules on fees for abstraction of water and waste-water discharge were inconsistent with the objectives of the WFD.

The WFD requires, as confirmed by a ruling in Joined cases C-105/18 to C-113/18, that the assessment of whether a Member State has appropriately fulfilled the obligation arising from article 9 paragraph 1 should be made when considering the entire water-pricing policy established by this Member State. Due to publication constraints, only the rules on fees for water abstraction and waste-water discharge have been analysed in this chapter, as these water services are most widely provided in Poland. It is also undisputed that these fees are representative of the whole Polish water-pricing policy and, therefore, can be used to evaluate the conformity of the Water Law Act with the WFD in this respect.

These fees for water services comprise two components: a variable fee and a fixed fee. The former is dependent on the actual provision of water services – volume of abstracted water and volume of particular pollutants present in discharged waste-water. The latter is determined based on the water permit and relies on the maximum volume of water to be abstracted or the maximum volume of waste-water to be discharged under this permit. In Case C-686/15, the CJEU stated that the requirement to consider the need to provide adequate incentives for users to use water resources efficiently does not oblige Member States to determine water-pricing policies based solely on the actual use of water. However, the Court emphasised that water-pricing policies should be established so that the cost recovery principle is taken into account. In the cited case, the CJEU approved the Croatian regulations, according to which pricing for water supplied to consumers included a fixed fee, corresponding to costs borne by the supplying company to ensure supply of water in sufficient quantity and of sufficient quality. The fixed fee established in Polish regulations does not reflect the costs of actually provided water services, as it is calculated exclusively based on the wording of the particular water permit. The fee is due even if no water services were actually provided. As a result, by such determination of regulations on fixed fees for water services, the Polish legislator did not consider the cost recovery principle to *any* extent.

Another issue relevant for evaluating the conformity of the analysed regulations with the relevant provisions of the WFD relates to abolishing of complete exemptions from the obligation to pay fees for certain water services. The Polish legislator justified the adoption of such a solution by indicating the European Commission's position, according to which it is indispensable that provision of all water services is subject to fees because only such an approach allows the cost recovery principle to be implemented. It appears that the legislator did not take note of the judgment of the CJEU in Case C-525/12, where the

Court did not share this position.[51] The CJEU held that it is admissible for a Member State to envisage some exemptions from the obligation to incur fees for water services. Consequently, Polish regulations which do not fully exempt from the obligation to pay water fees for abstraction of water and discharge of waste-water are compliant with the WFD in this respect, although, according to the CJEU, the WFD does not *require* the adoption of such severe regulations.[52] It is also worth noting that the legislator did not present a convincing rationale for exempting certain persons (e.g., churches and other religious associations) from the obligation to pay fees, which poses significant doubts as to the conformity of such a rule with the WFD.[53]

7. CONCLUSIONS

The conducted analysis enables both questions raised in the introduction of this chapter to be answered in the negative.

The new Polish rules on fees for water services envisage that the due fee comes in two components: a variable fee, depending on the actual scope of provided water services, and a fixed fee, calculated based on the wording of the water permit. The latter is not connected to the cost recovery principle. It is due even if the water permit-holder does not provide any water services. Also, completely abolishing the exemptions from the obligation to incur fees has negative outcomes – for instance, the costs of hydroelectric power generation have increased significantly, and consequently the operations of such power plants are less profitable, which is likely to cause a significant decline in investments in this field.

Therefore, in my opinion, the regulations of the Polish Water Law Act on fees for water services – water abstraction and waste-water discharge – do not comply with article 9 paragraph 1 of the WFD. In particular, these regulations do not encourage businesses to make their models of operation more sustainable, to save water or generate less waste-water. In fact, the former laws promoted such

51 Although legal scholars were pointing it out while commenting drafts of Water Law Act – see e.g. D. Wałkowski, 'Nowe Prawo wodne to mała rewolucja' (2016) 2 *Energetyka Wodna* p. 32, M. Robakowska and D. Wałkowski, 'Reforma Prawa wodnego wejdzie w życie 1 stycznia 2018' (2017) 3 *Energetyka Wodna* pp. 27–28.

52 The exemptions functions e.g. in Portugal – A. Aragão, 'Water Pricing and Cost Recovery in Water Services in Portugal' (2013) 10(4) *JEEPL* 333, p. 345.

53 Especially when comparing to doubts of Lindhout whether an exemption for small individual agricultural extractions established in Dutch law is compliant with the Directive – P.E. Lindhout, above n. 17, pp. 327–328 or concerns of Reese as to the compliance of German regulations exempting hydropower or mining activities from water abstractions levies – M. Reese, above n. 16, pp. 372–374.

actions to a greater extent, as the fee amount depended on the actual scope of performed services. Hence, the new Polish laws on fees for water services should be assessed as hampering the transition to a more sustainable economy, as the calculation mechanisms do not promote or encourage businesses to limit their environmental impact. Change of these laws should be preceded by analysis of water-pricing policies adopted by other Member States and wide public consultations – work on the discussed bill was conducted practically without the benefit of such actions.

ABOUT THE EDITORS

Marlon Boeve is Assistant Professor at the Utrecht Centre for Water, Oceans and Sustainability Law, Utrecht University, the Netherlands. Her research focuses on European and national environmental law and spatial planning law. She is particularly interested in how law can support the transition to a circular economy. She is coordinator of the interdisciplinary platform 'Towards a Circular Economy and Society' at Utrecht University and is a member of the editorial board of the Dutch Journal for Environmental Law.

Sanne Akerboom is Assistant Professor of Law and Politics of the Energy Transition at the Copernicus Institute of Sustainable Development (Faculty of Geosciences), Utrecht University, the Netherlands. Her work examines the energy transition from a legal, political and social sciences perspective. She publishes in legal, governance and energy and climate journals, both in English and Dutch. She is coordinator of the Utrecht University and TUEindhoven collaboration on the 'Fair Energy Transition' as well the hub on 'Decarbonising the Energy System' at Utrecht University.

Chris Backes is Professor of Environmental and Planning Law at the Utrecht Centre for Water, Oceans and Sustainability Law, Utrecht University, the Netherlands. Notably, he has acted as President of the Dutch Society for Environmental Law, a member of the Netherlands Council for Nature Protection (Natuurbeschermingsraad) and a member of the Netherlands Council of Housing, Spatial Planning and the Environment (VROM-Raad). He specialises in sustainability law as well as environmental and planning law with a special focus on law for circular economy and biodiversity law.

Marleen van Rijswick is Professor of European and Dutch Water Law and is Director of the Utrecht Centre for Water, Oceans and Sustainability Law, Utrecht University, the Netherlands. Her research focuses on the question of how law can contribute to a sustainable and equitable use of water resources based on shared responsibilities. Notably, she has acted as President of the Dutch Society for Environmental Law, a member of the Netherlands Council for Water legislation (Commissie van Advies voor de waterstaatswetgeving) and a member of the Wadden Sea Council (Waddenraad). Her research interests include water law and adaptation to climate change within the broader field of environmental law, spatial planning law, nature conservation law and European and constitutional and administrative law.

Milton Keynes UK
Ingram Content Group UK Ltd.
UKHW030628011224
451924UK00016B/76

9 781780 689296